D0283343

Hiking
the
North Cascades

by

Erik Molvar

FALCON®

HELENA, MONTANA

ᴀ FALCON GUIDE ®

Falcon® Publishing is continually expanding its list of recreational guidebooks. All books include detailed descriptions, accurate maps, and all information necessary for enjoyable trips. You can order extra copies of this book and get information and prices for other Falcon® books by writing Falcon, P.O. Box 1718, Helena, MT 59624, or by calling toll-free 1-800-582-2665. Also, please ask for a copy of our current catalog. Visit our website at www.Falcon.com or contact us by e-mail at falcon@falcon.com.

© 1998 Falcon® Publishing, Inc., Helena, Montana.
Printed in the United States of America.

2 3 4 5 6 7 8 9 10 MG 05 04 03 02 01 00

Falcon and FalconGuide are registered trademarks of Falcon Publishing Co., Inc.

All rights reserved, including the right to reproduce this book or parts thereof in any form, except for inclusion of brief quotations in a review.

Printed in the United States of America.

Cover photo by Eric Molvar.

Library of Congress Cataloging-in-Publication Data
    Molvar, Erik
        Hiking the North Cascades / by Erik Molvar.
            p. cm.
        Includes index.
        ISBN 1-56044-596-3 (pbk.)
        1. Hiking—Washington (State)—North Cascades National Park—
        Guidebooks. 2. Backpacking—Washington (State)—North Cascades
        National Park—Guidebooks. 3. North Cascades National Park (Wash.)
        —Guidebooks. I. Title
        GV199.42.W22N675   1998
        796.51'09797'73—dc21   97-30343
                                                                  CIP

CAUTION

Outdoor recreational activities are by their very nature potentially hazardous. All participants in such activities must assume the responsibility for their own actions and safety. The information contained in this guidebook cannot replace sound judgment and good decision-making skills, which help reduce risk exposure, nor does the scope of this book allow for disclosure of all the potential hazards and risks involved in such activities.

Learn as much as possible about the outdoor recreational activities in which you participate, prepare for the unexpected, and be cautious. The reward will be a safer and more enjoyable experience.

♻ Text pages printed on recycled paper.

For Bill Brockman,
whose influence extends across several generations
of conservationists in the Pacific Northwest

Contents

Acknowledgments

First, I would like to recognize Melanie Davidson for her constant companionship over hundreds of miles of trails, who maintained her humor and mine through the wind and the rain and the snow, on tedious forest treks and over the steepest passes. Melanie was in large part responsible for keeping our backcountry patrol reports up to date, and was indispensible in providing extra runs to town for supplies and in giving me a two-car shuttle capability that obviated the need for hundreds of miles of backtracking. Many thanks for a job well done.

Thanks to Hugh Dougher and Kelly Bush for allowing us to volunteer as backcountry rangers and for providing assistance in a thousand small but crucial ways. Thanks to Robes, Tony, and Adam for their hospitality during our exile from the Marblemount compound. Jim Archambeault provided information concerning trails on the Okanogan National Forest. Thanks to Marshall and Dawn Plumer for the logistical support and the rare treat of Hozomeen ice cream. The ranger staff at Stehekin provided much-needed assistance in helping us solve the transportation nightmare in that remote corner of the world. Mikhail and Vladimir at Northwest Boot Repair in Bellingham did yeoman work in keeping our expensive but disappointing footwear going.

This book, as well as *Hiking Olympic National Park*, would never have been written without Donna DeShazo's visionary handling of my Glacier manuscript. Background research was conducted at the North Cascades National Park interpreters' library in Newhalem, park headquarters at Sedro-Woolley, the University of Idaho, the Texas A&M University map collection, and the Wilderness district office in Marblemount. We appreciate the curators of these collections of texts and maps for their diligence in keeping this information available. Archaeological information was provided by Bob Mierendorf, who generously shared some of the results of his survey efforts.

Thanks to Craig Holmquist, Eli Warren, Kevin Kennedy, Margi Gromek, Barry George, Jim Hammer, and Jim Archeambeault of the Forest Service for providing mileage data, background information, and reviews for the trails that fell within their respective districts. John Rose and Jim Wiebe of BC Parks provided information and reviews for hikes in Canada. The park dispatchers, Gaylyn, Lynn, and Vicki will always have a special place in our memories as the friendly voices on the other end of the radio each morning and evening.

Finally, I would like to thank Little Joe Manley for just being himself.

Green Trails Topo Map Index

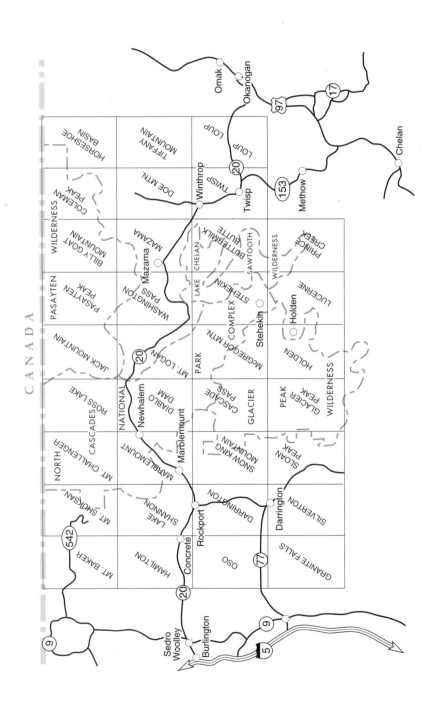

USGS Topo Map Index

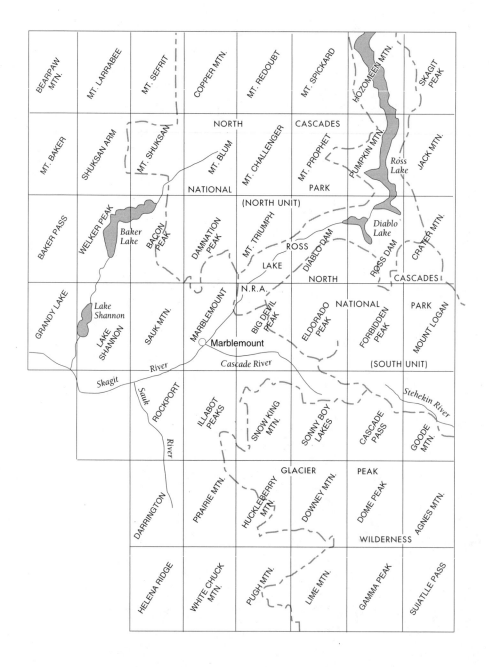

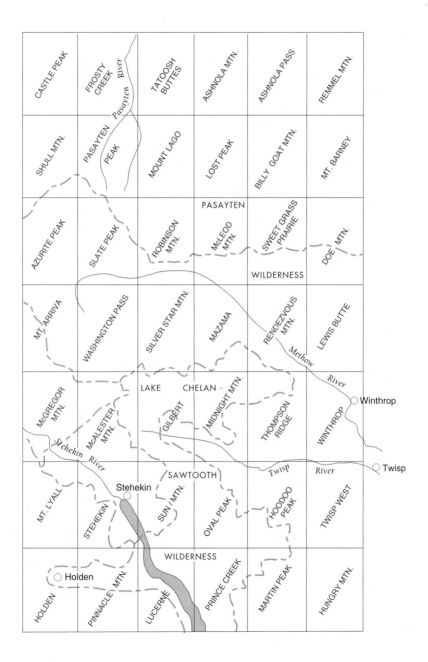

Map Legend

US Highway	2	Picnic Area	🏕
State or Other Principal Road	20 530	Campground (Fires allowed)	▲
Forest Service Road	4420	Campground (Fires prohibited)	▲
Interstate Highway	⟹	Horse Camp (Fires allowed)	⚑
Paved Road	⟹	Horse Camp (Fires prohibited)	⚑
Gravel Road	⟹	Automobile Camping	▲
Unimproved Road	=======⟹	Cabins/Buildings	▪
Trailhead	◯	Ruins	◪
Featured Trail(s)	– – – ⌢ –	Corral	↺
Secondary Trail(s)	– – – – –	Ski Lift	▪▪▪▪▪▪▪
Featured Route(s)	••••• ••••	Day-Use Area	⊠
Secondary Route(s)	····· ····	Peak	9,782 ft.
5,000 ft. Contour			
Pass	⌣	Locked Gate	•—•
Ranger Station	⚑	Overlook/Point of Interest	◨
Mine Site	⚒	National Forest/Park Boundary	⌐ ⌐
River	～	State/National Boundary	BRITISH COLUMBIA / WASHINGTON
Creek	～		
Intermittent Stream	–·–·–		
Falls	～⫝	Map Orientation	N
Lake	⬬		
Spring	⌀	Scale	0 0.5 1 Miles
Marsh/Wetlands	⸌ ⸜ ⸌		
Pacific Crest Trail	⬘		

North Cascades Overview Map

Hope

To Princeton

Chilliwack

1

Maple Falls

Glacier

542

SKAGIT VALLEY PROVINCIAL PARK

3

MANNING PROVINCIAL PARK

BRITISH

COLUMBIA

WASHINGTON

ROSS LAKE N.R.A.

NORTH CASCADES N.P.

PASAYTEN WILDERNESS

MT. BAKER WILDERNESS

Newhalem

Mazama

Sedro-Wooley

NOISY-DIOBSUD WILDERNESS

20

NORTH CASCADES N.P.

20

Hamilton

Concrete

Rockport

Marblemount

Winthrop

Twisp

20

LAKE CHELAN N.R.A.

Stehekin

530

Darrington

GLACIER PEAK WILDERNESS

Holden

LAKE CHELAN - SAWTOOTH WILDERNESS

Carlton

153

Arlington

Ferry

Everett

Lake Chelan

2

Monroe

Chelan

93

2

Skykomish

To Wenatchee

To Wenatchee

Derek Falls, Manning Provincial Park.

Introduction

East of Puget Sound, a jagged range of glacier-clad mountains rises skyward, walling off the rainy country of the coast from the arid plains of the Columbia River Basin. This is not a lofty range from the standpoint of altitude—most of the taller peaks are less than 9,000 feet at the summit. However, because they rise from sea level, these mountains have a vertical rise similar to that of the Rockies or the Sierra Nevada. The northern end of the Cascades has always been the most forbidding and impenetrable, replete with sawback ridges and dense jungles of brush, vast icefields and torrential rivers. This wilderness had never been conquered by "civilization," and offers a last retreat for those who seek to leave the encumbrances of the modern world behind and discover themselves in the simplicity of the untamed wilds. This is steep country, but the trails have been built along the same gradients as those in other mountainous parts of the United States, and most trails are suitable for intermediate-level backpackers.

North Cascades National Park is no tour-bus park. In contrast to many of our national parks, the scenic wonders in this part of the world cannot be reached by car, do not have paved sidewalks or boardwalks to them, and are not accompanied by interpretive plaques. To experience the raw grandeur and beauty of the North Cascades, it is necessary to shoulder a pack and travel into the wilderness by shoe-leather express. This is a backpacker's park, with hundreds of miles of pathways that penetrate deep into the forests and climb to the barren tundra of the mountaintops. These mountains offer unlimited possibilities to solitude-seeking hikers, from short day hikes to two-week expeditions. Along with surrounding wilderness areas administered by the Forest Service and neighboring parks and reserves in Canada, the park is part of a vast and complete ecosystem that supports mountain lions, elk, mountain goats, and even a few grizzly bears along with its annual influx of human visitors. Enjoy the wilderness and help to preserve its pristine quality for future generations.

THE ORIGINAL INHABITANTS

The first explorers to penetrate the North Cascades were indigenous hunter-gatherers who inhabited the surrounding lowlands and followed the retreat of the Pleistocene glaciers into the mountains. The oldest occupied site dates from 8,400 years before present, and further archaeological evidence indicates an uninterrupted human presence in the North Cascades ever since. These people came here in small groups to hunt mountain goats, elk, deer, and beaver, to fish the abundant salmon and steelhead of the Cascade streams, and to gather berries during the waning days of summer. Ranging from the forested lowlands to the alpine tundra, the earliest humans took advantage of seasonal abundances of plants and wild game. In summer they came to the high country in small groups and left before the coming of winter's cold winds and heavy snows.

These were Neolithic peoples, known for their great skill at knapping edged tools and weapons from native stone. Local deposits of chert and vitrophyre were commonly used by early stone knappers. High-quality obsidian points have also been found in the area. There is no local source for this "volcanic glass"; instead, indigenous peoples traded for the stone, which must have been a sought-after commodity in those times. Obsidian found in the North Cascades has been traced to sources as far away as northern California and Wyoming, indicating that these people were part of a trading network that stretched far to the east and south.

Today, there are few traces of these original inhabitants. Archaeologists have found widely scattered rock shelters, pits, and rock art, but never have found any evidence of a permanent settlement. Modern visitors are unlikely to come upon any traces of prehistoric peoples in the North Cascades backcountry. If you happen to find evidence of past inhabitants, leave it alone and notify the appropriate rangers. Bear in mind that all artifacts and sites (including stone points) are protected by the American Antiquities Act, a federal law that covers sites and relics of archaeological interest on all public lands. It is illegal to remove or damage artifacts or artwork.

By the 1800s, the North Cascades were home to a rich assemblage of Native Americans. The Skagit and Nooksack peoples lived west of the range. Their culture depended heavily on salmon, a characteristic that they shared with the Stolo (Chilliwack) and Nlakapamuks (Lower Thompson) tribes of the Fraser River valley in what is now Canada. East of the range were the interior Salish tribes, who hunted on the grasslands there. The tribe known to the French-speaking voyageurs as the Mitois inhabited the Twisp and Methow river valleys, and today they are known as the Methow Indians. Farther south, the Chelan tribe lived at the foot of Lake Chelan. These people, along with the Skagits, pioneered an early route over Cascade Pass that was used for trade in times of peace and by raiding parties in times of conflict.

EARLY HISTORY

The first recorded white man to penetrate this forbidding wilderness was Alexander Ross, an Englishman who explored the remote parts of the Pacific Northwest on behalf of the Hudson's Bay Company. He sought to establish trade contacts with the indigenous tribes and to survey the fur-producing potential of the region. Furbearers were never as abundant here as they were in the Rockies and the boreal forests of the far north, and lifeways of the natives were more strongly focused on salmon fishing than on hunting and trapping. As a result, the North Cascades became a backwater in the fur trade and soon slipped back into obscurity.

In the 1860s, a few enterprising traders tried to punch a pack trail through the range to link Puget Sound with the goldfields of interior British Columbia, but their route was too steep and rough for freight traffic and was soon abandoned. The North Cascades saw a brief flurry of gold prospecting between 1880 and 1900. A few found small fortunes, but most found only hardship and heartbreak. During the early 1900s, sheep ranching became a big business in the Okanogan Valley, and Basque herders immigrated from Spain to shepherd the huge flocks through the timberline meadows on the eastern side of the range. At the same time, timber barons were making fortunes by logging off the ancient stands of coastal forest that once grew in the Cascades' western foothills. In the heart of the range, however, steep slopes kept the loggers at bay.

The interior of the North Cascades has maintained its pristine quality because of its forbidding aspect: its soils are too thin for agriculture, winters too cold and snowy for livestock, slopes too steep for logging, and metal-bearing ores too low-grade for commercial exploitation. In a nation that prized economic growth and "progress" above all else, this country was left alone because it was perceived to be worthless. Today, to a society awash in materialism, the mountains of the North Cascades have become a haven from the excesses of civilization and a last refuge in which to re-establish our ties with the natural world.

GEOLOGY OF A YOUTHFUL RANGE

The North Cascades are merely a small part of a vast mountain chain that stretches unbroken along the western edge of the North American continent, from the tip of Baja California in the south to the Alaska Range, which crowds the Arctic Circle. The mountains have risen during the collision of great continental plates: Here, the Pacific plate subducts or dives beneath the North American plate. The zone of subduction is still geologically active, with active volcanoes such as Mount Baker and Glacier Peak rising

Looking south from Sahale Glacier.

5

above the lesser peaks, and occasional earthquakes attesting to the ongoing movement of the Earth's crust. The North Cascades are geologically distinct from the more southerly reaches of the range, in that they are typified by large formations of granite and other hard rocks that are resistant to weathering. These peaks of resistant stone have been sculpted by wind, ice, and water into an imposing wall of crags stretching from the center of Washington into southernmost British Columbia.

The oldest rocks of the formation appear at the western edge of the mountains, remnants of an ancient continental crust. This mélange of igneous and sedimentary rocks crops up in the vicinity of Mount Baker and also forms prominent landmarks of the western foothills, such as Sauk Mountain.

The heart of the Cascades is made up of a resistant belt of Skagit gneiss that forms many of the most imposing peaks of the range: Mount Redoubt, the Picket Range, Colonial Peak and its neighbors, Mount Logan and Goode Mountain. The Skagit gneiss is both volcanic and metamorphic in nature. The original metamorphic gneiss was fractured deep in the earth, where superheated water was forced upward through the interstices, turning the surrounding rock into granite.

To the east of the Skagit gneiss is a belt of younger sedimentary and volcanic rocks, typified by the sandstone ranges of the Pasayten Wilderness and the volcanics found at the base of Hozomeen Mountain and near Easy Pass.

About 55 million years ago, a series of magma upwellings led molten rock to flow upward from the Earth's mantle through faults in the crust. Pools of magma cooled below the surface, forming large batholiths of granite. These batholiths were often miles across, and as the weaker rock that over-topped them eroded, the resistant granite was exposed to the weathering of the elements. Today, the granite from these batholiths can be seen in Mount Spickard, Black Peak, and Liberty Bell Mountain.

During the Pleistocene epoch, vast icefields covered the region, completely burying the North Cascades in glaciers. Only the loftiest peaks rose as *nunataks* (Inuit for "lonely peaks") above the ice. The original valleys of the range, formed by erosion that followed faults and bands of weak or shattered bedrock, were deepened by immense glaciers that flowed downvalley, plucking and grinding at the bedrock as they surged. The glaciers planed the valley floors flat, while steepening the valley walls to create a characteristic U-shaped cross-section. Mountains that were carved on two sides became knife-edge ridges called *arêtes*. Later, smaller montane glaciers high on the slopes would scoop out cirques or natural amphitheaters. Some of these fell away into the deeper and older valleys that had been carved by larger valley glaciers long before, and these became hanging cirques and hanging valleys. Today the headwalls of these hanging basins bear the magnificent waterfalls for which the range is named.

FORESTS OF THE NORTH CASCADES

Below towering crags and glistening icefields, the lowlands of the North Cascades are part of a boreal forest that spans the northern third of the globe. Some of the isolated valleys have not been greatly disturbed in more than a thousand years, and the result is an old-growth community of outstanding diversity. Enormous specimens of coniferous trees can be found in fertile pockets of the bottomland, in stands that took root long before Europeans set foot on the North American continent. Visitors should take time to familiarize themselves with some of the most common trees and plants in order to gain a greater insight into the ecology of this wild mountain ecosystem.

The coastal forest region has great ecological importance. This area receives abundant rainfall, most of which occurs during winter months. Fertile soils and plentiful moisture create ideal growing conditions for conifers such as western red-cedar and western hemlock, which achieve towering proportions in areas that have been spared from clearcutting. Bigleaf and vine maples, as well as red alder, are the prominent hardwoods. Douglas-fir is prevalent in areas with a history of fire.

East of the divide, lowland forests are determined by frequent droughts and periodic fires that have molded the forest ecosystem for uncounted millennia. In some places, fire has thinned the forest to create a savannah of grassy clearings and isolated trees. Pockets of growth that receive more rainfall are similar to the bottomland forests of the western slope of the mountains.

Moving up in elevation, a montane forest dominates the lower slopes of the foothills. Western hemlock is dominant west of the Cascades' crest, and Douglas-fir is prevalent east of the divide. Lodgepole pines grow in pure stands on both sides of the range where intense wildfires once leveled the forest. Silver fir and Engelmann spruce make a showing as the montane forest becomes subalpine in character, occupying moist sites that remain

The white-tailed ptarmigan is found only in the high alpine zone.

Footbridge in old-growth forest.

undisturbed by fire or other disasters. Near timberline, lingering snows determine the distribution of trees, and the conical mountain hemlock (in the west) and subalpine fir (in the east) predominate. These spire-shaped trees shed winter snows easily by virtue of their slender growth form and downward-sloping branches. Subalpine larch grows on even more wind- and frost-prone sites in the eastern Cascades. It sheds its needles in autumn and weathers the storms of winter in a dormant state. The driest timberline communities east of the divide are dominated by whitebark pine.

Above timberline (5,500 feet west of the Cascade crest, and 6,500 feet east of it), plant communities are influenced strongly by minute differences in microclimate. The few conifers that grow here are sculpted into low-growing krummholz formed by windblown ice and snow. Lingering snowfields may promote the growth of plants such as avalanche lilies or bistort, and in extreme cases may prevent any plants from taking root at all. In contrast, well-drained sites may be as arid as a desert, and only water misers such as shrubby cinquefoil can survive in such places. Other plants, such as phlox and penstemon, specialize in colonizing cracks in the rock itself, where little or no soil is present. In general, timberline habitats in the Cascades are dominated by lush swards dotted with wildflowers, although a kind of alpine desert can be found in places on the eastern side of the mountains.

How To Use This Guide

The primary intents of this guide are to provide information that will help hikers choose backpacking trips according to their desires and abilities and to provide a detailed description of the trail system for interpretation of natural features found along the trails. This guide is intended to be used in conjunction with topographic maps, which can be purchased at ranger stations, local gift and sporting goods stores, or through the U.S. Geological Survey.

Each trail description begins with a statistical section, covering the physical characteristics of the trail for quick and easy reference. Overall distance is measured in miles, and an overview describes the hike type: day hike, backpack, extended trip, or wilderness route. Extended trips cannot be reached by road, while wilderness routes represent abandoned trails and cross-country routes where the only indication of a trail might be an occasional cairn. This description is followed by a difficulty rating. The rating can be interpreted as follows: Easy trails can be completed without difficulty by hikers of all abilities; moderate trails will challenge novices; moderately strenuous hikes will tax even experienced travelers; and strenuous trails will push the physical limits of the most Herculean hiker.

The best season entry provides an index of when the trail will be passable without special aids, like crampons, ice axes, or skis. It does not necessarily reflect a schedule of trail maintenance, which varies unpredictably from year to year. This is a relative measure, and late snowstorms may delay the opening of a trail beyond the time published here. Indeed, during years of heavy snowfall, some of the later-opening trails may never become passable without ice-axe and crampons. Use this guidebook to get a feel for the dates when the trail is usually open and check with local authorities before your trip to get the latest trail conditions.

A list of topographic quad maps that cover the trail is also provided. The most current topographic maps for the North Cascades belong to the Green Trails series. The USGS quads tend to be outdated, and the Trails Illustrated map that covers the region incorporates these errors. The main USGS maps were last updated in 1976; Forest Service topo maps that cover individual wilderness areas are slightly more current. The appropriate quadrangles (several are usually required) are listed for each featured hike in this guidebook, and the corresponding Green Trails map appears in italics.

Following this statistical section is a mile-by-mile list of landmarks, trail junctions, and gradient changes. Official mileages were used for all trails that had them. In the absence of official mileages, distances were measured by planimeter on 1:24,000 scale topographic maps.

The mileage section is followed by a detailed interpretive description of the trail, including geologic and ecological features, fishing opportunities, campsites, and other important information. Photographs have been included to give the reader a visual preview of some of the prominent features seen along the trial. An elevation profile accompanies each trail description, providing a schematic look at the major elevation gains and losses incurred during the course of the trip.

PLANNING YOUR TRIP

Gather as much current information as possible before starting out on a wilderness expedition. Permits are required for overnight expeditions into North Cascades National Park and the neighboring national recreation areas, and you must register your itinerary at a ranger station. Once the permit is issued, you must stick to the exact campsites and exact dates on the permit. Each backcountry camp has a limited number of campsites; staying in the wrong place could cause conflicts with other parties who have proper permits. Marblemount is the best source for backcountry permits and information, but Sedro-Woolley, Glacier, Hozomeen, Stehekin, Winthrop, and Twisp have ranger stations capable of issuing backcountry permits. A list of addresses and phone numbers for these ranger stations is provided in Appendix A.

There are no designated camping areas within the national forest lands that border the park, and no permits are required for overnight stays there. Campers are encouraged to use established campsites and to practice minimum-impact camping techniques where these are unavailable. In the wilderness, each of us is a passing visitor, and we should leave no trace of our travels to mar the wilderness experience of others. New trailhead user fees are now in effect for the Okanogan and Mount Baker–Snoqualmie national forests. Parking permits are available at nearby Forest Service ranger stations. This new fee system is a pilot program; tell your representatives in the U.S. Congress what you think of it.

The key to a quality hiking experience is good planning. Hikers who underestimate the distance or time required to complete a trip may find themselves hiking in the dark, a dangerous proposition at best. An experienced hiker traveling at a fast clip without rest stops can generally make 3 miles per hour on any terrain, perhaps more if the distance is all downhill. Hikers in less than peak physical condition or who are new to the sport have a maximum speed of 2.5 miles per hour. Note that these rates do not include stops for rest and refreshment, which add tremendously to a hiker's enjoyment and appreciation of the surroundings. Eight miles a day is a good goal for travelers new to backpacking, while old hands can generally cover at least 12 miles comfortably. We recommend traveling below top speed, focusing more attention on the surrounding natural beauty and less on the exercise of hiking itself.

CROSS-COUNTRY TRAVEL

In a wilderness of steep slopes, impassable cliffs, impenetrable brush, and rushing whitewater, cross-country travel is best left to the foolhardy, the insane, and the mountaineers. Even experienced wilderness travelers will discover that finding a passable off-trail route through the North Cascades backcountry is all but impossible. Bushwhacking through the

Cascades requires a special combination of stamina and obstinacy. Cross-country travelers must be constantly prepared to change their planned route or turn back when confronted with obstacles, such as sheer walls of stone that block the heads of many valleys, nettle-filled and alder-choked avalanche tracks that descend from the mountaintops to the valley floors, old burns where fallen timber litters the slopes, and flood-swollen streams. Common sense is a must in off-trail areas, where rescue is usually a do-it-yourself proposition.

Traveling cross-country is allowed in both national park and national forest lands. Most areas away from roadways are protected by wilderness status: the Stephen Mather Wilderness in North Cascades National Park and the adjoining recreation areas, as well as the Mount Baker, Noisy-Diobsud, Pasayten, Glacier Peak, and Lake Chelan-Sawtooth wilderness areas on adjoining Forest Service lands. Motorized and mechanized equipment (including mountain bikes) is expressly prohibited in these areas. The hinterlands of the national park have been divided into backcountry camping zones where dispersed camping is allowed 0.5 mile away from a trail and 1 mile from an established backcountry camp; permits are required and can be obtained at any ranger station. There are no restrictions on cross-country travel on the national forest. Please use minimum-impact techniques to avoid scarring the landscape.

CUSTOMS PROCEDURES AND THE INTERNATIONAL BORDER

Canada and the United States share the longest undefended border in the world, a narrow swath cut arrow-straight through the timber and across the mountaintops. Part of this border forms the boundary between North Cascades National Park and Manning Provincial Park, popular hiking destinations in their respective countries. Several trails cross the border in places where there are no permanent customs facilities, and the road from Hope, British Columbia, to Hozomeen, Washington, is similarly unguarded. For now, these border crossings are patrolled sporadically by the customs agents of both nations, and there is no formal protocol to cover border crossings. No special customs procedures are required for motorists driving into Hozomeen from the north, but hikers who plan to cross the border must make special arrangements before departing on their journey.

Neither country actively acknowledges the existence of trails that cross the border (with the possible exception of the Pacific Crest Trail), and using them is officially discouraged. Travelers who plan backcountry trips that carry them across the border must check in with customs agents of the country to be entered before beginning their trip. If you plan to start in Canada, dip into the United States, and finish your trip on Canadian soil, you must clear customs of both countries in advance. Customs agents from both countries can be found anywhere a highway crosses the international border. In addition, a customs agent from Canada makes periodic visits to the ranger station in Winthrop for the benefit of Pacific Crest Trail hikers. Contact the ranger station well in advance to be sure that a customs agent can be there to assist you when you arrive in the Winthrop area.

A FEW WORDS OF CAUTION

Weather patterns in the North Cascades can change frequently and without warning. Cold temperatures can occur even during the height of summer, and nighttime Fahrenheit temperatures routinely dip into the 40s and even 30s on clear nights. Thunderstorms may suddenly change cloudless days into drenching misery, so carry appropriate rain gear at all times. Ponchos are generally sufficient for day hikes, but backpackers should carry full rain suits; water from drenched vegetation will quickly soak travelers who rely solely on ponchos for protection. Snowfall is always a distinct possibility in the high country, and backpackers should carry clothing and gear with this in mind. Detailed short-range forecasts available at ranger stations are generally reliable.

In most years, snow lingers in the high country well into July. Hikers who head for the high country in early summer should check with local rangers for current trail conditions. In many cases, ice axes and crampons will be required, especially on high passes with northern exposures. The first serious snowstorms visit the high country in early September, and by mid-October a deep blanket of snow may cover the passes. October also marks the beginning of the rainy season in the low country, and the drizzle may not let up until late April.

Drinking water from the seemingly pristine streams and lakes of the North Cascades is quite refreshing, but all such sources may contain a microorganism called *Giardia lamblia*. Giardia is readily spread to surface water supplies through the feces of mammals and infected humans, causing severe diarrhea and dehydration when ingested. Water can be rendered safe for drinking by boiling it for at least 5 minutes or by passing it through a filter system with a mesh no larger than 2 microns. Iodine tablets and other purification additives are not considered effective against giardia. No natural water source is safe, and a single sip of untreated water can transmit the illness. Symptoms (gas, cramps, nausea, and diarrhea) usually appear within three weeks and demand medical attention.

Many of the **wild animals** in North Cascades National Park may seem almost tame. In the absence of hunting, these creatures have lost their natural fear of humans. However, they remain wild, finely attuned to their environment and sensitive to human disturbance. Feeding wildlife human food may cause digestive problems and may erase the wild instincts that keep the animals alive during times of scarcity.

Black bears can be particularly troublesome. Campers must hang their food in a tree or from a cache wire, at least 10 feet above the ground and 6 feet away from the tree trunk (There are also a limited number of bear-proof food canisters that can be checked out at the Marblemount Ranger Station). These bears are able climbers and will raid food containers that are hung too close to the trunk. In recent years, there have also been signs of grizzly bear activity in the North Cascades. There may be as many as ten to twenty animals within the range's thousands of square miles; travelers should assume that grizzlies are present and behave accordingly. In camp, hang all cosmetics and food-scented items well out of a bear's reach. On the trail, converse or make other noise to warn bears if visibility is limited by brush or fog.

Mountain lions are scattered sparsely throughout the North Cascades. Because of their reclusive habits, they are rarely seen by hikers. However, they can present a real threat if encountered at close range. The current wisdom is that hikers encountering a cougar should behave aggressively in order to scare it off. Remain standing and never turn your back on a cougar or attempt to run away. Such behavior may incite an attack. Report all sightings at the nearest ranger station.

Other animals are more a nuisance than a danger. Deer and mountain goats crave salt, and often hang around campsites and try to steal sweat-soaked clothing and saddle tack. At higher elevations, rodents dwelling in rockslides may chew their way into a pack in search of food or salt.

FORDING STREAMS AND RIVERS

There are only a few places in the North Cascades where trails cross substantial streams without the benefit of a bridge. Bear in mind, however, that these footlogs and bridges can be washed out during floods. Unbridged stream crossings are labeled as fords on the maps provided in this book. Streams are typically highest in early summer, when snowmelt swells the watercourses with silty discharge. Water levels also rise following rainstorms. Glacier-fed waterways rise on warm afternoons as meltwater surges downstream. Stream crossings should always be approached with caution; even a shallow stream can harbor slippery stones that can cause a sprained ankle, or worse. However, wilderness travelers can almost always make safe crossings by exercising good judgment and employing a few simple techniques.

When you get to the water's edge, the first thing you'll probably think is, "This is going to be really cold!" It will be even colder if you try to cross barefooted. Since most folks don't like to hike around in wet boots all day, we recommend bringing a pair of lightweight canvas sneakers or river sandals specifically for the purpose of fording streams. Wearing something on your feet will give you superior traction for a safer crossing. A walking staff adds additional stability when wading. Some manufacturers make a special wading staff with a metal tip, and some even telescope down to manageable proportions when not in use. If you use one of these, remember not to lean too hard on it; your legs should always bear most of the burden.

Before entering the stream, unclip your hip belt and other restrictive straps. Having the straps undone could save you from drowning. Water up to knee-depth can usually be forded without much difficulty; mid-thigh is the greatest safe depth for crossing unless the water is barely moving. Once you get in up to your crotch, your body starts giving the current a broad profile to push against, and you can bet that it won't be long before you are swimming.

When wading, discipline yourself to take tiny steps. The water will be cold, and your first impulse will be to rush across and get warm again. This kind of carelessness frequently results in a dunking. While inching your way across, your feet should seek the lowest possible footing, so that it is impossible to slip downward any farther. Use boulders sticking out of the streambed as braces for your feet; these boulders will have tiny underwater eddies on their upstream and downstream sides, and thus the force of the current against you will be reduced by a fraction. When emerging from the water, towel off as quickly as possible with an absorbent piece of clothing. If you let the water evaporate from your body, it will take with it additional heat that you could have used to warm up.

Some streams will be narrow, with boulders beckoning you to hopscotch across without getting your feet wet. Be careful, because you are in prime ankle-spraining country. Damp rocks may have a film of slippery algae on them, and even dry rocks might be unstable and roll out from underfoot. To avoid calamity, step only on boulders that are completely dry, and do not jump onto an untested boulder, since it may give way. The best policy is to keep one foot on the rocks at all times, so that you have firm footing to fall back on in case a foothold proves to be unstable.

HOW TO FOLLOW A FAINT TRAIL

Some trails that appear on maps of the North Cascades are quite faint and difficult to follow. Visitors should have a few elementary trail-finding skills in their bag of tricks, in case a trail peters out or a snowfall covers the pathway. A topographic map and compass—and the ability to use them— are essential insurance against disaster when a trail takes a wrong turn or disappears completely.

Maintained trails in the North Cascades are marked in a variety of ways. Signs bearing the name of the trail are present at most trail junctions. The trail signs are usually fashioned of plain wood, with script carved into them. They sometimes blend in well with the surrounding forest and may go unnoticed at junctions where a major trail meets a lightly traveled one. These signs may contain mileage information, but this information is often inaccurate.

Along the trail, several kinds of markers indicate the location of maintained trails. In forested areas, old blazes cut into the bark of trees may mark the path. In spots where a trail crosses a gravel streambed or rock outcrop, piles of rocks called cairns may mark the route. Cairns are also used in windswept alpine areas. These cairns are typically constructed of three or more stones placed on top of one another, a formation that almost never occurs naturally.

In the case of an extremely overgrown trail, markings of any kind may be impossible to find. On such a trail, the techniques used to build the trail serve as clues to its location. Well-constructed trails have rather wide, flat beds. Let your feet seek level spots when traveling through tall brush, and you will almost always find yourself on the trail. Old sawed logs from previous trail maintenance can be used to navigate in spots where the trail bed is obscured; if you find a sawed log, then you must be on a trail that was maintained at some point in time. Switchbacks are also a sure sign of

14

"Hall of trees" effect.

Author's Recommendations

Waterfalls		
	Agnes Gorge	North Fork Meadows
	Agnes Creek	Railroad Creek
	Holden Lake	Rainy Lake
	Horseshoe Basin	Three Falls Trail
	Little Beaver Creek	

Glacier Views		
	Cascade Pass	Park Creek
	Holden Lake	Ptarmigan Ridge
	Lake Ann	Railroad Creek
	North Fork Meadows	Whatcom Pass

Panoramic Vistas		
	Cascade Crest	Monogram Lake and Lookout Mountain
	Church Mountain	Maple Pass Loop
	Copper Ridge	Purple Pass
	Desolation Peak	Sahale Arm
	Devils Dome	Sauk Mountain
	Goode Ridge	Skyline Divide
	Granite Pass Highline	Skyline Trail
	Grasshopper Pass	Sourdough Mountain
	Hidden Lake Lookout	Table Mountain
	High Pass	Winchester Mountain
	McGregor Mountain	Yellow Aster Butte

Alpine Wildflowers		
	Cascade Crest	Jackita Ridge
	Center Mountain	Skyline Divide
	Chelan Crest Trail	South Pass
	Church Mountain	Stiletto Peak
	Devils Dome	Three Fools Trail
	Heather Trail	Welcome Pass and the High Divide

Solitude	Boulder Creek	Galene Lakes
	Buckskin Ridge	Monument Trail
	Center Mountain	Scaffold Ridge
	Company-Devore Creek Loop	Shellrock Pass
	East Creek	Silesia Creek
	Flat Creek	Three Fools Trail
Historical Features	Cady Pass	Horseshoe Basin
	Chancellor Trail	Skagit River Trail
	East Bank Trail	Thunder Creek
	East Creek	
Old-growth Forest	Big Beaver Creek	Little Beaver Creek
	Chilliwack River	Thunder Creek
Fall Colors	Blue Lake	Railroad Creek
	Chelan Crest Trail	Scatter Lake
	Monument Trail	

an official trail; wild animals travel in straight lines and rarely zigzag across hillsides.

Trail specifications often call for the clearing of all trees and branches for several feet on each side of a trail. In a forest situation, this results in a distinct "hall of trees" effect, where a corridor of cleared vegetation extends continuously through the woods. Trees grow randomly in a natural situation, so a long, thin clearing bordered by tree trunks usually indicates an old trail bed. On more open ground, look for trees that have lost all of their lower branches on only one side. Such trees often indicate a spot where the old trail once passed close to a lone tree.

When attempting to find a trail that has disappeared, ask yourself where the most logical place would be to build a trail given its source and destination. Trail builders tend to seek level ground where it is available, and often follow the natural contours of streamcourses and ridgelines. Bear in mind that most trails avoid up-and-down motion in favor of long, sustained grades culminating in major passes or hilltops. Old trail beds can sometimes be spotted from a distance as they cut across hillsides at a constant angle.

Zero Impact

One of the aims of this book is to encourage people to heft a pack and strike out on one of the wonderful trails in the North Cascades. But many of these same trails already receive moderate to heavy use, and they're showing signs of wear. Erosion is a problem where an army of boots has short-cut switchbacks. Litter seems to beget more litter, especially near trailheads and at backcountry campsites. Unofficial trails have proliferated across some alpine meadows, marring the otherwise pristine environment. Fortunately, all of these problems are avoidable—as are most impacts caused by backcountry visitors—if a few simple guidelines are heeded. Remember, the goal is to leave zero impact of your passing.

ADVANCED PLANNING TO MINIMIZE IMPACT

Much of the wear and tear that occurs in the North Cascades could be reduced by careful planning before the trip. Visitors should contact local authorities (see Appendix A) to find out about areas that are particularly sensitive to disturbance or receive heavy use. Since the goal of most wilderness travelers is to visit pristine and untrammeled areas, avoiding the most popular sites can only enhance one's wilderness experience.

The collared pika gathers grasses all summer to eat when snow covers the mountains.

We encourage travelers to plan their routes using established trails whenever possible, since these travel corridors are least susceptible to damage. Alpine habitats above the timberline are particularly fragile, and travelers who lack thorough training in minimum-impact techniques should cross them only on designated trails. Backcountry visitors can also travel more lightly by moving about in small groups. Small groups stress the landscape to a much smaller degree, especially around campsites, and they also lend themselves to greater flexibility in route choice and on-the-spot problem solving. Groups of two to four people are optimal, while groups larger than ten hikers have a much greater potential for environmental damage and should be split into smaller components.

The proper equipment can also help visitors reduce their visual presence and effects on the wilderness. Dark-hued or muted clothing, tents, and packs help make you less conspicuous to other travelers. Carry one bright yellow or orange shirt to attract attention in an emergency. Hiking shoes with a shallow tread design are gentler on plants and soils and also won't clog with mud. Backpackers can also carry a pair of smooth-soled camp shoes—sport sandals, boat shoes, or moccasins. These feel terrific after a day on the trail and they greatly reduce wear and tear on plants and soils around camp.

ON THE TRAIL

Please stay on established trails. Cutting switchbacks or crossing previously untracked ground leaves behind footprints and trampled plants—signs that may

Black bear.

invite the next person to follow in your footsteps. Eventually, enough footsteps lead to damaged plants and soils, erosion, and unwanted "social" trails.

Try to avoid travel when trails are saturated with rain or snowmelt. When muddy conditions are unavoidable (as is often the case in the Pacific Northwest), resist the temptation to skirt around puddles or boggy spots in the trail. This only widens the tread, and your feet will likely get soaked from brushing against ground plants anyway.

If you must travel off trail, look for trample-resistant surfaces: sand, gravel, snow (if it's not too steep), glacial till, or a streambed below the high water mark. Parties traveling cross-country should spread out in a line abreast rather than travel single file. This reduces the potential for creating new and unwanted trails and erosion in pristine areas. Leave your route unmarked— no blazes, cairns, flagging, or arrows scratched in the dirt.

As you hike along, always be conscious to reduce short- and long-term disturbances in the environment. Making loud noises can be helpful in avoiding encounters with bears and mountain lions where visibility is limited, but it also disturbs the less dangerous wildlife, as well as other travelers. If you do spot wildlife along the trail, be careful to stay outside the animal's comfort zone. If an animal changes behavior as a result of your presence, you are too close.

Be courteous and considerate to people you meet on the trail. Downhill hikers should yield to those going up. Motorbikers (where allowed) yield to all other trail users; mountain bikers yield to pack stock and hikers; and hikers yield to pack stock. Take the opportunity to say hello and exchange news of the trail. Remember, we are each in our own way pursuing the same goal of having fun in the backcountry.

SELECTING A CAMPSITE

Plan your route so that you can camp in established campsites that are officially listed in this guide. If you are traveling on National Park Service-managed lands, you must camp at the site designated on your permit. Pitch your tent in the center of the bare ground so as not to trample vegetation.

On national forest lands, established campsites may not be marked. If you cannot locate such a site, you will need to choose an impact-resistant spot to pitch your camp. Snow and river gravel bars, far as possible from the water, are preferable. Shorelines of lakes and streambanks are particularly sensitive to disturbance. Keep all campsites at least 200 feet from the nearest lake or stream. Alpine meadows are also very fragile and should be avoided by campers, especially heather and huckleberry meadows. Also camp well away from travel corridors. This will increase your own seclusion and help other parties preserve their wilderness experience.

When leaving any campsite, be sure that the area is returned to its natural state. Check around the area to be sure that you don't leave any belongings or litter. Leaves, duff, and twigs should be scattered about to camouflage your tent site and any high foot-traffic areas.

CAMPFIRES

Even where campfires are allowed, consider doing without one. The sudden cloudbursts found in this part of the country often make dry firewood a scarce commodity. A lightweight stove is a far superior alternative for cooking, and light can be supplied by a flashlight or candle lantern. Remember—within the national park complex, if there is no established fire grate, then fires are not allowed.

If you build a fire, do so only where downed, dead wood is abundant. Use sticks small enough to be broken by hand, and gather only as much as you need. Keep the fire small and brief. The fire should be built in an existing fire ring or in a fire pan (a metal tray or scrap of flame-resistant canvas under a 6-inch mound of dirt). Do not build new rock fire rings, and dismantle new ones that you find outside designated campsites.

A fire should never be left unattended, and once it's out, make sure the ashes are cold. The cold ashes should be scattered; leave the fire ring clean and pack out any unburned trash.

HUMAN WASTE DISPOSAL

Many people are surprised to learn that human waste, even when properly buried in a "cat hole" under ideal conditions, requires a year or more to decompose naturally. Any fecal bacteria present will remain viable (that is, infectious) for that length of time. The decomposition process is slowed even more when waste is concentrated (as in a group latrine) or deposited in excessively dry, wet, or cold conditions.

Once the traveler understands these facts, it is easy to see that natural composting can't always keep pace with the amount of human waste that is deposited, particularly at heavily used backcountry campsites. The problem is compounded when the site is near a lake or stream because runoff or groundwater can easily carry fecal material and disease into the surface water. Wildlife—and other campers—then use the contaminated source for drinking water. This can result in sickening consequences.

Most of the camping areas in national parks are provided with old-fashioned outhouses. Use these rustic facilities whenever nature calls, and practice minimum-impact disposal techniques where they are unavailable. Increasingly, land managers are asking (and in some places *requiring*) that people pack out human waste. Boaters on many western rivers have been doing this for years, and mountain climbers are now handed plastic bags for this purpose in several national parks. Thanks to the staff at Yosemite National Park, all backcountry visitors now have a clean, easy, and secure way to join the ranks and pack out waste. It's called the "poop tube."

You can make your own poop tube from a piece of 4-inch diameter PVC plastic pipe, the kind used for plumbing. Cut the pipe to length as needed for the number of days you'll be in the backcountry; a 2-foot section is enough for five to seven days for most folks. Then glue a cap on one end and a threaded adapter for a screw-on plug on the other end. Some travelers duct tape a piece of nylon webbing onto the side of the tube so that it can be strapped onto the outside of a pack.

To use the tube, defecate into a paper lunch bag. Then sprinkle in a handful of kitty litter to absorb moisture and reduce odors. Shake the bag to distribute the kitty litter, then roll it up and slide it into the tube. Used toilet paper can go in the tube as well. Screw in the plug and you're done. At the end of the trip, empty the contents into a non-flush vault or "pit" toilet (ask land managers beforehand to recommend a specific outhouse). The paper bags will quickly decay (use only unwaxed bags to ensure that they do) and won't clog the pump used to clean out the vault. Never put human waste into trash cans or dumpsters—it creates a health hazard and is illegal.

If you decide instead to use the cat hole method and bury your waste in the backcountry, follow a few simple guidelines:

- Look for an out-of-the-way site in stable soil at least 200 feet (about seventy paces) from surface water. Avoid places that show signs of flooding, carrying runoff, or groundwater seepage.
- Make sure the site is at least 200 feet from campsites, trails, and other centers of human activity.
- Look for a site with a healthy layer of topsoil at least 6 inches deep. The ground should be moist but not saturated and easy to dig in.
- With a small hand trowel, dig a cat hole 6 to 8 inches deep. Keep the sod lid intact. Set it aside and pile all the dirt next to the hole.
- Squat and aim for the hole. Deposit used toilet paper in the hole (burning it is unnecessary and risky in dry or windy conditions).
- When covering the waste, use a stick to stir in the first handful or two of soil. This hastens the decomposition process. Add the remaining soil and replace the sod lid. Scrape leaves and duff around the site to camouflage your efforts. Remember to clean your hands well before handling food or cooking utensils.
- It is better to pack out your toilet paper rather than burying it.

Unless local regulations state otherwise, it's usually best to dig individual cat holes rather than a group latrine. And always use the outhouse if one is provided.

WASHING

The key to cleaning up in the backcountry is to keep soap, oils, and all other pollutants out of the water. Mountain lakes and streams have a delicate balance of nutrients. Soaps and dishwater dumped into alpine waterways encourage the growth of microbes that can deplete dissolved oxygen in the water, making it inhospitable to many species of fish. In addition, aquatic plants and fish are extremely sensitive to soap, even the biodegradable kind, and can die from contact with it.

To wash cooking and eating utensils, carry water in a clean bowl or pot at least 200 feet from water sources. Use little or no soap—water warmed on the stove will unstick most food and grease. Use a plastic scrubber and a little muscle for stubborn residues. Scatter wash water over the ground in an out-of-the-way spot at least 200 feet from surface water and 100 yards from any likely campsite. This is bear country; pick out food scraps before scattering the water and pack them out with other garbage.

For personal bathing, a good dousing and scrubbing with a washcloth will suffice for all but extended trips. Again, carry the water at least 200 feet from surface water. There are also rinse-free soaps and shampoos on the market that are designed specifically for backpackers.

Regulations

REGULATIONS AND GUIDELINES SPECIFIC TO NORTH CASCADES NATIONAL PARK

- Backcountry campers must obtain a permit, which is available free of charge at ranger stations and many trailheads. Camp only at the site on your permit; changes in itinerary must be confirmed at a ranger station.
- Campfires are permitted only at camps with fire grates. See Appendix B for a complete listing.
- Pets are prohibited in the backcountry and in some frontcountry areas.
- The collection or removal of rocks or wildflowers is illegal.
- All trails in the park are closed to mountain bikes; some trails are off-limits to horses.
- The entire park backcountry has been designated by Congress as the Steven Mather Wilderness Area; mechanized and motorized equipment are prohibited.
- A Washington State fishing license is required for all fishing within the park, including minors and catch-and-release.
- Firearms are prohibited throughout the park.
- The group size limit for overnight trips is twelve people and/or eight head of stock.

REGULATIONS AND GUIDELINES SPECIFIC TO ROSS LAKE AND LAKE CHELAN NATIONAL RECREATION AREAS

- Backcountry campers must obtain a permit, which is available free of charge at ranger stations. Camp only at the site on your permit; changes in itinerary must be confirmed at a ranger station.
- Campfires are permitted only at camps with fire grates. See Appendix B for a complete listing.

- Pets are permitted throughout the recreation areas, even within designated wilderness. They must be leashed at all times.
- All trails in the recreation areas are closed to mountain bikes; some trails are off-limits to horses.
- Parts of both recreation areas fall within the Steven Mather Wilderness. Mechanized and motorized equipment are prohibited within wilderness areas.
- During hunting season, hunters are allowed to carry firearms and off-road throughout the area within both recreation areas, and hunting is permitted pursuant to Washington State regulations.
- A Washington State fishing license is required for all fishing within the recreation areas, including minors and catch-and-release.
- The group size limit for overnight trips is twelve, including stock (where permitted). Most cross-country zones have a party limit of six people.

REGULATIONS SPECIFIC TO NATIONAL FOREST WILDERNESS AREAS

- Mechanized vehicles and motorized equipment are prohibited.
- Overnight parking permits are required within the Okanogan National Forest. The Mount Baker–Snoqualmie National Forest requires a parking permit for day use as well. These permits also apply to non-wilderness trailheads within the forest.
- Campfires are discouraged above 5,000 feet elevation.
- Group size is limited to twelve people and/or eight head of stock.
- Livestock may not be tethered to trees or shrubs for more than thirty minutes.
- Transporting of unprocessed vegetative matter, such as hay or grain, is prohibited.

REGULATIONS SPECIFIC TO CANADIAN PROVINCIAL PARKS

- Backcountry permits are not required, but you must camp in an officially designated backcountry campsite.
- Open fires are permitted in the backcountry, except on the Heather Trail, where they are strictly prohibited.
- Firearms are prohibited.
- It is illegal to collect or remove any natural feature, including rocks and flowers.
- Pets must be on a leash at all times.
- Anglers must carry a valid British Columbia fishing license.

The Hikes

The Skagit River—Gateway to the North Cascades

The broad, green Skagit River, which courses down a fertile valley from thousands of snowfields and a hundred glaciers, was the original thoroughfare into the North Cascades. Trails used by the Skagit tribe became the pack-horse routes of prospectors and, later, a railway to support the building of hydroelectric dams on the river during the 1920s. Modern visitors follow the asphalt ribbon of Washington Highway 20, which finally breached the mountain fastness in 1972.

The Skagit Valley is a broad and lush basin fed by the abundant rains of Puget Sound. It is filled with fruit orchards and dairy farms, and bordered by broad clearcuts scythed from the forests by an aggressive timber industry. Surrounding the valley are the peripheral ranges of the North Cascades, where a multitude of short trails lead to the mountaintops. The climate here is distinctly maritime; fogs and rainstorms are the defining element of the landscape. Abundant moisture creates ideal growing conditions for conifers, such as mountain hemlock and western red-cedar, which attain mighty proportions in isolated pockets that were never logged off. Especially impressive stands occur at Rockport State Park and along the upper reaches of the Baker River Highway. Above timberline are lush meadows guarded by peaks where snowfields linger year-round. There are relatively few developed trails into the high country, though, and these are plagued by crowds on the weekends.

Because the Skagit Valley is close to both Seattle, Washington, and Vancouver, British Columbia, it receives quite a bit of weekend tourism. Many visitors never venture far from their cars, and the short hikes in the surrounding mountains are well-suited to the tight schedules of a whirlwind tour. Seek out the National Park Service ranger station at Marblemount, which is the information center for day hikes and backcountry excursions in the North Cascades National Park complex. This is where most backcountry permits are issued. Interpretive displays and presentations can be found at the large visitor center just south of Newhalem. Visitors approaching from the west can also obtain information at the joint Forest Service–Park Service station at Sedro-Woolley. The towns of Burlington and Mount Vernon provide all the services of a modern city, while a more limited selection of supplies can be found at Concrete and Marblemount. Rockport has gas and a country store, while Newhalem is a company town built by Seattle City Light for its dam workers and has only a small mercantile store.

Car campers will find public camping at Rockport State Park as well as large park campgrounds outside Newhalem. There are a number of Forest Service campgrounds along the Baker River Highway, a paved

Skagit River Overview

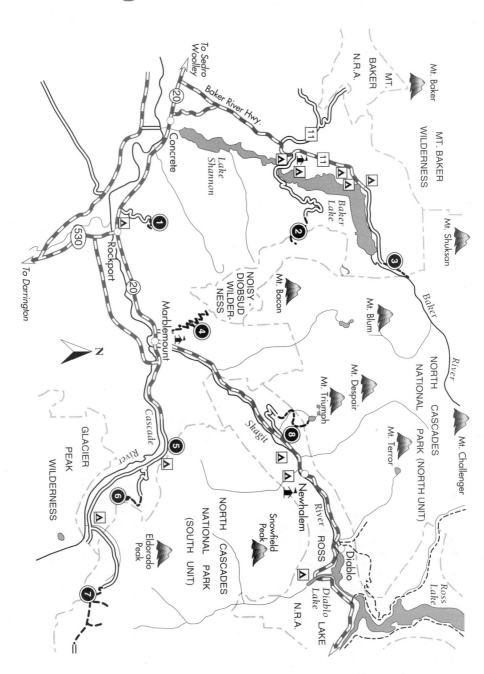

thoroughfare that originates west of Concrete, and along the Cascade River Road, a gravel trunk road that runs southeast from Marblemount. User fees are now in effect for all trailheads that fall within the Mount Baker–Snoqualmie National Forest.

1   Sauk Mountain

Overview: A half-day hike to Sauk Mountain, 4.2 miles round trip, or a day hike or short backpack to Sauk Lake, 6.2 miles round trip.

Best season: Mid-May to mid-October; Sauk Lake opens mid-June.

Difficulty: Moderate.

Elevation gain: 1,040 feet to Sauk Mountain.

Elevation loss: 1,170 feet to Sauk Lake.

Maximum elevation: 5,541 feet at the summit of Sauk Mountain.

Topo maps: Sauk Mountain; *Lake Shannon.*

Jurisdiction: Mount Baker–Snoqualmie National Forest.

Mount Baker from the top of Sauk Mountain.

Finding the trailhead: Follow Washington Highway 20 to Rockport State Park, just west of Rockport. Drive north on Sauk Mountain Road, an improved gravel road that winds upward for 8 miles to the trailhead.

Key points:
- 0.0   Sauk Mountain Trailhead.
- 1.4   Trail reaches ridge crest.
- 1.6   Junction with spur trail to Sauk Lake (1.5 miles, moderate). Bear left for summit of Sauk Mountain.
- 2.1   Trail ends atop one of the crags of Sauk Mountain.

The hike: This trail makes a short but challenging ascent to the summit of Sauk Mountain on the seaward edge of the North Cascades. Views are surprisingly inspiring from here, encompassing Mount Baker and Puget Sound as well as the glacier-carved peaks of the Cascades. A spur trail makes a long descent from the heights to reach Sauk Lake, where there are several camping spots. Both the lake and the summit of Sauk Mountain can be reached in a hard half day of hiking.

The trail begins at timberline, zigzagging steadily up a wide but steep couloir. Avalanches have cleared away the trees here, clearing a space for a magnificent display of alpine wildflowers. Glacier and avalanche lilies dominate the early season just after snowmelt, and are overtopped by lupine, Indian paintbrush, monkeyflower, penstemon, and many others as the summer progresses. From the slopes, one can look out across the Skagit and Sauk river valleys, with the lofty summit of Whitehorse Mountain rising to the southwest. The icebound volcanic cone of Mount Baker becomes visible near the top of the grade.

The path tops out in a grassy saddle in the rocky cockscomb of Sauk Mountain. Splendid westward views stretch from the high volcanic summit of Glacier Peak north along the western scarp of the Cascade Mountains and into Canada. Strange tors of basalt rise along the crest of Sauk Mountain itself, and small way trails wander among them. The main trail traverses high across the eastern face of the peak, and soon the Sauk Lake spur trail drops away to the right (see below). The Sauk Mountain route glides up to a bald knob that offers superb northward views of Mount Shuksan.

The trail then crosses the talus slopes beneath a series of sharp pinnacles. Watch for tiny pikas scurrying among the broken shards of rock. The path soon climbs into a saddle and then ascends one of the pinnacles, where it reaches its end. Hikers get an unobstructed vista of Mount Baker from this point, and on an exceptionally clear day one can see the Olympic Mountains to the west and Mount Rainier to the south.

Sauk Lake Option. From a signpost high on the flanks of Sauk Mountain, this spur path descends steadily across meadow-strewn slopes. The trail slumps away in spots, making for treacherous footing. The path soon seeks an eastward-trending spur ridge and follows it downward past odd sinkholes bordered by mats of pink heather. As it enters a sparse growth of trees, the trail passes several fine overlooks of the Skagit Valley. It then

Sauk Mountain

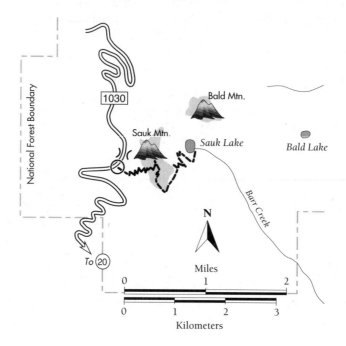

turns north, still descending, to pass through a notch that overlooks Sauk Lake. Beyond the notch, the trail traverses a talus slope where marmots make their dens. The path zigzags down toward the lake, then levels off and traverses small patches of brush to reach the low rise at its foot. This rise is an old terminal moraine, bulldozed into place by a long-extinct montane glacier that once gouged the lake basin out of the mountainside. Camping spots are secluded in the trees atop the moraine; camp so that your tent is not visible to hikers atop Sauk Mountain.

2 Watson Lakes

Overview:	A day hike to Anderson Butte (3 miles round trip), Anderson Lakes (5 miles round trip), Watson Lakes (6.2 miles round trip), or all three (9.4 miles total).
Best season:	Mid-June to mid-October.
Difficulty:	Moderate overall; moderately strenuous to Anderson Butte.
Elevation gain:	780 feet to Watson Lakes; 1,260 feet to Anderson Butte.
Elevation loss:	710 feet to Watson Lakes.
Maximum elevation:	5,380 feet at Anderson Butte.
Topo maps:	Bacon Peak; *Lake Shannon.*
Jurisdiction:	Noisy-Diobsud Wilderness (Mount Baker–Snoqualmie National Forest).

Finding the trailhead: Follow Washington Highway 20 west from Concrete for 5 miles to the Baker River Highway (Forest Road 11). Follow this road north for 14 miles, then turn right at signs for Baker Dam. Drive across the dam and turn north on Forest Road 1107, a logging road passable to passenger cars. Follow this road upward for 9.2 miles to a junction with FR 1107-022. Turn left onto this spur and follow it for 1.2 miles to the trailhead.

Key points:
- 0.0 Watson Lakes Trailhead.
- 0.8 Junction with Anderson Butte Trail (0.7 mile, moderately strenuous). Stay right for Watson Lakes.
- 1.6 Junction with Anderson Lakes Trail (0.9 mile, moderate). Stay left for Watson Lakes.
- 1.9 Trail crosses pass and enters Noisy-Diobsud Wilderness.
- 2.5 Camping area beside the westernmost of the Watson Lakes. Trail follows lakeshore.
- 2.9 Trail reaches foot of lake.
- 3.1 Foot of eastern Watson Lake. Trail follows lakeshore.
- 3.8 Head of eastern Watson Lake.

The hike: This network of short trails climbs to the timberline at the edge of the Noisy-Diobsud Wilderness, visiting alpine lakes and an old fire lookout site. Wildflower displays are impressive here, and black bears are commonly sighted. Travelers can choose to visit either Watson Lakes, Anderson Lakes, or Anderson Butte in a half-day hike, or combine all three in a long day trek. Fires are not allowed in the Noisy-Diobsud Wilderness, and campers must pitch their tents in a designated site.

Watson Lakes

The trail begins by ascending gradually across steep slopes robed in old-growth coastal forest. Mountain hemlock is the dominant conifer, but silver fir is also present. Observe the open nature of the forest and the rich mix of tree sizes: This complexity provides a multitude of ecological niches for forest animals, accounting for the ecological importance of old-growth to forest ecosystems.

After crossing sinuous finger ridges and low saddles, the path emerges unexpectedly into a luxuriant meadow of heather and sedges. The Anderson Butte trail (see below) splits away at the bottom of the meadow, while the main path ascends along it to reveal striking views of mounts Baker and Shuksan to the northwest. Meadows such as these occur in pockets that fill with deep snow, making for a short growing season that effectively excludes most conifers. A few clumps of mountain hemlock grow from the hillocks where the snow melts sooner. Wildlife enthusiasts can glass for pikas in the talus on the lower slopes of Anderson Butte. At the upper edge of the meadow, the trail crosses a pass and enters heavy timber once more. A faint spur path runs to an outcrop that faces southwest for views across Baker Lake.

The main trail descends through the trees to reach a boggy meadow, where the path to Anderson Lakes splits away to the right (see below). The Watson Lakes trail now climbs vigorously to reach a low notch, then descends into the Noisy-Diobsud Wilderness. Just beyond the boundary, open slopes face eastward across the Watson Lakes for views of majestic Bacon Peak. Hagan Mountain is visible farther to the north. The path now descends sharply to reach camping spots in the heavy timber on the north shore of the westernmost lake.

Our route continues around the lakeshore and crosses the logs at its outlet to reach camping spots amid the heather-sedge parks above the second lake (please camp only in designated spots). This lake is the larger of the two, with rocky peninsulas that jut out into the water. The track becomes more primitive as it crosses the log boom at the outlet of the lake and climbs and falls sharply across the hummocky heather. There are excellent views of Martin Peak along the way, and Anderson Butte is revealed in its rocky majesty from the trail's end on the eastern shore.

Anderson Butte Option. This steep trail begins by climbing eastward across the timbered slopes of Anderson Butte, in full view of the craggy summit. The path tops out in a saddle north of the butte and enters the Noisy-Diobsud Wilderness. Initial views feature Hagan Mountain and vistas up the Baker River valley toward the peaks of the Picket Range. Climbers can try for the summit, but the trail runs north along the ridgetop. It ends atop a rocky promontory that offers panoramic views that stretch across the head of Baker Lake to the regal summits of mounts Baker and Shuksan.

Anderson Lakes Option. This primitive trail wanders southward through heather parklands, then makes a rocky descent along talus slopes and through stands of hemlock. At the bottom of the grade is the lowermost of the Anderson Lakes. Sheer cliffs guard the head of the lake, while to the west is a broad shelf of heather and sedge meadows where good camping spots can be found. Black bears frequent the area, particularly in late summer when dwarf blueberries ripen. Only the lower lake is accessible by trail; the upper two lie to the southwest atop an elevated shelf.

3 Baker River

Overview:	A half-day hike along the Baker River to Sulphide Camp, 5.2 miles round trip.
Best season:	Mid-April to early November.
Difficulty:	Easy.
Elevation gain:	190 feet.
Elevation loss:	80 feet.
Maximum elevation:	900 feet.
Topo maps:	Mount Shuksan; *Mount Shuksan*.
Jurisdiction:	Mount Baker–Snoqualmie National Forest, North Cascades National Park.

Finding the trailhead: Follow Washington Highway 20 west from Concrete for 5 miles to the Baker River Highway (Forest Road 11). Follow this road

Baker River

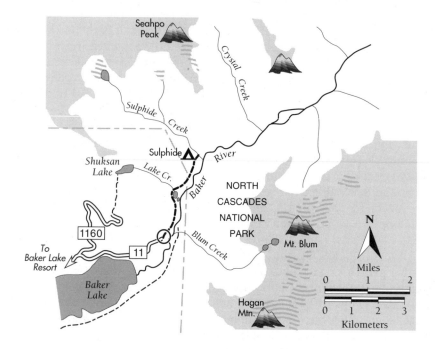

north. The pavement ends after 20 miles, and at mile 25 there is an unmarked intersection. Turn left for the final mile to the trailhead.

Keypoints:
- 0.0   Trailhead at end of road.
- 1.5   Trail crosses Lake Creek.
- 1.9   Trail enters North Cascades National Park.
- 2.6   Sulphide Camp (backcountry permit required).

The hike: This trail penetrates a remote and forgotten corner of North Cascades National Park, offering an easy stroll through the ancient forests along one of the wildest rivers in the Cascades. The trail begins as an old road that wanders along the riverbanks, which are robed in a young forest of mountain hemlock, western red-cedar, and red alder. Plentiful rainfall creates favorable growing conditions for club moss, which hangs like shrouding from the branches of the vine maples.

Soon there are views of the water. The Baker River is young in the geological sense of the word. As it brawls down its gravel-choked course, it splits into broad channels where floodwaters have built up new gravel bars and the water has sought a lower passageway. Watch for the glacier-clad fastness of Hagan Mountain, which peeks out above the steep foothills beyond the river.

As steep slopes crowd the riverbank, the trail threads its way among massive boulders covered with moss, and ancient cedars tower overhead. Gravel bars farther upstream have been colonized by groves of red alder, which invades flood-scoured riverbanks. Symbiotic bacteria in alder roots pump nitrogen into the soil, where it can nourish the seedlings of the shade-tolerant conifers that will eventually replace the alders. The trail soon splashes across several tributary streams. The largest of these is Lake Creek, and its alluvial fan supports a fine mixed forest of enormous cedars and moss-draped bigleaf maples.

After a final visit to the river's edge, the path turns inland to bypass an extensive wetland created by beavers. This is an excellent spot to glass for waterfowl and other marsh inhabitants. Returning to the bottomlands, the trail leads onward across the shady floor of a closed-canopy hemlock forest. The understory is suffused with green: mosses grow from every available surface. The trail reaches its end at a National Park Service camp beside Sulphide Creek. Visit the banks of this large tributary for northward views of Seahpo Peak at the end of Jagged Ridge.

4   Cow Heaven

Overview:	A day hike from the Skagit Valley to an alpine ridgetop, 11 miles round trip.
Best season:	Late June to mid-October.
Difficulty:	Moderately strenuous.
Elevation gain:	4,475 feet.
Elevation loss:	None.
Maximum elevation:	4,840 feet.
Topo maps:	Marblemount (trail not shown); *Marblemount.*
Jurisdiction:	Mount Baker–Snoqualmie National Forest.

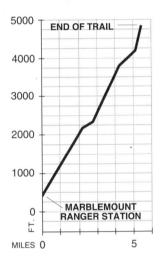

Finding the trailhead: In Marblemount, take Washington Highway 20 to Ranger Station Road, at the west edge of town. Follow this road north for a mile to the National Park Service compound. Park at the visitor center and walk east down the gravel road past the greenhouse to the horse barn. The new trailhead is a wide spot opposite the barn, and the route follows flagging to meet the original trail, which began on what is now private property.

Key points:
- 0.0   Trail begins opposite horse barn.
- 4.3   Camping spot.
- 5.5   Trail ends on ridgetop.

Cow Heaven

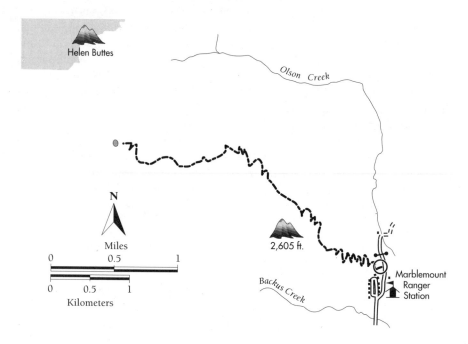

The hike: This trail offers a strenuous day hike from the floor of the Skagit Valley to the mountain heights north of Marblemount. For visitors who are pressed for time and find themselves at the Park Service ranger station, this trail offers a full day of hiking into alpine country without any additional driving. The trail has recently been rerouted to avoid private property along Olson Creek; the new trailhead across from the National Park Service barn should be complete by 1998.

The trail begins by climbing steadily through a closed-canopy forest of mountain hemlock. Ferns and mosses carpet the forest floor as the well-trodden trail zigzags up the steep slopes. An intermittent stream runs beside the trail during early summer, and the path crosses it several times during the initial ascent. Moss-covered logs and boulders provide a colorful counterpoint to the rushing waters. After a long climb, the trail abandons the watercourse and crosses a series of level benches where great rounded outcrops of a metamorphic rock called *schist* rise from the moss. Soon the path drops to cross a swampy dale where western red-cedars tower above a riot of underbrush.

The level terraces get smaller and smaller as the trail continues up the mountainside. Just beyond the 3-mile mark, the path reaches the wooded edge of a narrow ravine, and openings in the forest offer the first mountain views. Rushing water can be heard nearby during early summer, but the hidden stream is difficult to approach safely. The trail continues upward, following the steep toe of a spur ridge as it ascends into the subalpine zone. False huckleberry now crowds the overgrown path, while subalpine fir and mountain hemlock form a patchy forest. Views now encompass Mount Terror and the Crescent Creek Spires to the east as well as Teebone Ridge and El Dorado Peak to the south. The rocky outcrops that rise ahead are not the Helen Buttes, but minor outriders.

The path now follows the ridgeline upward, and the views improve with each passing step. A broad sweep of the Skagit Valley unfolds below, robed in a patchwork of clearcuts and surrounded by snowy peaks. The trail ultimately passes a camping spot tucked into a ridgetop hollow, but it lacks a reliable water supply. The trail continues up along the ridgecrest, yielding views of the brush-filled bowl below. This area burned years ago, and a lush growth of plants grew in the wake of the fire. Farmers are said to have driven their cattle here for summer pasture during the years that followed the blaze, and the basin came to be known as "Cow Heaven." Shrubs have since taken over the bowl, highlighted by white rhododendron, which blooms in early summer, and huckleberry bushes that bear fruit in August.

The path continues its dogged ascent, zigzagging up the head of the bowl to reach swards of alpine tundra on the mountaintop. As the trail ends, a series of rounded summits offers views in all directions. Helen Buttes rise stark and bare to the north, and the rocky crest of Diobsud Butte is visible farther east. The isolated massif of crags on the southwestern horizon is crowned by Whitehorse Mountain. Travelers with a thirst for even more adventure might attempt the cross-country ridge trek to the Helen Buttes and continue onward to Olson Lake.

5 Monogram Lake and Lookout Mountain

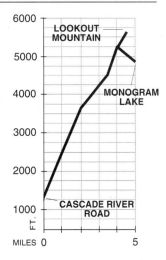

Overview:	A long day hike or backpack to either Monogram Lake (9.8 miles round trip) or Lookout Mountain (9.4 miles round trip).
Best season:	Mid-July to mid-October for Lookout Mountain; late July to mid-October for Monogram Lake.
Difficulty:	Strenuous.
Elevation gain:	4,095 feet to Monogram Lake; 4,444 feet to Lookout Mountain.
Elevation loss:	470 feet to Monogram Lake.
Maximum elevation:	5,699 feet at Lookout Mountain.

Looking into the Monogram Lake basin.

Topo maps: Big Devil Peak;
Marblemount.
Jurisdiction: Mount Baker–Snoqualmie
National Forest, North
Cascades National Park.

Finding the trailhead: From Marblemount, follow the Cascade River Road across the bridge. Follow this road past the pavement's end to the Monogram Lake trailhead at mile 9.1.

Key points:
    0.0 Trailhead on Cascade River Road.
    2.8 Trail junction. Bear left for Lookout Mountain (1.9 more miles)
         or turn right for Monogram Lake.
    4.9 Monogram Lake.

The hike: This trail enjoys enormous popularity as one of the fastest routes to the high country from the Marblemount Ranger Station. Legions of day hikers set out each weekend, bound for Monogram Lake, one of the true alpine gems of the North Cascades, and for the old fire tower atop Lookout Mountain. Few make it; the tedious 2,500-foot climb up the forested walls of the Cascade River valley is merely a prelude to the near-vertical angler's trail that leads to Monogram Lake. The climb to the lookout is gentler, but no peach either. A volunteer organization maintains the fire tower, and it is open for overnight stays on a first-come first-served basis. Monogram Lake

Monogram Lake • Lookout Mountain

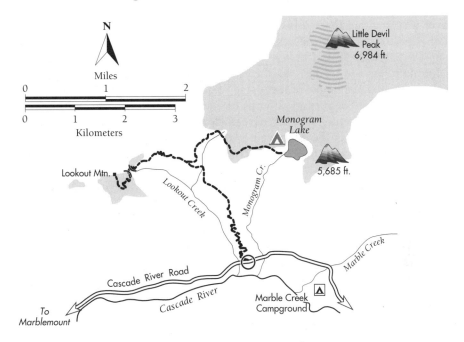

lies just within the national park boundary, and permits are required for backpackers. Cutthroats inhabit the lake and offer spectacular fishing.

The trek begins with a relentless, zigzagging climb through heavy timber. Mature hemlocks provide unbroken shade for the ascent, and moss carpets the forest floor. About halfway up the grade, views down the valley can be had from the top of a stone outcrop. As the trail continues to gain altitude, rushing streams can be heard on both sides of the trail, but there is no easy way to get to the water.

At the top of the initial slope, the trail passes a spring and a pitiful little camping spot at the edge of a landslide scar. To the west, conifers are tilted at crazy angles, attesting to the downhill slumping of the soil beneath them. The trail climbs through a brushy avalanche swath that is filled with cow parsnip, salmonberry, and stinging nettle. A backward glance yields views of the southwestern buttress of Eldorado Peak. At the top of the brushy stretch, the trail turns west and the gradient eases for a while. The forest is now dominated by ancient hemlocks intermixed with younger silver firs, which are even more shade-tolerant. The trail crosses a substantial stream, then rounds a finger ridge to reach a trail junction on the slope beyond. The main trail continues straight ahead toward Lookout Mountain; lake-bound travelers should turn right onto the fainter trail.

The rough track to Monogram Lake ascends through the subalpine forest with brutal uphill pitches. It passes along the edge of an old burn, then resumes its merciless ascent through the trees. The path ultimately levels off and turns eastward, and flowery glades begin to interrupt the forest. A meadow-strewn bowl stretches ahead, and the trail crosses it before climbing over a spur ridge that yields mountain views that stretch from horizon to horizon. To the north the rugged crags of Bacon Peak are dwarfed by the snowy massif of Mount Baker, and close at hand is the tower atop Lookout Mountain. As the trail crests the ridge, astounding views open up to the east, encompassing most of the glacier-clad summits that guard the Cascade River as well as the distant summit of Glacier Peak far to the south.

The trail descends steadily across slopes of heather and glacier lilies, making a beeline for the deep waters of Monogram Lake. The lake is situated beneath a small peak of its own, from which waterfalls descend into the basin. Marmots are abundant here, and black bears are sighted frequently. Campers and anglers should tread lightly as they enjoy the fragile lakeshore environs, where alpine plants are easily damaged by trampling.

Lookout Mountain Option. Upon leaving the high trail junction, this route climbs gradually through the forest on a westward heading. The trees are soon interrupted by pleasant glades filled with alpine wildflowers. The path ultimately reaches a steep meadow, richly carpeted with blossoms throughout the summer. There are good views of Little Devil Peak from this point. At the far edge of the slope, the trail zigzags up to a wooded saddle, then begins its assault on the eastern face of Lookout Mountain. Open meadows on the way up reveal outstanding views of Eldorado Peak. The lookout tower rises from the summit, commanding views of the Skagit Valley and the innumerable peaks of the North Cascades. The lookout is no longer staffed but is open to public use, with priority given to lookout maintenance crews.

6   Hidden Lake Lookout

Overview:	A day hike to Hidden Lake Lookout, 7.4 miles round trip.
Best season:	Mid-July to mid-October (expect snow in upper reaches).
Difficulty:	Moderately strenuous.
Elevation gain:	3,210 feet.
Maximum elevation:	5,699 feet at Hidden Lake Lookout.
Topo maps:	Eldorado Peak, Sonny Boy Lakes; *Diablo Lake, Cascade Pass.*
Jurisdiction:	Mount Baker–Snoqualmie National Forest, North Cascades National Park.

Elevation profile chart: horizontal axis in MILES from 0 to 5; vertical axis in FT. from 3000 to 7000. Labels on the profile: TRAILHEAD, PASS ABOVE HIDDEN LAKE, LOOKOUT.

Eldorado Peak from ridge below Hidden Lake Lookout.

Finding the trailhead: From Marblemount, follow the Cascade River Road across the bridge. Follow this road past the pavement's end to mile 10.2 and a junction with Forest Road 1540. This steep and narrow road winds upward for 4.7 miles to reach the trailhead.

Key points:
- 0.0 Hidden Lake Trailhead.
- 0.5 Trail crosses the East Fork of Sibley Creek.
- 3.4 Pass overlooking Hidden Lake.
- 3.7 Hidden Lake Lookout.

The hike: This popular day hike starts near timberline and climbs to the mountaintops for superb views of the glacier-clad peaks that line the Cascade River. The old fire lookout atop Hidden Lake Peak is now maintained by a volunteer group for overnight stays. There is no fee (although donations are welcome); get there early if you plan to sleep in the lookout, because it's a first-come first-served proposition. Hikers who wish to camp in the basin of Hidden Lake must have a National Park Service permit and be prepared for the scrambling required to descend to level ground.

From the parking lot, the trail crosses some brushy streams, then zigzags upward through a climax forest of silver fir. After 0.4 mile, the path breaks into an open basin where the East Fork of Sibley Creek has its origins. The trail soon climbs out of a riot of cow parsnip, fireweed, and false hellebore to reach the sloping meadows of the bowl. The upper slopes support a riot of wildflowers, and hoary marmots and black bears are often spotted here. High in

Hidden Lake Lookout

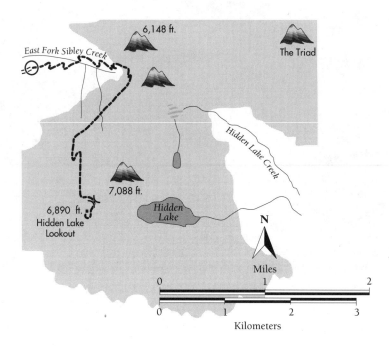

the basin, the lofty cone of Mount Baker becomes visible far to the northwest, while the lesser cockscomb of Sauk Mountain rises in the middle distance.

After a long and vigorous climb, the trail reaches alpine slopes robed in heather and dwarf blueberry. It now levels off on a southward heading, and sparkling brooks of all descriptions course down through the boulder-strewn meadows. Snowy summits rise above sawback ridges to the north. A spur trail soon leads westward to a campsite on a high perch, while the main trail continues a gentle ascent toward a spur ridge clad in full-grown mountain hemlock. Upon gaining the ridge, look eastward for spectacular views featuring the western summits of Eldorado Peak.

The trail now climbs across a dome of bedrock, and the glacier-clad summit of Snowking Mountain becomes visible to the southwest. There is another high camp in this area, near snowmelt pools that thaw in late summer. Listen for the kazoo-like warning call of the pika, a short-eared member of the rabbit clan. The path now snakes upward along ridges of frost-riven granite, and a ragged summit rises ahead. The trail, often covered in snow here, climbs into the saddle to the north of the peak and ends.

This rocky col offers superb views of Hidden Lake in its basin of fractured rock, with Forbidden Peak and Sahale Mountain ranged beyond it to the east. The broad icefield between the peaks is the Quien Sabe Glacier. To the southwest is a crowd of imposing summits: Johannesburg Mountain, Spider

Mountain and Middle Cascade Glacier, Mount Formidable rising in front of it, Sentinel Peak with its snow domes, Dome Peak, and finally Spire Peak embracing Spire Glacier.

Adventurous travelers might opt to undertake the steep and hazardous scramble from the pass down the snowfields and talus slopes to the shores of Hidden Lake. According to legend, trout of mythic proportions can be found here during the brief ice-free season.

A cairn- and paint-marked route leads south across the mountainside, then climbs to reach the old Hidden Lake fire lookout. The structure was built in 1933, and is currently maintained as a public shelter. The lookout boasts superb views that encompass Eldorado Peak to the north and Glacier Peak far to the south. On a clear day, Mount Rainier can be seen just to the left of Snowking Mountain.

7 Cascade Pass and Sahale Arm

Overview: A day hike to Cascade Pass, 7.4 miles round trip; a long day trip or backpack to Sahale Glacier (10.8 miles round trip); or a backpack to the Stehekin Valley Road, 8.4 miles total.

Best season: Mid-July to mid-October.

Difficulty: Moderate west to east; moderately strenuous east to west and Sahale Arm.

Elevation gain: 1,740 feet to Cascade Pass; 4,060 feet to Sahale Arm.

Elevation loss: 2,625 feet to Cottonwood Camp.

Maximum elevation: 5,380 feet at Cascade Pass; 7,700 feet at Sahale Glacier.

Topo maps: Cascade Pass, Goode Mountain; *Cascade Pass, McGregor Mountain.*

Jurisdiction: North Cascades National Park.

Finding the trailhead: From Marblemount, follow the Cascade River Road across the bridge. Follow this road about 24 miles to the trailhead at its end. The last several miles may be rough and potholed.

Key points:
0.0   Cascade Pass Trailhead.
2.6   Junction with abandoned Diamond Mine Trail. Bear right.
3.7   Cascade Pass.
3.8   Junction with Sahale Arm spur (see below). Bear right for the Stehekin Valley Road.
4.4   Pelton Basin Camp.
5.5   Trail crosses Doubtful Creek.
6.1   Junction with Horseshoe Basin Trail. Main trail doglegs down to the right.
7.0   Trail crosses Basin Creek.
7.1   Basin Camp.
8.4   Cottonwood Camp, at the end of the Stehekin Valley Road.

Sahale Arm

0.0   Junction with Cascade Pass Trail.
0.7   Trail reaches ridgeline of Sahale Arm. Junction with Doubtful Lake spur trail (0.5 mile, moderately strenuous). Bear left for Sahale Glacier.
1.2   Trail maintenance ends; follow cairns upward through the rocks.
1.6   Sahale Glacier Camp.

The hike: Perhaps the best-loved trail in the North Cascades, this path follows the ancient trade route used by the Skagit and Chelan tribes to breach the lofty peaks of the divide. Alexander Ross is thought to have bumbled through Cascade Pass during his 1814 explorations on behalf of the Hudson's Bay Company. Today, a rugged road leads into the upper basin of the Cascade River's north fork, from which a moderate trail climbs through the pass and into the headwaters of the Stehekin River. The main route descends from Cascade Pass to the valley of the Stehekin, providing one of the quickest hiking routes to the river. As of this writing, flood damage had closed Stehekin Valley Road at Flat Creek; from there, hikers can connect with a shuttle bus for a ride to the settlement of Stehekin on the shores of Lake Chelan.

A challenging mountaineer's trail leads upward from Cascade Pass, following Sahale Arm to the dizzying heights of the camp at the toe of Sahale Glacier. Travelers bound for the camp should start the trek no later than 2 p.m. A steep spur path drops from Sahale Arm to Doubtful Lake for fishing opportunities and a chance to view the oldest gold-mining site in the Stehekin district.

The Cascade Pass Trail begins in the upper basin of the North Fork, which has its own history of gold-mining activity. The cliffs of Johannesburg Mountain and Cascade Peak tower above the far side of the valley, rising to neck-stretching heights. To the northwest is the rocky summit of the Triad, and west of it is Eldorado Peak, mantled in glaciers. The path soon ascends into a mature forest of spruce, fir, and hemlock, zigzagging upward at a modest pace.

After climbing high up the wall of the valley, the path swings eastward for the level approach to Cascade Pass. The trees dwindle away, allowing fine views of the surrounding peaks. Looking ahead, the steep horn framed by the pass belongs to Magic Mountain.

Watch for marmots as the trail crosses the final talus slopes and alpine meadows before the pass. Cascade Pass is mantled in verdant meadows punctuated by wind-torn copses of subalpine fir. A viewing bench faces east toward Magic Mountain and Pelton Peak, which flank Yawning Glacier. Farther down the valley is the summit of Glory Mountain. The trail now begins to descend, and soon passes a junction with the Sahale Arm spur trail (discussed below).

The main trail continues to drop, then angles eastward across the hanging valley known as the Pelton Basin. At the first stringer of trees, a side path descends to a camping area. The main trail stays high in the forest, and soon swings north above steep slopes that drop away into the head of the Stehekin Valley. The snowy summit of Sahale Mountain rises to the north, and to the east is a long view down the brushy valley of the Stehekin River. The path drops steeply at first, then adopts a more moderate grade as it zigzags through heavy brush. To the north are the many waterfalls of Doubtful Creek, and to the south the incipient Stehekin River drops through a similar series of cascades. Look south for final views of Yawning Glacier.

The path fords Doubtful Creek below a striking waterfall, then runs eastward across arid slopes, dropping gently toward a junction with the Horseshoe Basin Trail (See p.275). Patient visitors might spot pikas among the shattered

The approach to Cascade Pass.

Cascade Pass • Sahale Arm

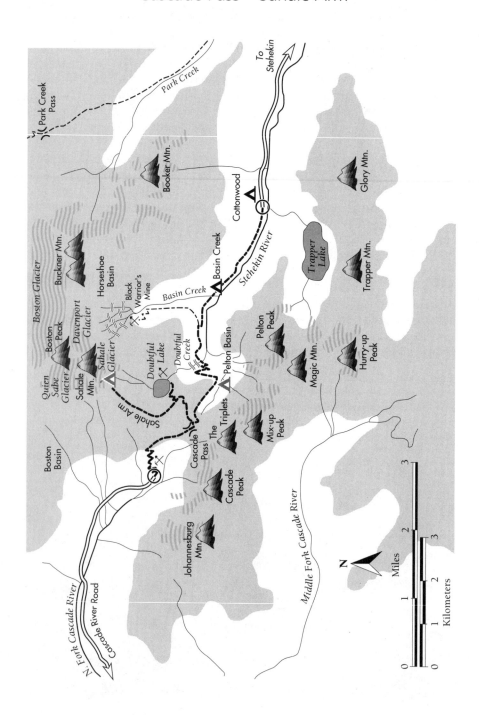

rocks. At the junction, the trail encounters the old road built in 1943 to serve the Black Warrior Mine, and follows it down to cross Basin Creek. Rusting bits of old mining machinery line the trail at Basin Camp. During the boom years of gold mining, this was a thriving tent city known as Rouse's Camp, but it is now the exclusive domain of hikers.

Watch out for stinging nettle as the old roadbed follows the river through brushy bottoms. As the path skirts the edge of an old rockslide, look back for a fine view of Sahale with Davenport Glacier spread below its eastern face. A few stout cottonwoods rise from the brush as the trail approaches the end of the Stehekin Valley Road. The trek ends at Cottonwood Camp, once served by shuttle buses but now isolated by flood damage to the road, which has yet to be repaired.

Sahale Arm Option. From Cascade Pass, this primitive trail climbs steeply northward through grassy meadows. Views are superb all the way up, featuring Cascade Peak, The Triplets, Magic Mountain, Yawning Glacier, Pelton Peak, and Glory Mountain. The trail tops out on the toe of Sahale Arm (pronounced suh-HAH-lee). This rounded, verdant ridge arcs southward from the base of Sahale Mountain, a name that translates as "high up" in the Skagit dialect. The summit rises impressively to the north, mantled in glaciers. Far below is the round mere of Doubtful Lake with its barren isle, surrounded by sheer walls and slender waterfalls. A steep path drops away from a large signpost on the main route, bound for the foot of the lake. The Quien Sabe mining claim was staked on the lakeshore in 1886. A mineshaft was blasted into the cliffs opposite the island, and several cabins were built at the foot of the lake.

The trail follows the crest of Sahale Arm, climbing moderately at first then more insistently. Heather mats are interspersed with swards of herbaceous plants, creating ideal summer habitat for herbivores. Hoary marmots are particularly abundant here, and a dozen may be in view at one time. Golden-mantled ground squirrels and mule deer are often spotted amid the lush meadows. As the trail skirts west-facing slopes, hikers get superb views of Forbidden Peak, with its mantle of glacial ice. The rocky summit to its left is Mount Torment, and Mount Baker appears in the distance.

The trail follows the ridgetop to the base of the mountain, then climbs straight up the slopes onto the broken talus of the south face. Great mounds of rock have been pushed up by the Sahale Glacier, and the path scrambles upward across the face of these moraines, following a series of cairns. A southward glance reveals the first views of Trapper Mountain, Spider Mountain, Dome Peak, and the distant edifice of Mount Rainier. After gaining more than 2,300 feet from Cascade Pass, the trail reaches a series of camping spots at the toe of Sahale Glacier, each one atop its own mound of rubble and protected against the winds by a stonework ring. This is the loftiest developed camp in North Cascades National Park and looks out across a sea of jagged peaks. Vistas like these are usually reserved for mountaineers, following demanding and dangerous ascents.

8   Thornton Lakes

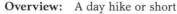

Overview: A day hike or short backpack to Thornton Lakes, 10.8 miles round trip.

Best season: Late July to mid-October.

Difficulty: Moderate.

Elevation gain: 2,560 feet.

Elevation loss: 400 feet.

Maximum elevation: 5,060 feet.

Topo maps: Mount Triumph; *Marblemount.*

Jurisdiction: Ross Lake National Recreation Area (National Park Service).

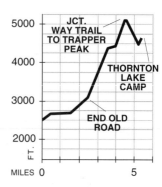

Finding the trailhead: Take Washington Highway 20 to the Thornton Lakes Road, 3 miles west of Newhalem. This narrow gravel road winds upward for 5.4 miles to reach the trailhead at its end.

Key points:
- 0.0 Trailhead at road's end.
- 2.3 Trail leaves old logging road and starts to climb.
- 3.6 Trail leaves Ross Lake National Recreation Area and enters North Cascades National Park.
- 4.5 Junction with unmarked path to Trapper Peak. Bear left for the lakes.
- 4.7 Trail crests the ridge above Thornton Lakes.
- 5.4 Thornton Lake Camp.

The hike: An old logging road leads from the Skagit Valley just west of Newhalem high into the foothills to the north, and from there the Thornton Lakes trail leads into a surprisingly spectacular landscape of majestic peaks and glacier-carved lake basins. The trek to the lowermost of the Thornton Lakes can be accomplished in a long day of hiking, and a backcountry campsite is available for folks who desire a more leisurely pace. A popular (and elementary) cross-country route leads from the high point of the trail to the summit of Trapper Peak, just across the valley from Mount Terror and the other sheer pinnacles of the southern Picket Range.

The first part of the hike follows a closed logging road, which was punched across the steep mountainside prior to the creation of Ross Lake National Recreation Area. After the slopes were clearcut, the barren soil was left to reforest itself by natural means. Shrubs were quick to exploit the abundance of direct sunlight, and formed impenetrable thickets. Later, conifer seedlings took root, and a mixture of mountain hemlock, silver fir, and Douglas-fir is now pushing up through the brush. The roadway itself, scoured bare of topsoil, became a seedbed for alders. These enterprising shrubs specialize in colonizing badly disturbed sites, and symbiotic bacteria that live in alder roots act as natural fertilizers, returning nitrogen to the soil. The roadbed traverses the slope to reach Thornton Creek, then begins a gradual ascent. Along the way, gaps in the recovering forest offer views of Teebone Ridge beyond the Skagit River.

At the end of the road, a footpath snakes upward into a loose forest of mature hemlocks. The ascent has a few steep pitches, but is quite moderate overall. Springs and seeps dot the mountainside, providing enough moisture to support bog plants, such as skunk cabbage and devil's club. Eventually the path finds its way up into a subalpine vale, where a tiny rill courses through heather meadows. The trail skirts the meadows' northern edge, then resumes its climb. Near the top, a loose parkland of mountain hemlock allows superb views of Eldorado Peak to the south. At a signpost, a rough way trail makes the ridge-running ascent to the top of Trapper Peak for views of Mount Terror and all three of the Thornton Lakes.

Meanwhile, the main trail turns west to cross a low saddle. As it does so, Mount Triumph towers ahead, with the lowermost of the Thornton Lakes spread beneath it like a giant sapphire. The trail plummets down the mountainside to reach the foot of the lake, then makes a tricky crossing of the outlet stream atop huge boulders and floating logs. The camping area is on the far bank; a difficult cross-country bushwhack leads along the western shore of the lake and onward to the two upper lakes.

Lower Thornton Lake and Mount Triumph.

Thornton Lakes

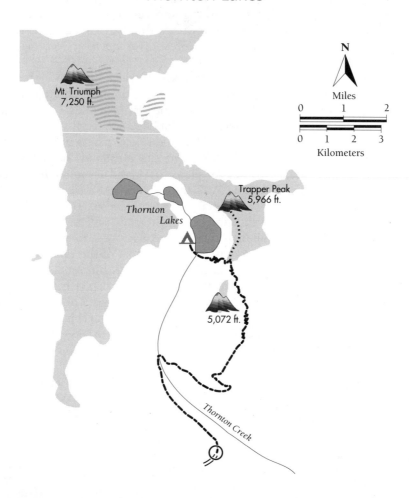

ADDITIONAL TRAILS

The **Baker Lake Trail** follows the eastern shore of the lake to the Baker River, which has to be forded to complete the hike (a new bridge is planned for this crossing).

An extremely steep path leads up to **Shuksan Lake**, a remote subalpine tarn.

The **Diobsud Creek trail** is almost impossible to find these days. It follows Diobsud Creek for a short distance into the foothills.

Old trails run up the **South Fork** and the **Middle Fork of the Cascade River**. They receive sporadic maintenance, and have become quite brushy.

Ross Lake and Vicinity

Ross Lake National Recreation Area lies at the heart of the North Cascades, splitting the national park into two separate units. The hydroelectric potential of the Skagit River was recognized by early pioneers: a small Pelton-wheel powerhouse was built in 1900 on the current site of Diablo Dam to power a lumber mill. Big corporations soon moved in, and between 1924 and 1961, the Seattle City Light Company impounded the waters of the Skagit River to form Gorge Lake, Diablo Lake, and Ross Lake itself. The company also built a spur railway to aid in the construction of the dams. More than 40 miles of valley were flooded during the creation of the reservoirs, which have become the defining features of the landscape.

Although much of the ecologically important bottomland was lost, the reservoirs have proved to be a boon to recreational visitors. The turquoise waters of Diablo Lake, tinted by the effluvium of melting glaciers, have become a popular spot for powerboaters, with campgrounds along the shore for backcountry stays.

The long and fjordlike finger of Ross Lake projects deep into the heart of the snowcapped peaks, and its lack of an accessible motorboat launch site makes it largely the domain of canoeists and kayakers. Campgrounds with boat landings are scattered at regular intervals along the lakeshore and on its small islands. Plan to paddle during the mornings and evenings; midday winds build up immense swells that make boating both laborious and dangerous. Easiest access for canoeists is by paddling Diablo Lake from Colonial Campground to its head, then portaging up a 1-mile gravel road to surmount Ross Dam. The Ross Lake Resort will drive your boat up or down this road at prices that reflect its monopoly. The resort also rents canoes by the hour and provides motorboat shuttles to lakeside trailheads for a fee. The lakeshore can also be accessed through Hozomeen, after a long drive through Canada that includes 40 miles of gravel forest roads.

Backpackers will find a well-developed network of trails, following both shores of Ross Lake and radiating deep into North Cascades National Park to the west and south and into the Pasayten Wilderness to the east. Many lakeside camps are also accessible by foot, and inland camps are the exclusive province of the land-based traveler. Visitors can combine boating and backpacking for a multifaceted wilderness experience.

Ross Lake National Recreation Area is administered by the National Park Service, and all its backcountry and boat-accessed camps require a permit that can be obtained at any permanently staffed ranger station. Beyond the lakeshore, most of the recreation area falls within the Steven Mather Wilderness, where motorized devices and mechanized transportation are prohibited. In contrast to national park lands, recreation area lands allow visitors to bring pets if they are properly leashed.

Ross Lake Overview

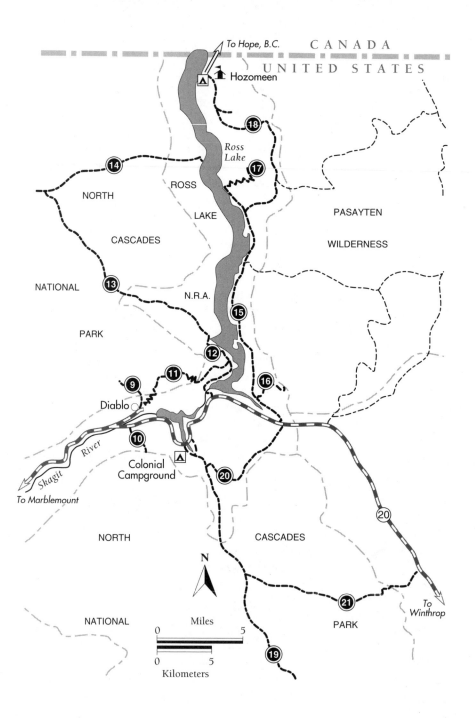

To Hope, B.C.

CANADA

UNITED STATES

Hozomeen

Ross Lake

ROSS

LAKE

NORTH

CASCADES

N.R.A.

NATIONAL

PARK

PASAYTEN

WILDERNESS

Diablo

Skagit River

To Marblemount

Colonial Campground

NORTH

CASCADES

NATIONAL

PARK

To Winthrop

N

Miles
0   5

Kilometers
0   5

Ranger stations at Marblemount and Hozomeen are the primary sources for backcountry information. There is also a National Park Service visitor center in Newhalem that offers interpretive displays and multimedia programs. The town of Newhalem is a company town built entirely by Seattle City Light; it has a small general store that is stocked with a few bare essentials. The nearest true grocery and motels are in Marblemount, and for backpacking equipment one must venture even farther down the Skagit Valley to Burlington or Mount Vernon. The Ross Lake Resort offers remote lodgings but no restaurant in its complex of floating cabins near Ross Dam.

9 Stetattle Creek

Overview:	A day hike up Stetattle Creek, 2.8 miles to trail's end.
Best season:	Mid-May to late October.
Difficulty:	Easy along Stetattle Creek; moderate beyond.
Elevation gain:	1,260 feet.
Elevation loss:	60 feet.
Maximum elevation:	2,100 feet.
Topo maps:	Diablo Dam, Mount Prophet; *Diablo Lake, Ross Lake.*
Jurisdiction:	Ross Lake National Recreation Area, North Cascades National Park.

Finding the trailhead: From Newhalem, drive east on Washington Highway 20 to mile 126, where a spur road runs into the company town of Diablo. Park in the parking area beside the bridge, just within town. The trail starts on the opposite side of the road.

Key points:
- 0.0 Trailhead in the settlement of Diablo.
- 0.8 Trail leaves Ross Lake NRA, enters North Cascades National Park, and starts to climb.
- 1.6 Trail crosses Bucket Creek.
- 2.4 Trail crosses Camp Dayo Creek.
- 2.8 Trail peters out.

The hike: Stetattle Creek is an ancient tribal boundary. To the Skagit people it marked the start of a dangerous hinterland, the domain of their enemies the *Ntlakyapamuks* or Thompson Indians. Modern visitors can approach the lower reaches of the creek as an easy introduction to the coastal forests of the Cascades, or can penetrate deeper into the hinterlands for a more challenging day trip.

Stetattle Creek

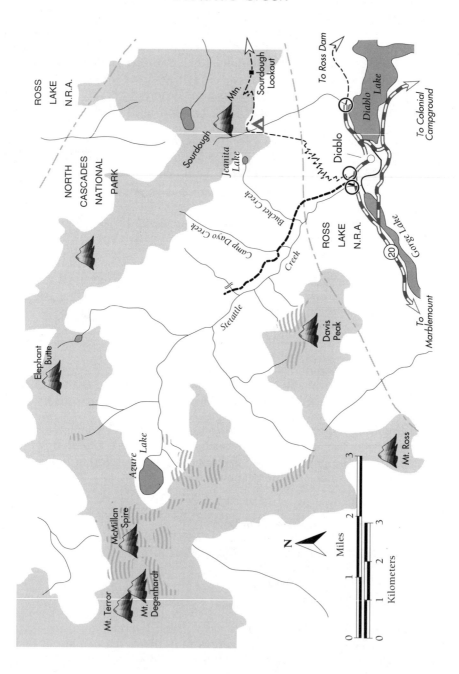

Stetattle Creek.

The first 0.8 mile of trail is an easy stroll along the streambank. As the houses of Diablo fall behind, a riparian woodland closes in around the stream. This diverse forest community includes mountain hemlock, western red-cedar, bigleaf maple, and red alder. The damp climate provides superb growing conditions for epiphytes, plants that grow from aerial perches on the trunks or limbs of trees. Of these, club moss is particularly abundant, and licorice fern also can be found. Watch the boulders in the stream for the water ouzel, a tiny waterbird that dives into the current in a quest for aquatic insects.

The bottomland sojourn ends with a series of breath-stealing switchbacks that carry hikers up the steep slopes east of the creek. The trail soon resumes its northward trek, crossing numerous tributaries. Some are no more than gurgling freshets that course through the moss, while others are quite substantial and hurry through stairstep cascades. The young forest of hemlock and lodgepole pine underlain by salal bushes arose following a forest fire in the early 1900s. Gaps in the trees reveal the towering east face of Davis Mountain. This young stand of trees is soon replaced by a mature forest underlain by a carpet of fern moss. The trail becomes more primitive after passing a large waterfall on Camp Dayo Creek, where sheets of water pour over a broad sill of Skagit gneiss. As the valley widens, a few huge and ancient cedars and hemlocks tower above their lesser neighbors. The trail ultimately peters out in this forest, where deer do more for trail maintenance than the National Park Service does.

10 Pyramid Lake

Overview:	A half-day hike to Pyramid Lake, 2.1 miles round trip.
Best season:	Late June to mid-October.
Difficulty:	Moderate.
Elevation gain:	840 feet.
Elevation loss:	None.
Maximum elevation:	2,640 feet.
Topo maps:	Diablo Dam, Ross Dam; *Diablo Lake*.
Jurisdiction:	Ross Lake National Recreation Area, North Cascades National Park.

Finding the trailhead: Take Washington Highway 20 east from Newhalem to mile 126.9, where there are several parking pulloffs. The marked trail begins across the road.

Key points:
    0.0 Pyramid Lake Trailhead.
    0.9 Trail crosses a tributary of Pyramid Creek.
    2.1 Pyramid Lake.

The hike: This trail offers a moderate half-day hike to a small woodland mere below Pyramid Peak. This lake is unique; unlike most lakes in the region, it has never been stocked with trout. Here is found a pristine aquatic community, unaltered by the activities of mankind: a complex web of herbivorous and predatory insects, insect-eating sundew plants growing upon floating logs, and newts at the top of the food chain. The lake environment has been designated a Research Natural Area in recognition of its ecological significance.

The trail begins with a vigorous ascent across a sparsely forested slope where spindly Douglas-firs and lodgepole pines arose in the wake of a small forest fire. In the generation of trees that follows, the sun-loving lodgepoles will be replaced by the Douglas-firs, which are more shade-tolerant. The Douglas-firs will ultimately give way to western hemlock, which has the greatest shade tolerance and is considered the climax dominant tree at this elevation. The hemlock forest, in the absence of fire or other natural disasters, can replace itself perpetually.

At mile 0.9, the path crosses a branch of Pyramid Creek. This mossy brook wanders through a pocket bottomland populated by tall and graceful western red-cedars. A few of them are old enough to be considered mature, a status that they attain after about five hundred years. The path soon resumes its climb as the forest grades into a lush montane stand of mountain hemlock and silver fir. After a number of steep spurts, the trail reaches the deep, green pool of Pyramid Lake. The graceful summit of Pyramid Peak presides over this tiny but self-contained ecosystem.

Pyramid Lake

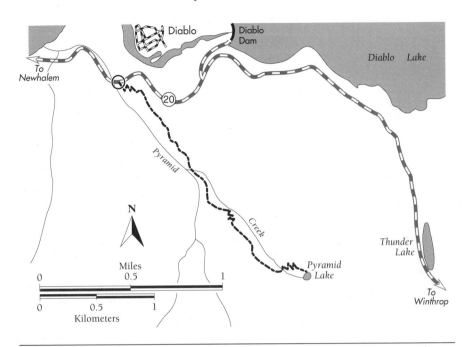

11 Sourdough Mountain

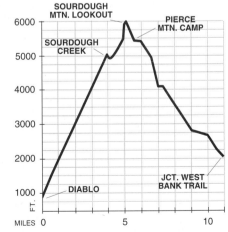

Overview:	A long day hike to Sourdough Mountain Lookout, 10.4 miles round trip, or a backpack to the West Bank trail, 11.1 miles one way.
Best season:	Mid-July to mid-October.
Difficulty:	Moderately strenuous.
Elevation gain:	5,095 feet, west to east.
Elevation loss:	3,895 feet, west to east.
Maximum elevation:	5,985 feet at Sourdough Mountain Lookout.
Topo maps:	Diablo Dam, Ross Dam, Pumpkin Mountain; *Diablo Lake, Ross Lake.*
Jurisdiction:	Ross Lake National Recreation Area, North Cascades National Park.

Sourdough Mountain

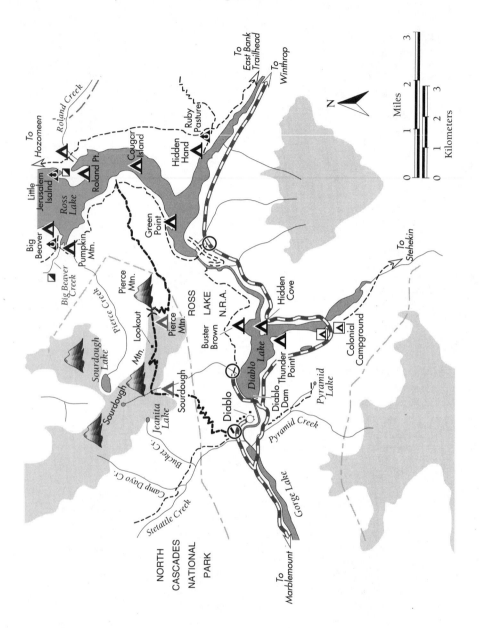

To
East Bank
Trailhead

To
Winthrop

To
Hozomeen

Roland Creek

Little
Jerusalem
Island

Big
Beaver

Ross
Lake

Roland Pt.

Cougar
Island

Hidden
Hand

Ruby
Pasture

N

Miles

Kilometers

Big Beaver
Creek

Pumpkin
Mtn.

Pierce
Creek

Green
Point

Sourdough
Lake

Mtn. Lookout

Pierce
Mtn.

Pierce
Mtn.

ROSS

Buster
Brown

LAKE

Hidden
Cove

N.R.A.

To
Stehekin

Colonial
Campground

Sourdough

Sourdough

Jeanita
Lake

Diablo

Diablo
Lake

Thunder
Point

Diablo
Dam

Pyramid
Lake

Bucket Cr.

Camp Dayo Cr.

Stetattle Creek

Pyramid Creek

Gorge Lake

NORTH
CASCADES
NATIONAL
PARK

To
Marblemount

Finding the trailhead: Follow Washington Highway 20 to mile 126 and take the paved access road to Diablo. Park across from the swimming pool; the trail begins beside the pool. The trail ends at mile 3.8 on the West Bank Trail.

Key points:
   0.0   Trailhead in the settlement of Diablo.
   3.2   Trail leaves Ross Lake NRA and enters North Cascades National Park.
   4.1   Sourdough Creek Camp.
   4.2   Trail crosses Sourdough Creek.
   5.0   Trail reaches top of Sourdough Mountain.
   5.2   Sourdough Mountain Lookout. Trail begins to descend.
   6.2   Pierce Mountain Camp.
   6.4   Trail leaves the ridgecrest and descends into an old burn.
   7.4   Trail leaves North Cascades National Park and enters Ross Lake NRA.
  11.1   Trail ends at a junction with West Bank Trail.

The hike: This popular trail can be approached via a long ascent from the town of Diablo or by a longer (9.7 miles one way) but easier route via the West Bank trail. The trail makes a nice two-day loop when combined with the West Bank and Diablo Lake trails; hike it counterclockwise for easiest traveling. Atop Sourdough Mountain, an active fire lookout offers superb views of Diablo Lake and snowcapped peaks stretching in all directions. One of the first fire lookouts in the nation was built here in 1917 by Glee Davis. The original log cabin with its 6-foot-square cupola was replaced with the current structure during the Great Depression.

From Diablo, the trail embarks immediately on a long and vigorous ascent up the steep mountainsides above Stetattle Creek. After a steep initial pitch, a grassy slope reveals southward views of Colonial and Pyramid peaks. The gradient eases as the trail settles into a steady zigzagging ascent across dry slopes covered with lodgepole pine. Small ravines and hollows here have a moister microclimate, favoring water-loving plants, such as sword fern, Douglas maple, and red alder. As the trail climbs higher, the sparse forest canopy reveals fine views of Davis Peak and Mount Terror beyond the Stetattle Creek valley. The path ultimately climbs onto south-facing slopes covered in large Douglas-firs. The lower limbs of these trees are draped with old man's beard, a lichen that is a winter staple for browsing deer.

At mile 3.0, the path crosses a sparsely wooded ridgetop overgrown with huckleberry bushes. A faint track climbs to a microwave relay station, while the main trail makes its way onto east-facing slopes within the national park boundary. Here, an open subalpine forest reveals views of Ruby Mountain and later of Diablo Lake. The peculiar turquoise tint of the lake is derived from fine glacial sediments, known as *gletschermilch*, suspended in the water. The sediments diffract light that enters the water in such a way that only blue and green light escapes.

The path traverses steep slopes to Sourdough Creek, where a camping spot is nestled amid heather meadows. It is common for snowdrifts to linger in this area well into July. Sourdough Creek follows a major fault in the bedrock, the same rift that accounts for the larger Thunder Creek valley to the south. Movement along such faults weakens the bedrock along the rift, hastening erosion and thus prompting the formation of linear drainages along the fault line.

The trail now turns east, climbing through stands of mountain hemlock to reach open swards of wildflowers beyond. The views from these slopes are superb, encompassing a broad arc of mountainous country to the south. Of particular note is Boston Glacier, a broad icefield that mantles the slopes at the head of the Thunder Creek watershed. The path zigzags steadily upward to reach the high alpine country of the ridgetop, where snow lingers well into July. Look northwest for a view of Sourdough Lake, with the Picket Range rising beyond it.

The path climbs along the ridgeline to its zenith at the lookout, with spectacular views in all directions. In addition to the now-familiar scenery to the west and south, the tall edifice of Jack Mountain rises beyond Ross Lake, with the jagged granite spires of the Golden Horn Batholith crowding the eastern horizon.

The trail continues down the far side of the ridge, marked by cairns where snows linger late into summer. Snowslips and broken talus gradually give way to a rock garden of heather and mountain hemlock as the ridgetop levels off somewhat. Pierce Mountain Camp occupies a rocky shelf in the parklands, with a small snowmelt pool to provide drinking water. Filter plenty of water for the arid descent to Ross Lake. The trail descends to the low saddle behind Pierce Mountain, then drops onto south-facing slopes. An intense fire burned here in 1978, and the fallen snags and overgrown

Diablo Lake from Sourdough Lookout.

60

shrubs make for difficult traveling. The views are rewarding, though, featuring Jack and Ruby mountains as well as the glacier-mantled summit of Colonial Peak.

Upon returning to the forest, the trail follows an eastward-trending finger ridge across the boundary into Ross Lake National Recreation Area. The path tracks the rounded crest of this ridge, sometimes descending steeply, otherwise leveling off for extended periods. The loose forest of hemlocks affords few distant views, but hikers get a final look at Jack Mountain near the bottom of the grade. Here, the route joins the West Bank Trail and a faint path drops to the shore of Ross Lake.

12 West Bank Trail

Overview:	A connecting trail linking Washington Highway 20 with Big Beaver Creek, 7.1 miles overall.
Best season:	Mid-May to early November.
Difficulty:	Moderate.
Elevation gain:	840 feet.
Elevation loss:	1,250 feet.
Maximum elevation:	2,100 feet.
Topo maps:	Ross Dam, Pumpkin Mountain; *Diablo Lake, Ross Lake.*
Jurisdiction:	Ross Lake National Recreation Area, North Cascades National Park.

Finding the trailhead: The trail begins at the Ross Dam Trailhead at mile 134 on Washington Highway 20, 4 miles east of Colonial Campground.

Key points:

    0.0 Trailhead above Ross Dam.
    0.7 Trail runs onto dam access road. Turn left.
    0.9 Trail crosses Ross Dam and follows the shore of Ross Lake.
    1.6 Spur trail descends to Ross Lake Resort.
    1.9 Spur trail descends to Green Point Camp.
    3.8 Junction with Sourdough Mountain Trail. Continue straight ahead.
    6.0 Trail crosses Pierce Creek.
    6.9 Spur path descends to Pumpkin Mountain Camp.
    7.0 Trail crosses Big Beaver Creek.
    7.1 Junction with Big Beaver Trail.

The hike: This connecting trail links WA 20 with the Big Beaver Trail via Ross Dam. It follows the western shore of Ross Lake, with occasional views of the water and access to the Ross Lake Resort, Green Point and Pumpkin

Along the West Bank Trail.

Mountain camps, and the east end of the Sourdough Mountain Trail. Seldom hiked as a trip unto itself, this trail is an important link for backpackers on extended journeys into the mountains west of Ross Lake.

The Ross Dam Trailhead sits on a bluff high above the lakeshore, and from its large parking lot the path wanders downward through storm-wracked Douglas-firs. The path passes a small cascade on Happy Creek, then drops across an open and rocky face that yields views of Pyramid Peak to the southwest. The trail bottoms out on a service road; turn left and then right, following signs for Ross Dam. The route then leads across the top of the dam, its curving façade of concrete rising 540 feet above the Skagit River. The dam was constructed between 1937 and 1949, and flooded the Skagit Valley for 21 miles upstream.

On the far shore, the trail begins a brisk ascent as it turns eastward above the lake. An opening atop the initial grade yields views of Ruby Mountain and a waterfall on the far shore. These falls are not natural, but were created when engineers diverted part of Happy Creek to enter Ross Lake above the dam, thus increasing the water available for hydropower. The trail maintains a constant elevation above the shoreline as it passes through a mixed woodland of birch and conifers. Steep side paths descend to the lakeshore at Ross Lake Resort and later at Green Point Camp.

Just beyond the campground junction is a rocky overlook that commands a fine panorama, highlighted by views up the Ruby Arm of Ross Lake and down-valley to Colonial and Pyramid peaks. The path soon enters a burn dating from 1926 that has grown up in a doghair stand of lodgepole pine and Douglas-fir. This forest community arises when thickets of fire-adapted seedlings spring up "thicker

West Bank Trail • East Bank Trail

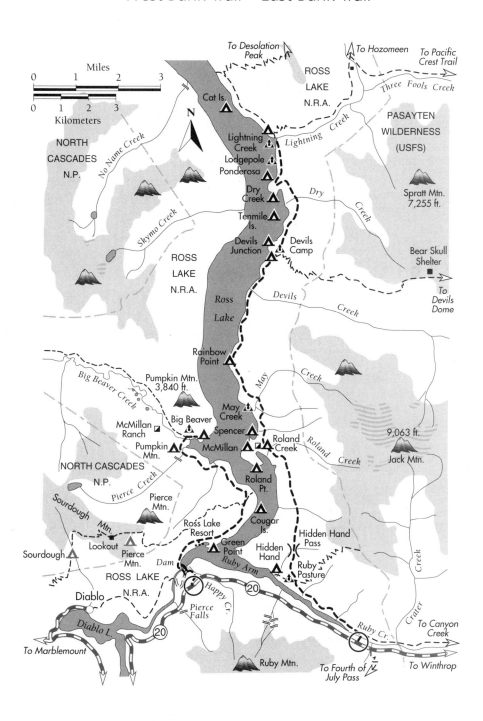

To Desolation Peak

To Hozomeen

To Pacific Crest Trail

ROSS LAKE N.R.A.

Three Fools Creek

PASAYTEN WILDERNESS (USFS)

Cat Is.

Miles
0   1   2   3

Kilometers
0   1   2   3

N

NORTH CASCADES N.P.

No Name Creek

Lightning Creek

Lightning Creek

Lodgepole

Ponderosa

Dry Creek

Dry Creek

Spratt Mtn. 7,255 ft.

Skymo Creek

Tenmile Is.

Devils Junction

Devils Camp

Bear Skull Shelter

ROSS LAKE N.R.A.

Ross Lake

Devils Creek

To Devils Dome

Rainbow Point

May Creek

Big Beaver Creek

Pumpkin Mtn. 3,840 ft.

Big Beaver

May Creek

Spencer

Roland Creek

Roland Creek

9,063 ft.

McMillan Ranch

McMillan

Pumpkin Mtn.

Jack Mtn.

NORTH CASCADES N.P.

Pierce Creek

Pierce Mtn.

Roland Pt.

Cougar Is.

Hidden Hand Pass

Sourdough Mtn.

Lookout

Pierce Mtn.

Ross Lake Resort

Green Point

Hidden Hand

Ruby Pasture

Sourdough

Dam

Ruby Arm

Crater Creek

ROSS LAKE N.R.A.

Diablo

Happy Cr.

20

Pierce Falls

Ruby Cr.

To Canyon Creek

Diablo L.

20

To Marblemount

Ruby Mtn.

To Fourth of July Pass

To Winthrop

than the hair on a dog's back" on mineral-rich ashes after a blaze. Numerous openings offer views of the lake, with Jack Mountain towering above it.

As the trail rounds the headland, the young trees give way to old Douglas-firs that block out the views. The Sourdough Mountain Trail soon climbs away to the west, while the West Bank Trail winds onto north-facing slopes. Here, a cool, moist forest of hemlock and western red-cedar is underlain by a verdant carpet of fern moss. Stony promontories with dry, shallow soils harbor stands of lodgepole pine, and allow the first northward views of Pumpkin Mountain's wooded dome. The trail now begins a gradual ascent as the peaks flanking Big Beaver Creek come into view. The trail tops out above a spectacular cataract on Pierce Creek, where water thunders through a perilous gorge.

The trail then descends vigorously to the banks of Big Beaver Creek, passing the woodland campground of Pumpkin Mountain along the way. A suspension bridge spans Big Beaver Creek, and beyond it is a junction where trails run westward along the creek and east to Big Beaver Camp on the lakeshore.

13 Big Beaver Creek

Overview:	A backpack (with boat shuttle) or extended trip from Big Beaver Camp to Little Beaver Creek, 16.8 miles total.
Best season:	Mid-May to early November to Luna Camp; mid-June to mid-October beyond.
Difficulty:	Moderate.
Elevation gain:	2,080 feet.
Elevation loss:	1,260 feet.
Maximum elevation:	3,660 feet at Beaver Pass.
Topo maps:	Pumpkin Mountain, Mount Prophet, Mount Redoubt; *Mount Challenger, Ross Lake*.
Jurisdiction:	Ross Lake National Recreation Area, North Cascades National Park.

Finding the trail: The beginning of the trail can be reached by boat or by a 7-mile hike on the West Bank Trail. The Big Beaver Trail ends at a junction with the Little Beaver Trail.

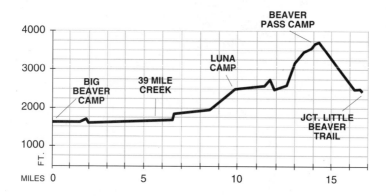

A beaver pond along the Big Beaver.

Key points:

0.0 Big Beaver camping area.

0.3 Spur trail to horse camp. Stay left.

0.4 Junction with West Bank Trail. Turn right to begin hiking up the Big Beaver valley.

5.5 Thirtynine Mile Creek. Horse camp on near bank, hiker camp on far bank.

7.1 Trail leaves Ross Lake NRA, entering North Cascades National Park.

9.8 Luna Camp.

12.4 Trail begins the final climb toward Beaver Pass.

13.9 Beaver Pass horse camp.

14.1 Beaver Pass hiker camp.

16.6 Junction with spur trail to Stillwell Camp (0.2 mile, easy). Bear left.

16.8 Trail crosses footbridges over Little Beaver Creek and joins Little Beaver Trail.

The hike: Big Beaver Creek occupies a broad, glacier-carved valley known for the pockets of old-growth cedar in its lower reaches. The creek's gentle gradient and the low altitude of Beaver Pass make it a good site for early season treks and for visitors who are new to backpacking.

The trail begins by running west from Big Beaver Camp, following the shallow bay where Big Beaver Creek pours into Ross Lake. The young stand of lodgepole pine here arose following a severe forest fire in 1926. Turn right at a junction with the West Bank trail as the route follows Big Beaver Creek northwest into its glacier-carved valley. As the trail climbs a small hill, a scattering of old Douglas-firs rises above the younger pines. These trees were able to survive the blaze by virtue of their thick bark.

After descending from the hillside, the trail wanders close to the banks of Big Beaver Creek. Somewhere beyond the far bank lie the ruins of the McMillan Ranch, a small homestead that was carved out of the forest by John McMillan, one of the most colorful pioneers of the Skagit Valley. McMillan never filed the papers on his homestead, but it was so remote that the authorities never challenged his right to settle here.

The sluggish, turquoise waters of Big Beaver Creek swirl lazily through its deep channel, now shaded by stout red-cedars. Some of the oldest trees approach a thousand years of age. As the path makes its way up the valley, old beaver ponds interrupt the forest to allow views of the surrounding mountains. By damming up lowland waterways, beavers serve as architects of ecological change, killing timber by flooding and creating sunny openings for swamp plants, such as willow, skunk cabbage, and sundew. The sundew is a tiny, carnivorous plant whose padlike leaves are coated with sticky hairs that ensnare ants and other insects. As time wears on, the beaver ponds fill with silt to become brushfields, and these are ultimately invaded by trees to complete the cycle.

At mile 5.5, the trail reaches Thirtynine Mile Creek, with camps on both banks beneath the shade of old hemlocks. Beyond the stream, the trail rises and falls with the undulating terrain. The mixed forest is often interrupted by boggy brooks and by beaver ponds in the bottomlands. Cedar swamps along the way offer more viewing of gigantic trees.

The trail passes the confluence of Big Beaver and McMillan creeks, and here it makes a minor ascent to avoid a narrow gorge. As the trail climbs, hikers get fine views of Elephant Butte across the valley. After the trail levels off, it reaches Luna Camp, with campsites scattered down the course of a steep tributary stream. Beyond the camp, the forest grades into an almost pure stand of silver fir. The trees are interrupted by two avalanche slopes. The first opening offers views of a waterfall coursing down an eastern bulwark of Luna Peak. The second brushfield yields a glimpse of Mount Challenger.

The trail now begins its climb to Beaver Pass, and views through the trees are inspiring. Mount Challenger can now be seen in all its glory, with Crooked Thumb Peak to the left of it in the Luna Cirque. The climbing is largely over by the time the trail reaches the Beaver Pass shelter; the hiker camp is a short distance farther up the trail. Beyond it, young conifers are replaced by an impressive stand of tall timber that lasts as far as the summit of the pass. At the summit are a series of snow course markers, once used by hydrologists on skis to determine the winter snowpack so that spring runoff waters could be efficiently released through Ross Dam.

Beyond the crest of the divide, a loose forest of mountain hemlock is underlain by a dense mat of huckleberry bushes. The descent is gradual until the path reaches the rim of the Little Beaver valley. Switchbacks lead down through widely spaced hemlocks that grow from the steep slope. At the bottom of the grade, a spur path runs east to a grove of ancient hemlocks where Stillwell Camp sits beside Little Beaver Creek. The main trail crosses several footbridges over the stream to meet the Little Beaver Trail near its midpoint.

Big Beaver Creek

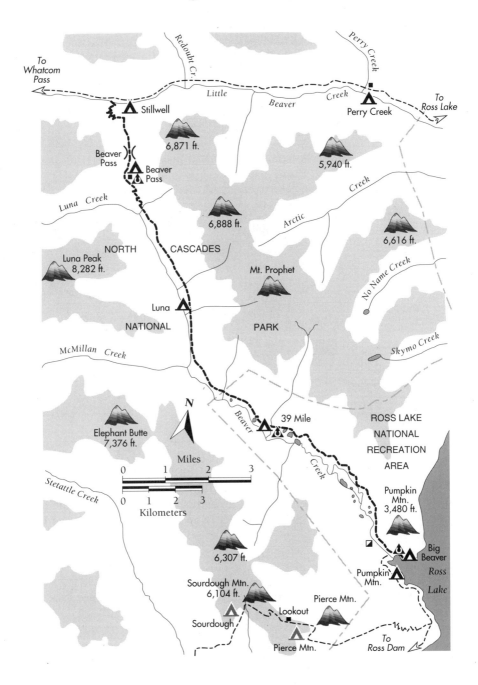

To Whatcom Pass

Redoubt Cr.

Perry Creek

To Ross Lake

Stillwell

Little   Beaver   Creek

Perry Creek

6,871 ft.

5,940 ft.

Beaver Pass

Beaver Pass

Luna   Creek

Arctic   Creek

6,888 ft.

6,616 ft.

NORTH   CASCADES

Luna Peak
8,282 ft.

No Name Creek

Mt. Prophet

Luna

NATIONAL   PARK

McMillan   Creek

Skymo Creek

Elephant Butte
7,376 ft.

N

Beaver

39 Mile

ROSS LAKE
NATIONAL
RECREATION
AREA

Miles

0   1   2   3

Stetattle Creek

0   1   2   3

Kilometers

Creek

Pumpkin
Mtn.
3,480 ft.

6,307 ft.

Pumpkin
Mtn.

Big
Beaver

Ross
Lake

Sourdough Mtn.
6,104 ft.

Pierce Mtn.

Lookout

Sourdough

Pierce Mtn.

To
Ross Dam

14 Little Beaver Creek

Overview:	An extended trip from Ross Lake to Whatcom Pass, 17.5 miles one way.
Best season:	Mid-June to late October to Stillwell Camp; mid-July to mid-October beyond.
Difficulty:	Moderate to Twin Rocks Camp; moderately strenuous beyond.
Elevation gain:	4,146 feet.
Elevation loss:	560 feet.
Maximum elevation:	5,206 feet at Whatcom Pass.
Topo maps:	Hozomeen Mountain, Mount Redoubt, Mount Spickard, Mount Challenger; *Mount Challenger, Ross Lake.*
Jurisdiction:	Ross Lake National Recreation Area, North Cascades National Park.

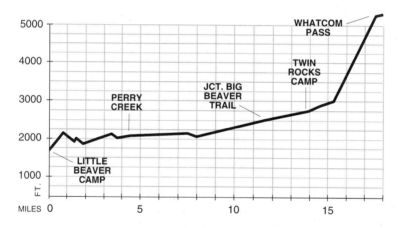

Finding the trail: The trail begins at Little Beaver Camp, which can be reached only by boat. The end of the trail can be reached via a 17-mile hike from the Nooksack Valley. A 24-mile trek from Ross Dam reaches the trail near its midpoint.

Key points:
- 0.0 Little Beaver Camp.
- 3.2 Trail leaves Ross Lake NRA and enters North Cascades National Park.
- 4.5 Perry Creek Camp and shelter.
- 4.6 Trail crosses Perry Creek.
- 9.3 Trail crosses Redoubt Creek.
- 11.4 Junction with Big Beaver Trail. Bear right for Whatcom Pass. (Left leads to Stillwell Camp.)
- 13.9 Twin Rocks hiker camp.
- 14.0 Twin Rocks horse camp.

15.6 Trail begins final grade to Whatcom Pass.

17.5 Whatcom Pass. Whatcom Pass Trail descends into Brush Creek valley.

The hike: This long bottomland trek leads from a remote spot on Ross Lake to a high alpine pass at the edge of the Chilliwack River watershed. The eastern terminus of the trail can be reached only by boat. This wilderness route through the remote Little Beaver country features miles of unbroken old-growth forest that opens up in a basin deep in the mountains where waterfalls plunge from melting glaciers and hurtle to the valley floor. Trails leading over Beaver Pass and down Brushy Creek offer options for even longer backcountry expeditions. Spring runoff may result in dangerous stream crossings on this trail during early summer.

From Little Beaver Camp, the trail skirts northward above the shore of Ross Lake. Landslides along the lakeshore have created broad openings that allow views of Jack Mountain to the south and Hozomeen Mountain above the ridgetop across the lake. The path soon begins to zigzag up the hillside, gaining altitude to avoid the gorge at the mouth of Little Beaver Creek. The Douglas-fir savannah on these arid slopes is maintained by rapid evaporation and frequent ground fires.

As the trail turns the corner to enter the Little Beaver drainage, hikers get superb views of Jack Mountain, with the Nohokomeen Glacier crowning its north face. As the path runs westward, the distant views are replaced by heavy undergrowth and stands of young conifers. This regenerating forest

Hiking through cedar forest near Perry Creek.

Little Beaver Creek

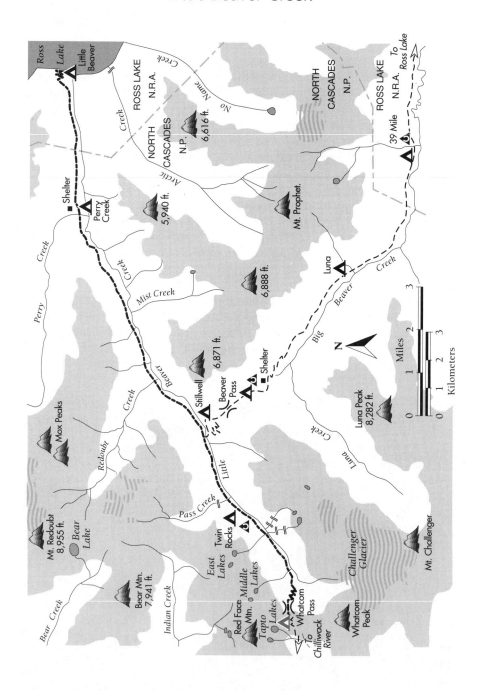

soon gives way to a climax coniferous forest that is for many visitors the highlight of the Little Beaver trek. Dominated by western red-cedar, Douglas-fir, and western hemlock, this rich and varied forest is underlain by a diverse array of mosses, ferns, and woodland flowers. The stand replaces itself one tree at a time: When a dead or dying tree falls to the forest floor, it creates an opening in the canopy that allows sufficient sunlight for new seedlings to take root and grow skyward. Though the stand is of indeterminate age, one 4-foot diameter Douglas-fir that fell here was more than five hundred years old.

After some distance, the trail passes fallen boulders that have broken free from the stark cliffs that line the valley. A verdant carpet of moss has grown over the boulders, lending an ancient feel to the landscape. After a long trek through the forest, the path crosses a second talus slope, then runs out onto the bottoms where Perry Creek enters the valley. This stream was named for Bill Perry, an early day muleskinner. A shelter rests in the midst of the towering cedars, with campsites along the sluggish, green waters of Little Beaver Creek. The trail then crosses the many channels of Perry Creek via an assortment of footlogs and shallow fords.

The trek next carries the traveler along the edge of the Little Beaver flood-plain, which is now a primordial swamp of devil's club, skunk cabbage, and other water-loving plants. The trail passes through damp glades where ferns grow taller than a man's head, then returns to the forest. It emerges at mile 7.0, where a brushy avalanche slope reveals the nameless crags that rise above the head of Mist Creek. Dense shrubbery makes route-finding a challenge, and stinging nettles and hidden boulders keep things lively.

The trail crosses several such avalanche paths before encountering a broad bottomland. After a considerable woodland trek, you will reach a logjam that has been modified to bridge Redoubt Creek. On the far side, the path enters a maze of enormous boulders, covered in moss, with mighty conifers growing from their surfaces. This boulder garden soon gives way to a monotonous forest of young hemlock that lasts as far as the junction with the Big Beaver trail. Travelers bound for Stillwell Camp should turn left at this junction; the path ahead leads to Whatcom Pass. The trail continues through the forest, breaking out at an avalanche track where Pass Creek plummets down a steep cliff. Whatcom Peak can be glimpsed ahead.

The trail reaches the Twin Rocks Camps in a grove of hemlocks that faces a rugged ridge. Farther up the valley, the forest gives way to brushfields choked with salmonberry, alder, and other tanglesome delights. Route-finding can be difficult here if the trail has not been brushed out recently. To the south, dozens of breathtaking waterfalls course down the face of the cliff, and Whatcom Peak is an inspiring presence at the head of the valley.

The path ultimately finds its way to one last grove of giant cedars, which marks the beginning of the ascent to Whatcom Pass. The trail snakes upward at a steady pace, climbing the sheer north wall of the valley. Stands of old mountain hemlocks alternate with talus slopes and small patches of brush. There are outstanding views throughout the ascent: Mount Challenger rises just across the valley, with Challenger Glacier forming a broad apron below it. There are long views down the valley and up the steep, nameless peaks that flank it. The U-shaped cross-section of the valley betrays its glacial origins: an enormous valley glacier once gouged this deep channel that runs all the way to the Skagit Valley. The Challenger Glacier may represent a minor remnant of that great river of ice.

Near the top of the grade, the trail enters an alpine vale of heather and chuckling brooks. This defile leads to the summit of Whatcom Pass. Whatcom Peak towers above the pass, with the long arm of Easy Ridge stretching northward above the valley of Brushy Creek. There is a backcountry camp just beyond the pass, and the trail that descends from this point to the Chilliwack Valley is discussed on p.125.

15 East Bank Trail

See Map on Page 63

Overview:	A backpack along Ross Lake to the mouth of Lightning Creek, 16 miles overall.
Best season:	Early June to late October.
Difficulty:	Easy.
Elevation gain:	1,297 feet.
Elevation loss:	1,525 feet.
Maximum elevation:	2,520 feet at Hidden Hand Pass.
Topo maps:	Crater Mountain, Ross Dam, Pumpkin Mountain; *Diablo Lake, Mount Logan, Ross Lake.*
Jurisdiction:	Ross Lake National Recreation Area, North Cascades National Park.

Finding the trailhead: The trail leaves from Washington Highway 20 at the East Bank Trailhead, at mile 138.2 (19 miles east of Newhalem).

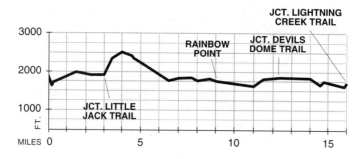

Key points:

0.0 Trailhead on WA 20.

0.3 Trail crosses Ruby Creek to meet Ruby Creek Trail. Turn left.

2.8 Junction with spur trail to Ruby Pasture Camp, Hidden Hand Camp, and Ruby Arm overlook (0.6 mile, easy). Turn right for East Bank Trail.

2.85 Junction with Little Jack Trail. Bear left as main trail starts to climb.

3.9 Hidden Hand Pass.

6.5 Trail crosses Roland Creek to reach Roland Creek Camp.

7.8 Trail crosses May Creek. Spur trail runs downstream to horse camp.

8.7 Rainbow Point Camp. Trail follows shore of Ross Lake.

11.0 Bridge over mouth of Devils Creek. Trail leaves lakeshore.

12.4 Junctions with Devils Dome Trail and spur paths to Devils Creek and Devils Junction camps. Continue straight ahead for Lightning Creek.

14.0 Trail crosses Dry Creek.

15.6 Spur trail descends to Lodgepole horse camp.

15.8 Lightning Creek horse camp.

15.9 Trail crosses mouth of Lightning Creek.

16.0 Trail ends at junctions with Desolation Peak Trail, Lightning Creek Trail, and spur to Lightning Creek hiker camp.

The hike: This trail makes a long trek through the forest, roughly following the eastern shore of Ross Lake. The lake is in view only sporadically, with the best vistas coming between Rainbow Point and the mouth of Devils Creek. The East Bank Trail is an integral leg of the Devils Dome loop trek, and can also be combined with the Lightning Creek and Three Fools trails for longer trips.

The trail begins with a descent from the highway to the confluence of Ruby and Panther creeks. Interpretive signs tell of the Ruby Creek gold rush of 1879, when the banks of Ruby Creek were staked from end to end with placer claims. A prospect pit, or "glory hole," lies beside the interpretive display. A suspension bridge leads across Ruby Creek, and beyond it the trail climbs to an old roadbed and follows it downstream. This road was built in 1938 in a failed effort to breach the Cascades Divide via Harts Pass and link the mines on Slate Creek with markets to the west. The old road traverses the slopes high above Ruby Creek, passing through a mixed woodland of birch, red alder, and Douglas-fir.

As the creek pours into the Ruby Arm of Ross Lake far below, the roadbed passes above the flooded site of the Ruby Mining Company's ill-fated operation. The company was formed in 1906 in a vain attempt to reap fortunes by consolidating the small placer claims and mining them on a large scale with giant hydraulic cannons and diversion flumes. After a $300,000 investment in capital yielded only $3,000 in gold, the company folded. Watch the gaps in the forest for views of Ruby Mountain, with the cascades of Lillian Creek tumbling down its flanks.

The trail ultimately reaches a well-marked junction. The wide trail straight ahead leads past the Ruby Pasture and Hidden Hand camps to a clifftop overlook of Ross Lake. The smaller trail that climbs to the north is the East Bank trail, from which the Little Jack trail soon breaks away. The main trail now skirts the upper edge of Ruby Pasture, where the Forest Service once built an extensive guard station using lumber from the ruins of the Ruby Mining Company. The guard station was itself abandoned, and the pastures have become overgrown with brush.

A short climb leads to Hidden Hand Pass, where a swampy forest occupies the long gap behind a stony hillock. According to local legend, prospector

Jack Rowley was prospecting near this spot when he had a dream in which a hidden hand guided him to the spot on Canyon Creek where he was to make the gold strike that started the Ruby Creek rush. After passing through the gap, the trail maintains its altitude as it charts an inland course through a diverse array of forest habitats. Open stands of Douglas-fir alternate with groves of birch and bigleaf maple, cedar swamps, and corridors of moss-hung vine maple suffused with green.

The trail encounters a camping area on the far bank of Roland Creek, and an unmarked path descends on a westward heading to the shore of Ross Lake. Tommy Rowland's homestead once occupied the base of a small peninsula nearby. Perhaps the isolation was too much for the Irish settler; he insisted that he was an incarnation of the Prophet Elijah, and took to calling his home "Little Jerusalem." His prophetic ravings earned him a trip to the lunatic asylum, but he escaped and returned here before he was finally committed for good.

A short distance beyond Roland Creek, the trail approaches the shore of Ross Lake for the first time, with views of the mountains flanking Big Beaver Creek. The path then journeys inland once more, ultimately crossing May Creek in the deep shade of a mossy defile. This stream carries the meltwater of Nohokomeen Glacier, which sits high on the flanks of Jack Mountain, obscured by trees. The path that runs down the south bank leads to a horse camp, while the main trail continues northward. The latter trail emerges from the timber at Rainbow Point, where a camp commands beautiful views up and down Ross Lake.

The East Bank Trail now hugs the lakeshore, yielding the finest views of the trek. Just south of Devils Creek, the route has been blasted out of sheer cliffs, and solid bedrock overhangs the pathway in several places. A suspension bridge spans the narrow cove where Devils Creek enters the lake. On the far side, the trail climbs for several hundred feet, then levels off amid a woodland of birch and grand fir. The path plods along through the forest to reach a junction with the Devils Dome Trail, and below the junction is a camp spot on a high and wooded knoll.

For the next several miles, the only sights that break the monotony of the forest are provided by the tributary streams that tumble down through the timber. As it passes a shallow bay, the trail reveals brief glimpses of the lake, then climbs through a low saddle. A gradual descent leads past Lodgepole Camp to the mouth of Lightning Creek, where the trek ends and trails continue northward to Desolation Peak and Hozomeen Lake. There is a horse camp on the south side of Lightning Creek's mouth, while a hiker camp lies north of the suspension bridge.

16 Little Jack Trail

Overview: A very long day hike from Washington Highway 20, 14.8 miles round trip, or a more manageable day trip from the East Bank trail, 9.2 miles round trip.
Best season: Early July to mid-October.
Difficulty: Moderately strenuous.
Elevation gain: 4,130 feet.
Elevation loss: None.
Maximum elevation: 6,060 feet.
Topo maps: Ross Dam, Crater Mountain; *Diablo Lake, Mount Logan.*
Jurisdiction: Ross Lake National Recreation Area.

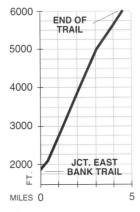

Finding the trail: The trail can be reached via a 2.8-mile hike on the East Bank Trail from its trailhead at mile 138.2 on Washington Highway 20.

Key points:

0.0   Junction with East Bank Trail near Ruby Pasture. Little Jack Trail climbs eastward.
4.6   Trail peters out at viewpoint of Jack Mountain.

Jack Mountain from the Little Jack Trail.

The hike: This odd little trail climbs from Ruby Pasture to the top of a lofty spur ridge for excellent views of Jack and Crater mountains. The trail can be approached as a long and difficult day hike from the East Bank Trailhead on WA 20, or more reasonably as a side trip for backpackers based out of Ruby Pasture or Hidden Hand camps. The old campsite at the end of the trail has been closed permanently for rehabilitation. Bring plenty of drinking water; the only surface water along the way is provided by high alpine rills that run only during early summer.

To begin the trek from the highway, follow the East Bank Trail across Ruby Creek and then head westward along the Ruby Arm of Ross Lake. Upon reaching the junction at Ruby Pasture, make two consecutive right turns as the Little Jack Trail charts a rather faint and unkempt course eastward through the forest. It soon begins to zigzag upward through Douglas-fir, and tall underbrush limits views through the trees. After a substantial climb, the trail reaches arid, south-facing slopes where grassy meadows provide views of Ruby Mountain and the crags of Elija Ridge. Looking westward, Davis Peak stands sentinel over the Skagit Valley. It is a long and wearisome slog, growing steeper with each passing mile. On a sunny day, hot temperatures on these open slopes can pose a very real health hazard; drink plenty of water.

The trail ultimately ascends into the subalpine zone, where spire-shaped subalpine firs replace the Douglas-fir found on the drier slopes below. The openings now contain lush swards of wildflowers, highlighted by lupine, Indian paintbrush, and tiger lily. The trail continues to zigzag upward, yielding glimpses of Ross Lake. Intermittent streams may offer water here during early summer; be sure to purify it before drinking. After gaining most of its elevation, the trail turns east and levels off, traversing meadow-strewn slopes and wooded spur ridges. A final walk through the forest leads to a spectacular overlook high above Crater Creek. The stark summit of Crater Mountain rises directly across the void, while the majestic south face of Jack Mountain presides over alpine parklands to the north.

The official trail ends here, but a well-trodden way trail continues northward along the ridgetop, visiting swales and pocket meadows filled with heather and dwarf blueberry. This path soon peters out amid a tangle of game trails at the base of an imposing hillock.

Little Jack Trail

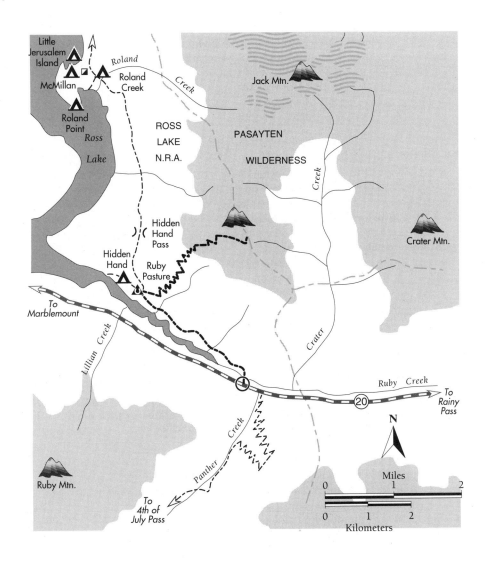

17 Desolation Peak

See Map on Page 83

Overview: A day hike from Lightning Creek Camp to the summit of Desolation Peak, 13.6 miles round trip, or from the Jack Point boat landing to the summit, 9.8 miles round trip.

Best season: Late June to mid-October.

Difficulty: Moderately strenuous.

Elevation gain: 4,532 feet.

Elevation loss: 80 feet.

Maximum elevation: 6,102 feet at Desolation Peak.

Topo maps: Hozomeen Mountain; *Ross Lake.*

Jurisdiction: Ross Lake National Recreation Area.

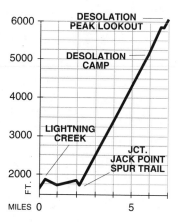

Finding the trail: The hike can be approached from Lightning Creek Camp (14.1 miles by trail from Hozomeen; 16 miles from Washington Highway 20) or from a poorly marked boat landing on Ross Lake, about 2 miles north of the mouth of Lightning Creek.

Key points:
- 0.0 Junction with Lightning Creek Trail. Bear north.
- 2.1 Junction with spur trail to Jack Point boat landing. Turn right as the trail begins to climb Desolation Peak.
- 5.8 Trail tops the ridgeline at Desolation Camp.
- 6.8 Desolation Peak Lookout.

The hike: This trail makes a good day trip for hikers based at the mouth of Lightning Creek. Visitors who are traveling Ross Lake by boat may access the trail by hauling out at a poorly marked trailhead in a small cove 2 miles north of Lightning Creek. The trail presents a challenging climb to the summit of Desolation Peak, where a fire lookout station commands fine views of the surrounding ranges. During the tinder-dry summer of 1926, a wildfire ignited in the Big Beaver Creek valley and spread rapidly eastward, expanding to engulf this low peak that guarded what was then the eastern bank of the Skagit River. The mountain was named Desolation Peak in the wake of this blaze, and a fire lookout was built atop it to help prevent future wildfires.

The lookout has been the summer home to a succession of writers and artists over the years. The best-known luminary to stand watch here was Jack Kerouac, beatnik novelist and inveterate wanderer. His season as a fire lookout in 1956 inspired him to write the novel *Desolation Angels*.

From the bridge that spans the mouth of Lightning Creek, hike northward on the trail that runs above the shore of Ross Lake. Bear right as a spur path descends to the Lightning Creek hiker camp, then continue straight ahead as the Lightning Creek trail climbs away to the right. You are now on the trail to Desolation Peak, which maintains a constant altitude above the lakeshore as it charts a level northward course. Openings in the forest are plentiful, first yielding views down Ross Lake and later revealing Cat Island and the waterfalls on the far shore. After 2.1 miles, a spur trail descends to an unimproved boat landing on the lakeshore; waterborne hikers can start the trek at this point.

The trail now begins its upward journey, climbing through an open forest that shows scars of the blaze that once razed the trees on Desolation Peak. Colonizing shrubs such as ceanothus and wild rose grow in the abundant sunlight of the forest openings. About a third of the way up the mountain, the open meadows give way to a dense growth of young conifers. The drier conditions of the lower slopes prevented rapid reforestation, but here the trees are making a strong comeback, aided by ample moisture.

The trail stays in the forest as it climbs vigorously between brush-choked avalanche paths. When it emerges into flowery pocket meadows, it offers outstanding views of Ross Lake, highlighted by the distant massif of Colonial

Ross Lake from Desolation Peak Trail.

Peak, with Paul Bunyan's Stump to the right of it and Colonial Glacier at its foot. Later, there are excellent vistas of Jack Mountain, with spectacular Nohokomeen Glacier gracing its north face. The trail soon finds its way into a steep-sided bowl covered in a mixture of alpine wildflowers and shrubs. This area is particularly favored by foraging black bears during early summer. The path zigzags up to the ridgetop, where a short spur runs south to Desolation Camp. The camp offers superb views of Jack and Spratt mountains, but water can be hard to come by.

Meanwhile, the main trail turns north toward a false summit robed in meadows and dotted with copses of subalpine fir. After cresting the top of this rise, hikers can see the rocky summit of Desolation Peak ahead, crowned with its fire lookout station. Here the trail ends with views in all directions, described by Kerouac as "hundreds of miles of snow-covered rock all around, looming Mount Hozomeen on my north, vast snowy Jack to the south, the encharmed picture of the lake below to the west and the snowy hump of Mount Baker beyond, and to the east the rilled and ridged monstrosities humping to the Cascade Ridge." Even the loo has a view: the open-air toilet is perched on the edge of a cliff, looking out over the Lightning Creek valley toward Freezeout Mountain and other barren peaks of the Pasayten Wilderness.

18 Lightning Creek and Hozomeen Lake

Overview:	A day hike to Hozomeen Lake, 7.8 miles round trip, or a backpack to Ross Lake, 14.1 miles overall.
Best season:	Early June to late October.
Difficulty:	Moderate, north to south; moderately strenuous, south to north.
Elevation gain:	2,530 feet.
Elevation loss:	2,570 feet.
Maximum elevation:	2,900 feet.
Topo maps:	Hozomeen Mountain, Skagit Peak; *Ross Lake, Jack Mountain.*
Jurisdiction:	Ross Lake National Recreation Area.

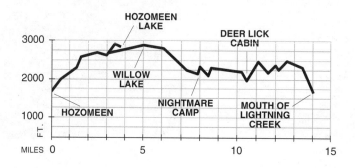

Hozomeen Lake. PHOTO BY MELANIE DAVIDSON

Finding the trailhead: From the western edge of Hope, British Columbia, follow the Silver-Skagit Road south for 38 miles to the U.S.-Canada border. This road has a broad, gravel surface that may have numerous potholes and washboards. Once in the United States, drive past the ranger station and take the second left, which accesses a campground loop. The trailhead is at the end of this road, beside a historic customs station.

Key points:
- 0.0 Trailhead at old Hozomeen Customs cabin.
- 3.0 Trail crosses Hozomeen Creek.
- 3.1 Junction with spur trail to Hozomeen Lake (0.8 mile, easy). Bear right for Lightning Creek.
- 5.1 Head of Willow Lake and spur trail to Willow Lake Camp.
- 5.5 Trail leaves Willow Lake.
- 7.8 Nightmare Camp. Trail crosses Lightning Creek and follows its east bank.
- 10.2 Deer Lick Camp.
- 10.3 Junction with Three Fools Trail. Bear right for Ross Lake.
- 10.4 Trail crosses Lightning Creek to reach Deer Lick Cabin.
- 12.7 Top of grade that descends to Ross Lake.
- 14.1 Trail ends at junction above Lightning Creek hiker camp.

The hike: This trail offers a northern route to the eastern shore of Ross Lake, and provides access to several lowland lakes along the way. The largest of these, Hozomeen Lake, reflects the striking crags of Hozomeen Mountain, and it is a popular day hike from Hozomeen. The longer trail along Lightning Creek makes an easy circuit around Desolation Peak, passing through fine stands of old-growth timber along the middle reaches of the creek before climbing above a narrow canyon to reach Ross Lake. This trail links up with the Three Fools Trail, the East Bank Trail, and the Desolation Peak Trail for extended forays into the backcountry.

The trail begins beside a historic U.S. Customs cabin, and ascends briskly through the timber above the Hozomeen Campground. The forest soon thins to a sparse growth of spindly Douglas-firs and lodgepole pines, the sure sign of an old burn. The thin and stony soil is covered with mosses and foliose lichens, which are related to the caribou moss of the Arctic tundra. At the top of the initial grade, the trail reaches a level upland where stately cedars grow. The gradient is gentler now, and it remains so as far as the junction with the spur path to Hozomeen Lake. This side trail leads 0.6 mile through a broad watershed divide to reach the lake, a vast lowland pool that lies at the foot of Hozomeen Mountain. *Hozomeen* means "sharp like a knife" in the local Native dialect, an appropriate description of the several sheer crags that rise from the massif. Mule deer are abundant (and sometimes pestiferous) here, and loons commonly are spotted on the still waters. There is a pretty campground at the south end of the lake, and visitors will find fair fishing for brook trout.

Meanwhile, the Lightning Creek Trail continues eastward through the forest, rising and falling gently with the folds in the terrain. The trees

Desolation Peak • Lightning Creek • Hozomeen Lake

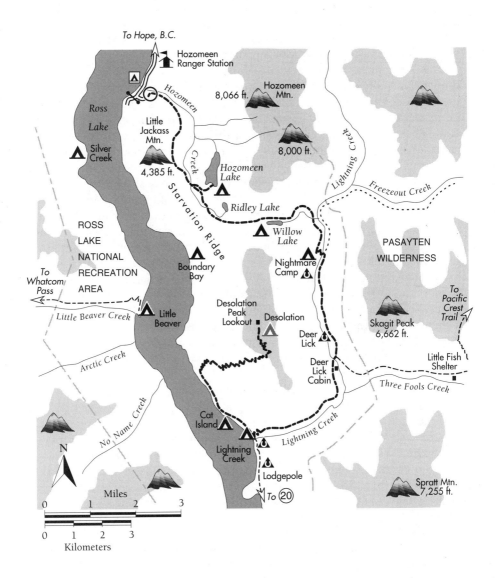

To Hope, B.C.

Hozomeen Ranger Station

Ross Lake

Silver Creek

Little Jackass Mtn.
4,385 ft.

Hozomeen

Creek

8,066 ft.

Hozomeen Mtn.

8,000 ft.

Hozomeen Lake

Ridley Lake

Starvation Ridge

Willow Lake

Lightning Creek

Freezeout Creek

ROSS
LAKE
NATIONAL
RECREATION
AREA

Boundary Bay

Nightmare Camp

PASAYTEN
WILDERNESS

To Whatcom Pass

Little Beaver Creek

Little Beaver

Desolation Peak Lookout

Desolation

Deer Lick

Skagit Peak
6,662 ft.

To Pacific Crest Trail

Arctic Creek

Deer Lick Cabin

Little Fish Shelter

Three Fools Creek

No Name Creek

Cat Island

Lightning Creek

Lightning Creek

N

Lodgepole

To 20

Spratt Mtn.
7,255 ft.

Miles

0   1   2   3

0   1   2   3
Kilometers

ultimately thin out, and huckleberry bushes grow abundantly in the sunny understory. The path soon reaches the head of Willow Lake, where a campsite shaded by cottonwoods guards the shallow woodland pool. The lake is gradually filling in with sediment, and shrubs are encroaching at its margins. The lake will ultimately become a brushy meadow, which will in turn give way to conifers as forest succession runs its course.

The trail follows the north shore of the mere, then strikes out through tall timber. The path strikes the outlet stream at a pleasant waterfall and follows the brook downward toward Lightning Creek. Its valley is level at first, with immense cedars that tower above an undergrowth of salmonberry and devil's club. Then the gradient steepens, and the stream plunges through mossy cascades shaded by a mature forest of hemlock. After a vigorous descent, the trail turns south along the edge of the Lightning Creek valley. A few steep drops carry the trail down into the bottomlands, where it reaches Nightmare Camp. This camp is set amid the massive boles of old-growth cedars.

A footbridge spans Lightning Creek, and beyond it the trail follows the stream downward. Convoluted hillsides soon give way to level terraces, their ancient sediments laid down by glaciers to form the ancestral valley floor. Lightning Creek has since cut down through them, leaving them stranded high above the new bottomlands. A dense growth of hemlock saplings now borders the trail, which occupies a wide swath cut through the forest.

Just before the junction with the Three Fools trail, Deer Lick Camp occupies a small clearing in the forest above the creek. Beyond the junction, the trail descends to a stock bridge over Lightning Creek. On the far bank is the Deer Lick Cabin, built for the Forest Service by a prominent Native American pioneer named Leonard Bacon.

Beyond the cabin, the trail climbs steadily through the forest. The towering cedars of the bottomlands are soon replaced by trees that grew in the wake of the 1926 fire that started along Big Beaver Creek and burned much of the upper Skagit Valley. The streamcourse is now far below, and the trail follows it, bending around the mountainside onto an eastward heading. There are periodic openings where old Douglas-firs grow sparsely, and these allow views down into the steep-walled canyon. Spratt Mountain is the massive peak beyond the canyon. The path rises and falls, maintaining a level gradient as the chasm grows deeper. Soon the trail is more than a thousand feet above the rushing water.

Near the mouth of the creek are fine views of Ross Lake and the snowclad peaks that surround it. The trail then switchbacks steadily downward to the lakeshore. Bear left at the two trail junctions to reach the suspension bridge that spans the cove where Lightning Creek empties into Ross Lake.

19 Thunder Creek

Overview:	A day hike to McAllister Camp, 12.5 miles round trip, or a backpack to Park Creek Pass, 19 miles one way.
Best season:	Mid-April to early November as far as Tricouni Camp; Late July to mid-October for Park Creek Pass.
Difficulty:	Easy to Tricouni Camp; moderately strenuous beyond.
Elevation gain:	6,540 feet.
Elevation loss:	1,660 feet.
Maximum elevation:	6,100 feet at Park Creek Pass.
Topo maps:	Ross Dam, Mount Logan, Forbidden Peak; *Diablo Lake, Mount Logan.*
Jurisdiction:	Ross Lake National Recreation Area, North Cascades National Park.

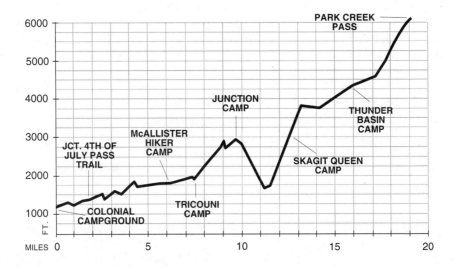

Finding the trailhead: Follow Washington Highway 20 to Colonial Campground at mile 130.2, 11 miles east of Newhalem. The trail begins at the south end of the campground, next to the amphitheater.

Key points:

0.0 Trailhead in Colonial Campground south unit.
0.6 Junction with Thunder Woods Nature Trail. Stay left for Thunder Creek.
0.9 Bridge over Thunder Creek. Trail now follows east bank.
1.4 Spur trail descends to Thunder Camp.
1.7 Junction with Fourth of July Pass Trail. Continue straight ahead.

1.9   Spur trail descends to Neve Camp.
5.9   McAllister horse camp.
6.2   Spur trail leads across stream to McAllister hiker camp.
6.6   Trail leaves Ross Lake NRA and enters North Cascades National Park.
7.5   Trail crosses Fisher Creek to arrive at Tricouni Camp.
9.7   Junction Camp. Fisher Creek Trail splits away to left. Continue straight ahead.
13.3 Trail crosses upper Thunder Creek above an impressive waterfall.
13.5 Skagit Queen Camp.
16.4 Thunder Basin Camp.
19.0 Park Creek Pass.

The hike: This trail was originally blazed by prospectors bound for the gold-bearing veins along Skagit Queen Creek. A number of hard rock claims were staked, shafts blasted into the mountainsides, and by 1905 the first of a series of mining consortiums were incorporated to scratch out fortunes in precious metals from this remote mountain wilderness. Equipment and supplies had to be packed in from Marblemount by mule train, across the narrow ledges of Devils Elbow and through the deep forests that led along the Skagit and up Thunder Creek itself. But the veins were shallow and the ore played out quickly, so the mining companies went bankrupt and the prospectors went away penniless. The wilderness has since swallowed up most signs of their vain efforts.

Today, the Thunder Creek valley offers a long trek through old-growth conifers to the remote alpine basins near Park Creek Pass, deep in the North Cascades backcountry. The trek begins by following an arm of Diablo Lake, with periodic views of its turquoise water. This unique coloration is the result of glacial silt, which flows down into the lake from the Boston, Klawatti, and Neve glaciers. Glacial silt is so fine that it floats suspended in the water, refracting light so that only aquamarine colors escape. After

Peaks above the Thunder Basin.

0.9 mile, the trail reaches a suspension bridge spanning the mouth of Thunder Creek. The original bridge, built in 1913, was packed overland piece by piece by mule. Its site, 3 miles downstream, was flooded in 1928 during the construction of Diablo Dam.

On the far bank, the trail crosses low-lying, sandy flats that are flooded periodically when high runoff or glacier melt causes the creek to swell. These floodplains are covered with water-tolerant shrubs, such as thimbleberry, salmonberry, and devil's club. The path soon ascends onto well-drained terraces, where it enters an old-growth forest of hemlock, western redcedar, and Douglas-fir. The twin camps of Thunder and Neve occupy particularly striking stands of timber on both sides of the junction with the Fourth of July Pass Trail. Beyond the camps, the Thunder Creek Trail climbs gradually along steep hillsides, and a sturdy bridge spans a tumultuous feeder creek to reveal Thunder Creek far below, coursing noisily through a rugged canyon.

The path then ascends onto stony slopes that burned in 1970 and again in 1990. Colonial Peak can now be seen up the valley of Neve Creek. After dropping into the trees, the track ascends onto a second open slope, which faces up the drainage of McAllister Creek. The path then drops into the bottomlands, passing the McAllister horse camp and the short spur trail that leads to the hiker camp across Thunder Creek. Beyond this point, heavily timbered bottoms are littered with nurse logs that provide seedbeds for shrubs and young trees.

At mile 7.5, the trail crosses Fisher Creek to reach Tricouni Camp, which has views of Tricouni Peak. The views improve as the main trail climbs a burned ridgetop along Fisher Creek, and now Snowfield Peak is visible to the northwest. As the trees close in, watch for a thundering waterfall on Fisher Creek. At the top of the grade, the trail reaches a lofty shelf where the Fisher Creek trail joins in from the east. Junction Camp is located here, at the edge of a wooded scarp with views through the trees of Forbidden and Tricouni peaks. At the far edge of the shelf, an unmarked spur descends steeply to the ruins of old log cabins at the edge of a swampy meadow.

The trail then begins to descend across a steep mountainside wooded in Douglas-fir. Openings in the forest are frequent, revealing Tricouni and Forbidden peaks and offering glimpses of Boston Glacier through the trees. At the bottom of the grade, the path crosses a substantial stream and flirts with Thunder Creek before turning inland for a vigorous ascent. After much climbing, the trail returns to Thunder Creek at an impressive waterfall. Above the falls, a bridge leads to the far bank. The path now surmounts the ridge that divides the Thunder and Skagit Queen watersheds.

After a short distance, Skagit Queen Camp occupies a loose grove of mature silver fir. Just beyond the camp, watch the slopes below the trail for the ruins of the Skagit Queen generator house, which dates from 1905. Water was piped downhill from Thunder Creek to run a Pelton wheel, which used the flow of the water to generate electricity for the mill that served the Skagit Queen Mine. The mill and pipeline are of great archaeological interest,

Thunder Creek

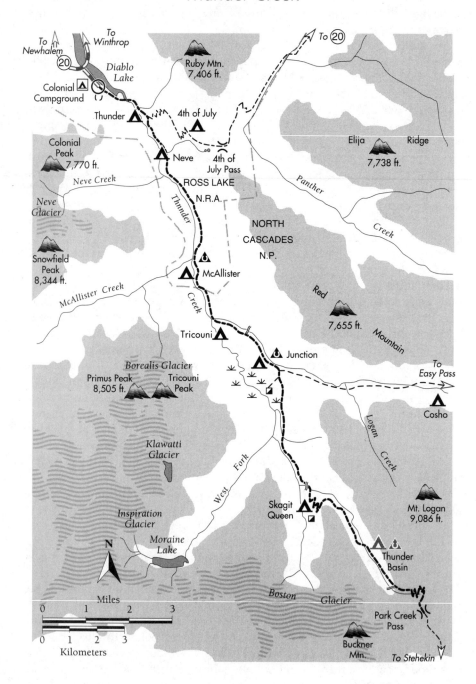

and are protected by federal law. Feel free to observe them, but don't disturb the ruins or the pipeline.

The trail now zigzags aggressively up the slope, making frequent crossings of the pipeline. The path ultimately swings east into the hanging valley that bears the headwaters of Thunder Creek. The forest is now distinctly subalpine, and numerous rockfalls have built up piles of talus below the rugged cliffs. These boulderfields provide homes for hoary marmots, which are abundant in this high basin. After a mile of gentle climbing, the roaring creek is replaced by glassy runs that glide through logjams. The trail levels off as well, and avalanche slopes offer tantalizing glimpses of the peaks that line the valley. The largest of these clearings is just below Thunder Basin Camp, and it reveals the mountains in their full glory.

The trail then crosses Thunder Creek to reach the camp, which occupies a dense grove of subalpine fir with limited views. Where the trail continues upvalley, avalanches have all but erased the trees from the west side of the basin, making for spectacular vistas. The trail sticks to the forest edge, then zigzags lazily upward through copses of subalpine fir and mountain hemlock. The trees give way to swards of avalanche lilies on the steeper slopes, with views of Thunder Glacier to the west. The trail tops out in a high alpine cirque, flanked by talus slopes below sheer cliffs of Skagit gneiss. The trail then traverses steep and rocky slopes (ice axes are a must here if the snow has not melted), approaching Park Creek Pass through a scattering of subalpine larches.

From the pass's alpine meadows and rockfields, hikers get superb views of Booker Mountain to the west. Northward views stretch all the way to mounts Redoubt and Spickard on the Canadian border, and south views find the shining summit of Glacier Peak presiding above a turbulent sea of craggy summits. Ahead, the Park Creek Trail descends toward Stehekin.

20 Fourth of July Pass

Overview:	A day hike or short backpack that follows Panther Creek, then climbs over Fourth of July Pass to Thunder Creek, 9.7 miles overall.
Best season:	Early July to early October.
Difficulty:	Moderately strenuous.
Elevation gain:	2,190 feet, east to west.
Elevation loss:	2,850 feet, east to west.
Maximum elevation:	3,530 feet.
Topo maps:	Crater Mountain, Ross Dam; *Diablo Lake, Mount Logan.*
Jurisdiction:	Ross Lake National Recreation Area, North Cascades National Park.

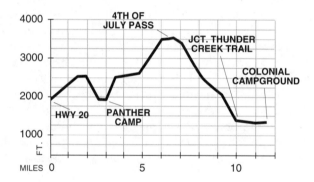

Finding the trailhead: Park at the East Bank Trailhead at mile 138 on Washington Highway 20, and walk east on the highway for 60 yards to reach the beginning of the trail. The trek ends at the trailhead at the southern edge of Colonial Campground. Through-hikers will need to arrange a car shuttle.

Key points:
- 0.0 Trail leaves the highway just east of East Bank Trailhead.
- 1.5 Top of initial grade. Trail begins descent to Panther Creek.
- 3.1 Trail crosses Panther Creek to reach camping area.
- 6.5 Fourth of July Pass.
- 7.2 Fourth of July Pass Camp. Trail begins descent toward Thunder Creek.
- 9.7 Trail ends at junction with Thunder Creek Trail, 2.1 miles south of Colonial Campground.

The hike: This popular trail offers an accessible overnight trek through the low

Tricouni Peak from Fourth of July camp.

pass behind Ruby Mountain. Heavy forests yield views of the surrounding grandeur grudgingly and at infrequent intervals. The trek along Panther Creek is a delight in itself, however, with foaming rapids and boisterous cascades, and perhaps the chance to spot a mink or a water ouzel. Travelers who hike this trail as a loop should post cars at both trailheads since hitchhiking can be a difficult proposition in this part of the country.

The trail leaves the highway in full sprint up the mountainside, zigzagging rapidly up the toe of a ridge. A long and wearying ascent carries hikers hundreds of feet above Panther Creek. After a brief traverse the path plummets through the timber to reach the streamside. Panther Creek courses through its narrow valley in a continuous series of rapids and cascades, rarely pausing to languish in a shady pool. The trail ascends the stream steadily, tracking its gradient and occasionally climbing onto steep hillsides to avoid a tricky impasse. Early on, the few brushy openings reveal no peaks, but do give the nettles a chance to inflict pain on the unwary.

Just below the confluence of Stillwell and Panther creeks, a footbridge spans the waters to carry the trail to an island camp in deep timber. The trail now follows the west bank of Panther Creek to an avalanche slope opposite the mouth of Stillwell Creek. From here, one can look eastward up the side valley to glimpse the stony pinnacles of Elija Ridge. From the upper edge of the clearing are views down Panther Creek of the lofty summit of Crater Mountain.

From this point on, the gradient of Panther Creek lessens, and peaceful hemlock woodlands line its banks. Occasional avalanche slopes interrupt

Fourth of July Pass

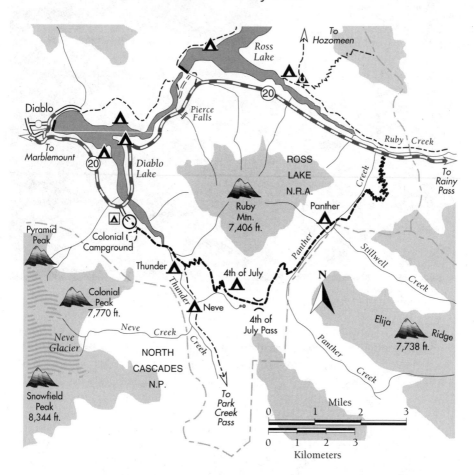

the timber, but there are no views here. After 4.8 miles, the trail abandons Panther Creek and climbs westward along a finger ridge to begin the ascent to Fourth of July Pass. The lowland hemlocks are soon replaced by silver firs. Views are scarce as the path climbs steadily, then traverses southward to enter the pass. The drainage divide is a low and broad saddle, protected from prevailing winds. It fosters a rich and robust forest of hemlock that mirrors the forest community of the Panther Creek bottoms.

After passing through the gap, the trail climbs onto well-drained, stony slopes where Douglas-fir and hemlock form a sparse woodland. A short spur path soon descends to an outcrop of gneiss that overlooks the Panther Potholes, a pair of small woodland lakes that are reputed to offer fine fishing for cutthroat trout to adventurous souls who survive the descent. Just beyond this point is Fourth of July Camp, which occupies an old burn grown up in young lodgepole pine and Douglas-fir. The camp offers the best view of the trek, facing west toward Snowfield and Colonial peaks with Neve

Glacier between them. Farther south are Tricouni and Primus peaks, framing Borealis Glacier.

After passing the camp, the trail begins its long and zigzagging descent into the Thunder Creek valley. After dropping through the timber for some distance, the path levels out and traverses northward. Openings in the forest reveal Snowfield Peak and the summit of Colonial Peak, as well as Davis Peak to the north. The trail soon resumes its descent, passing numerous openings in the timber. Elephant Butte is now visible to the north, and McMillan Spire flanks Davis Peak. At the bottom of the grade, the trail joins the Thunder Creek trail between Neve and Thunder camps. Turn right to follow the flat bottomlands of Thunder Creek to Colonial Campground, where the hike ends at a marked trailhead.

21 Easy Pass and Fisher Creek

Overview:	A day hike to Easy Pass, 7.4 miles round trip, or a backpack to the Thunder Creek Trail, 14.2 miles overall.
Best season:	Late July to early October.
Difficulty:	Moderately strenuous.
Elevation gain:	2,950 feet.
Elevation loss:	3,520 feet.
Maximum elevation:	6,540 feet at Easy Pass.
Topo maps:	Mount Arriva, Mount Logan, Forbidden Peak; *Diablo Lake, Mount Logan.*
Jurisdiction:	Okanogan National Forest, North Cascades National Park.

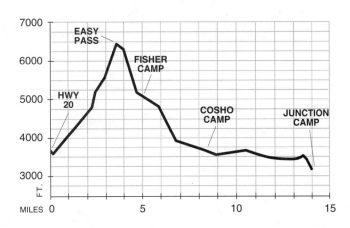

Finding the trailhead: The trailhead is at mile 151.5 on Washington Highway 20, 6 miles west of Rainy Pass.

Easy Pass • Fisher Creek

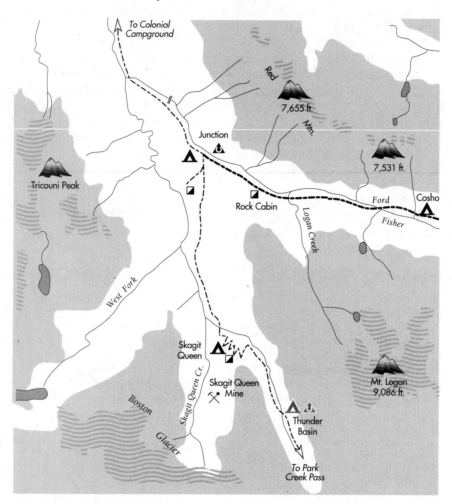

Key points:
- 0.0 Trailhead on WA 20.
- 0.1 Trail fords Granite Creek.
- 3.7 Easy Pass. Trail enters North Cascades National Park and begins to descend.
- 4.7 Trail bottoms out in Fisher Creek valley.
- 5.1 Fisher Basin Camp.
- 8.6 Cosho Camp.
- 9.1 Trail fords Fisher Creek.
- 12.1 Trail crosses Logan Creek.
- 12.9 Trail passes Rock Cabin site.
- 14.1 Junction with spur trail to Junction horse camp.
- 14.2 Trail ends at junction with Thunder Creek Trail. Junction hiker camp is just to the south.

Easy Pass • Fisher Creek

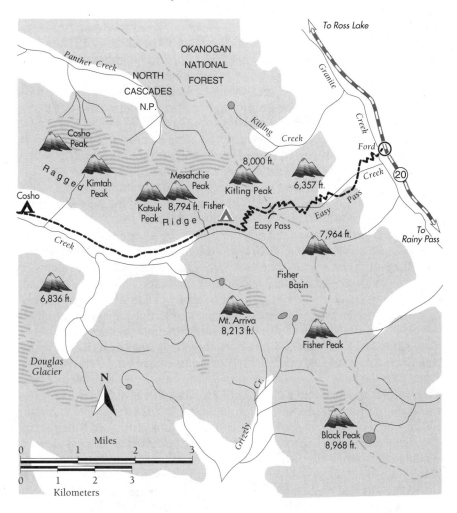

The hike: This route climbs from WA 20 over a high divide to enter the southern quadrant of North Cascades National Park. A day trip leads to the alpine country and mountain grandeur of Easy Pass, and backpackers can continue down Fisher Creek to intersect the Thunder Creek Trail for longer trips to Colonial Campground or Stehekin. Easy Pass is perhaps one of the best places in the Cascades to watch for mountain goats, and black bears commonly are spotted in the upper basin of Fisher Creek.

The trail begins with a crossing of Granite Creek, a knee-deep ford of swift-flowing water that will be necessary until a footlog is emplaced. On the far bank, the trail makes a few upward switchbacks through a sun-dappled forest of mountain hemlock to reach an open basin below Easy Pass. Stark and nameless crags guard the basin, and as the trail climbs upward there are southward views of Mount Hardy. The trail crosses talus slopes, then zigzags up beside noisy waterfalls of Easy Pass Creek. Above the lower headwall is a hanging basin of alpine tundra and frost-shattered rock.

The path steepens as it zigzags up the talus to reach Easy Pass and the boundary of North Cascades National Park. Here, loose groves of subalpine larch and fir rise from the midst of broad heather meadows. Hikers get superb views of the Fisher Creek Basin, guarded by the massive granite summits of Fisher Peak at the head of the valley and Mount Arriva directly across the deep gulf of air. Descending from the pass, the trail traverses westward across a steep and flower-strewn mountainside interrupted by scattered clumps of fir. The westward views are outstanding here. The jagged horn of Mesahchie Peak presides over the north side of the valley, while Mount Logan rises in full view to the southwest, robed in the rumpled ice of Douglas Glacier. Looking father down the valley, Tricouni Peak sends thin jawbones of naked rock above a thick cloak of glacial ice.

The trail zigzags down to the valley floor in short order, then follows the gentle downward flow of Fisher Creek through orderly subalpine meadows. Fisher Camp is soon reached, nestled into a narrow band of firs steeped in the mountain grandeur. The views continue unabated for a mile as the path makes its way down the valley. A mature forest closes in around the trail, which begins to descend in earnest. A brushy avalanche slope yields a final view of Mount Logan before the path disappears into the forest for good.

The slope levels off into a broad bottomland, shaded by a deep forest of silver fir and hemlock. Cosho Camp occupies a streamside site about 1.3 miles down the valley. Soon after passing the camp, the trail fords Fisher Creek, which has become a deep, lazy stream with translucent turquoise waters. As the path continues down the valley, avalanche slopes interrupt the forest on a periodic basis, revealing the summits of Ragged Ridge across the valley. A particularly broad brushfield at mile 10.6 has the best views of the peaks that crown the ridgetop.

Mountain hemlock and silver fir give way to western red-cedar and western hemlock as the trail nears Logan Creek, and evidence of old rockfalls can be seen on both sides of the valley. Logan Creek itself sports a series of turbulent cascades over a channel of mossy boulders, providing an excellent place for rest and rejuvenation. As the trail continues onward, watch for the enormous rockslide scar on the south face of Ragged Ridge, and the great pile of rubble at its foot. Soon after passing a foaming cascade on Fisher Creek, the path climbs into a maze of mossy boulders. It then leaves the streamside, descending steadily to reach its end at an intersection with the Thunder Creek Trail at Junction Camp.

ADDITIONAL TRAILS

The **Freezeout Creek Tail** once departed from Lightning Creek at Nightmare Camp, but it has been abandoned and is now hard to find.

The **Ruby Creek Trail** is a connector that parallels the highway between the East Bank and Canyon Creek trailheads.

The **Happy Creek Forest Walk** is a 0.3-mile interpretive trail just east of the Ross Dam overlook. It is wheelchair-accessible.

The **Newhalem Creek Trail** follows an old logging road. It has been abandoned and is overgrown with alder.

The **Ladder Falls Trail** is a short walk from the town of Newhalem or the East Bank and Canyon Creek trailheads.

Other short strolls around Newhalem are the **River Loop**, the **Trail of the Cedars**, and the **Rockshelter Trail**.

Mount Baker and the Chilliwack Watershed

The North Fork of the Nooksack River drains an isolated corner of the North Cascades, backed up against the Canadian border and guarded by the immense volcanic cone of Mount Baker and the equally imposing crags of Mount Shuksan. Originally the domain of the Nooksack tribe, the valley saw a brief flurry of gold prospecting and is now a year-round vacation retreat for world-weary tourists from all over the globe.

The town of Glacier is the hub of activity in the valley, with lodges and inns, fine restaurants, and a small mercantile store. Stop at the Glacier Ranger Station for information on hiking in the area. Washington Highway 542 follows the river up from the town into Forest Service domain, climbing through the forested valley to end in the Heather Meadows Recreation Area, designed for day use and replete with a network of well-built trails. Just below it is the Mount Baker Ski Area, where deep (though water-saturated) snows of the windward Cascades draw a mostly local crowd.

The area is known for its spectacular alpine meadows and easy access. Mountain vistas rival those of the Alps, drawing photographers from the far corners of the planet to morning and evening displays of alpenglow. The

The white paintbrush is endemic to the alpine meadows of the Nooksack River watershed.

Chilliwack Watershed Overview

high ridges that border the Nooksack sometimes get so crowded that they often seem like city parks. Mercifully, most of the tourists stick to the easier trails, and solitude can be found on the more demanding routes even at the height of the tourist season. For a true wilderness experience, stop at the Glacier ranger station and get a permit to visit the backcountry of North Cascades National Park, which is easily accessible by trail through the low gap of Hannegan Pass. Visitor numbers within the park are effectively limited by the few available campsites. All trailheads in the area fall within the Mount Baker–Snoqualmie National Forest, which charges a user fee for day and overnight parking.

22 Skyline Divide

Overview: A short day hike to the top of Skyline Divide, 4 miles round trip, or a longer day hike to the base of Chowder Ridge, 11.6 miles round trip.

Best season: Late July to mid-October.

Difficulty: Moderate.

Elevation gain: 2,690 feet.

Elevation loss: 680 feet.

Maximum elevation: 6,570 feet near the base of Chowder Ridge.

Topo maps: Mount Baker, Bearpaw Mountain; *Mount Baker*.

Jurisdiction: Mount Baker Wilderness (Mount Baker–Snoqualmie National Forest).

Finding the trailhead: Follow Washington Highway 542 to the east end of Glacier, then turn right onto the Glacier Creek Road (Forest Road 39). Make an immediate left onto Forest Road 37. This forest trunk road is paved the first 10 miles before winding upward for the remaining 5.4 miles to the trailhead.

Mount Baker from the Skyline Divide.

Skyline Divide

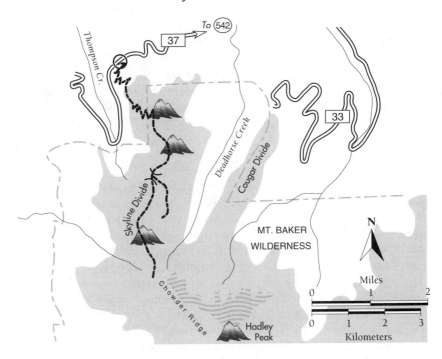

Key points:
  0.0 Trailhead.
  2.0 Top of Skyline Divide.
  3.5 Trail junction. Left-hand trail descends into meadowy basins
       (1 mile, moderate). Right-hand trail (moderately strenuous)
       continues up the divide.
  5.8 Base of Chowder Ridge.

The hike: This popular trail climbs to a meadowy ridgetop at the base of
Mount Baker. Its easy access makes it popular with the jet-set crowd that
bases itself out of the resort town of Glacier. The alpine meadows atop the
divide are crowded with tourists on weekends; midweek and early morning
visitors have a better chance of finding solitude.

The first third of the trail is devoted to a moderate climb through a forest
of mountain hemlock. Due to the moderate climate found in the western
foothills of the Cascades, the trees grow tall and full near the timberline,
and the understory plants are the same species that are found in the river
bottoms on the eastern side of the range. As the trail approaches the ridgetop,
small glades interrupt the trees, and soon the route climbs through lush
pocket meadows filled with wildflowers. Lupine, arnica, bistort, and vale-
rian are the principal species. Westward views from the openings are not so
engaging, featuring a patchwork of large clearcuts linked by the ragged
stitchwork of logging roads.

Near the summit of the ridge, there are southwesterly views of the Twin Sisters, their jagged summits etched in contrasting shades of tan and umber. As the trail finally reaches the top of the divide, it enters a vast meadow that stretches from the ridgeline far down the slopes to the east. Hikers get magnificent southward views of Mount Baker, its great volcanic cone hidden beneath a rumpled blanket of glacial ice. To the east is the craggy wall of Mount Shuksan, while the distant teeth of mounts Redoubt and Spickard rise along the eastern horizon. The trail follows the ridgetop southward through tidy lawns of wildflowers. Watch for the distinctive blossoms of white Indian paintbrush, which is common in these alpine areas but seldom seen elsewhere.

The path soon climbs vigorously to surmount a high knoll fringed with trees. There are northward views on the way up, with the jagged backbone of Mount Larrabee and the Border Peaks stretching north into Canada. Beyond the first knoll is a second bald prominence. A rough track climbs to its summit, but the main trail swings across its western slope to bypass the high point. On the far side is an unobstructed vista of Chowder Ridge and Dobbs Cleaver, which unite at the low but craggy summit of Hadley Peak. Mount Baker rises to dizzying heights behind it, dwarfing the closer peak.

The path now descends gently along an increasingly barren ridgeline to reach its official terminus in a low saddle. A steep track climbs along the rugged ridgeline into wilder and more remote country beyond, ending after 5.8 miles at a sheer wall that marks the toe of Chowder Ridge. Here, the views stretch all the way to Puget Sound and beyond. A better-tended trail descends from the saddle onto the eastern slope of the ridge. This trail passes several marmot colonies as it crosses slopes covered in a fragile mat of heather and blueberry. After rounding a spur ridge, the path crosses a series of east-facing bowls. It peters out beside a tent spot with flowing water nearby and fine views of Mount Baker.

23 Table Mountain

Overview:	A short day hike to the top of Table Mountain, 1.6 miles round trip.
Best season:	Early August to mid-October.
Difficulty:	Moderate.
Elevation gain:	420 feet.
Elevation loss:	None.
Maximum elevation:	5,520 feet.
Topo maps:	Shuksan Arm; *Mount Shuksan.*
Jurisdiction:	Mount Baker–Snoqualmie National Forest.

Finding the trailhead: The hike begins at the west edge of the Artist Point parking lot, at the end of Washington Highway 542 (mile 57).

Key points:
- 0.0 Artist Point parking area.
- 0.4 Top of Table Mountain.
- 0.8 Trail peters out to become a cairn-marked route.

The hike: This short trail climbs atop the surface of an ancient flow of hot

Mount Shuksan from Table Mountain.

103

Table Mountain

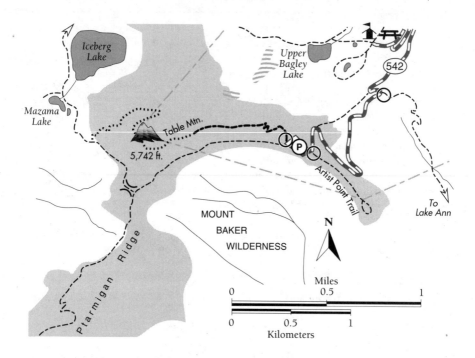

ash that once rolled down from a fissure on Mount Baker. This is a popular and heavily used trail, principally the domain of weekend tourists. It offers some of the best views of mounts Shuksan and Baker to be had in the Heather Meadows area. The trail climbs along sheer cliffs with no guardrails, and families with children should approach the trek with extreme caution. The official trail ends atop Table Mountain, but it is possible to follow the southern edge of the rims to a steep scramble route that leads down across talus slopes and links up with the Galena Chain Lakes Trail (see p.105).

The trail begins by wandering westward toward the base of Table Mountain, passing through a moonscape of naked basalt pocked with snowmelt pools. Upon reaching the mountain, the trail snakes upward steeply along a course blasted into the cliffs with dynamite. In addition to views of the surrounding peaks, the trail overlooks the upper basin of Swift Creek. This stream has cut down through a deep layer of volcanic ash, belched forth by Mount Baker during its violent past. The path passes among wind-torn mountain hemlocks as it works its way onto north-facing slopes, with fine views of the lake basin below.

Upon reaching the level surface of Table Mountain, the path runs westward through the heather, with fine views of the basalt cliffs that mark the northern edge of the old lava flow. Views are panoramic: The several lobes of Curtis Glacier cascade down the slopes of Mount Shuksan in a jumble of séracs and crevasses; a sliver of Baker Lake appears to the south, and to the southwest the dormant cone of Mount Baker is locked in the ice of Park, Mazama, and Roosevelt glaciers. The trail soon runs out onto the bare and jumbled surface of the lava flow; snowfields commonly persist here well into August. The maintained trail ends at the edge of the bare rock; adventurous hikers can follow cairns along the south rim to reach the scramble route that descends westward to the Galena Chain Lakes Trail.

24 Galena Chain Lakes Loop

Overview:	A day hike visiting the subalpine lakes of the Heather Meadows area, 6.7 miles one way or 7.7 miles as a loop hike.
Best season:	Late July to mid-October.
Difficulty:	Moderate clockwise; moderately strenuous counterclockwise.
Elevation gain:	880 feet clockwise.
Elevation loss:	1,740 feet clockwise.
Maximum elevation:	5,440 feet.
Topo maps:	Shuksan Arm; *Mount Shuksan*.
Jurisdiction:	Mount Baker Wilderness (Mount Baker–Snoqualmie National Forest).

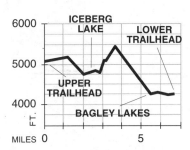

Finding the trailhead: The hike begins at the west edge of the Artist Point parking lot, at the end of Washington Highway 542 (mile 57). It ends at the Lower Bagley parking lot, an unmarked, paved turnoff on the right side of the road just beyond the Picture Lake roundabout. Through-hikers will need to arrange a car shuttle or hike the Wild Goose trail 1 mile back to the Artist Point Trailhead.

Key points:
- 0.0 Artist Point parking area.
- 0.3 Trail enters Mount Baker Wilderness.
- 1.2 Junction with Ptarmigan Ridge Trail. Bear right for Galena Chain Lakes.

Galena Chain Lakes Loop

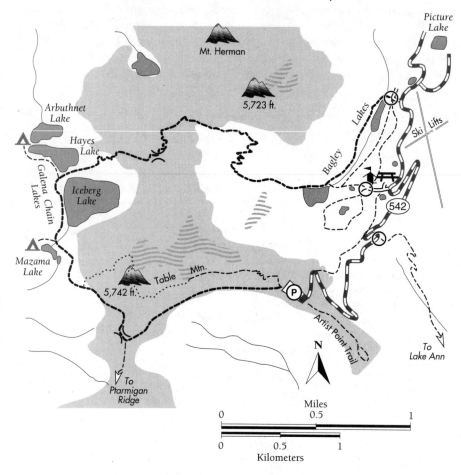

2.1   Mazama Lake.

2.4   Trail reaches foot of Iceberg Lake.

2.7   Junction with trail to Arbuthnet Lake. Bear right to complete the loop.

3.7   Trail crosses pass to enter Bagley Creek watershed and leaves Mount Baker Wilderness.

5.4   Head of upper Bagley Lake.

5.8   Junction with spur trail to visitor center. Stay left to complete the hike.

6.3   Head of lower Bagley Lake.

6.6   Trail crosses dam at foot of lower Bagley Lake.

6.7   Lower trailhead.

The hike: This trail takes in the many lakes, meadows, and brooks of the Heather Meadows area. Although part of it passes through the Mount Baker Wilderness, do not come here seeking a wilderness experience: the trail is teeming with tourists, many of them unfamiliar with backcountry etiquette.

There are camping spots near Mazama and Hayes lakes, but because the area receives such a high volume of day hikers, it is hard to justify pitching a tent in the midst of the traffic.

The hike begins by following the path westward beneath the lava cliffs of Table Mountain. Open slopes reveal both Mount Shuksan and Mount Baker, as well as deep deposits of volcanic ash that have been exposed by waters that feed Swift Creek. A gentle uphill grade leads to a barren saddle, where the Ptarmigan Ridge trail splits away and runs southward.

The Galena Chain Lakes trail now turns northwest and descends steadily across the talus slopes at the foot of Table Mountain. It bottoms out in a meadowy pocket of mountain hemlocks. Here, the smallest of the chain lakes, Mazama Lake, is bordered by carpets of wildflowers. A spur path runs westward toward Mazama Falls, with campsites along the way. The main trail runs north through a wooded gap to reach Iceberg Lake, the largest of the Chain Lakes. This deep tarn is surrounded by hemlock parks lit with wildflowers, and mirrors the tall cliffs that gird the northwestern flank of Table Mountain.

After skirting the western shore of Iceberg Lake, the trail reaches a narrow isthmus that separates it from Hayes Lake. A spur path runs north along Hayes Lake to reach camping spots beside Arbuthnet Lake. Each of the three northernmost lakes support populations of brook trout. The main trail climbs across the hilly neck of land to the north of Iceberg Lake, then makes a steady ascent of the slopes beyond. Views open up as the trail climbs, featuring Ptarmigan Ridge, the summit of Mount Baker, and finally the deep blue waters of Iceberg Lake. Grassy pocket meadows give way to rocky country as the trail works its way upward, and soon the path leads through narrow corridors in the stone.

The trail then surmounts the narrow col below the northern corner of Table Mountain and continues to climb northward across the slopes of Mazama Dome. After a brief ascent, the trail begins the long and foot-pounding grade down to the Bagley Creek basin, in full view of Mount Shuksan. Heather slopes give way to a vast apron of broken rock that has fallen from Mazama Dome. Near the bottom of the grade, the trail reaches several brooks that are bordered by a fringe of pink monkeyflower. When in bloom, this bounty of blossoms attracts nectar-seeking hummingbirds.

The grade bottoms out at the marshy head of Upper Bagley Lake, and a faint pathway departs to the right to round the head of the lake. The main trail runs north to the foot of the lake, where a stone footbridge leads toward the visitor center and connects with the Wild Goose and Bagley Lakes trails (turn right for a shorter loop). Our route continues to follow the western edge of the valley, becoming rougher as it rounds the shore of Lower Bagley Lake. Goat Mountain is the prominent summit to the north. The trail finally crosses the dam at the foot of the lower lake to reach an extensive parking lot that marks the lower trailhead.

25 Ptarmigan Ridge

Overview:	A day hike from the Artist Point Trailhead to Sholes Glacier, 11.8 miles round trip.
Best season:	Early August to mid-October. Ice axe recommended.
Difficulty:	Moderate.
Elevation gain:	1,470 feet.
Elevation loss:	495 feet.
Maximum elevation:	6,160 feet.
Topo maps:	Mount Baker, Shuksan Arm; *Mount Shuksan.*
Jurisdiction:	Mount Baker Wilderness (Mount Baker–Snoqualmie National Forest).

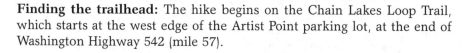

Finding the trailhead: The hike begins on the Chain Lakes Loop Trail, which starts at the west edge of the Artist Point parking lot, at the end of Washington Highway 542 (mile 57).

Key points:
    0.0 Artist Point parking area. Follow Galena Chain Lakes Trail.
    0.3 Trail enters Mount Baker Wilderness.
    1.2 Ptarmigan Ridge Trail splits away from Chain Lakes Trail. Turn left.
    2.4 Trail reaches pass at the head of Wells Creek drainage.
    4.3 Overlook above Camp Kaiser.
    4.7 Saddle behind Coleman Pinnacle.
    5.9 Trail peters out beside Sholes Glacier.

The hike: This trail follows a barren ridgetop through the high alpine country that leads upward to the glaciers of Mount Baker. For a modest day hike, the trek gives a real feeling of a high mountain traverse across country that is ordinarily the domain of mountaineers. There are several potential campsites near the end of the trail, but the heavy volume of day use in the area makes solitude a rare commodity.

The trek begins on the Galena Chain Lakes loop, which runs westward from the parking lot across the open skirts of Table Mountain. Hikers get superb views of mounts Shuksan and Baker as the trail makes its way to the barren saddle at the head of Wells Creek. It is here that the Ptarmigan Ridge trail departs south, descending into a barren and rocky basin. The fields of snow and shattered stone appear lifeless at first, but closer inspection reveals tiny mats of saxifrage on drier spots and vigorous clumps of pink monkeyflower along watercourses. The trail descends across the rolling washes of the basin, then makes a steady ascent to a saddle on the crest of Ptarmigan Ridge.

Viewing the Rainbow Glacier from Ptarmigan Ridge.

The vegetation is more vigorous on the ridgetop and on the southeast-facing slopes beyond it, forming fragile heather meadows and copses of mountain hemlock. The sharp spire of Coleman Pinnacle rises ahead along the ridgeline. The trail traverses beneath its eastern face, climbing gently across snowfields and talus slopes. It reaches a superb overlook south of the pinnacle. From here, excellent views stretch westward, featuring the regal crest of Mount Shuksan with a collection of lesser-known summits south of it: stout Mount Blum, the jagged teeth of Hagan Mountain guarding its broad glacier, and Mount Bacon farthest south. To the east is the towering summit of Mount Baker, and pouring down its flanks are Park and Rainbow glaciers, separated by the snaggletooth spires of the Lava Divide. Below the overlook is Camp Kaiser, perched on a pair of high knolls on the rim of Avalanche Gorge.

Most hikers turn around here, but the trail continues northward across dense sedge meadows on the back side of Coleman Pinnacle. Lupine, bistort, and aster provide the trail's finest floral displays. Nearing the next saddle, the path descends through wind-torn firs and crosses a small rill to reach eroded slopes beyond. After working its way around the head of the basin, the faint track now climbs westward toward a dark and jagged ridge of rhyolite. The billowy icefields of Sholes Glacier lie ahead as the path climbs through a volcanic moonscape. Even here, hardy plants such as dwarf fireweed and silky phaecelia have taken root amid the fractured lava. The trail ends as a definable entity at the edge of Sholes Glacier; ahead lies a mountaineer's route to Mount Baker.

Ptarmigan Ridge

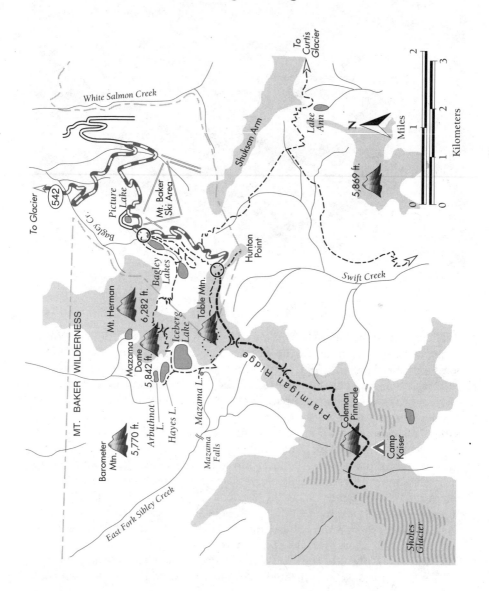

White Salmon Creek

To Curtis Glacier

Shuksan Arm

Lake Ann

N

Miles

Kilometers

5,869 ft.

To Glacier

542

Picture Lake

Mt. Baker Ski Area

Bagley C.

Bagley Lakes

Hunton Point

Table Mtn.

Swift Creek

MT. BAKER WILDERNESS

Mt. Herman

6,282 ft.

Iceberg Lake

Mazama Dome

5,842 ft.

Arbuthnot L.

Hayes L.

Mazama L.

Ptarmigan Ridge

Coleman Pinnacle

Camp Kaiser

Barometer Mtn.

5,770 ft.

Mazama Falls

East Fork Sibley Creek

Sholes Glacier

26 Lake Ann

Overview:	A day hike to Lake Ann, 7.4 miles round trip, or to the toe of Curtis Glacier, 9.4 miles round trip.	
Best season:	Late July to mid-October.	
Difficulty:	Moderate.	
Elevation gain:	1,540 feet.	
Elevation loss:	1,200 feet.	
Maximum elevation:	5,200 feet near Curtis Glacier.	
Topo maps:	Shuksan Arm; *Mount Shuksan.*	
Jurisdiction:	Mount Baker Wilderness (Mount Baker–Snoqualmie National Forest), North Cascades National Park.	

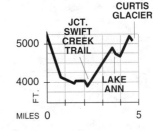

Finding the trailhead: From the town of Glacier, drive east on Washington Highway 542, past Picture Lake to mile 56, where a paved parking area on the left side of the road announces the beginning of the Lake Ann Trail.

Key points:

0.0 Lake Ann Trailhead.
0.8 Trail reaches upper basin of Swift Creek and enters Mount Baker Wilderness.
1.4 Trail crosses Swift Creek.
2.2 Junction with Swift Creek Trail. Stay left as Lake Ann Trail starts to climb.
3.5 Trail crosses a pass to enter the Shuksan Creek drainage.
3.7 Lake Ann. Trail becomes a primitive climber's path.
4.5 Path enters North Cascades National Park.
4.7 Trail reaches lower end of Curtis Glacier.

The hike: Lake Ann is one of the truly awe-inspiring destinations in the North Cascades, with the soaring towers of Mount Shuksan rising above it and the crevasse-riddled surface of Curtis Glacier just across a small valley. The lake itself makes a fine day hike; from its shore, adventurous travelers can traverse the head of Shuksan Creek on a primitive climber's trail to reach the glacier's toe. There are a few campsites among the copses of mountain hemlock above the eastern shore, but they fill up quickly at the height of the summer season.

The trail begins with a steady descent into the head of a hanging valley. Widely spaced mountain hemlocks rise from a dense growth of huckleberry bushes. Folds in the hillsides bear dry streamcourses that are crowded with alpine flowers. At the bottom of the initial grade is a beautiful subalpine

Lake Ann and Mount Shuksan.

basin where sedge meadows are lit by the lavender blossoms of spiraea. The piping of marmots and the bleats of pikas rise from talus slopes on both sides of the basin. In late August the blueberries ripen, offering good pickings as the trail continues down the valley beneath the brooding walls of Shuksan Arm. Small but snowy summits rise ahead, and Mount Shuksan itself is revealed as the trail crosses a second clearing that is slowly being colonized by conifers.

At the lower end of this opening, the path crosses the nascent waters of Swift Creek and begins a level traverse across slopes forested in silver fir and hemlock. Mount Baker can be glimpsed through the treetops, and it emerges into full view as the path descends gently into an open bowl. A signpost on the floor of the bowl marks the intersection with the primitive Swift Creek Trail, which is no longer maintained by the Forest Service.

The Lake Ann Trail is the well-beaten track that ascends the far side of the basin. A vigorous grade leads upward through alpine meadows and heather to reach a gap in the ridgetop. Mount Shuksan cannot be seen from the pass, but Mount Baker is in full view to the west.

The trail now makes its shallow descent to the foot of Lake Ann, which commands a jaw-dropping view of the west face of Shuksan. The peak presents a dynamic and ever-changing landscape, with huge chunks of ice periodically breaking away from the lobes of Curtis Glacier, and slender waterfalls dropping down the lower flanks of the mountain into the depths of the Shuksan Creek valley. Lake Ann itself occupies a shallow and barren pocket near the ridgetop, and hardy saxifrage blooms amid the outcrops

Lake Ann

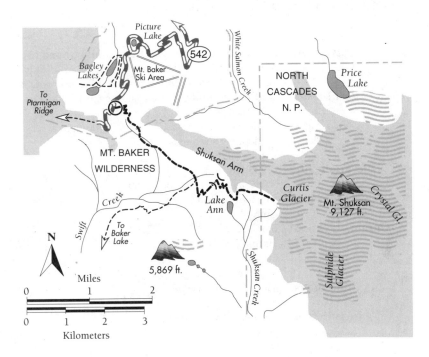

and boulders surrounding the water. A handful of campsites are huddled amid mountain hemlocks at the eastern edge of the lake, perched high above Shuksan Creek. A climber's access trail traverses around the headwall of Shuksan Creek, entering North Cascades National Park on its way to Curtis Glacier.

27 Hannegan Pass and Hannegan Peak

Overview:	A day hike to Hannegan Pass (8 miles round trip) or Hannegan Peak (10 miles round trip), or a short backpack to Boundary Camp, 5 miles one way.
Best season:	Mid-July to mid-October. Hannegan Peak opens in late July.
Difficulty:	Moderate to the pass; moderately strenuous to the peak.
Elevation gain:	1,926 feet to the pass; 3,047 feet to the peak.
Elevation loss:	616 feet to Boundary Camp.
Maximum elevation:	5,066 feet at Hannegan Pass; 6,187 feet at Hannegan Peak.
Topo maps:	Mount Sefrit; *Mount Shuksan.*
Jurisdiction:	Mount Baker Wilderness (Mount Baker–Snoqualmie National Forest).

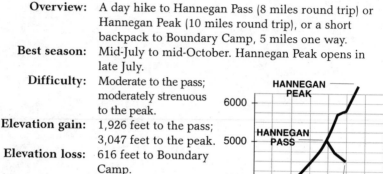

Finding the trailhead: From Glacier, drive east on Washington Highway 542 to mile 46.5. Turn left onto Forest Road 32, and after a mile bear left at the split for Forest Road 34, following signs for Hannegan Pass. It is 5.4 miles from the highway to the campground/trailhead at the end of this improved gravel road.

Key points:
- 0.0 Trailhead at Camp Hannegan.
- 3.4 Hannegan Pass camping area.
- 4.0 Hannegan Pass. Junction with Hannegan Peak Trail (1 mile, moderately strenuous). Continue straight ahead for Boundary Camp.
- 5.0 Boundary Camp. Trail reaches North Cascades National Park and a junction with the Copper Ridge and Chilliwack River trails.

The hike: This well-traveled trail leads up Ruth Creek to Hannegan Pass, the gateway to the northwest corner of North Cascades National Park. The route leads through Forest Service lands, with no special permit required for overnight stays. However, the trail ends at the national park boundary, and backpackers bound for Boundary Camp, Copper Ridge, or the Chilliwack Valley will need to secure a free backcountry permit at Glacier Ranger Station. From Hannegan Pass, a spur trail climbs westward to the bare summit of Hannegan Peak, which makes an excellent day trip.

The trail begins with an easy stroll up the Ruth Creek valley, gouged out of bedrock eons ago by the grinding of deep glaciers. Stands of Engelmann spruce and mountain hemlock are widely scattered; most of the valley is dominated by heavy brush sprinkled liberally with stinging nettle. Views are superb from the outset, featuring the jagged backbone of Nooksack Ridge across the valley. This great wall of metamorphic rock has been carved into arêtes and horn peaks by glacial ice, and slender waterfalls course down its lower flanks. The lofty summit that rises above the trail is Granite Mountain.

After a mile or so, the trail begins a gradual ascent of the valley's north wall. The timber is heavier in the upper reaches of the valley, and now the ice-mantled summit of Ruth Mountain can be seen above the head of the drainage. The gradient steepens as the trail nears Hannegan Pass, and a couple of switchbacks lead upward through the forest to the edge of a meadowy bowl. A spur path now leads southward to a camping area that affords fine views of the surrounding summits. The main path continues its steady ascent, passing through stands of timber and flower-strewn glades to reach the low saddle of Hannegan Pass.

The east-facing meadows of the pass offer views of Copper Ridge and Indian Mountain, with glimpses of the more distant summits of Bear Mountain and Mount Redoubt. To the left is the spur trail to Hannegan Peak (see below), and to the right a way trail runs south to round a tall summit and ends in alpine meadows. From Hannegan Pass, the Chilliwack River valley stretches out ahead, and the main trail makes a brief but steady descent into its headwaters to reach Boundary Camp at the edge of an open basin. The

Looking into the northern Pickets from Hannegan Peak.

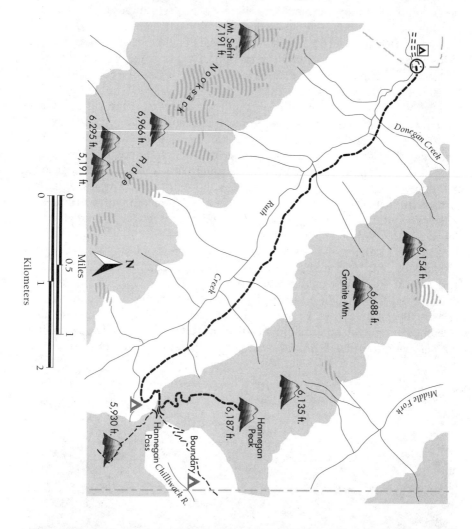

trek ends here, at a junction just beyond the park boundary with trails leading to Copper Ridge and the Chilliwack River.

Hannegan Peak Option. This spur trail begins in a loose woodland of large mountain hemlocks, but soon rises onto steep slopes mantled with wildflowers. Early views are dominated by Ruth Mountain and Nooksack Ridge, with glimpses of East Nooksack Glacier beneath the spires of Jagged Ridge. Before long, the path swings onto east-facing slopes for views of Mineral Mountain and the northern reaches of the Picket Range. The trail then zigzags to the top of a high spur, where a small pond may offer drinking water. It then continues straight up the ridgeline at a calf-burning pace. These slopes are subject to severe winter weather, a fact that is reflected in the sparse mats of heather and wind-torn clumps of mountain hemlock.

The trail ultimately crests a series of bald domes covered in frost-shattered rock. Mountains stretch away in all directions, featuring the steep summit of Granite Mountain to the west, and a long vista down the Chilliwack River toward the lofty and remote summits of Mount Redoubt and Bear Mountain along the Canadian border. To the south is the immense summit of Mount Shuksan, sending its sheer walls and spires above a collar of glacial ice. The trail ends upon reaching the penultimate summit of Hannegan Peak, where a pocket of fir and hemlock krummholz provides shelter from the elements.

28 Copper Ridge

Overview:	A backpack from the Hannegan Pass Trailhead to Egg Lake (8.5 miles one way) or Copper Lake (11.4 miles one way) or, an extended trip from Boundary Camp to the Chilliwack River, 13.9 miles overall.
Best season:	Late July to mid-October.
Difficulty:	Moderately strenuous south to north; strenuous north to south.
Elevation gain:	2,820 feet (south to north).
Elevation loss:	4,930 feet (south to north).
Maximum elevation:	6,260 feet at Copper Ridge Lookout.
Topo maps:	Mount Sefrit, Copper Mountain; *Mount Shuksan, Mount Challenger.*
Jurisdiction:	North Cascades National Park.

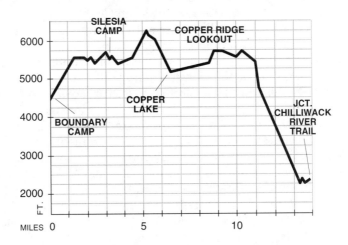

Finding the trail: The trail begins at Boundary Camp, which can be reached by a 5-mile hike over Hannegan Pass. The end of the trail is accessed by a 6.9-mile hike up the Chilliwack River or a 16-mile jaunt over Hannegan Pass (see Hike 27).

Key points:
- 0.0 Trail begins at Boundary Camp. Junction with Hannegan Pass and Chilliwack River trails.
- 1.7 Trail crosses upper Hells Gorge.
- 1.9 Spine of Copper Ridge.
- 3.0 Silesia Camp.
- 3.2 Junction with spur trail to Egg Lake Camp (0.3 mile, moderate). Bear right.
- 5.2 Copper Ridge Lookout.
- 6.4 Copper Lake. Junction with spur trail to Copper Lake Camp. Bear right.
- 11.0 Trail enters old burn and begins long descent into Chilliwack Valley.
- 13.6 Chilliwack River ford.
- 13.9 Junction with Chilliwack River Trail.

The hike: This trail follows an alpine ridge through the northwest corner of the North Cascades. Since it lies entirely within the national park, permits are required and all park regulations apply. This is one of the few trails in the North Cascades that stays above timberline for a significant distance, and along its length are superb mountain views, abundant wildlife, and a diverse array of alpine flowers. Silesia Camp and Egg Lake can be reached in a long two-day backpack over Hannegan Pass (see Hike 27). Destinations farther north along Copper Ridge require a multi-day expedition.

From the signpost in the meadows above Boundary Camp, the Copper Ridge trek begins with an eastward traverse into heavy timber. Level stretches alternate with spurts of climbing, and soon the trail is high above the valley floor. The dense forest of mountain hemlocks thins out as the trail rises higher, revealing views of Ruth Mountain and Mineral Peak. A series of switchbacks lead up toward the ridge crest, and at the top of the grade the trail crosses a steep and eroded gully known as Hells Gorge. Lingering snowdrifts in this area make for a hazardous crossing until midsummer.

The trail crosses several steep meadows before climbing into the heather-blueberry parklands of the ridgetop. The path crests the ridgeline at an open saddle and hikers can look north across the headwaters of Silesia Creek, with fine views of Copper Mountain beyond the forested basin. As the trail follows the top of Copper Ridge, there are excellent views of Ruth Mountain and Mineral Peak across the Chilliwack valley, while the craggy summit of Mount Shuksan rises above Nooksack Ridge to the southwest. Due south, the sharp horn of Mount Blum is visible through Chilliwack Pass.

After climbing vigorously to surmount several low summits, the trail reaches Silesia Camp. Here, tent sites are perched on a high knoll overlooking the Chilliwack Valley. Looking down the valley, hikers can now see the summits of Bear Mountain and Mount Redoubt. In the next low saddle, a spur path descends northward to reach the shore of Egg Lake. This aquamarine tarn is cupped in a rocky hollow high above Silesia Creek. The main trail rounds the next high point to another saddle, then begins the final, calf-burning climb to Copper Ridge Lookout, which is staffed throughout the summer. The lookout occupies the highest point on the trail, commanding views in all directions. The structure itself is not open to the public. Scan the surrounding fellfields for marmots and white-tailed ptarmigan.

The trail then descends along the ridgeline beyond the lookout, skirting perennial snowdrifts as it descends. A barren moonscape of broken granite awaits in the next saddle, overlooked by brooding summits that stretch northward to Copper Mountain itself.

The trail next drops onto east-facing slopes, snaking downward at a vigorous pace toward the foot of Copper Lake. Along the way, several spots offer excellent aerial perspectives on the lake, with its deep azure waters embracing a single rocky peninsula. The lake basin was scooped out of the granite by a small hanging glacier during the most recent ice age. The camp spur leads to the lakeshore, where copses of mountain hemlock rise from the basin's heather-covered terminal moraine. Pikas live in the boulderfields around the lake, and their antics are on display for nature watchers who have the requisite patience.

The main trail angles downward across the lake's outlet stream, then ascends gradually through open parks where mountain brooks tumble down through boulder-strewn meadows. A vigorous climb then leads upward through the timber to reach the bare top of a finger ridge. Superb views across the Chilliwack Valley are punctuated by the soaring summits of Mount Redoubt and Bear Mountain, as well as the multiple peaks of Red Mountain, gathered around the headwaters of Indian Creek. After dropping through an open bowl of heather-blueberry meadows, the trail traverses steep slopes upholstered with herbaceous wildflowers. It soon reaches a north-facing viewpoint, which takes in the cluster of sharp horn peaks west of Chilliwack Lake.

The trail then drops to negotiate a snow-covered talus slope. After a tricky crossing, it traverses above more slopes of broken rock to reach a spot below a wooded saddle. From here, the route leads steeply downward onto timbered slopes, descending on a northward tangent through a climax forest of hemlock. It soon passes through the edges of an old burn. Here, a growth of young Alaska cedar and hemlock is striving to fill the gap. Hikers get parting views of Bear and Red Face mountains as the path drops steeply across the burn. Beyond it is the first in a long series of switchbacks that leads to the valley floor, descending through monotonous forest at a modest pace.

Near the bottom of the grade, the trail strikes a woodland stream and follows it downward into the diverse forest of the Chilliwack bottomlands. The trail soon crosses the streamcourse, then runs south along the base of the ridge to a ford of the river channels. Travelers who make the thigh-deep crossing in mid-August will find spawning salmon in their path. The trail is faint where it crosses an alder grove between the channels, but becomes distinct again on the far side of the water. It follows the bank upstream for a short distance, then turns inland to meet the Chilliwack River Trail (see p.121) just north of Indian Creek Camp.

Copper Ridge • Chilliwack River
to Chilliwack, B.C.

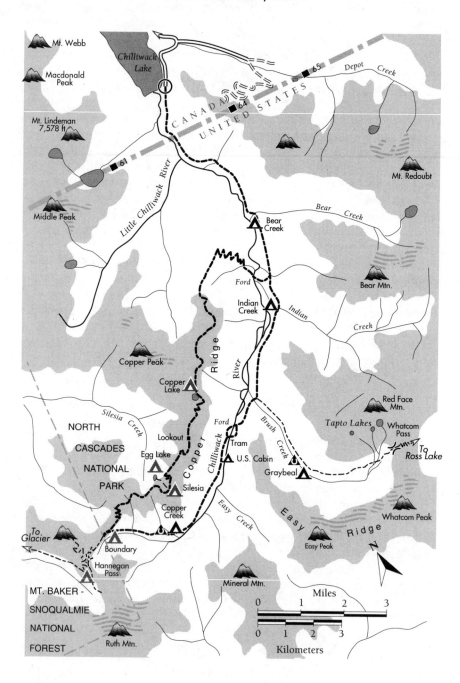

Mt. Webb

Macdonald Peak

Chilliwack Lake

Mt. Lindeman 7,578 ft

Middle Peak

CANADA
UNITED STATES

61

64

65

Depot Creek

Mt. Redoubt

Little Chilliwack River

Bear Creek

Bear Creek

Bear Mtn.

Ford

Indian Creek

Indian Creek

Copper Peak

Ridge

Copper Lake

River

Red Face Mtn.

Silesia Creek

NORTH

CASCADES

NATIONAL

PARK

Lookout

Egg Lake

Ford

Tram

U.S. Cabin

Tapto Lakes

Whatcom Pass

To Ross Lake

Brush Creek

Copper

Chilliwack

Graybeal

Silesia

Copper Creek

Easy Creek

Easy Ridge

Whatcom Peak

To Glacier

Boundary

Hannegan Pass

Mineral Mtn.

Easy Peak

N

MT. BAKER -

SNOQUALMIE

NATIONAL

FOREST

Ruth Mtn.

Miles
0 1 2 3

0 1 2 3
Kilometers

29 Chilliwack River

See Map on Page 120

Overview:	A backpack following the Chilliwack River from Chilliwack Lake in Canada to Boundary Camp in North Cascades National Park, 17.9 miles overall.
Best season:	Mid-June to mid-October.
Difficulty:	Easy to Copper Creek; moderately strenuous beyond.
Elevation gain:	3,440 feet (north to south).
Elevation loss:	1,016 feet (north to south).
Maximum elevation:	4,450 feet at Boundary Camp.
Topo maps:	Copper Mountain, Mount Sefrit, Skagit River-CGS; *Mount Shuksan, Mount Challenger.*
Jurisdiction:	British Columbia Ministry of Forests, North Cascades National Park.

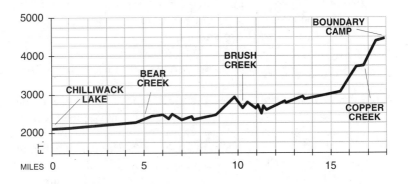

Finding the trailhead: From Chilliwack, British Columbia, take Vedder Road south to the edge of town. Turn left before crossing the bridge over the Chilliwack River, following signs for Chilliwack Lake Provincial Park. The road is paved for the first 32 km (20 miles), then turns to gravel for the final 13 km (8 miles). At Chilliwack Lake Provincial Park, bear left onto the Chilliwack River Forest Road, a narrow and potholed road that follows the lakeshore. Park at the barrier at the head of the lake and follow the closed road to the marked trailhead.

Key points:
0.0 Trail begins at head of Chilliwack Lake.
1.7 Trail crosses U.S.-Canada border to enter North Cascades National Park.
2.7 Chilliwack Camp.
5.1 Trail crosses Bear Creek to arrive at Bear Creek Camp.

6.9	Junction with Copper Ridge Trail. Keep going straight ahead.
7.4	Indian Creek Camp.
7.5	Bridge over Indian Creek.
10.2	Junction with Whatcom Pass Trail. Bear right for Hannegan Pass.
10.3	Trail crosses Brush Creek.
11.0	Junction with horse ford trail. Bear left for aerial tram over river.
11.2	Aerial tram spans Chilliwack River. Trail now follows west bank.
11.3	Horse ford trail rejoins hiker route. Bear left.
12.1	Spur trail descends to U.S. Cabin hiker camp.
12.3	Spur trail descends to U.S. Cabin horse camp.
15.4	Copper Creek. Hiker camp on north bank; horse camp on south bank.
16.7	Trail crosses mouth of Hells Gorge.
17.9	Trail ends at Boundary Camp. Junctions with trails to Hannegan Pass and Copper Ridge.

The hike: This remote valley-bottom trek wanders among some of the finest stands of old-growth timber that remain in the Pacific Northwest. Local wags note with wry humor that "It always rains in the Chilliwack," and the abundance of rainfall gives the ancient forest the ambience of the temperate rainforests of coastal Washington and British Columbia. Travelers who access this trail from Chilliwack Lake should notify Customs authorities of their itinerary. The trail is more commonly accessed from the south via Hannegan Pass, and often is hiked as part of a longer extended journey through the northwestern reaches of North Cascades National Park.

From the Canadian trailhead on the south shore of Chilliwack Lake, follow the closed road past the lakeshore campsites to reach a post marked "Upper Chilliwack Trail." Turn left as the rough and often muddy pathway meanders through old-growth cedar and brushy clearings. The trail skirts the estuary where the river enters Chilliwack Lake, a beautiful 6-mile long mere guarded by lofty peaks. The estuary is a rare mountain wetland where waterfowl and aquatic mammals thrive. The woodland that surrounds the mouth of the river has many of the hallmarks of a rain forest: vine maples draped with club moss, seedlings growing from arboreal perches atop nurse logs and decaying stumps, and tree frogs singing from the branches at night.

The international border is marked by an arrow-straight swath cut through the timber, long since overgrown by dense brush. North Cascades National Park begins at the far side of the opening. The path now makes frequent visits to the riverbank, where the crystalline waters of the Chilliwack glide through a sandy course strewn with driftwood. Chilliwack Camp occupies a riverside site at mile 2.7, and already the forest has begun to take on a younger aspect. The rich soils of the bottomland support a riot of under-growth, and the trail often forces its way through dense thickets.

After several miles, the trail climbs out of the bottoms for the first time, emerging into a mossy forest where a few ancient Douglas-firs tower above their younger neighbors. The next little climb supports a stand of even larger western red-cedars, with some of the boles exceeding 10 feet in diameter. Just beyond this impressive stand, snowslides have cleared a broad path

Nurse log in the Chilliwack valley.

through the forest. The brush is tall, however, and it is difficult to gain views of the surrounding mountains.

The trail soon returns to the bottomland forest, and the underbrush disappears almost entirely. Upon crossing Bear Creek, the trail skirts a sandbar that offers the first river views in many miles. There is a small camp on the far bank. The trail turns inland again, climbing toward the steep slopes that bound the valley. Reaching them, the path turns southward once more. Cedars and hemlocks dominate the mossy woodland, but the few ancient Douglas-firs that overtop them are most striking. A well-marked junction announces the northern terminus of the Copper Ridge trail. A short detour down this trail leads to the banks of the river, where spawning salmon may be viewed during mid-August.

Meanwhile, the Chilliwack River trail continues southward to Indian Creek Camp and the suspension bridge that spans this substantial stream. The forest is now grading into a montane stand dominated by silver fir, a deep-shade specialist. The path skirts sloughs where beavers once dammed side channels of the river; they have since become choked with thickets of willow. The mossy forest is ultimately broken by a broad and brushy slope, and beyond this clearing the silver firs are replaced by hemlocks that thrive on a warmer southwesterly exposure.

The path then descends to Brush Creek, where the Whatcom Pass Trail runs eastward toward the shores of Ross Lake. After a bridge spans Brush Creek, the trail continues southward through the forest, dipping and rising across the lower slopes of the foothills. It crosses several substantial brushfields, courtesy of avalanches that routinely course down the toe of Easy Ridge during winter. The trail soon splits, the lower trail bound for a ford of the river while the upper trail accesses an aerial tram that carries hikers high above the water. In midstream, look south for the first views of Ruth Mountain. The trails rejoin on the far bank, and the trail continues south into a broad clearing for superb views of Mineral Mountain ahead and Bear Mountain down your back trail.

Just beyond this opening, trails run down into the bottoms to reach the U.S. Cabin camps. These camps are sited within damp riverside stands of hemlock that receive little sunlight and are always a bit gloomy. In camp, look for nurse logs that form seedbeds for young saplings, colonnades of mature trees that originated atop such decaying logs, and stilted trees that got their starts atop rotting stumps.

The main trail continues up the valley, through a young but mossy forest that offers a few openings for mountain views. A spur path descends to the river opposite Easy Creek, while the main trail surmounts a low shoulder of Copper Ridge. The path then descends gradually to the valley floor, where boggy forests are underlain by a sparse growth of salmonberry and devil's club. The trail passes the two Copper Creek camps on either bank of that small stream, then begins a vigorous ascent toward Hannegan Pass. It climbs through an open woodland of Douglas-fir that bears the mark of low-intensity fire; huckleberries grow abundantly in the understory. The canopy opens at the mouth of Hells Gorge, where small waterfalls tumble down across sills in the eroded rock.

After more hard climbing, the trail enters a forest of mountain hemlock and levels off. A small clearing that bears a trickle of water affords eastward views of Easy and Whatcom peaks above a shoulder of Mineral Peak. The path soon enters the flowery meadows below Hannegan Pass, and reaches its terminus at a trail junction above Boundary Camp. From here, hikers can take the Copper Ridge Trail to the north, or continue southward into national forest land on the Hannegan Pass Trail.

30 Whatcom Pass

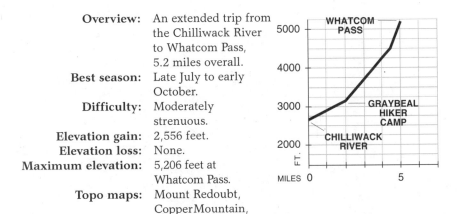

Overview:	An extended trip from the Chilliwack River to Whatcom Pass, 5.2 miles overall.
Best season:	Late July to early October.
Difficulty:	Moderately strenuous.
Elevation gain:	2,556 feet.
Elevation loss:	None.
Maximum elevation:	5,206 feet at Whatcom Pass.
Topo maps:	Mount Redoubt, Copper Mountain, Mount Blum, Mount Challenger; *Mount Shuksan, Mount Challenger.*
Jurisdiction:	North Cascades National Park.

Finding the trail: The beginning of the trail can be reached via an 10.2-mile trek up the Chilliwack River or a 11.9-mile hike over Hannegan Pass. Its terminus can be reached via a 17.5-mile trek up Little Beaver Creek.

Looking up Brushy Creek.

Whatcom Pass

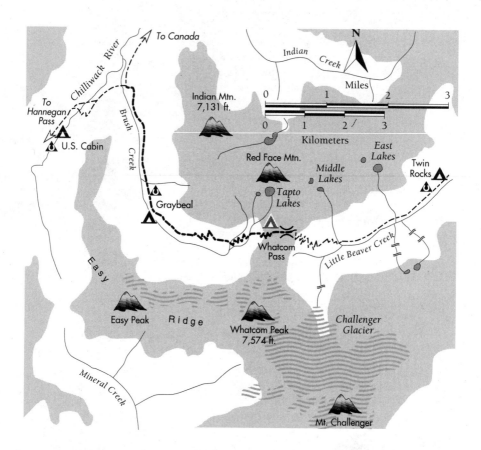

Key points:

    0.0 Junction with Chilliwack River Trail.
    2.0 Graybeal horse camp.
    2.2 Graybeal hiker camp. Trail begins climb toward Whatcom Pass.
    3.9 Tapto Creek crossing.
    4.9 Whatcom Camp.
    5.2 Whatcom Pass. Little Beaver Trail leads downward toward Ross Lake.

The hike: This remote trail follows Brush Creek from its confluence with the
Chilliwack River to Whatcom Pass. From the pass, hikers get spectacular views
of glaciers and waterfalls. This trail follows an old route once used by the
Chilliwack Indians to trade with the Skagit people farther to the south. Euro-
American pioneers adopted the route as part of the short-lived Whatcom Trail,
which linked Bellingham, Washington, with the goldfields of interior British
Columbia. This trail is the only link between the Chilliwack River valley and
the Ross Lake basin, and thus forms an important leg of many extended

journeys through the northwest quadrant of North Cascades National Park.

From its origins in the Chilliwack Valley, the trail begins with a gentle ascent along Brush Creek. The loose forest is often interrupted by brushy clearings, and from the broader ones you can see the rocky summits of Easy Ridge. After several miles of easy traveling, the path arrives at the Graybeal horse camp, amid a bottomland stand of silver fir. The hiker camp is at the upstream end of the same stand of timber, and its excellent views up the creek toward Whatcom Peak with its necklace of glaciers are well worth a side trip.

The main trail now begins its ascent toward Whatcom Pass, traversing steep slopes above Brush Creek. The grade increases as the path crosses steep brushfields that face the many waterfalls that descend like threads of silver from the cliffs of Easy Ridge. Whatcom Peak presides over the head of the valley, graced with several small glaciers.

The trail rises into the trees, and soon strikes a small woodland stream known as Tapto Creek. After crossing it, the path winds upward through mountain hemlocks and huckleberry bushes on its final ascent to the pass. After crossing a second stream, the path ascends beside an open basin, then continues its upward trek through brushy forest. A spur path to the left soon leads through wet meadows of cottongrass (not a true grass, but a sedge) to reach Whatcom Camp. Campsites are perched atop a wooded knoll. The main trail continues upward into the flower-studded meadows of the pass itself. The vast Challenger Glacier awaits in the basin beyond; for a better view, hike 0.3 mile down the Little Beaver trail to an overlook at the edge of a steep slope.

31 Goat Mountain

Overview:	A day hike to a timberline overlook on the shoulder of Goat Mountain, 8 miles round trip.
Best season:	Early July to mid-October.
Difficulty:	Moderately strenuous.
Elevation gain:	3,110 feet.
Maximum elevation:	5,880 feet where the trail peters out.
Topo maps:	Mount Larrabee; *Mount Shuksan.*
Jurisdiction:	Mount Baker Wilderness (Mount Baker— Snoqualmie National Forest).

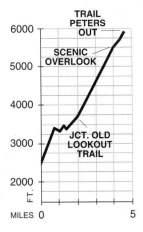

Finding the trailhead: From Glacier, follow Washington Highway 542 to mile 46.5, where Forest Road 32 splits off. Follow this improved gravel road for 1 mile, then turn left on Forest Road 34, following signs for Hannegan Pass. Follow this road for another mile to the Goat Mountain Trailhead.

Mount Shuksan from the Goat Mountain Trail.

Key points:
- 0.0 Goat Mountain Trailhead.
- 1.9 Junction with old trail to lookout site. Stay left.
- 4.0 Trail reaches high overlook. Primitive trail continues upward.
- 4.6 Primitive trail peters out on slopes below summit of Goat Mountain.

The hike: This trail once served a fire lookout on the lower slopes of Goat Mountain. The lookout tower and the spur trail that accessed it have been abandoned, but a trail still climbs to the timberline, where an old burn yields spectacular views of Mount Shuksan and excellent berry-picking in late summer. It is a long and steady climb, avoided by tourists who prefer to stay in their cars until they reach timberline.

The trail begins by zigzagging up a moderate grade, shaded by a dense growth of hemlock. The early-season fire that swept across the southern slopes of Goat Mountain in 1958 destroyed the fire lookout before it was manned for the summer. A few charred stumps remain amid the regenerating forest to mark its passage. After gaining 900 vertical feet, the path swings westward for a long and almost level traverse of the mountainside. It passes a number of seeps and springs where cedars have taken root, then resumes its ascent through a drier woodland of Douglas-fir. After a few upward switchbacks, the old lookout spur runs eastward, abandoned now and completely overgrown with stout alders.

As the trail continues upward, the forest thins out and dense thickets of alder grow between the conifers. Soon a substantial stream can be heard as it tumbles down slopes west of the trail. The trail ultimately approaches this

Goat Mountain

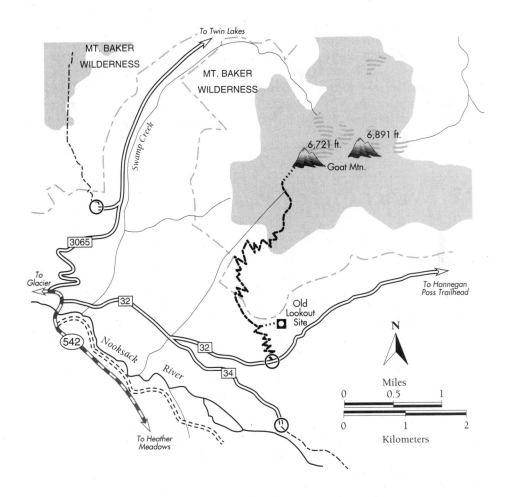

watercourse, and a spur path leads to a cliffside overlook of the stream. The main trail now swings east, climbing steadily through dense thickets of alder and willow. The shrubs part occasionally for southward vistas of Mount Shuksan, and the shining summit of Mount Baker peers over the rocky crest of Mount Herman.

The alders thin with altitude and are finally replaced by huckleberries, fireweed, and dwarf blueberries. The trail swings into an open basin, then climbs to the top of a rocky spur with a primitive tent spot above the timberline. A spur path descends to a rocky overlook high above the North Fork of the Nooksack. Price and White Salmon glaciers are in full view, and the north face of Mount Shuksan rears its crags and cliffs above the ice. Closer at hand, the rocky towers of Mount Sefrit rise from the steep, heavily timbered slopes above Ruby Creek. Mount Baker now rises in regal majesty above the intervening peaks.

From the eastern side of the campsite, a steep and primitive track ascends the ridgeline. The crest of this ridge is blanketed with heather and dwarf blueberries, and mountain hemlocks rise in isolated copses above the ground cover. Upon reaching steeper slopes, the trail zigzags up toward the western summit of Goat Mountain. This route is overgrown with sedges in places, and the tread has suffered from slumping. It does reward adventurous hikers with superb views of Mount Baker and eastward glimpses of the Picket Range. The path peters out several hundred feet below the summit, and an upward scramble across steep meadows is required to gain the top.

32 Winchester Mountain Lookout

Overview:	A short day hike from Twin Lakes to the top of Winchester Mountain, 3.8 miles round trip.
Best season:	Late July to early October.
Difficulty:	Moderate.
Elevation gain:	1,310 feet.
Maximum elevation:	6,510 feet.
Topo maps:	Mount Larrabee; *Mount Shuksan.*
Jurisdiction:	Mount Baker Wilderness (Mount Baker–Snoqualmie National Forest).

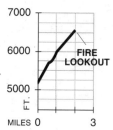

Finding the trailhead: From Glacier, drive east on Washington Highway 542 to mile 46, where a major gravel road (Forest Road 3065) branches away beside a highway maintenance compound. Follow this road 4.5 miles to the Gold Run Pass Trailhead. Visitors with four-wheel drive can continue up the road for the remaining 4.5 miles to reach Twin Lakes; otherwise, walk the road. The trail begins at the trailhead between the two lakes.

Key points:
- 0.0 Twin Lakes Trailhead.
- 0.2 Junction with High Pass Trail. Turn left.
- 1.9 Winchester Mountain Lookout.

The hike: This short trail climbs from Twin Lakes to the summit of Winchester Mountain, where a historic fire lookout is now maintained for overnight stays. There is no way to reserve the cabin except by getting there early; overnight visitors should bring a tent in case the lookout is occupied. Accessing the trailhead requires four-wheel drive; visitors who wish to save wear and tear on their vehicles can hike the road for 4.5 miles from the

Tomyhoi Lake trailhead.

The trail begins by zigzagging up through flowery meadows above the sapphire waters of Upper Twin Lake. The earliest mountain vistas feature the bare knuckles of the Skagit Range, rising to the north beyond the West Fork of Silesia Creek. A lesser pathway that leads to High Pass soon splits away to the right, while the main trail continues upward across a series of meadowy terraces bordered by tall mountain hemlocks. The stark and snow-dappled peaks to the south belong to Goat Mountain, and soon the taller summit of Mount Shuksan can be seen between them. Look southwest down the valley of Swamp Creek for an unobstructed view of Mount Baker.

The trees fall away as the path gains elevation, and soon both of the Twin Lakes can be seen, as well as the mining road that leads northward from their shores toward the Lone Jack Mine. Upon approaching the northern corner of the mountain, the trail offers an early look at Mount Larrabee and the stone towers of The Pleiades. The trail then levels off and traverses over to the south side of the mountain, where it seems to end at an exposed buttress of stone. A steep and treacherous scramble leads over the spur, whereupon the trail swings west to begin a circuit of the summit.

Bushlike krummholz of hemlock and subalpine fir flanks the trail as it climbs steadily. Hardy alpine flowers bloom from every crevice in the rock as the trail reveals Tomyhoi Peak, crowding the lake of the same name. Upon reaching west-facing slopes, hikers face a surreal panorama of vertical rock ahead, with the stone pyramid of Mount Larrabee flanked to the left

Goat Mountain and Twin Lakes from Winchester Mountain.

Winchester Mountain Lookout

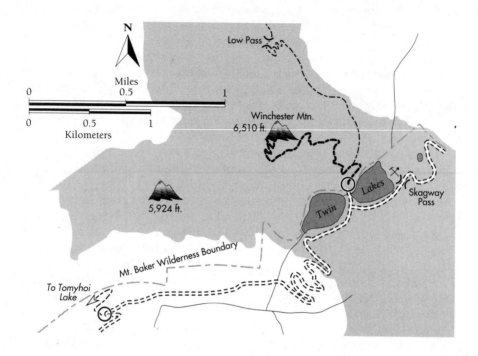

by the twisted spires of the Border Peaks and to the right by the razorback ridges of The Pleiades. An old fire lookout awaits at the end of the climb, built during the 1930s and now relegated to the role of a shelter for hikers. Views stretch to the distant horizons, encompassing the Picket Range to the west, Mount Redoubt to the northwest, and a sea of remote crags in the heart of the Canadian Cascades to the north.

33 High Pass

Overview:	A day hike from Twin Lakes to The Pleiades overlook, 8 miles round trip.
Best season:	Late July to early October.
Difficulty:	Moderate.
Elevation gain:	1,845 feet.
Elevation loss:	305 feet.
Maximum elevation:	6,740 feet at trail's end.
Topo maps:	Mount Larrabee; *Mount Shuksan.*
Jurisdiction:	Mount Baker Wilderness (Mount Baker–Snoqualmie National Forest).

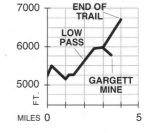

Finding the trailhead: The hike begins at the Twin Lakes Trailhead; see Winchester Mountain Lookout, Hike 32, for details.

Key points:

- 0.0 Twin Lakes Trailhead.
- 0.2 Junction with Winchester Mountain Trail. Turn right.
- 2.1 Low Pass.
- 3.0 High Pass. Junction with Gargett Mine spur (0.3 mile, moderate). Keep right to complete the trek.
- 4.0 Trail ends at overlook of The Pleiades.

Looking south from the slopes of Mount Larrabee.

High Pass • Silesia Creek

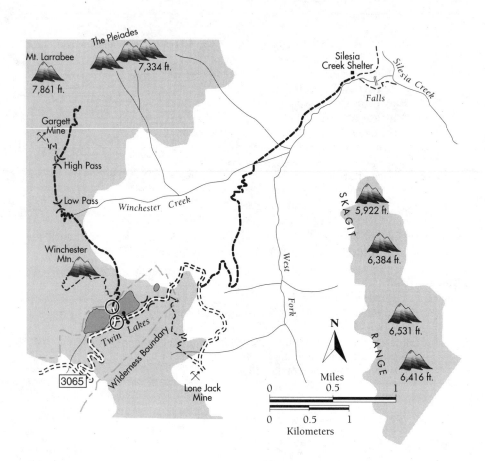

The hike: This trail makes a challenging half-day hike from Twin Lakes; travelers who cannot drive all the way to the trailhead will have difficulty completing the trek in a single day. On the way to its terminus high on the flanks of Mount Larrabee, the trail passes the old Gargett Mine, which was worked unsuccessfully for gold during the early 1900s.

The path begins by ascending flower-strewn slopes above Upper Twin Lake. It soon splits away from the larger Winchester Mountain Trail and runs north to cross the low divide that leads into the Winchester Creek watershed. The pyramid-shaped summit that rises ahead is Mount Larrabee, streaked with a rusty red from the oxidizing iron in its bedrock. This summit will be a constant companion as the trail makes its way northward.

The trail now descends steeply across slopes that offer the best floral displays of the hike. Still high above the valley's head, the path levels off and traverses beneath the rocky eastern slopes of Winchester Mountain.

Fine eastward views feature the naked domes of the Skagit Range as well as the sharp horn peaks that rise beyond the Canadian border. The trail ultimately reaches the bottom of a wide and heathery couloir and switchbacks up it to gain the meadowy col of Low Pass. Looking westward, hikers get good views of Tomyhoi Peak, and Mount Baker becomes visible as the path climbs the rocky knoll to the north.

After a brief but vigorous ascent, the trail rounds the knob to reach the long and lofty saddle of High Pass. Examine the northern slopes of the basin below to view the rusting wreckage of the Gargett Mine. For visitors who would like a closer look, a good trail descends into the basin then climbs briefly to reach the mine site. Do not damage or remove any part of this historical site; it is protected by federal law.

From High Pass, the main trail gets rougher as it climbs steeply up the ridgeline toward the base of Mount Larrabee. Southward views open up as the path gains altitude, revealing a sea of sharp horn peaks: Winchester Mountain, Goat Mountain, Mount Sefrit, and finally the lofty crest of Mount Shuksan. After a few switchbacks across bare and unstable scree, the path ascends across the heather to a high and barren col that overlooks the jagged spires of The Pleiades. Run the ridgetops southward for panoramic vistas that encompass such distant peaks as Mount Redoubt to the east and those of the Picket Range to the southeast.

34 Silesia Creek

See Map on Page 134

Overview:	A long day hike or short backpack from Twin Lakes to the Silesia Creek Shelter, 13 miles round trip.
Best season:	Mid-July to mid-October.
Difficulty:	Moderately strenuous.
Elevation gain:	None.
Elevation loss:	2,620 feet.
Maximum elevation:	5,240 feet at Skagway Pass.
Topo maps:	Mount Larrabee, Mount Sefrit; *Mount Shuksan.*
Jurisdiction:	Mount Baker Wilderness (Mount Baker–Snoqualmie National Forest).

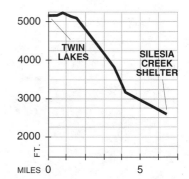

Falls below the Silesia Creek shelter.

Finding the trailhead: Drive or walk to the Twin Lakes camping area; see Winchester Mountain Lookout, Hike 32, for details. The hike begins on the closed road that runs north along the shore of the upper lake.

Key points:
    0.0 Twin Lakes camping area. Hike north on Lone Jack Mine road.
    0.2 Head of upper Twin Lakes. Road enters Mount Baker Wilderness.
    1.9 Trail departs from road on northward bearing.
    4.6 Trail crosses Winchester Creek
    6.5 Silesia Creek shelter.

The hike: This trail has been all but forgotten as the trails along the border have been abandoned and the early reaches of the route have been overrun by the newly rebuilt road to the Lone Jack Mine. At the end of the trail is the Silesia Creek shelter, within a stone's throw of a magnificent waterfall on the West Fork of Silesia Creek. This bottomlands of the West Fork are perhaps the only trail-accessed spot in the Mount Baker Wilderness where the primeval landscape has remained unaltered by man.

The trail begins on the road to the Lone Jack Mine, which follows the eastern shore of Upper Twin Lake. At the head of the lake, an angler's path runs around the north shore, visiting a lakeside mine tunnel that makes a worthwhile side trip. The Silesia Creek route continues to follow the road through the low gap of Skagway Pass and onto the ridgetop beyond. This area bears the scars of extensive mining activity in the past, but its heather meadows still harbor a healthy population of marmots, and its poisoned ponds reflect the spectacular crags of Mount Larrabee and The Pleiades. The road follows the ridgetop until it falls away into the deep valley below; turn right at the intersection. An overgrown trail leads down the ridgeline, but it soon returns to the road. The road now descends on a southeasterly heading, and soon reaches the edge of an open bowl lined with talus.

The Silesia Creek Trail leaves the road at the near edge of the opening, where the road first ventures onto the broken rock. It zigzags down through a shady stand of ancient hemlocks, dropping through the forest at a leisurely pace. At one point, the path wanders into the opening created by snowslides from the bowl above, but views are otherwise blocked by the forest canopy. After a long descent, the trail runs northward across slopes robed in silver fir, the deep shade specialist. It begins to drop more sharply as it descends along the ridge that divides the valleys of Winchester Creek and Silesia Creek's West Fork.

At the bottom of the grade, the trail enters the bottomland forest of Winchester Creek. A footlog spans the stream, and beyond it the trail follows the West Fork of Silesia Creek around the end of the Skagit Range. A broad clearing soon interrupts the forest, and the path threads its way thickets of willow, alder, and thimbleberry. Watch out for stinging nettle here. After returning to the forest, the path runs through forest wracked by floods during the winter of 1995-1996. During the deluge, the West Fork cut itself a new channel, and now the path follows downed logs across the new waterway to a long island of timber.

The path ultimately runs out into primeval forestland that borders the main fork of Silesia Creek. Trail maintenance ends at the Silesia Creek shelter, but old paths can be followed on both sides of the creek to reach the waterfall on the West Fork, just downstream. This mighty cataract thunders down into a rock-walled amphitheater, overgrown with ferns and other water-loving vegetation. Watch your footing—it is difficult and dangerous to get an unobstructed view of the falls.

35 Gold Run Pass and Tomyhoi Lake

Overview: A day hike to Gold Run Pass (5.4 miles round trip) or a longer day hike or short backpack to Tomyhoi Lake (10 miles round trip).
Best season: Early June to mid-October for Gold Run Pass; mid-July to mid-October for Tomyhoi Lake.
Difficulty: Moderately strenuous.
Elevation gain: 1,820 feet.
Elevation loss: 1,760 feet to Tomyhoi Lake.
Maximum elevation: 5,460 feet at Gold Run Pass.
Topo maps: Mount Larrabee; *Mount Shuksan*.
Jurisdiction: Mount Baker Wilderness (Mount Baker–Snoqualmie National Forest).

Finding the trailhead: From Glacier, drive east on Washington Highway 542 to mile 46, where a major gravel road branches away beside a highway maintenance compound. Turn left on this road (Forest Road 3065) and follow it for 4.5 miles to the Gold Run Pass trailhead.

Key points:
0.0 Gold Run Pass–Tomyhoi Lake Trailhead.
0.6 Trail enters Mount Baker Wilderness.
2.7 Gold Run Pass.
4.4 Trail crosses Tomyhoi Creek and follows east bank.
5.0 Head of Tomyhoi Lake.

The hike: This trail makes a challenging climb over a narrow notch, then drops into the valley of Tomyhoi Creek, which drains northward into Canada. At the end of the trek is Tomyhoi Lake, a large lowland lake that stretches into Canada, where the clearcuts march southward to the border. Tomyhoi Lake drains through subterranean passages beneath its bed, and in late summer the water is drawn down far below the high water mark. The hike to the lake is fairly moderate, but the return trip is a more strenuous proposition. Biting insects are abundant throughout the trek; bring lots of repellant.

Mount Larrabee as seen from Gold Run Pass.

Gold Run Pass • Tomyhoi Lake • Yellow Aster Butte

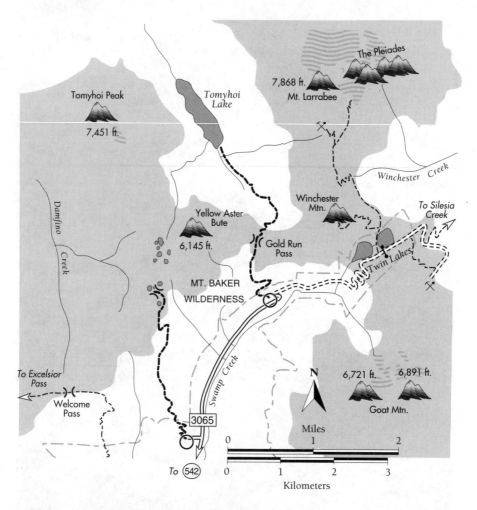

The trail begins with a steady climb, switchbacking upward across brushy slopes that face southward toward Mount Baker. After a vigorous ascent, the path levels off and heads southwest. A mature stand of hemlock and silver fir shades the journey to a false pass on a ridgetop that divides Swamp Creek from a tributary stream that rises on the slopes of Yellow Aster Butte. The ridgetop is home to hemlocks that reach old-growth proportions.

The trail then climbs gently into subalpine parks that line the head of the tributary stream. The warning whistles of marmots can be heard from the slopes of Yellow Aster Butte, but the animals themselves are hard to spot without binoculars. A steep final ascent leads upward across flower-strewn meadows that offer a fine parting view of Mount Baker and the closer summit of Goat Mountain. The path then leads over Gold Run Pass, a high col that bears a sparse growth of mountain hemlock. Northward views from the pass encompass Mount Larrabee and the Border Peaks, splashed with red and yellow hues that derive from iron and sulfur compounds within the bedrock.

The path then begins an insanely steep descent toward the headwaters of Tomyhoi Creek. The still waters of Tomyhoi Lake can soon be seen, guarded by the hulking massif of Tomyhoi Peak. Beyond the lake, clearcuts and logging roads cover the hillsides beyond the international border. The path dives down the mountainside, ultimately leveling off on a meadowy shelf. There are campsites at the lower end of the shelf. Beyond this point, the trail adopts a more reasonable descent. The trail now threads its way down through the heather, overgrown boulders, and a sparse growth of hemlock. Marmots are often sighted along this stretch of the trail. The path soon enters the shade of mature forest. The trees part occasionally at wet meadows, and huckleberry bushes provide a tasty diversion when they ripen in mid-August.

The trail ultimately strikes a brushy stream and follows it down to Tomyhoi Lake. Just before reaching the lakeshore, the path crosses a snowslide swath that is choked with downed logs. It then tracks the stream down through a heavy growth of willows to the head of the lake. Tents can be pitched amid the driftwood on the lakeshore.

36 Yellow Aster Butte

See Map on Page 140

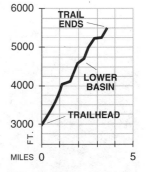

Overview:	A day hike to the divide below Yellow Aster Butte, 7 miles round trip.
Best season:	Late July to mid-October.
Difficulty:	Strenuous.
Elevation gain:	2,440 feet.
Elevation loss:	None.
Maximum elevation:	5,440 feet at trail's end.
Topo maps:	Mount Larrabee; *Mount Shuksan.*
Jurisdiction:	Mount Baker Wilderness (Mount Baker–Snoqualmie National Forest).

Finding the trailhead: From Glacier, drive east on Washington Highway 542 to mile 46, where a major gravel road branches away beside a highway maintenance compound. Turn left on this road (Forest Road 3065) and follow it for 2.3 miles to an unmarked intersection. Turn left onto the spur road and follow it 0.5 mile to the Yellow Aster Butte trailhead.

Key points:
- 0.0 Yellow Aster Butte Trailhead.
- 0.8 Trail enters Mount Baker Wilderness.
- 2.2 First subalpine basin.
- 3.5 Trail ends in a maze of social trails on the ridgetop.

The hike: This steep path was pioneered by prospectors who sought gold in the veins of quartz high atop the divide to the north of the Nooksack watershed. The trail can be managed readily in a day trip. The trail ends in tundra atop the divide, and numerous social paths run in all directions, visiting the many alpine tarns that dot the landscape. Use no-trace techniques as outlined at the beginning of this book when traveling or camping off-trail in the alpine zone. Travelers bound cross-country to the top of Yellow Aster Butte or to the base of Tomyhoi Peak should allow several days to complete the trip.

The area surrounding the trailhead was logged off fairly recently and the trail begins by following an old skid road bulldozed across the lower slopes to haul away the timber. The overgrown clearcut soon gives way to a stand of silver fir, and the trail continues to zigzag upward through the shady forest. The large, old Douglas-firs that once overtopped the canopy were removed by selective cutting in the 1940s.

At the wilderness boundary, the old road gives way to a steep prospector's trail. This track is little more than a stairway of roots and rocks that climbs as rapidly as the landscape allows. There is a brief respite about halfway up the initial grade as the steep slopes level off at a series of woodland fens. The trail then resumes its ascent, passing several waterfalls on a small

Goat Mountain from Yellow Aster Butte Trail.

mountain rivulet as it nears the top.

The forest thins out as the trail shoots northward, and soon pocket meadows interrupt the trees. Mountain views open up as the trail reaches a bowl, with Mount Larrabee rising beyond the shoulder of Yellow Aster Butte to the north and clear views of Goat Mountain and Mount Shuksan to the east and south, respectively. Snowmelt patterns determine the distribution of vegetation here, with sedges and herbaceous plants growing in the low-lying pockets where snow lingers late while heather, blueberries, and copses of mountain hemlock occupy the higher mounds that melt off sooner. Expect muddy traveling as the path crosses the basin, then begins a calf-burning pitch to the top of the divide.

Here, a rolling plain of alpine tundra is interrupted by rocky knobs, alpine ponds, and the "glory holes" dug into the bedrock by miners in a vain search for precious metals. The maintained trail ends at a signpost atop the divide. It is possible to run the ridges southwest to Welcome Pass, northwest to Tomyhoi Peak, or northeast to Yellow Aster Butte. Campers should choose a secluded spot that other explorers are unlikely to find.

37 Welcome Pass and the High Divide

Overview:	A day hike to Welcome Pass, 5 miles round trip, or a longer day hike when combined with the Excelsior Pass Trail (car shuttle required), 11.3 miles overall.
Best season:	Mid-June to mid-October for Welcome Pass; mid-July to mid-October for High Divide.
Difficulty:	Strenuous to Welcome Pass; moderate beyond.
Elevation gain:	2,740 feet to Welcome Pass; 3,891 feet overall.
Elevation loss:	25 feet to Welcome Pass; 986 feet overall.
Maximum elevation:	5,790 feet along High Divide.
Topo maps:	Mount Larrabee, Bearpaw Mountain; *Mount Baker, Mount Shuksan.*
Jurisdiction:	Mount Baker Wilderness (Mount Baker–Snoqualmie National Forest).

Finding the trailhead: From Glacier, drive east on Washington Highway 542 to mile 45, where a primitive road (Forest Road 3060) runs north. Fol-

143

Welcome Pass • High Divide

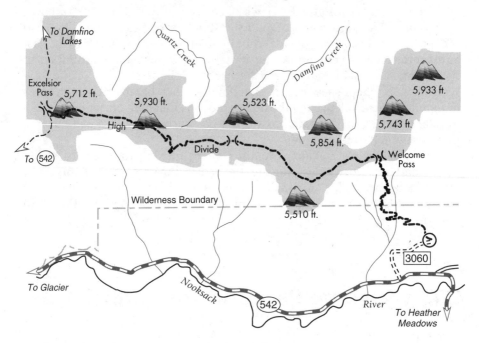

low this road for 1 mile to the trailhead at its end; hikers without high-clearance vehicles should walk it.

Key points:
    0.0   Welcome Pass Trailhead.
    1.0   Old road ends and trail steepens.
    2.5   Welcome Pass. Trail turns west along High Divide.
    7.1   Excelsior Pass. Junction with Excelsior Pass and Damfino Lakes trails.

The hike: This mercilessly steep trail leads from the valley floor to the summit of the Nooksack River divide, where alpine meadows stretch westward to Excelsior Pass. The High Divide segment of the trail offers a spectacular diversity of wildflowers, as well as views that encompass both Mount Shuksan and Mount Baker. Alternate routes to the High Divide include the Excelsior Pass Trail (which can be combined with this route for a good day semi-loop) and the Damfino Lakes Trail, which begins at the head of Canyon Creek. Bring lots of water, because surface water is hard to find along the route.

The trek begins on an old logging road that climbs moderately through dense coastal forest. After 1 mile, the roadbed ends and an old prospector's trail of surpassing steepness heads up the mountainside. As it climbs, the western hemlocks are replaced by silver fir. After sixty tight hairpins and an unrelenting grade, the trail breaks out onto steep meadows that offer south-ward views of the mountains. Mount Shuksan reigns above the North Fork

144

of the Nooksack, with Icy Peak and Ruth Mountain to the left of it. The trail then climbs the final steep switchbacks to Welcome Pass. Trees screen off views to the south, but open meadows lead down into the head of Damfino Creek. Its valley is lined with barren crags, tallest of which is Tomyhoi Peak to the northwest.

High Divide Option. The trail now turns westward atop the meadowy crest of the High Divide, lit with the blossoms of bistort and arnica. The trail climbs along a small rift vale, passing several frog ponds as it runs south of the next high point. Look eastward for views that feature Goat Mountain and Mount Larrabee. The trail reaches its highest point at the next saddle, which overlooks a western branch of Damfino Creek. It then descends moderately across south-facing slopes, where the meadows reveal superb views of Mount Baker, with Mazama and Roosevelt glaciers pouring down its north face.

The trail next meets the ridgeline at a lower saddle, perched above the gentler, forest-robed terrain of the Quartz Creek watershed. The path climbs and falls as it follows the divide, crossing deep swales filled with lupine and aster as well as colder exposures robed in mats of heather. The trail ends a signpost in the flat saddle of Excelsior Pass, where the Damfino Lakes Trail runs north across the meadows and the Excelsior Pass Trail (see below) drops away toward the North Fork of the Nooksack.

38 Excelsior Pass

Overview:	A day hike or short backpack to Excelsior Pass, 8.4 miles round trip.
Best season:	Early June to mid-October.
Difficulty:	Moderately strenuous.
Elevation gain:	3,538 feet.
Elevation loss:	None.
Maximum elevation:	5,365 feet at Excelsior Pass.
Topo maps:	Bearpaw Mountain; *Mount Baker*.
Jurisdiction:	Mount Baker Wilderness (Mount Baker–Snoqualmie National Forest).

Finding the trailhead: Follow Washington Highway 542 east from Glacier to a pulloff at mile 41.2. The marked trail begins across the road.

Key points:
  0.0 Excelsior Pass Trailhead.
  4.2 Excelsior Pass. Trails run north to Damfino Lake and east along the High Divide.

Flowers along the Excelsior Pass Trail.

The hike: This trail presents a steady climb from the North Fork of the Nooksack River to the western end of the High Divide, where alpine meadows cover the rolling ridgetops. The trail receives heavy use from horse parties, which have severely impacted the fragile upper reaches of the trail. Hikers should be prepared to travel on deeply gullied trails and through broad mud pits. Most of the ferns native to the west slope of the Cascades can be found along the lower stretches of this trail.

The trek begins on an old logging road that climbs gently through second-growth timber of the valley bottoms. As steeper slopes rise ahead, a trail breaks away from the road and climbs to reach the wilderness boundary after 0.3 mile. Watch for an old bear den just beyond the boundary marker. The path approaches a substantial stream, then begins a long but moderate ascent to the east of it. The route leads upward through an old burn. The regenerating forest is just reaching the self-thinning stage, when less-vigorous saplings die from lack of sunlight and their more robust peers rise into the forest canopy. As the path rises above the burn, it passes onto slopes that were logged off circa 1915. Watch for sawed-off stumps that indicate lumbering activity.

The trail approaches the stream again at mile 1.6, and a single tent site occupies a trailside grove of conifers. The path continues its zigzagging climb for another 1,000 vertical feet, passing through heavy timber that is under-lain by a diverse array of shade-tolerant wildflowers. Near the top of the grade, it finally emerges from the trees into brushy clearings. Mount Baker can now be seen to the south. Signs of heavy horse traffic soon become evident: badly eroded trailbeds, mudholes, and multiple trails become the

146

Excelsior Pass

rule. Subalpine parklands beckon ahead, but hikers must first climb through a dense stand of silver fir and then a widely spaced grove of ancient, moss-hung mountain hemlocks.

The trail then enters a subalpine basin upholstered in a diverse array of blossoms: pink monkeyflower, fireweed, arnica, aster, and lupine are all abundant. The trail arcs upward through the basin to reach Excelsior Pass, atop the High Divide. Views to the south are fantastic with the craggy summit of Mount Shuksan rising farther to the east and the glacier-clad cone of Mount Baker soaring skyward beyond the North Fork of the Nooksack. The Black Buttes are the dark pinnacles that rise from the eastern slopes of Mount Baker; they represent the ancient eruptive center of the volcano, long dormant and now whittled away by glaciers. From a signpost at the pass, trails run north to Damfino Lakes and east along the crest of the High Divide toward Welcome Pass.

39 Church Mountain

Overview: A day hike to a former lookout site on a high spur of Church Mountain, 8.4 miles round trip.

Best season: Early June to mid-October (snow lingers later in the Deerhorn Creek basin).

Difficulty: Moderately strenuous.

Elevation gain: 3,787 feet.

Elevation loss: None.

Maximum elevation: 6,100 feet at the lookout site.

Topo maps: Bearpaw Mountain, Glacier; *Mount Baker*.

Jurisdiction: Mount Baker–Snoqualmie National Forest.

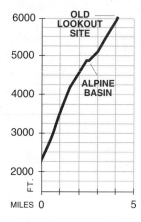

Finding the trailhead: From Glacier, follow Washington Highway 542 east to a junction with Forest Road 3040 at mile 38.7. Follow this narrow but passable logging road upward for 3 miles to reach the trailhead.

Looking toward the Border Peaks from Church Mountain.

Church Mountain

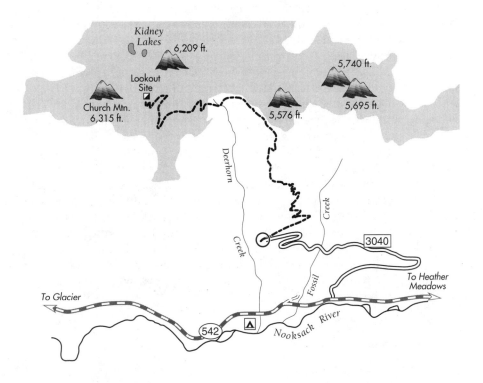

Key points:
    0.0   Church Mountain Trailhead.
    2.5   Upper basin of Deerhorn Creek.
    4.2   Trail reaches site of Church Mountain fire lookout.

The hike: A long climb through the timber leads up to alpine meadows on the slopes of Church Mountain, and from here the trail climbs to the former site of a fire lookout atop one of the mountain's eastern buttresses. The trail makes an excellent day hike, with outstanding views of the surrounding peaks and good berry pickings on the slopes below the peak.

The trek begins on an old logging road that climbs through a regenerating clearcut. After a short distance, the Church Mountain Trail departs from the roadbed and climbs into tall timber that grew in the wake of logging. Views through the canopy are limited to ridges that border the North Fork of the Nooksack River, which themselves bear the scars of the timber industry. A long and tedious ascent leads up through mature hemlocks and Douglas-firs, zigzagging upward at a steady and relentless pace.

Near the top of the initial grade, the trail runs westward into a fold in the hills that bears many small streams. Steep and narrow snowslide meadows alternate with ribbons of timber. The trail ultimately breaks out into a broad basin overlooked by the upthrust buttresses of Church Mountain. The path runs westward across the floor of the basin, passing through a diverse assemblage of wildflowers and dwarf shrubs. Mount Baker and the Twin Sisters show themselves immediately, and Mount Shuksan is visible from the far side of the basin.

The trail now zigzags upward once more, passing over a spur ridge then continuing its ascent above a smaller bowl. Visits to the crests of various spur ridges yield northwesterly views of Tomyhoi Peak and the Border Peaks, with an ever-increasing sea of snowcapped summits spreading westward. The trail ultimately reaches the nose of a rocky pinnacle, then threads its way up a steep course through the rock to reach the lookout site.

The fire lookout was torn from its moorings and dashed against the mountainside during a recent winter storm; its former perch yields fantastic views in all directions. The aquamarine Kidney Lakes occupy the shallow and barren basin to the north; adventurous hikers can attempt to scramble down through cliffs to the water. To the west is the rocky summit of Church Mountain, with a broad reach of salt water beyond it. Sighting eastward down the tree-mottled crest of the High Divide, the tallest of the distant crags is Mount Redoubt. The northern horizon is crowded with the snowy summits of the Coast Mountains in British Columbia, which rise beyond the deep trench of the Fraser River Valley.

ADDITIONAL TRAILS

The **Heliotrope Ridge Trail** is an overcrowded pathway that runs for 3 miles across alpine meadows to the foot of Coleman Glacier.

A primitive trail along the north divide of **Canyon Creek** is open to motorbikes, but is maintained infrequently and is prone to deadfalls.

The **Damfino Lakes Trail** runs for 3 miles between the head of Canyon Creek and Excelsior Pass, providing back-door access to the High Divide.

A primitive route runs along the North Fork of the Nooksack River to the **Nooksack Cirque**. The trail ends after 2 miles and the rest is a gravel bar trek with many dangerous fords.

An administrative trail fords the Chilliwack River above U.S. Cabin Camp and climbs to a radio repeater station atop **Easy Ridge**.

The **Fire and Ice Trail** is an interpretive loop that begins near the Heather Meadows visitor center.

The **Wild Goose Trail** is a 1-mile connector that links Lower Bagley Lake with the Artist Point parking area.

The **Artist Ridge Trail** is a 0.5-mile paved walkway to a high overlook above the valley of Swift Creek. It is wheelchair-accessible.

The Canadian Cascades

Often overlooked by backpackers from the United States, the Canadian end of the North Cascades has been set aside in a series of provincial parks and recreation areas replete with fine hiking trails. Permits are not required for backcountry camping within provincial parks, but campers must pitch their tents in officially designated sites. Some of the more popular backcountry campgrounds fill up during weekends—be prepared to hike onward to the next camp if no sites are available. The provincial parks are managed more intensively than their U.S. counterparts, with heavily engineered trails and camping areas. Don't be surprised if you find wooden tent pallets or even picnic tables in backcountry camps, particularly in Manning Provincial Park.

Established in 1941, Manning Provincial Park covers most of the land area within the Canadian Cascades. It is managed to provide a broad spectrum of recreational opportunities. In addition to its extensive hiking trails, it hosts trails open to mountain bikes and horses. Lightning Lake attracts canoeists and beachgoers, and downhill and cross-country skiing trails start at Gibson Pass. Most of its trails are best suited to day trips. Backpackers can try longer routes, such as the Frosty Mountain Loop, the Skyline Trail, and the Heather Trail. There are automobile campgrounds at Lightning Lake and scattered along British Columbia Highway 3, a major thoroughfare that splits the park and provides year-round access. Limited supplies can be purchased at the Manning Park Lodge; the nearest town is Hope, British Columbia, 26 km (16 miles) from the west entrance. Park headquarters are a short distance east of the lodge, with a visitor center that provides information.

The Skagit Valley did not become a provincial park until 1996, but it has long been the focal point of environmental concern. In 1941, a wartime plan to raise Ross Dam would have flooded the valley by the resulting expansion of Ross Lake. The Skagit found an unlikely ally, though, in the person of Curley Chittenden, a logger who had contracted to clearcut the forests of the valley floor to make way for the reservoir. Chittenden recognized the uniqueness of the Skagit Valley forests and spearheaded an international effort that ultimately quashed the High Ross project and resulted in creation of the Skagit Valley Recreation Area. With funds provided through a settlement between a Canadian hydropower company and the United States government, new campgrounds and trailheads were created and the recreation area became a provincial park.

To access the valley, drive south from Hope on the Silver-Skagit Road. This gravel trunk road once served primarily as a thoroughfare for logging trucks, and there is still some logging activity in the area. The road condition varies from excellent to poor with potholes and washboards, depending on how long it has been since the last grader passed through. There are a number

Canadian Cascades Overview

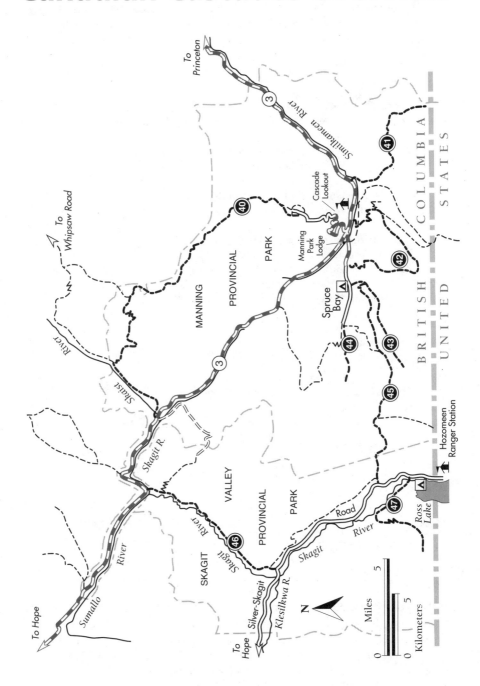

of auto-accessible campgrounds along the road; these are fee areas. Travelers can also use the Silver-Skagit Road to cross the international border and reach Hozomeen at the head of Ross Lake, with its boat launches and free camping areas. There are no stores or gas stations in the Skagit Valley; load up on essentials before leaving Hope.

40 Heather Trail

Overview:	A day hike to the top of First Brother, 22.2 km (13.8 miles) round trip, or a backpack to the mouth of the Skaist River, 42.5 km (26.5 miles) overall.
Best season:	Mid-June to mid-October.
Difficulty:	Moderate east to west; moderately strenuous west to east.
Elevation gain:	933 m (3,060 feet).
Elevation loss:	2,115 m (6,940 feet).
Maximum elevation:	2,272 m (7,453 feet) at the summit of First Brother.
Topo maps:	Manning Park-CGS.
Jurisdiction:	Manning Provincial Park.

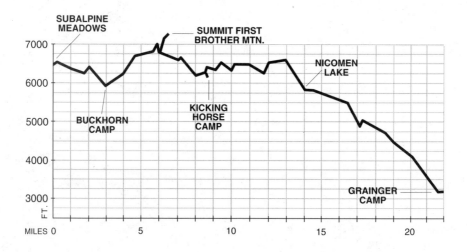

Finding the trailhead: Take British Columbia Highway 3 to the junction at the Manning Park Lodge. Turn north onto the Cascade Lookout Road. Follow this paved road as it climbs for 15 km (9.5 miles). After passing behind the summit of Blackwall Peak, park at the trailhead on the left just before the end of the road. The hike ends at Cayuse Flats Trailhead, 20 km (12.5 miles) east of the West Gate of Manning Provincial Park on BC 3.

Looking across meadows to Mount Winthrop.

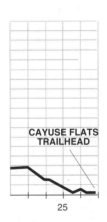

25

Key points:

km	miles	
0.0	0.0	Heather Trailhead.
1.3	0.8	Junction with cutoff to Sub-Alpine Meadow area. Bear left.
5.0	3.1	Buckhorn Camp.
7.4	4.6	Junction with Bonnevier Trail. Bear left.
10.0	6.2	Junction with spur to First Brother (1.1 km/0.7 mile, moderately strenuous). Continue straight ahead.
13.5	8.4	Spur trail to Kicking Horse Camp. Continue straight ahead.
21.0	13.1	Top of Nicomen Ridge.
22.5	14.0	Camping area at head of Nicomen Lake.
23.0	14.3	Shelter at foot of Nicomen Lake. Junction with trail to Marmot City. Bear left, following Grainger Creek Trail across outlet of lake.
27.7	17.2	Grainger Creek crossing.
34.6	21.5	Junction with Hope Pass Trail. Turn left to finish hike.
38.6	24.0	Taboo Creek. Trail now follows old roadbed.
41.0	25.5	Trail leaves old road on westward heading.
42.0	26.1	Trail crosses bridge over Skaist River.
42.5	26.5	Cayuse Flats Trailhead.

The hike: This trail penetrates the rolling uplands to the north of the Similkameen River, crossing endless subalpine meadows that offer views of the distant peaks of the Cascades. The trail is wide and heavily developed as far as Buckhorn Camp. It receives heavy foot traffic up to the First Brother, which is a popular day-hiking destination. Allow several days for the full journey, and avoid the trail on weekends when the backcountry campsites are likely to be full.

From its inception on the back side of Blackwall Peak, the path descends gently along rounded ridgetops that are clothed in a spruce-fir parkland. Lush glades between the trees have a rich upholstery of wildflowers; the blossoms peak in midsummer. Descending into the headwaters of Buckhorn Creek, the trail passes a camping area complete with picnic tables and tent pallets, then climbs vigorously onto slopes that burned in 1945.

The path soon rises above the trees into an arid alpine grassland where blooms of anemone and white Indian paintbrush are accompanied by broad views to the south that encompass Mount Winthrop, Frosty Mountain, and the jagged towers of Hozomeen Mountain. After passing a junction with the Bonnevier Trail, the main trail makes its way across the tawny shoulders of Big Buck Mountain. Dense carpets of blossoms cover the moisture-bearing folds, featuring lupine, arnica, Indian paintbrush, and elephant heads. Hikers soon find themselves on the lip of a steep cliff that overlooks a glacier-carved cirque. First Brother is the prominent peak that rises ahead.

At the base of the peak, a steep and primitive spur trail splits away en route to the summit. This side trail gains most of its elevation early on, then follows the narrow and sinuous ridgetop to the top of the peak. Here, in a barren alpine desert of lichens, krummholz, and juniper, a well-built cairn faces northward across the undulating forests and distant prairies of interior British Columbia.

Meanwhile, the Heather Trail traverses westward across the grassy slopes of the Three Brothers. It then pops through a saddle that leads into a north-facing bowl, where heather finally becomes abundant as ground cover. The trail now descends past pleasant brooks to reach expansive lower meadows interspersed with stands of spruce and fir. After passing Kicking Horse Camp, the path climbs gradually onto the grassy shoulders of Fourth Brother Mountain. In addition to southward vistas, there are now views of the westerly ranges: Mox Peaks and Mount Spickard to the southwest with the glistening cone of Mount Baker beyond them, the lone horn of Silvertip Mountain with its hanging glacier, and the lower but more colorful summits of mounts Ford and Dewdney to the northwest.

After a long stretch in the uplands, the trail drops into a loosely wooded saddle. It then climbs back into the meadows, passing several meltwater pools along the way. Back in the high country, the trail passes along the rim of the Copper Creek drainage. Nicomen Ridge is the rocky bluff that rises ahead, and the trail rises onto its southern tail and follows it northward through the heather. Here are the last views of the distant mountains, along with a fine view of Nicomen Lake. The trail zigzags down into the heavily

Heather Trail

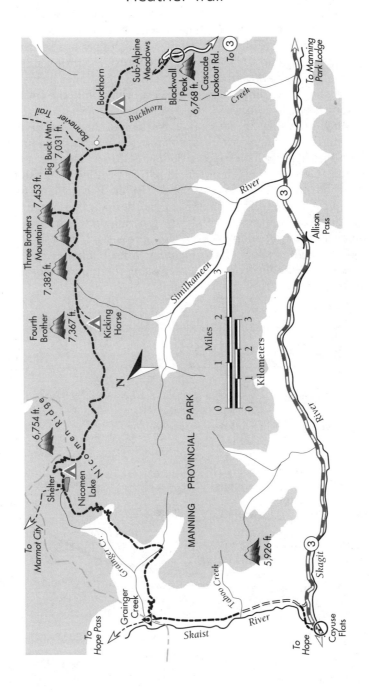

timbered lake basin. The best spots to camp are at the head of the lake, while there is a log shelter at the lake's foot, beside the trail that runs north to Fido Camp. Nicomen Lake offers fine fishing for rainbow trout.

Our trek now follows the Grainger Creek Trail, which crosses the outlet stream then runs across a talus slope where pikas are sometimes seen. Descending gently into a brushy subalpine forest, the trail bends southward around a ridge, high above the valley floor. It then snakes its way down to a footlog crossing of Grainger Creek. After a brief climb, the trail turns west for the long traverse across the thickly timbered slopes above the creek. At the mouth of the valley, there is a fine overlook of the Skaist River drainage.

The path then snakes down across timbered benches to a junction with the Hope Pass Trail, which follows the Skaist River. There is a horse camp on Grainger Creek just north of this junction; turn left to finish the trek as the trail runs southward above the Skaist River. The lowland forest found here is typical of the west slope of the Cascades: a mix of western hemlock and western red-cedar, with Douglas-fir growing on the drier exposures. At Taboo Creek, the trail adopts an old fire access road and follows it toward BC Highway 3. Just short of the highway, a trail splits away to the right, climbing and falling vigorously, then crossing the footlog over Snass Creek that leads to the Cayuse Flats Trailhead.

41 Monument 83

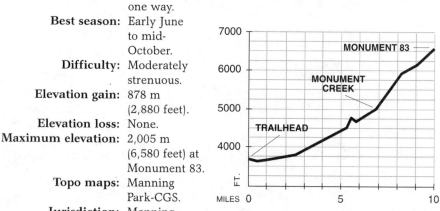

Overview: A backpack to Monument Spring, 17 km (10.6 miles) one way.

Best season: Early June to mid-October.

Difficulty: Moderately strenuous.

Elevation gain: 878 m (2,880 feet).

Elevation loss: None.

Maximum elevation: 2,005 m (6,580 feet) at Monument 83.

Topo maps: Manning Park-CGS.

Jurisdiction: Manning Provincial Park.

Finding the trailhead: The trail begins at the Monument 78/83 Trailhead, 4 km (2.5 miles) east of the Manning Provincial Park Visitor Centre.

158

Key points:

km	miles	
0.0	0.0	Monument 78/83 Trailhead. Trail runs east.
1.0	0.6	Bridge over Similkameen River.
1.1	0.7	Junction with Boyd Meadow Trail. Bear right.
1.3	0.8	Bridge over Chuwanten Creek.
1.9	1.2	Junction with Monument 78 Trail. Bear left.
4.7	2.9	Chuwanten Creek ford.
6.0	3.7	Trail enters Monument Creek valley.
11.1	6.9	Monument Creek crossing. Trail begins final climb.
13.4	8.3	Trail reaches ridgetop.
16.0	10.0	Monument 83. Trail enters United States.
17.0	10.6	Campsite at Monument Spring.

The hike: This trek follows a closed road that traverses the forested lowlands along the Similkameen River, then climbs high onto a meadow-topped foothill for superb mountain views and interesting historical structures.

The trail runs eastward along the highway, and soon it reaches a bridge over the Similkameen River. On the far bank, a spur track runs east to Boyd Meadows, while the main roadway swings west to cross Chuwanten Creek. The route climbs onto the pine-clad benches between Chuwanten and Castle creeks, and soon the Monument 78 route splits away to the right, following Castle Creek to the U.S. border. The Monument 83 route sticks to the bottoms along Chuwanten Creek, richly forested in spruce and cottonwood. After a connecting road climbs away toward Castle Creek, the road to Monument

Old fire lookout at Monument 83.

Monument 83

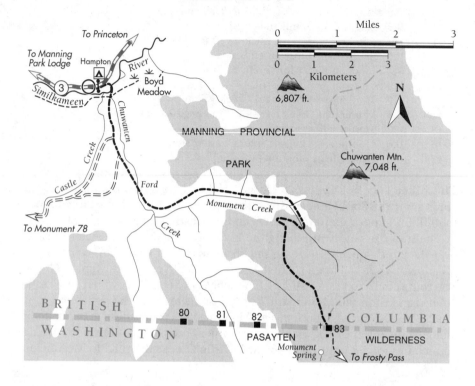

83 makes a knee-deep ford of Chuwanten Creek and climbs briskly onto the wooded benches on the east side of the valley.

Here, the trail levels off through lodgepole pines until it reaches the mouth of the Monument Creek valley. A series of sharp climbs leads the trail eastward along this tributary before the old roadbed settles into a gentle ascent up the heavily timbered valley. The real climbing begins after the route crosses Monument Creek, as the road grinds steadily upward through the trees. Breaks in the pines reveal an endless succession of timbered ridges. As the trail crests the ridgetop, a spur path runs west for a fine view of Mount Winthrop. The level ridgetop offers easy traveling through a woodland of lodgepole pine and subalpine fir that is transitional between the montane forest of the valley bottoms and subalpine stands of the timberline.

After a mile, the road steepens to make the final ascent to Monument 83 through open glades splashed with wildflowers. At the top, broad meadows offer panoramic views highlighted by Mount Winthrop to the west, with Castle Peak visible beyond it. To the southwest are the Smoky Mountain massif and Three Fools Peak, with the lofty summit of Jack Mountain to the right of them. Looking southwest, hikers can see a crowd of high peaks rising in the heart of the Pasayten Wilderness, crowned by Ptarmigan Peak,

Mount Lago, Mount Carru, and Osceola Peak. A 1920s-era fire lookout on the Canadian side of the border has the same cabin-and-cupola construction that typified the first generation of fire lookouts on both sides of the border, a style that has all but vanished. A more modern fire tower on the U.S. side dates from the 1950s. Between the two structures is the grave of Pasayten Pete, a character of mysterious (but perhaps canine or equine) identity. Travelers seeking a camp spot can continue along the trail as it enters the United States and descend through grassy meadows to Monument Spring.

42 Frosty Mountain Loop

Overview:	A long day hike or backpack to the east summit of Frosty Mountain, 27 km (16.8 miles) overall.
Best season:	Late June to mid-Ocotber.
Difficulty:	Moderately strenuous.
Elevation gain:	1,173 m (3,850 feet) west to east.
Elevation loss:	1,234 m (4,050 feet) west to east.
Maximum elevation:	2,408 m (7,900 feet) at the summit of Frosty Mountain.
Topo maps:	Manning Park-CGS; the rebuilt trail is not shown.
Jurisdiction:	Manning Provincial Park.

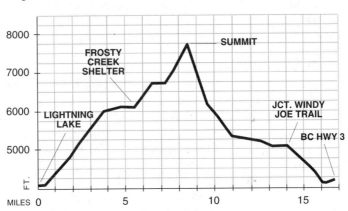

Finding the trailhead: Take British Columbia Highway 3 to the junction at the Manning Park Lodge. Turn south on Gibson Pass Road for 3 km (2 miles), then turn left at the Lightning Lake day-use area and park. The trail begins by crossing the dam at the lake's outlet. It ends at the Pacific Crest Trail (PCT) trailhead, 1 km east of the Manning Provincial Park Visitor Centre on BC 3. Through-hikers can arrange a car shuttle, or hike 4 km (2.5 miles) on the Similkameen River Trail to complete the loop.

Key points:

The hike: This popular route climbs from Lightning Lake to the eastern summit of Frosty Mountain for views deep into the heart of the Pasayten Wilderness. It then descends along a ridgetop to intersect the old fire road to Windy Joe Mountain, which it follows down to a trailhead on BC 3. The trek ends here for hikers who use a two-car shuttle; alternately, the loop can be closed by trails that follow the Similkameen River back to Lightning Lake. The trip can be completed in a single day by hikers of great stamina, but two camping areas along the way allow the trek to be approached at a more comfortable pace.

From the Lightning Lake day-use area, the trail crosses a dam to reach a marked junction on the far shore of the lake. Turn left as the Frosty Mountain Trail begins a steady climb through a forest of spruce and hemlock. As the path switchbacks upward, these conifers are replaced by lodgepole pine. Several openings reveal Lightning and Flash lakes in the valley below. As the trail approaches the ridgetop, the pines are in turn replaced by subalpine fir. The path ultimately reaches level country atop the ridge, and sun-splashed clearings interrupt the forest at regular intervals. The first views of Frosty Mountain come from these rolling uplands. Subalpine firs and whitebark pine close ranks around the trail as it approaches Frosty Creek camp, where a log shelter stands beside a spring-fed trickle of water.

The trail soon begins to climb again, rising above the forest onto a higher ridgetop where open meadows are guarded by sparse stands of subalpine larch. Larches are unique among conifers in that their needles turn brilliant gold in autumn and fall off with the onset of winter. The twin summits of Frosty Mountain now rise impressively to the south, and the trail wanders toward them through open country. The long meadows ultimately end as the path climbs through a bleak landscape of bedrock domes to reach the foot of the mountain. A precipitous climb leads up across a slope of frost-riven boulders to reach a wind-blasted signpost.

From here, the trail to the summit is little more than a pale track through the boulders where hikers' boots have worn off the black crust of lichens. Expect slow going as the path leads up the ridgeline to the eastern summit of Frosty Mountain, where a rockwork ring beside a large cairn provides

Castle Peak from Frosty Mountain.

shelter from the wind. Views are limitless from this highest point in Manning Provincial Park, featuring Castle Peak and Mount Winthrop guarding the emerald parks of Castle Creek. To the west are the sharp crags of Hozomeen Mountain with the summit of Mount Spickard beyond them. The lesser summits of the northernmost Cascades are spread in an arc to the north. From west to east, the principal summits are Silvertip Mountain, Snass Mountain, Three Brothers Mountain, and finally Chuwanten Mountain beyond Castle Creek.

Meanwhile, the loop trail descends northward from the signpost, zigzagging downward with impressive views of Castle Peak along the way. The trail bottoms out in broad meadows where anemones and lupines bloom, and larch and fir form stately clusters along the margins. The trees become more numerous with northward progress along the level ridgetop, forming an enchanting parkland that offers fine views of Mount Winthrop. This subalpine woodland, a mixture of fir, whitebark pine, and spruce, ultimately yields to a montane stand of Douglas-fir and lodgepole pine as the trail drops steadily from the ridgetop to reach the timbered saddle at the base of Windy Joe Mountain.

Here, the Pacific Crest Trail (PCT) rises up from the lowlands of Castle Creek to join the Frosty Mountain route; a 1-km jaunt down this trail leads to PCT Camp. The loop trail now traverses northwest and soon encounters the old Windy Joe fire access road, now closed to motorized traffic. Diehard hikers can hike up the road to the summit of Windy Joe Mountain, where interpretive panels identify the surrounding peaks. Windy Joe Mountain was named for a local trapper who vociferously claimed that

Frosty Mountain Loop

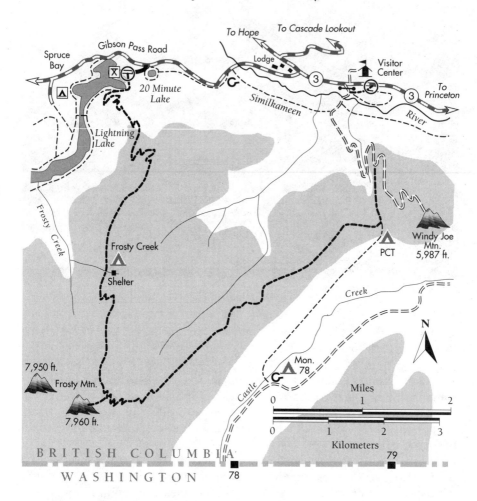

high winds kept the summit free of snow all winter.

To complete the hike, follow the road downward through lodgepole pines growing on slopes that burned in the 1800s. The road soon encounters a small stream; the moist bottomlands were spared by the blaze and contain a mixture of spruce and hemlock that is representative of the pre-fire forest. The road then descends steadily into the valley of the Similkameen River. Near the bottom of the grade, the Similkameen Trail departs from the road and runs westward; hikers completing the loop on foot should turn left here. To reach the highway, follow the road across the river to the horse corrals, then turn east past the sewage lagoons to reach the PCT Trailhead.

43 Lightning Lakes Chain

Overview:	An array of possible day hikes and loops, 20 km (12.4 miles) to Thunder Lake and back.
Best season:	Mid-May to late October.
Difficulty:	Easy to Strike Lake; moderate beyond.
Elevation gain:	None.
Elevation loss:	73 m (240 feet) to Thunder Lake.
Maximum elevation:	1,250 m (4,100 feet) at Lightning Lake.
Topo maps:	Manning Park-CGS; not all trails are shown.
Jurisdiction:	Manning Provincial Park.

Finding the trailhead: Take British Columbia Highway 3 to the junction at the Manning Park Lodge. Drive south on Gibson Pass Road for 6 km (4.2 miles), then turn left at Spruce Bay turnoff and park at the trailhead.

Key points:

km	miles	
0.0	0.0	Spruce Bay Trailhead.
0.3	0.2	Junction with angler's trail. Bear right and follow "Main Trail" signs.
1.1	0.7	Junction with Skyline II Trail. Bear left.
2.0	1.2	Head of Lightning Lake. Junction with Lightning Lake Loop Trail. Stay right.
2.3	1.4	First junction with Flash Lake Loop Trail. Stay right.
2.4	1.5	Head of Flash Lake.
3.4	2.1	Foot of Flash Lake.
3.7	2.3	Second junction with Flash Lake Loop. Keep right.
4.5	2.8	Head of Strike Lake.
5.8	3.6	Foot of Strike Lake.
6.9	4.3	Strike Lake Camp.
9.3	5.8	Head of Thunder Lake.
10.0	6.2	Trail ends.

The hike: In the heart of Manning Provincial Park, a chain of lakes at the head of Lightning Creek occupies a timbered low spot on the Cascades divide. Lightning Lake is the largest of these, and because it is accessible by road, it is a popular spot for picnics and canoe trips. A network of trails rings the lakes, allowing a diverse array of day-hikes of varying lengths. One could hike completely around both Lightning and Flash lakes, while the

Storm at Strike Lake.

main trail follows the western shores of the lakes and also visits the more remote waters of Strike Lake and Thunder Lake. These boreal lakes are outstanding spots for wildlife viewing, with waterfowl and beaver active on the water and opportunities to view spawning rainbow trout at the outlet of Lightning Lake during early summer.

The trail begins by wandering through the towering Engelmann spruce that border Spruce Bay. These trees are narrow and spire-shaped to shed heavy accumulations of winter snow. The wide path soon nears the shore of Lightning Lake; a narrow angler's trail runs along the lakeshore while the broad Lightning Lakes Chain path charts an inland course. The Skyline trail soon splits away to the right, while the main trail continues to the foot of the lake. A loop trail leads around the far shore, and a short distance along it leads to a bridge over the spot where the rainbow trout spawn.

Ahead lies Flash Lake, beyond a short stretch of bottomland forest. This picturesque lake is endowed with islands and peninsulas robed richly in spruce. Choose either shore to pass around the lake. Beyond it, a short jog through the forest leads to open marshes of emerald green sedge, created by the past flooding activities of beaver. These industrious animals have since moved on, leaving the gemlike wetland to smaller creatures. After wandering through the lowland forest, the trail arrives at Strike Lake, a clone of the two upper lakes. There are several bare spots along the shoreline, but backpackers should continue on past the foot of the lake for 1 km (about 0.62 mile) to reach Strike Lake Camp in a grove of fir.

The trail passes through the midst of the camp, then onward through an increasingly dry and open landscape. Early talus slopes reveal the bare flanks

Lightning Lakes Chain

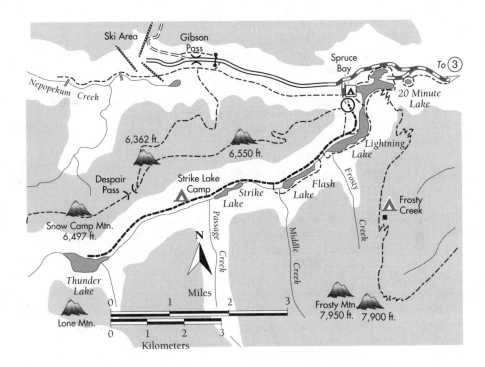

of Snow Camp Mountain ahead, and the stately spruces are replaced by Douglas-firs that are better suited to this arid landscape. The path crosses a broad apron of scree as it approaches Thunder Lake. The lake's bleak basin is fringed by tall cottonwoods, and the water level often drops well below the shoreline as the waters drain through underground channels in the shattered basin rock. The trail wanders halfway around its shore to end in the trees west of the lake.

44 Three Falls Trail

Overview:	A half-day hike to Derek Falls, 9 km (5.6 miles) round trip.
Best season:	Early June to late October.
Difficulty:	Easy to Shadow Falls; moderate beyond.
Elevation gain:	None.
Elevation loss:	177 m (580 feet) to Derek Falls.
Maximum elevation:	1,365 m (4,480 feet) at Gibson Pass Trailhead.
Topo maps:	Manning Park-CGS.
Jurisdiction:	Manning Provincial Park.

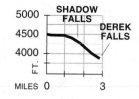

Finding the trailhead: Take British Columbia Highway 3 to the junction at the Manning Park Lodge. Drive south on Gibson Pass Road for 10 km (7 miles) to reach the Strawberry Flats Trailhead at the locked gate to the ski area.

Key points:

km	miles	
0.0	0.0	Trailhead.
0.3	0.2	Strawberry Flats.
0.9	0.5	Junction with Skyline I Trail. Continue straight ahead.
1.8	1.1	Trail passes beneath ski lift.
3.1	1.9	Shadow Falls overlook.
3.5	2.2	Nepopekum Falls viewpoint.
4.5	2.8	Derek Falls viewpoint and end of trail.

The hike: This trail offers a half-day trip from Gibson Pass, visiting three striking waterfalls along Nepopekum Creek. The trail begins in a lodgepole pine savannah that covers the flats of Gibson Pass. The pines got their start following a forest fire, and now a young crop of shade-tolerant spruce seedlings is growing up to replace them. After passing a junction with the Skyline I Trail, the wide track enters the grassy clearings of Strawberry Flats. In addition to wild strawberries, the flats are home to a diverse mixture of flowering plants, featuring tiger lily, monkshood, and lupine. The peak blooming occurs in late July.

As flower-studded meadows give way to subalpine forest, the path runs beneath one of the chairlifts of Gibson Pass Ski Area. After climbing across the ski run, the trail returns to a virgin stand of subalpine fir. The timber is dense as far as Shadow Falls, where an overlook is cordoned off by a split-rail fence. The falls are most spectacular in early June, and taper off to a trickle by late summer.

Beyond the overlook, the path begins a steady descent into the deep canyon of Nepopekum Creek. Early in the descent, talus slopes reveal the green sail

Three Falls Trail

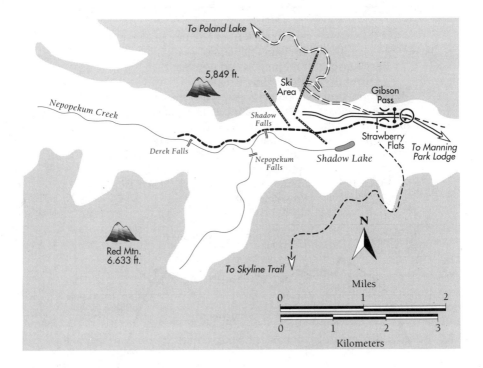

of Snow Camp Mountain and the bleaker summit of Red Mountain. Nepopekum Falls soon appears on the far side of the valley, a slender cascade that plummets from a hanging basin down a sheer wall of stone. Continuing downhill, the trail makes its way into timbered bottoms, where the silver fir and western hemlock so typical of the coastal forest are dominant. Soon, rushing Derek Falls can be heard, and the trail makes its way out onto a talus slope for a striking view of the cataract. Evidence of avalanches and rockslides is everywhere, and the trail ends at a warning sign just beyond the viewpoint.

45 Skyline Trail

Overview:	A backpack from Lightning Lake to the Skagit Valley, 36.2 km (22.5 miles) overall.
Best season:	Mid-June to mid-October.
Difficulty:	Moderately strenuous.
Elevation gain:	1,353 m (4,440 feet) east to west.
Elevation loss:	2,091 m (6,860 feet) east to west.
Maximum elevation:	1,932 m (6,340 feet).
Topo maps:	Manning Park-CGS (Skyline I and Hozameen Ridge trails not shown); Skagit River-CGS (trail location approximate).
Jurisdiction:	Manning Provincial Park, Skagit Valley Provincial Park.

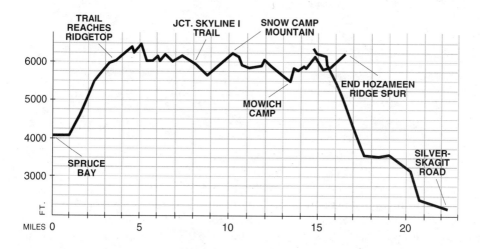

Finding the trailhead: The trail begins at the Spruce Bay Trailhead (see Lightning Lakes Chain, p.165), and ends at the Whitworth Meadow Trailhead, an unmarked pullout at km 54 (mile 33.6) on the Silver-Skagit Road. Through-hikers will need to arrange a car shuttle.

Key points:

km	miles	
0.0	0.0	Spruce Bay Trailhead. Follow signs for "Main Trail."
1.1	0.7	Junction with Skyline II Trail. Turn right to begin the ascent.
6.3	3.9	Trail reaches the ridgetop.
14.2	8.8	Junction with Skyline I (cutoff to Gibson Pass). Turn left.
15.1	9.4	Despair Pass.
17.7	11.0	Snow Camp Mountain.
23.2	14.4	Mowich Camp.
23.8	14.8	Junction with Hozameen Ridge Trail (5.3 km/3.3 miles, moderate). Continue straight ahead for the Silver-Skagit Road.

The hike: The crown jewel of Manning Provincial Park, this trail follows alpine ridgetops from Lightning Lake to the Skagit River valley, offering astounding views of Hozomeen Mountain as well as Castle Peak to the east. The trail will be described along its original route, although it might also be approached from Gibson Pass via a newer trail that climbs to the ridgetop from the north. This new trail (now known as Skyline I) can be combined with the old trail (Skyline II) for a day trip from Gibson Pass to Lightning Lake. Backpackers can pitch their tents at the remote Mowich Camp and make southward forays on the Hozameen Ridge Trail (see below). The trail from Hozameen Ridge down to the Skagit Valley was once quite steep, but has been rebuilt recently and is now quite manageable.

From the Spruce Bay parking area, follow the Lightning Lakes Chain Trail southward around the shore of Lightning Lake. Follow signs marked "Main Trail" as the wide pathway crosses spruce bottoms to reach its junction with the Skyline Trail. This route initially follows an old road grade that ascends steadily through dense stands of spruce and hemlock as it winds onto the north side of the ridge. The footpath begins here, making a long but moderate climb through the trees before a sharp hairpin leads back to the ridgeline. Sharp ascents alternate with level stretches as the path follows the ridgetop upward to a series of burns. Lightning strikes are common on these high ridges, and when the forest is dry they ignite small wildfires. The burns yield fine views of Frosty Mountain, the northernmost peak of the rugged and glacier-carved crest of the Cascades.

As the trail climbs to timberline, hikers get views of Flash Lake, distant Thunder Lake, and finally Strike Lake in the valley below. A bald and rocky knob marks the top of the initial grade; beyond this point, the route rises and falls with the changing pitch of the ridgetop. The eastern slope is covered in an arid parkland punctuated by subalpine fir and whitebark pine, but the north-facing bowls are robed in lush meadows. Northward views encompass Gibson Pass Ski Area, as well as the solitary horn of Silvertip Mountain with its diadem of glacial ice.

After surmounting the first three knolls, the trail drops onto south-facing slopes to cross a broad and flower-spangled grassland. One can now look straight up Passage Creek at the summit of Castle Peak, which lies just south of the international border. The trail enters a woodland of impressive subalpine firs as it continues across the mountainside. After a short distance, the rim of a steep dropoff commands views of Thunder Lake. The lake is guarded by the meadowy dome of Lone Mountain, with the spires of Hozomeen Mountain rising beyond.

The Skyline I segment of the trail now rises from Gibson Pass to join the main trail at a marked signpost; hikers bound for Mowich Camp will now switchback down into Despair Pass. The pass is wooded in spruce and fir, with a dense understory of shrubs that includes huckleberry and dwarf blueberry. After bottoming out, the path climbs to the north of the ridgecrest,

Skyline Trail

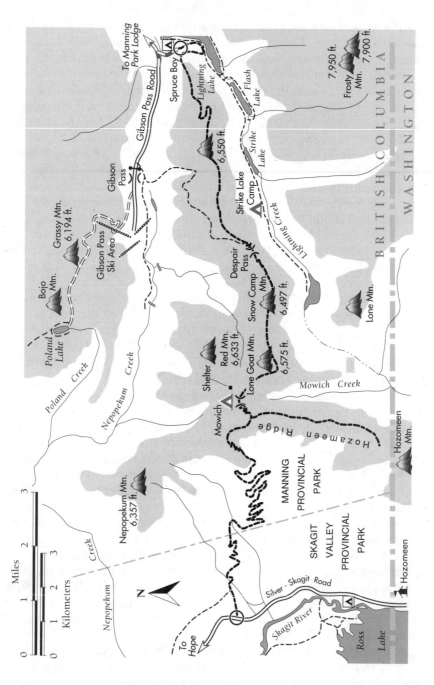

rising through tidy heather meadows that are protected by the trees. Suddenly, the trail breaks out onto the high and windswept grasslands atop Snow Camp Mountain. These heights face straight down Lightning Creek at the cathedral spires of Hozomeen Mountain, and also offer fine views of the peaks to the east. Looking west across the divide formed by Hozameen Ridge, the summits of Mox Peaks, Mount Spickard, and Custer Ridge crowd the distant horizon.

After traversing below the summit of Snow Camp, the trail drops into a saddle at the base of Lone Goat Mountain. Red Mountain now rises to the west. Late summer berry pickings can be good where the trail climbs across the face of Lone Goat, then rounds the peak and makes a northward descent across open bowls. Mowich Camp occupies the low saddle at the head of Mowich Creek, boasting a log shelter beside a pair of picturesque wet meadows.

An easy grade now leads to the top of the Hozameen Ridge, where the Hozameen Ridge Trail (see below) splits away to the south. The main trail drops onto the western slope of the ridge and traverses northward, first through an open subalpine woodland and then onto open slopes. There are superb parting views of Hozomeen Mountain, as well as of the head of Ross Lake and the peaks that rise beyond it. A long finger ridge extends into the Skagit Valley, and the trail follows it to begin its long descent.

The path enters heavy timber upon rounding the end of the ridge. Douglas-firs are draped with goat's beard on the southwest exposures, while hemlocks dominate the cooler north-facing slopes. After a long descent, the trail crosses a major stream. It then enters Skagit Valley Provincial Park as it climbs onto a series of timbered terraces. Another substantial descent leads to the valley floor, and after passing a junction with the Centennial Trail, the path makes its way to the Silver-Skagit Road at the site of the old Whitworth Ranch.

Hozameen Ridge Option. This trail began as a climber's route to Hozomeen Mountain, and follows the ridgetop southward through subalpine parks to the international border. The pace is moderate, but includes several killer grades to discourage the fainthearted. Leaving the Skyline Trail, the route meanders across rounded hillocks and through pocket vales ringed by subalpine fir. Westward views feature Mox Peaks, Mount Spickard, and Custer Ridge beyond the head of Ross Lake. Straight ahead, the north peak of Hozomeen rises like a beacon. The path dodges to the east side of the ridge while surmounting the first high point, and open slopes yield excellent views of Castle Peak. The trail tackles the second summit head-on, and after a long descent it reaches the first rocky battlement of Hozomeen Mountain. The trail snakes upward at an insanely steep angle and, between gasps, visitors may notice a subtle shift from subalpine fir to the mountain hemlock and Alaska cedar typical of the coastal subalpine zone. The path peters out atop this high spur, with full-face views of the north peak of Hozomeen.

46 Skagit River Trail

Overview: A day hike or short backpack along a roadless reach of the Skagit River, 14.5 km (9 miles) one way.

Best season: Early May to late October.

Difficulty: Easy.

Elevation gain: 216 m (710 feet) south to north.

Elevation loss: 122 m (400 feet) south to north.

Maximum elevation: 643 m (2,110 feet) opposite Silvertip Creek.

Topo maps: Skagit River-CGS.

Jurisdiction: Manning Provincial Park, Skagit Valley Provincial Park.

Finding the trailhead: To reach the trailhead, drive south from Hope for 42.5 km (29.8 miles) to reach an unmarked pulloff just beyond the 26 Mile Bridge. The trail ends at the Sumallo Grove picnic area, 12 km (8.4 miles) east of Manning Park's West Gate on British Columbia Highway 3. Through-hikers will need to arrange a car shuttle.

Key points:

km miles
- 0.0 0.0 26-Mile Bridge Trailhead.
- 0.9 0.5 Junction with Centennial Trail. Turn left.
- 10.8 6.7 Delacey Camp.
- 12.9 8.0 Trail crosses Silverdaisy Creek.
- 13.5 8.4 Junction with Silverdaisy Trail. Continue straight on old road.
- 14.3 8.9 Trail crosses bridge over Skagit River.
- 14.5 9.0 Old road reaches Sumallo Grove Trailhead.

The hike: This trail follows the last wild and free-flowing stretch of the Skagit River, linking Manning and Skagit Valley provincial parks. The original route, known as the Whatcom Trail, was blazed in 1858 by Captain Walter DeLacy. Trail boosters hoped that they could avoid paying import taxes by bypassing the customs house in Vancouver, and thus make the town of Whatcom, on Bellingham Bay, the principal supplier for the goldfields of interior British Columbia. The route soon proved too steep and arduous for commercial transport, and it was abandoned after only two months. Today, hikers can follow in the footsteps of the explorers through a remote corner of the mountains that has changed little in two hundred years.

Waterfall and mine portal on Silverdaisy Creek.

The trail begins in the broad valley where the Skagit and Klesilkwa rivers mingle their waters. It initially follows an old roadbed across a fertile lowland of flood channels and river bars. Nearing the base of the mountains, the path climbs onto an old glacial terrace, where it meets the Centennial Trail. The Skagit River trail runs north from the junction, passing through a sparse post-fire forest of lodgepole pine and Douglas-fir. The Hozameen Range soon constricts around the Skagit River. The river is older than the range, and as the land rose, the water cut down through the ridges to form a narrow canyon through the mountains. At the mouth of the canyon, Pacific rhododendrons light the forest with their enormous pink blossoms.

Following the river into the canyon, the trail makes a short but steep ascent along an old talus slope that has been overrun by moss. Southward views on the way up feature the ranges that rise beyond the Klesilkwa, including the sharp horn of Whitworth Peak. From the heights, one can look across the river at the pinnacles and glaciers of Silvertip Mountain. The trail then drops into the lowland forest, following the eastern edge of the bottomlands. The Skagit occasionally loops across the lowlands to approach the trail, its translucent green waters sliding silently through smooth runs. The path climbs again opposite the mouth of Marmot Creek, this time to avoid a landslide scar. There are final views of the mountains before the trail descends into the forest for good.

The path now follows the riverbank, and soon the first stands of old-growth timber appear: giant red-cedars that rise like stout pillars from the floodplain. The brush is initially heavy, but lessens as the trail continues

175

Skyline Trail

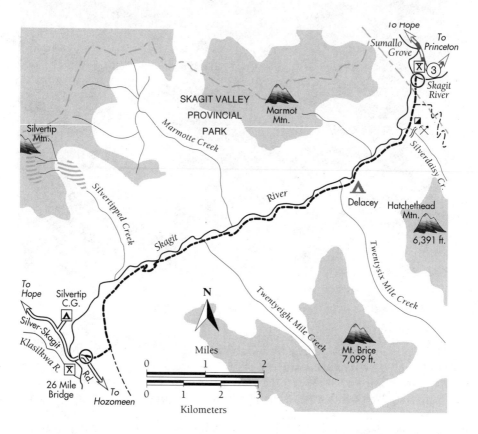

northward. Hemlocks now dominate the overstory. Shortly after crossing Twentysix Mile Creek, the trail reaches Delacey Camp in its sandbar grove of giant cedars. The forest reaches its climax in a stand of superb Douglas-firs and cedars, and the river provides a noisy accompaniment as it churns through riffles and boulder-strewn pools.

The trail then swings away from the river, continuing northward along the edge of the valley. From the crossing of Silverdaisy Creek, a short jog to the east leads to a pleasant waterfall beside the mouth of an abandoned mineshaft; look eastward from the bridge to see a swath cut across the forested slopes of Silverdaisy Mountain. The swath once bore a tramway that served the old Silverdaisy Mine, which produced a moderate amount of high-grade copper ore between the turn of the century and 1938. After crossing the bridge, the Skagit Valley route soon passes its junction with the Silverdaisy trail, and the mountains open out into the broad east-west valley that bears BC 3. A footbridge spans the Skagit River near its confluence with the Sumallo River, and soon the trail reaches its end at the Sumallo Grove day-use area.

47 Galene Lakes

Overview: A long day hike or backpack from the Skagit River to a group of subalpine lakes, 26 km (16.2 miles) round trip.

Best season: Early July to mid-October.

Difficulty: Strenuous.

Elevation gain: 1,234 m (4,050 feet) to Galene Lakes; 1,580 m (4,740 feet) to the ridgetop.

Elevation loss: None.

Maximum elevation: 1,954 m (6,410 feet) at the ridgetop.

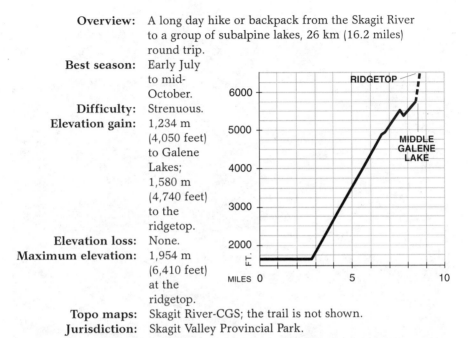

Topo maps: Skagit River-CGS; the trail is not shown.

Jurisdiction: Skagit Valley Provincial Park.

Finding the trailhead: From Hope, follow the bumpy, gravel ribbon of the Silver–Skagit Road south for 58.7 km (41 miles) to reach the suspension bridge that leads to Chittenden Meadow. The hike begins by crossing the bridge.

Key points:

km	miles	
0.0	0.0	Suspension bridge over Skagit River.
1.3	0.8	Junction in Chittenden Meadow. Turn right for Galene Lakes.
4.3	2.7	Trail enters dry course of Galene Creek.
6.3	3.9	End of old logging road.
7.2	4.5	Galene Creek ford.
10.5	6.5	Top of ridge.
13.0	8.1	Trail ends at the middle Galene Lake. Route continues upward from outlet.
13.7	8.5	Mountaintop meadows.

The hike: This nearly forgotten trail in the southern end of Skagit Valley Provincial Park climbs from the river bottoms to a series of subalpine lakes, with scramble routes that ascend above the timberline for phenomenal views. The trail has not been maintained in several years (hence the "trail closed" designation, which means no maintenance rather than no entry), and the

Middle Galene Lake.

portion of the trail that follows the Skagit River is quite overgrown with brush. Once you reach the Galene Lakes outlet stream, however, the trail grade to the lakes is in fine shape and poses little route-finding difficulty. Lowland mosquitoes are intolerable from August through September.

After crossing the suspension bridge over the Skagit River, follow the broad track of the Chittenden Meadow nature trail as it runs westward to a signpost at the edge of Chittenden Meadow. The meadow is of great ecological significance: ponderosa pine are ordinarily restricted to locales east of the Cascade divide, but they thrive here beside the Skagit. The meadow was once part of a turn-of-the-century cattle ranch, and was later named for Curley Chittenden, a Canadian logger who spearheaded the effort to thwart a higher dam on Ross Lake that would have flooded the valley far into Canada.

Turn north at the signpost; the trail follows abandoned logging roads across valley bottoms where a regenerating forest of Douglas-fir provides ample shade. The going is easy until the trail approaches the Skagit River. Here, it makes its way through thickets of red alder and cottonwood saplings; watch for flagging that marks the route. Although the brush is not heavy by Cascades standards, it is thick enough to be a nuisance when dry and to provide a free bath during wet weather. After passing along the crumbling and undercut banks of the Skagit, the path drops into a small flood channel that carries water during spring runoff. The trail then climbs onto the foot of a mossy hillside, charting a hardscrabble course among fallen logs and stumps before returning to the brushy bottomlands.

The path soon acquires the dry channel of Galene Creek (the waters flow under the gravel here) and follows it upward. It soon emerges onto the north bank of the watercourse and ascends gently into coniferous forest to meet an old logging road. The trail adopts the roadbed, ascending steeply in places where the road has washed out. Leaving the devil's club thickets of the streamcourse, the road swings north across the mountainside, and soon gives way to a well-built pack trail. This trail climbs southward through Douglas-fir, ultimately emerging beside Galene Creek for a tricky upper crossing. Erosion has created a 4-foot cutbank, which must be negotiated to reach the stream, and a rock-hop leads across to the other side.

On the slopes beyond, the trail enters a mossy forest of young hemlock, then switchbacks upward along the crest of a prominent ridge. As the ridgetop levels off, the hemlocks are replaced by subalpine firs with an understory of heather and huckleberries. The trail runs west along the ridgetop, then climbs vigorously to surmount a high point. As the path swings onto the point's south slope, open meadows reveal a stunning panorama centered around Ross Lake, guarded to the east by the ramparts of Hozomeen Mountain and to the west by Mount Raeburn. After gaining the top of the point, the trail returns to the ridgeline and drops into the next saddle. The lowermost of the Galene Lakes is now visible in the forested basin below, while the meadowy massif of Mount Wright guards the head of the valley.

The trail climbs steeply to gain the top of the next high point, then traverses north, away from the ridgeline. It reaches a sudden end at the middle Galene

Galene Lakes

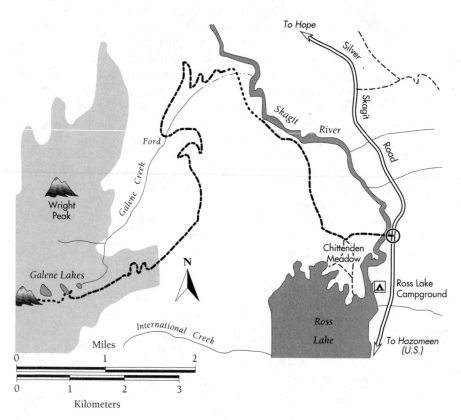

Lake. This beautiful tarn is set amid subalpine parks, once hard-used by campers who found tent spots on the narrow strip of level ground east of the water. From here, a steep and brushy scramble leads back to the ridgetop, then continues past the upper lake to reach the glorious meadows of the mountaintops. Westward views are stunning, featuring close looks at the Mox Peaks and Mount Spickard, with the rocky backbone of Custer Ridge stretching northward into Canada.

ADDITIONAL TRAILS

The 16-km (9-mile) **Dewdney Trail** is a section of the historic route blazed in 1860, and follows Snass Creek to Dry Lake and Paradise Valley.

A hiker-only alternate to the Dewdney Trail, the **Whatcom Trail** runs over a high pass to visit the Punch Bowl.

The **Skagit Bluffs Trail** follows BC Highway 3 and is primarily for horses.

The 20-km (12.4-mile) **Silverdaisy Trail** is a muddy mine access road from Cayuse Flats to Silverdaisy Mountain, and a hiking trail from there to Sumallo Grove. There is active mine drilling on the trail in its upper reaches.

The **Hope Pass Trail** follows the Skaist River and crosses the high country to reach Marmot City and the Whipsaw Road.

The **Nicomen Lake Trail** is a cutoff trail for horses that links Nicomen Lake with the Hope Pass route.

A closed fire access road runs for 8 km (5 miles) through the ski lifts at Gibson Pass to reach **Poland Lake**, which is well-stocked with rainbow trout.

The **Similkameen Trail** parallels the highway and is used mostly by equestrians.

The 7.5-km (5.3-mile) **Windy Joe Mountain Trail** follows a closed fire access road to the summit of Windy Joe Mountain, where interpretive signs identify the landmarks in a panorama that is essentially the same as at Cascade Lookout.

The primitive **Bonnevier Trail** runs for 29 km (18 miles) between the Heather Trail and east gate of the park. It is best suited to experienced backpackers.

The **Monument 78 Trail** is a 12-km (7.4-mile) hike on a muddy access road to reach the international border and join the Pacific Crest Trail (see Extended Journeys).

The **Centennial Trail** was designed for horse use and follows the floor of the Skagit Valley from Whitworth Meadow to Twentysix Mile Bridge and then west along the Klesilkwa River. It is maintained only sporadically.

The **Chittenden Meadow Nature Trail** is a short loop that visits the ponderosa pine savannahs at the head of Ross Lake.

The Pasayten Wilderness

The vast and remote Pasayten Wilderness stretches eastward from the crest of the Cascades to encompass arid ranges and wooded basins, untamed rivers and peaceful alpine lakes. Overshadowed by national park lands to the west, the Pasayten receives relatively few visitors. It is vast in extent, more than half a million acres in all. Hikers can go for weeks here without crossing a road or their own tracks. The long trails of the Pasayten Wilderness lead deep into the mountains, offering excellent opportunities for solitude that improve with distance from the Pacific Crest Trail and the Harts Pass area. Many of the trails that appear on maps receive little or no maintenance, and backpackers who wish to test their wilderness skills will find that the Pasayten country offers ample challenges.

The mountains east of the Cascade crest have a more continental climate than that west of the divide, with hotter summers and colder, drier winters. Lowland forests typically are dominated by Douglas-fir, with dense stands of lodgepole pine or open savannahs of ponderosa pine in drier areas where wildfires have shaped the landscape. Near the timberline, Engelmann spruce and subalpine fir are the dominant trees, while whitebark pine is prevalent in arid areas. Stands of subalpine larch can be found in some of the highest and most windswept locales. Alpine meadows above treeline are typified by a greater number of grasses and fewer flowering plants than are found farther west, although there can be stunning displays of wildflowers in locales that receive plenty of moisture.

The Pasayten is truly a multiple-use wilderness. It is popular with horse parties, and a few trunk trails receive heavy use by horse traffic. The area has been used as a summer range for domestic sheep since the early 1900s, and grazing is still permitted in some parts of the wilderness. Some of the alpine lakes provide outstanding fishing for trout, and the neighboring Methow River is also well known for its fly-fishing. In late September, deer hunters stalk the ridges and streams of the Pasayten in pursuit of deer. Travelers who enter the Pasayten at this time should wear blaze orange clothing. During the winter months, the Methow Valley is a mecca for cross-country skiing, but the steep country of the Pasayten itself is too avalanche-prone for backcountry ski trips.

Backcountry permits are not required, although there is a new fee for each night of parking on national forest lands that surround the wilderness. The fees are part of an experimental pilot program; be sure to voice your opinions about the fees to your congressional representatives.

The main access route to the Pasayten is the Harts Pass Road (Forest Road 5400), which runs 18.5 miles from Mazama to Harts Pass, near timberline. The road is wide and well maintained through the Methow River valley, but becomes narrow and steep as it climbs the valley walls and winds up past Deadhorse Point to reach the high country to the west. Potholes and fallen

Pasayten Wilderness Overview

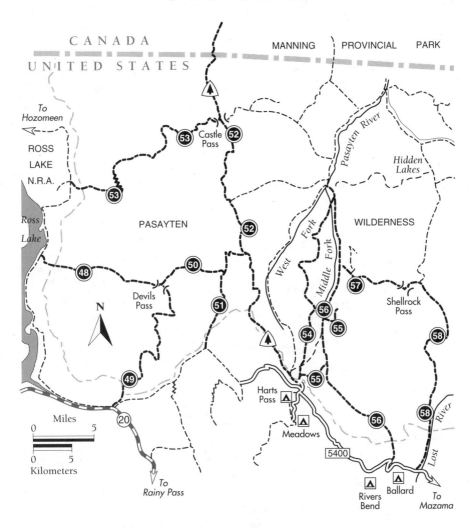

rocks can make for challenging driving, particularly for vehicles with low clearance. From Harts Pass, a good road winds up toward Slate Peak, and a narrow and rutted track descends along Slate Creek to end at the Cady Pass trailhead, where the road has been washed out and abandoned (Chancellor Campground can no longer be reached by car). The Pasayten can also be accessed from Washington Highway 20 via the Jackita Ridge and Chancellor trails (Hikes 49 and 65). The wilderness can be approached from the west via trails that follow Ross Lake; travelers who begin their journey in Ross Lake Recreation Area must have a free permit to camp on national park lands. Trails also penetrate the wilderness from Canada; hikers who approach from the north should obtain the appropriate clearance from U.S. and Canadian Customs.

There is little in the way of services near the Pasayten Wilderness. Gas and limited supplies can be obtained at the small mercantile store in Mazama. Eleven miles east of Mazama is the resort town of Winthrop, where visitors will find backpacking supplies, excellent restaurants, bed-and-breakfast lodgings, and a laid-back atmosphere that hearkens back to the days of the Old West. Travelers who seek a more rustic experience will find several Forest Service campgrounds along the West Fork of the Methow River as well as two alpine campgrounds in the vicinity of Harts Pass. There is a Forest Service visitor center in Winthrop, and a ranger cabin at Harts Pass is staffed sporadically during the summer.

48 Devils Dome

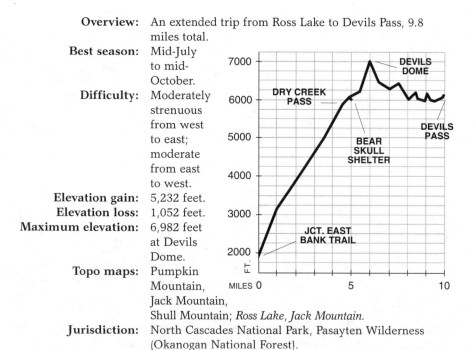

Overview: An extended trip from Ross Lake to Devils Pass, 9.8 miles total.

Best season: Mid-July to mid-October.

Difficulty: Moderately strenuous from west to east; moderate from east to west.

Elevation gain: 5,232 feet.

Elevation loss: 1,052 feet.

Maximum elevation: 6,982 feet at Devils Dome.

Topo maps: Pumpkin Mountain, Jack Mountain, Shull Mountain; *Ross Lake, Jack Mountain.*

Jurisdiction: North Cascades National Park, Pasayten Wilderness (Okanogan National Forest).

Finding the trail: The west end of the trail can be reached by boat at Devils Junction Camp, or on foot via the East Bank Trail from Washington Highway 20 (12.4 miles) or Hozomeen (17.7 miles). The east end of the trail can be reached via the Jackita Ridge Trail (Hike 49, 15.2 miles) or the Deception Pass Trail (Hike 50, 19.7 miles) from Harts Pass.

Key points:

    0.0 Junction with East Bank Trail at Devils Camp. Trail climbs eastward.
    1.2 Trail leaves North Cascades National Park and enters Pasayten
        Wilderness.
    4.5 Dry Creek Pass.
    4.8 Spur trail runs north to Bear Skull shelter. Bear right for Devils Dome.
    6.2 Summit of Devils Dome.
    9.8 Devils Pass. Trail to Deception Pass and Devils Pass shelter runs north;
        Jackita Ridge Trail runs southeast.

The hike: This trail is one of the best known and most popular treks in the Pasayten country, climbing from Ross Lake to the ridgetops and following them eastward to Devils Pass. Its panoramic scenery is highlighted by grandstand views of Jack Mountain, and lush alpine meadows splashed with wildflowers accompany hikers along most of the route. Shelters wait near Dry Creek Pass and Devils Pass; surface water is hard to come by between the summit of Devils Dome and Devils Pass.

    Departing from the East Bank trail, the Devils Dome trek begins with a long and tedious climb through stands of young conifers, particularly western red-cedar and Douglas-fir. Upon reaching the boundary of the Pasayten Wilderness, the trail enters an old burn choked with hemlock saplings. The path enters a more open stand of Douglas-fir as it climbs, and soon it turns eastward to traverse the mountainside high above Devils Creek. Gaps in the trees reveal the massive edifice of Jack Mountain on the far side of

The peaks of Jackita Ridge from the Devils Dome Trail.

Devils Dome

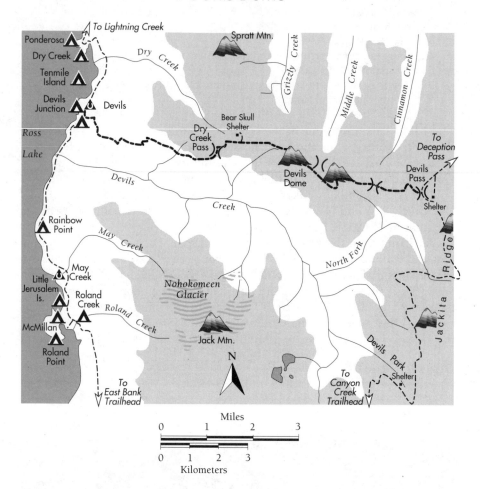

the valley, with the rumpled ice of Nohokomeen Glacier cupped within its northern buttresses.

Thickets of Douglas maple crowd the trail as it continues eastward. The path ultimately breaks out onto an arid, open slope where ceanothus, service-berry, kinnikinnick, and arrowleaf balsamroot are the dominant plants. As the path continues its gentle ascent, it enters an extensive stand of lodge-pole pine. Finally reaching the subalpine zone, the path enters open parklands where flower-strewn meadows are punctuated with stands of conical firs. An east-facing slope yields the first views of Devils Dome to the east, and soon the trail zigzags up to Dry Creek Pass.

The path now follows a narrow ridgecrest eastward, climbing heartily. A spur path soon runs northward to end at the Bear Skull Shelter, while the main trail continues east and levels off amid a broad swath of alpine tundra.

The verdant shelf falls away rapidly to the south, and ahead is the valley of a small but reliable brook. Views are superb from this area. Jack Mountain rises just across the valley with small glaciers adorning its northeast face. A thrust fault runs horizontally through this massive peak; the base of the mountain is composed of schist, a volcanic rock, while above the fault the rocky heights are made of much younger phyllite. Farther to the east are Crater Mountain and the many jagged summits of Jackita Ridge. The trail now follows the brook up to a grassy saddle, then zigzags up the final pitch to reach the bald summit of Devils Dome. Here, a level pad of tundra commands views that stretch to all horizons.

The trail drops southward from the summit, then tracks a narrow ridgeline eastward above precipitous cliffs. Phlox and other alpine wildflowers bloom profusely as the path makes its way down into a saddle at the base of a prominent summit. The trail swings south to bypass this prominence, traversing the alpine parks. Crater Mountain and Jackita Ridge now dominate the scenery straight ahead, while a backward glance reveals Jack Mountain in all its majesty. The path ultimately crosses a second saddle, then doglegs sharply to the northwest to traverse above a meadowy bowl. The path soon winds around onto timbered, south-facing slopes above the North Fork of Devils Creek. Openings are plentiful, revealing fine views of the surrounding peaks.

Reaching a low point on the ridgetop, the path crosses through grassy meadows surrounded by subalpine forest. The path drops through several prominent saddles, such as this one, before it finally reaches its end at Devils Pass. Here, watchful hikers may spot the well-hidden trail signs that point the way eastward to Deception Pass and southward to Jackita Ridge. To reach the Devils Pass shelter and its small but dependable spring, follow the Deception Pass trail north to an unmarked junction where a spur path descends several hundred feet to reach the shelter in a small subalpine basin.

49 Jackita Ridge

Overview:	A day hike to Crater Lake (8.4 miles round trip) or a long backpack to Devils Pass (15.2 miles one way).
Best season:	Early August to mid-October.
Difficulty:	Strenuous.
Elevation gain:	6,977 feet.
Elevation loss:	2,277 feet.
Maximum elevation:	6,840 feet.
Topo maps:	Crater Mountain, Jack Mountain, Shull Mountain; *Jack Mountain, Mount Logan.*
Jurisdiction:	Pasayten Wilderness (Okanogan National Forest).

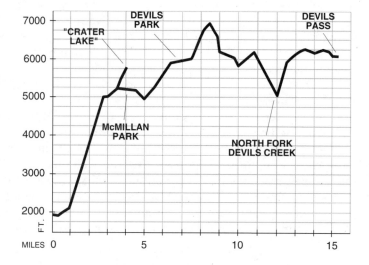

Finding the trailhead: The trail begins at the Canyon Creek trailhead, at mile 141.2 on Washington Highway 20, 16 miles west of Rainy Pass.

Key points:
- 0.0 Canyon Creek Trailhead.
- 0.1 Bridge over Granite Creek. Trail turns southwest.
- 0.2 Junction with Chancellor Trail. Keep going straight ahead.
- 0.3 Old guard station and bridge over Canyon Creek. On the far bank, turn right at junction with Ruby Creek Trail.
- 0.9 Trail begins to climb the initial grade.
- 3.3 Junction with spur trail to Crater Lake (0.9 mile, moderate). Continue straight ahead.
- 3.5 Trail enters McMillan Park.
- 4.4 Trail leaves McMillan Park.
- 5.1 Pass at the head of Nickol Creek.
- 6.0 Trail enters Devils Park.
- 6.4 Devils Park Shelter.

7.3 Trail leaves Devils Park and resumes climbing.

8.7 Top of grade. Trail descends steeply.

10.8 Trail crests next spur ridge.

12.0 Trail crosses North Fork of Devils Creek and begins next grade.

13.1 Junction with abandoned trail to Anacortes Crossing. Bear left.

15.2 Devils Pass. Trails depart for Devils Dome and Deception Pass.

The hike: This long and demanding trail climbs from the banks of Canyon Creek into the alpine country of Devils Park, then makes a series of sharp climbs and descents as it follows the sawtooth peaks of Jackita Ridge northward to Devils Pass. When approached from the south, the long and tedious grade up to McMillan Park is a daunting proposition. Hikers who follow the trail southward from Devils Pass will be staring at the steepest grades along Jackita Ridge from an uphill perspective. There is no easy way to hike this trail. But the displays of alpine wildflowers are superb throughout the high country, and the inspiring mountain vistas more than compensate for the grueling climbs. Visitors who seek a challenging day hike will discover that the small tarn known locally as Crater Lake makes an ideal destination.

To begin the hike, follow the main trail over the bridge than spans Granite Creek, then turn westward to the old cabin that guards the mouth of Canyon Creek. This cabin was built by a prospector during the Ruby Creek gold rush, and was later dismantled and moved to this spot to serve as a Forest Service guard station. Beside the cabin is a footlog over Canyon Creek; cross it and turn right immediately on the far bank. You are now on the Jackita Ridge trail, which soon ascends from the lush bottomlands, gaining altitude steadily as it crosses timbered slopes above the creek. After crossing several brushy openings, the trail meets the Pasayten Wilderness boundary and begins a long series of upward switchbacks.

A sparse stand of Douglas-fir accompanies the trail on its upward journey. Gaps in the tree trunks reveal the rugged summit of Beebe Mountain far to the south, as well as McKay Ridge and the many tops of Majestic Mountain to the east. Unobstructed views of all of these summits can be had at an overlook just beyond the 3-mile mark. Soon after, the trail reaches a series of picturesque waterfalls that course downward through a rocky cleft. The trail zigzags upward beside the falls, then turns east and continues its ascent into the subalpine zone.

The trail soon reaches a second small stream, where a poorly marked spur trail climbs away to the northwest. This 0.9-mile track leads to a small tarn, referred to locally as Crater Lake, beneath the snowfields of Crater Mountain. Abandoned trails lead upward from both sides of the lake toward old fire lookout sites.

Meanwhile, the main trail continues eastward into the swampy meadows of McMillan Park. The park occupies a high, flat shelf on a shoulder of Crater Mountain, which can be seen from the south end of the meadows. Hummocky openings are covered in a low-growing mat of huckleberry and heather, and copses of spire-shaped spruce and fir grow from low hillocks. Camping here is a dubious proposition: The park abounds with stagnant

Jackita Ridge

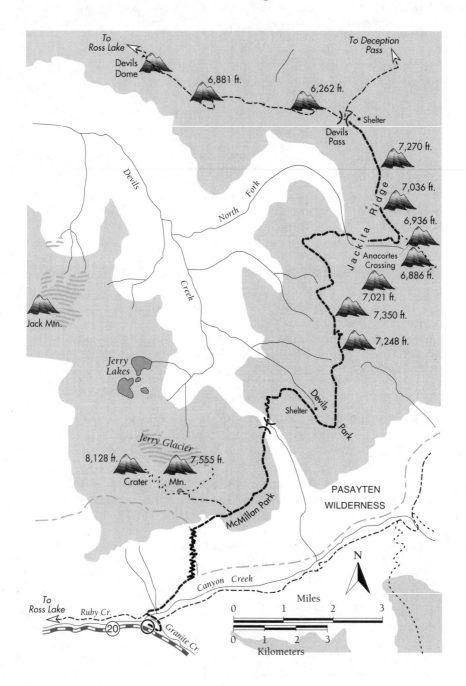

pools and sedge bogs that are a breeding ground for hordes of mosquitoes. The trail navigates across the shelf, then descends gradually through a brushy forest to reach the saddle at the head of the Nickol Creek drainage.

A vigorous climb leads up the brushy slopes toward Devils Park. Of particular interest along the way are white rhododendrons, which bloom in July, as well as huckleberries, which bear fruit in August. Some of the most spectacular views of Crater Mountain can be had from the top of the grade. The path then enters a subalpine forest and wends its way into Devils Park. This broad and flower-spangled grassland is punctuated by tidy clusters of subalpine fir. A shelter stands within the lower end of the park, and from it the trail follows small rills upward on an eastern heading.

Near the edge of this elevated terrace, the trail doglegs northwest and starts to climb across the meadowy shoulders of Jackita Ridge. Mountain views in all directions now feature the lofty summit of Jack Mountain to the west. The trail approaches a high shoulder of the ridge, then rounds it, bearing north across the alpine tundra. Scattered patches of krummholz can be seen throughout these high and windswept slopes. This dwarfed form of subalpine fir results when windblown snow abrades away the growing points at the tips of the branches that grow above the snowline, and this natural pruning creates a squat and bushy growth form.

The trail continues to ascend, reaching its highest elevation just below a sharp peak. Looking west, one can now see the lower of the Jerry Lakes cupped within a northern arm of Crater Mountain, and Jerry Glacier spread across the northeast face of the peak. The trail then zigzags down scree slopes into the basin beyond, following stringers of hardy subalpine larch to the floor of the bowl. After skirting a finger ridge, the path descends farther into a second basin. Following a steep descent, the trail climbs steadily to gain a sparsely wooded ridgetop.

It follows the ridge crest westward, then drops into a lush alpine cirque guarded by a rocky peak. After crossing the meadows of this final bowl, the trail enters the forest, then zigzags down at an exceedingly steep pace, following an avalanche path toward the North Fork of Devils Creek. After a rock-hop across the stream, hikers follow its north bank upward, sometimes climbing straight up the mountainside. Rising above the timberline, the trail reaches an unmarked junction with the abandoned Anacortes Crossing trail, which leads to the crest of Jackita Ridge. The main trail angles northward, climbing across open slopes where marmots and ground squirrels make their homes.

After gaining considerable elevation, the trail reaches the northern end of Jackita Ridge. Here, an overlook above the North Fork of Canyon Creek yields northward views of Shull Mountain. The trail then follows the open ridgeline down to Devils Pass, where the trek ends at a junction with the Devils Dome and Deception Pass trails.

50 Deception Pass

Overview:	A connecting trail that links Devils Pass with the Center Mountain and Cascade Crest routes, 8.2 miles overall.
Best season:	Mid-July to mid-October.
Difficulty:	Moderate west to east; moderately strenuous east to west.

Elevation gain:	2,405 feet (east to west).
Elevation loss:	1,445 feet (east to west).
Maximum elevation:	6,300 feet at Sky Pilot Pass.
Topo maps:	Shull Mountain, Pasayten Peak; *Pasayten Peak, Jack Mountain.*
Jurisdiction:	Pasayten Wilderness (Okanogan National Forest).

Finding the trail: The west end of the trail can be reached via an 11.2-mile jaunt on the Cascade Crest route (Hike 52), while the eastern end of the trail

Clearing storm along Deception Pass Trail.

joins the Jackita Ridge Trail (Hike 49) 15.2 miles from Washington Highway 20. The trail can also be accessed via Devils Dome (Hike 48) and Center Mountain (Hike 51).

Key points:
    0.0 Devils Pass. Junction with Jackita Ridge and Devils Dome trails.
    0.1 Spur trail descends 0.3 mile to Devils Pass Shelter. Bear left.
    1.4 Campsite in cirque above North Fork of Canyon Creek.
    3.7 Trail bottoms out at Deception Pass.
    5.4 Sky Pilot Pass. Junction with Center Mountain Trail. Continue straight ahead.
    6.2 Campsite in elevated basin.
    7.5 Canyon Creek crossing.
    8.2 Holman Pass and junction with Cascade Crest Trail.

The hike: This remote trail links Devils Pass with the Cascade Crest trail, enabling hikers to combine the Devils Dome or Jackita Ridge trails with other alpine ridge treks for a spectacular extended traverse across some of the most remote high country of the Pasayten Wilderness. The trail itself is pleasant but unspectacular, with mountain vistas at regular intervals. Camping spots can be found below Devils Pass or in the nameless basin 1.4 miles east of it.

From its beginning at Devils Pass, the Deception Pass trail runs northeast across open meadows dominated by phlox and other alpine wildflowers. The spur path to Devils Pass shelter soon drops away to the right, while the main trail maintains its altitude across the mountainside. There are fine views of the multiple summits of Jackita Ridge, which rises beyond a small valley that bears the North Fork of Canyon Creek. The scars of avalanches and rockslides extend from the far slopes down to the valley floor, where a small and inaccessible lake is nestled amid meadows and timber.

In time, the path begins a gradual ascent and soon works its way around to the floor of a rocky cirque. A nameless summit rises high above the bowl, and hoary marmots may be spotted among the boulders closer at hand. After passing good camping spots, the trail descends into a rather brushy subalpine forest, where in late summer an abundance of huckleberries compensates for the lack of views. The path flirts briefly with the ridgetop as it works its way down, then drops onto south-facing slopes to round the next mountainside. On its slopes, the forest is interrupted periodically by sunny meadows, populated by a vigorous growth of flowering plants.

The path soon begins a steady descent into the low and timbered saddle of Deception Pass, which divides Shull Creek from the North Fork of Canyon Creek. Here, hikers get limited views of Shull Mountain to the north. The trail now climbs onto the boggy slopes to the east, crossing several rivulets before breaking out into the open meadows below Sky Pilot Pass. As the trail climbs higher through the meadows, views open up to the west and south. The jagged peaks beyond Shull Creek are nameless, while to the southwest are the jumbled spires of Jackita Ridge. Between these two groups of nearby summits, the much taller miter of Jack Mountain can be seen through the low gap of Devils Pass.

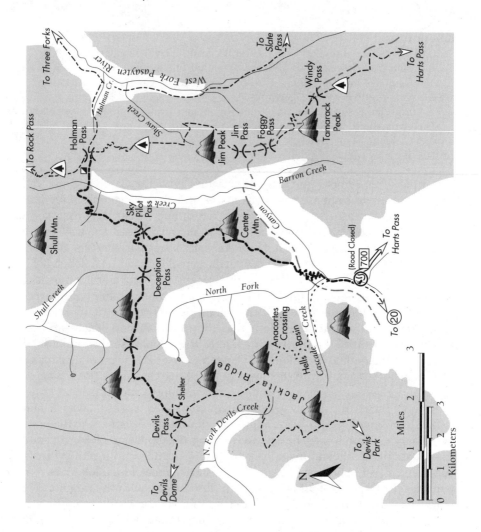

The trees close in as the trail climbs the final pitch to Sky Pilot Pass, and the pocket meadows of the pass itself offer no distant views. From atop the divide, the Center Mountain trail runs southward, while the main trail continues through the pass and turns north above the valley of Canyon Creek. Heather parklands give way to subalpine forest as the trail descends steadily, and openings in the forest face down the valley toward the mighty summit of Mount Ballard. Clumps of lupine light the way in midsummer; this member of the pea family has tiny hairs on its leaves that collect moisture from the clouds. A small stream beneath a northern spur of Shull Mountain offers fine camping spots in the high country.

As the trail begins its descent to the valley floor, openings reveal Holman Pass, with the barren summits of Gold and Buckskin ridges framed within the low gap. After many downward switchbacks, the path reaches a shallow ford of Canyon Creek, with a small trailside camping spot on the far bank. Beyond it the trail ascends gently through a flooded forest of old spruce, then makes the short climb to Holman Pass. Along the way is a small log shed that has been attributed to trappers Henry Bihart and Henry Kuykendall. Within the wooded flats of the pass, the trail links up with the Pacific Crest Trail (see Hike 52), and a connecting trail continues eastward to the West Fork of the Pasayten River.

51 Center Mountain

See Map on Page 194

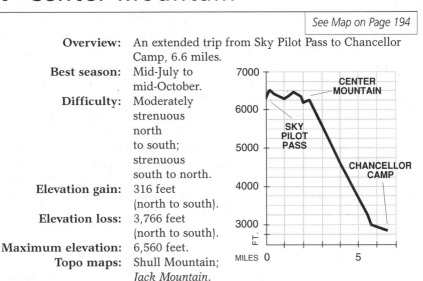

Overview:	An extended trip from Sky Pilot Pass to Chancellor Camp, 6.6 miles.
Best season:	Mid-July to mid-October.
Difficulty:	Moderately strenuous north to south; strenuous south to north.
Elevation gain:	316 feet (north to south).
Elevation loss:	3,766 feet (north to south).
Maximum elevation:	6,560 feet.
Topo maps:	Shull Mountain; *Jack Mountain.*
Jurisdiction:	Pasayten Wilderness (Okanogan National Forest)

Finding the trail: The north end of the trail is reached via a long trek on the Deception Pass Trail from the Jackita Ridge, Devils Dome, or Cascade Crest routes (see Hikes 48, 49, and 50). The south end of the trail can be reached via the Chancellor Trail (Hike 65, 8.3 miles) or by hiking 3.5 miles down the old Slate Creek Road (Forest Road 5400-700) from the washout. This road is reached via Harts Pass (see Cady Pass, p.252).

Key points:
- 0.0 Sky Pilot Pass.
- 1.6 Trail passes summit of Center Mountain.
- 5.6 Bottom of grade.
- 5.7 North Fork of Canyon Creek and junction with the old Anacortes Crossing trail. Turn left.
- 6.6 Bridge to Chancellor Camp. Junction with Chancellor Trail.

The hike: This remote trail links Sky Pilot Pass with the old Chancellor Camp at the confluence of Slate and Canyon creeks. Visitors cross spectacular meadows with panoramic views on the upper reaches of the trail, while the lower section features a long and tedious descent from the top of Center Mountain to the valley bottoms. It's a horse-killer from south to north; travelers are advised to approach the route from Sky Pilot Pass. The trail receives little maintenance, offering a few route-finding challenges and downed trees to negotiate. For this reason, it is an excellent place to avoid crowds.

From the junction at Sky Pilot Pass, the trail climbs southward along an open ridgeline. Look north for views of Shull Mountain; Joker Mountain appears far to the northwest while the grassy summits of Holman Peak guard the upper basin of Canyon Creek to the northeast. Before reaching the first summit on the ridgeline, the trail turns onto east-facing slopes and traverses the meadowy steeps. Watch for marmots among the boulders below the trail. On the far side of the summit, the path returns to the ridgeline. The gray tooth of Pasayten Peak now appears above an intervening ridgetop to the east, and the glacier-carved horns of Jackita Ridge rise to the west beyond the low divide of Deception Pass.

The trail now descends onto open meadows that crown the level surface of Center Mountain. Orderly groves of subalpine fir and spruce create a parklike setting here. The trail may disappear in places, overgrown with grasses and wildflowers. It sticks generally to the ridgeline, dipping slightly to cross a low saddle and then climbing a bit to crest the next high point. The summit of Center Mountain now mounds up directly ahead, while the regal crest of Jack Mountain can be seen above the lesser summits of Jackita Ridge. To the south is a broad panorama of peaks, dominated by Mount Ballard with the lower crest of Majestic Mountain rising beyond it.

Dipping into a low saddle, the path becomes quite faint as it traverses westward across the grassy slopes of Center Mountain, passing beneath a scattering of subalpine larch that finds good growing conditions on this cold exposure. After rounding the mountainside, the trail turns south again and traverses along gentle, meadowy slopes. Before reaching the ridgeline, it dips into the trees. The meadows decrease in size and frequency until the trail drops steadily across slopes timbered in a loose subalpine forest. Grouse whortleberry grows on the forest floor as the trail angles down the mountainside on a vaguely southerly course.

The path ultimately returns to the ridgeline for a near-vertical descent. Huckleberry bushes soon encroach into the pathway, but they thin out as subalpine firs give way to Douglas-firs of the montane forest. After a considerable drop in elevation, the trail reaches the first in a long series of switchbacks (reportedly there are sixty-four). The descent now eases to a more reasonable pace, and ultimately the forest canopy opens a bit to reveal glimpses of Cady Point and Jackita Ridge. The trail bottoms out in the deep shade of a cedar forest at the confluence of the main and north forks of Canyon Creek. Follow the North Fork to find a shallow ford or logjam crossing

Looking along Center Mountain toward Mount Ballard.

to the west bank. Here, an abandoned trail runs westward, climbing through Hells Basin to reach Anacortes Crossing.

The main trail continues south along the streambank, surmounting small rises and crossing a brushy clearing where thimbleberries may obscure the trail. Hikers must make a vigorous climb before the trail crosses the foot of a large talus slope to reach its end at a bridge that leads to Chancellor Camp. The Chancellor Trail continues southward along Canyon Creek for 8.3 miles to reach WA 20.

52 Cascade Crest–Pacific Crest Trail

Overview:	A day hike to Tamarack Peak (8.2 miles round trip) or a long backpack to Manning Provincial Park in Canada (37.2 miles overall).
Best season:	Late July to mid-October.
Difficulty:	Moderate.
Elevation gain:	4,564 feet (south to north).
Elevation loss:	7,104 feet (south to north).
Maximum elevation:	7,090 feet atop Devils Stairway.
Topo maps:	Slate Peak, Pasayten Peak, Shull Mountain, Castle Peak; Manning Park-CGS; *Washington Pass, Jack Mountain, Pasayten Peak.*
Jurisdiction:	Pasayten Wilderness (Okanogan National Forest), Manning Provincial Park.

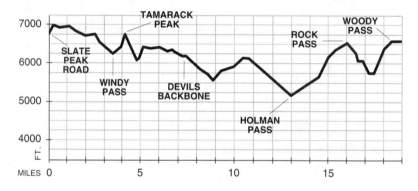

Finding the trailhead: Take Washington Highway 20 to the Mazama cutoff road, 11 miles west of Winthrop. After a mile, there is a T-intersection. Turn left, passing the Mazama General Store. This is the Harts Pass Road (Forest Road 5400), which is paved as far as the Lost River, about 5 miles. It then becomes gravel and is narrow and winding with many potholes as it makes the steep climb past Deadhorse Point to reach Harts Pass, 18.5 miles from Mazama. Turn right onto Forest Road 5400-600 and follow it 1.5 miles to the Pacific Crest Trail (PCT) Trailhead at the first switchback.

Key points:
- 0.0 Slate Peak PCT Trailhead.
- 3.5 Trail crosses through Windy Pass and enters Pasayten Wilderness.
- 4.1 Trail crosses high col behind Tamarack Peak.
- 5.0 Foggy Pass.
- 5.5 Jim Pass.
- 7.3 Devils Backbone. Bear left.
- 7.6 Trail crosses headwaters of Shaw Creek.
- 13.0 Holman Pass. Junction with Deception Pass and Holman Creek trails. Continue straight ahead.

16.2 Rock Pass.

18.0 Junction with Rock Creek Trail. Bear left.

18.5 Woody Pass.

21.3 Crest of Lakeview Ridge.

22.0 Devils Stairway.

23.2 Spur trail to Hopkins Lake. Bear left.

23.5 Hopkins Pass. Spur trail descends to camp. Continue straight ahead.

25.7 Junction with trail to Frosty Pass. Turn left.

25.9 Castle Pass. Junction with Three Fools Trail. Continue straight ahead.

29.7 Monument 78. Trail enters Manning Provincial Park.

30.3 Monument 78 Camp. Turn left at corral and cross Castle Creek.

33.4 PCT Camp.

33.6 Junction with Frosty Mountain Trail. Bear right.

34.2 Old Windy Joe Mountain Road. Turn left.

36.9 Junction with Similkameen River Trail. Stay on old road and cross Similkameen River.

37.2 PCT trailhead on British Columbia Highway 3.

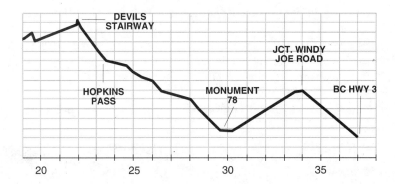

The hike: The northernmost section of the Pacific Crest Trail is one of the most awe-inspiring stretches of this storied route. It follows the ridgetops for almost the entire length between Harts Pass and the Canadian border. The Pasayten Wilderness presents a sea of barren peaks that stretch to the far horizons, and bordering the trail are brilliant constellations of meadow wildflowers. Water can be hard to find along the route, and well-worn camping spots are uncommon. Locate your campsite on grassy spots or atop snowbanks to ease your impact on the landscape.

Travelers who hike this trail into Canada must obtain special permission from Customs officials. Through-hikers tend to arrive at the north end of the PCT in mid-September, but solitude reigns during the summer months, at least in areas more than 5 miles from Slate Peak. Bring an ice axe if you plan to travel between Rock and Woody passes before mid-August.

The trek begins with a moderate climb through alpine meadows on the shoulder of Slate Peak. The summit of the peak is visible ahead, crowned with a fire lookout tower. During the Cold War, the top of the peak was razed and flattened to make space for a radar installation; when the new fire lookout was built on the site, it was built so that the floor of the cabin was at the altitude of the original summit. The trail levels off as it traverses northward across the steep and open slopes of the peak. Lupine and Indian paintbrush bloom in the moist meadows, while the drier slopes are home to phlox and cinquefoil. Panoramic westward views encompass the heart of the North Cascades. The dominant summit amid a crowd of peaks to the southwest is Mount Ballard. Due west, the two snowy peaks are Crater and Jack mountains. As the trail continues northward, the distant volcanic cone of Mount Baker appears between them, clad eternally in ice and snow.

The trail soon crosses the shallow, grassy basin that bears the headwaters of Benson Creek. It then makes its way over a meadowy shoulder of the mountain, unveiling views of the extensive mine workings in the Indiana Basin. During the late 1800s, miners worked their way upstream from placer gold deposits in Canyon Creek, seeking the mother lode. Alec Barron found the lode in this basin in 1891, igniting a boom of hard-rock mining in the area. Shafts were blasted into the heart of the mountain as miners followed the veins of quartz and gold. Enormous heaps of waste rock, called tailings, were piled beneath the portals of the shafts, and they can still be seen today.

The path descends to cross through Windy Pass, then traverses the east-facing slopes beyond it. There are now views of the barren ridge of crags beyond the West Fork of the Pasayten. The tallest of the crags is Pasayten Peak. The rocky summit that rises above the trail is Tamarack Peak, named for the abundance of tamarack, or subalpine larch, on its northern slopes. The path soon zigzags up to a high saddle behind a rocky spur of the peak,

Shull Mountain and meadows.

then begins the long descent to Foggy Pass. Looking northward beyond the grassy summit of Jim Peak, one can see the forbidding countenance of Shull Mountain. To the west, the sharp summits of Jackita Ridge rise beyond the meadowy domes of Center Mountain.

The trail ultimately slips through Foggy Pass onto the west-facing slopes beyond. Here, copses of subalpine fir rise among flower-strewn meadows. After rounding the next knob, Jim Pass leads the trail back into the West Fork Pasayten drainage. The trail passes beneath the vast grasslands on the south face of Jim Mountain, then enters an open woodland of fir and mountain hemlock. It emerges at the base of the Devils Backbone, a bare spine that extends northward into the valley, hemming in the Shaw Creek watershed. A faint path follows the meadowy crest of the Backbone, while the main path zigzags down to cross the many rills that join to form Shaw Creek. Bouldery meadows offer habitat to marmots. Later, avalanche chutes allow growing space for white rhododendrons.

The trail soon enters a full-blown subalpine forest, and the views disappear as the path climbs steadily across the mountainside. At the north end of the ridge, openings in the trees reveal a rank of spectacular summits rising to the north: Shull Mountain, Powder Mountain, and Three Fools Peak. The path then embarks upon a long and tedious descent into Holman Pass. These moist, north-facing slopes are protected from forest fires, creating conditions that favor Engelmann spruce as the dominant tree. At the bottom of the grade is a well marked junction in the deeply wooded pass. To the right, a connector trail descends to the West Fork of the Pasayten; to the left the Deception Pass Trail runs westward toward Devils Dome; and straight ahead lies the Cascade Crest trail. The heavily timbered flats of Holman Pass are well suited to camping, but water is hard to find.

The trail now jogs northwest, climbing across an open and rocky slope with southward views and a chance to spot diminutive pika among the rocks. The path then climbs moderately along the timbered slopes above the headwaters of Canyon Creek. Upon reaching the stream that drains the Goat Lakes, the trees take on the spire-shaped subalpine growth form and small openings reveal views of Shull Mountain. Higher in the drainage, the trees thin out into isolated groves, and broad expanses of meadow offer unrestricted views of the surrounding grandeur. The trail makes its way into the rolling meadows atop a high plateau, and Mount Ballard comes into view to the south. Ground squirrels and marmots are abundant here. Camp in the bare spots amid the trees at the edge of the meadows, not on the fragile alpine tundra.

From here, the trail arcs around the head of the drainage, climbing briskly at first then leveling off for the approach to Rock Pass. This spectacular divide sits at the base of Powder Mountain, offering superb views both north and south. The rocky summit of Holman Peak can now be seen to the east, while to the north are Three Fools Peak and Woody Pass. The trail makes a brief descent, then turns north across steep talus slopes below the craggy face of Powder Mountain. Snowfields may persist in this area well into August,

Cascade Crest

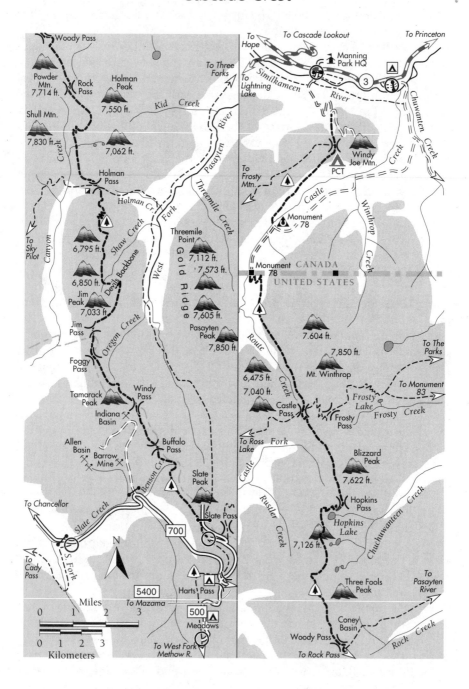

and ice axes will be needed until the trail is snow-free here. After traversing the head of the Rock Creek basin, the trail zigzags up to a junction with the Rock Creek trail. A short detour leads to the Coney Basin, nestled at the foot of Three Fools Peak.

The main trail continues to climb through a larch-heather parkland, passing a small campsite on its way to Woody Pass. This high saddle is choked with broken rock and completely bereft of trees. A sparse growth of larches soon gives way to steep meadows as the trail continues north, revealing the first westward vistas in many miles. Due west is the northern end of the Picket Range, adorned with many glaciers. Farther north, the lofty points that crowd the horizon belong to the Mox Peaks, Mount Spickard, and Custer Ridge. As the trail progresses northward, the great prow of Jack Mountain appears to the southwest. Straight ahead are the bare crags that line the international border: Hozomeen Mountain, Joker Mountain, Freezeout Mountain, Castle Peak, and Frosty Mountain.

The trail ultimately winds around a spur ridge and traverses above a grassy basin to reach the crest of the divide atop Lakeview Ridge. Here, swards of alpine tundra and copses of dwarf fir provide ever-expanding vistas, now encompassing the jagged teeth of the Mount Terror massif in the southern Pickets as well as the glacier-bound summit of Mount Baker, rising beyond the northern end of the range. A backward glance reveals the towering horn of Three Fools Peak, with Soda Peak and Smoky Mountain rising east of it. The path surmounts a grassy summit for the finest scenery on this stretch of the trail, with excellent views of the 1996 Elbow Basin burn in the Castle Fork drainage to the west.

The trail now drops along the Devils Stairway onto a level ridgetop. Mount Winthrop is the cliff-bound tricorn that rises beyond Blizzard Peak to the north, while Hopkins Lake occupies the basin below. The trail swings eastward, following the dwindling ridge toward the foot of the lake. Here, spur paths descend to the water's edge. Though lacking in fish and harboring an overabundance of mosquitoes, the lake is a popular spot to pitch a tent. The main trail swings north to Hopkins Pass, where an abandoned trail descends to fine camping spots beside springs and wet meadows. Continuing north, the PCT glides downward across the lower slopes of Blizzard Peak. Early on, openings reveal Castle Peak and Frosty Mountain, and Freezeout Mountain can be seen a little farther along. The slopes to the north of the Castle Fork bear the scars of the Elbow Basin fire, and this is the closest that the trail will get to the burned-over area.

The trees soon close in, blocking mountain views as the path descends to a confusing junction above Castle Pass. Straight ahead, the well-worn path marked "Pasayten River 16" leads eastward over Frosty Pass. The PCT doglegs sharply to the southwest, descending along the floor of a gulch before returning to a northward course that carries it into Castle Pass. Here, the Three Fools trail arrives from the west, while the main trail descends into the headwaters of Route Creek.

Grassy parks at the head of the drainage reveal little more than the neighboring summits, a collection of rocky but nondescript peaks. But as the valley empties out into the Castle Creek drainage, gaps in the timber reveal home-stretch views of Castle Peak. The path descends gently to reach the cleared swath that marks the border with Canada, and a series of switchbacks leads down to Monument 78, a boundary marker. The trail now enters Manning Provincial Park.

Follow the bulldozer track for a short distance to reach a horse corral. Turn left onto a footpath that runs past a campsite then crosses Castle Creek. A long but gentle incline leads to the saddle behind Windy Joe Mountain, with a campsite just below the pass. Bear northwest to reach the old fire road that leads to Windy Joe Peak. Nostalgic hikers might want to hike up the road to the summit of the mountain for one last view of the surrounding peaks. Outbound travelers will follow the road down through the timber, then cross the Similkameen River to reach a trailhead on BC Highway 3.

53 Three Fools Trail

Overview:	An extended trip from Lightning Creek to Castle Pass, 17.6 miles overall.
Best season:	Late July to mid-October.
Difficulty:	Strenuous.
Elevation gain:	7,161 feet (west to east).
Elevation loss:	4,101 feet (west to east).
Maximum elevation:	6,635 feet.
Topo maps:	Skagit Peak, Castle Peak; *Jack Mountain*.
Jurisdiction:	Pasayten Wilderness (Okanogan National Forest).

Finding the trail: The western end of the trail is reached via a 10.3-mile

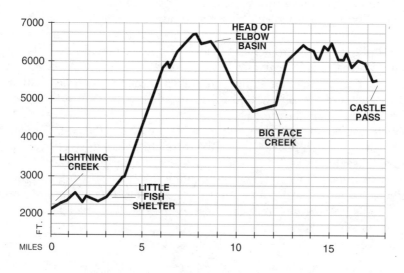

trek from Hozomeen on the Lightning Creek Trail. The east end is easiest to reach via a 10.8-mile trek from Manning Provincial Park in Canada on the Pacific Crest Trail (PCT).

Key points:
   0.0 Junction with Lightning Creek Trail near Deer Lick Cabin.
   0.8 Trail leaves Ross Lake NRA and enters Pasayten Wilderness.
   3.1 Little Fish Shelter. Trail starts climbing.
   5.7 Top of switchbacks.
   6.4 Pass behind Skagit Peak.
   7.1 Trail reaches ridge above Freezeout Lake.
   8.2 Seasonal spring.
   9.0 Trail crosses divide to enter Big Face watershed.
   11.9 Big Face Creek crossing.
   12.0 Big Face Camp. Trail starts climbing.
   13.5 Trail reaches top of ridge.
   16.1 Pass above Queen Creek.
   17.6 Castle Pass. Junction with Cascade Crest segment of PCT.

The hike: This primitive trail links Ross Lake with the spectacular high country of the Cascade Crest. It lies almost entirely within the Pasayten Wilderness, and is sought out only by a few travelers who seek solitude on a long and challenging trek. Expect blow-downs in the timbered low country, and route-finding challenges as the trail crosses overgrown alpine meadows. The Elbow Basin Fire of 1996 burned 3,687 acres of timber in the Castle Fork of the Three Fools drainage, but it burned across only about 10 percent of this route.

According to local legend, Three Fools Creek and the peak of the same name were named in honor of three prospectors who were convinced by claim jumpers to abandon their claim along Ruby Creek to pursue rumors of a new strike on the streams along the Canadian border. Their ill-fated venture is reflected in the names of local landmarks: Blizzard Peak, Freezeout Creek, and Nightmare Camp.

The trek departs from the Lightning Creek Trail just north of Deer Lick Cabin and climbs gently as it makes its way around the base of Skagit Peak to enter the Three Fools Creek valley. The forest here is regenerating after a massive wildfire that leveled it in 1926. The trail then glides down to reach the banks of Three Fools Creek, a roaring torrent that churns down a wide and rocky channel between heavily forested banks. A few stark cliffs rise above the path, and from time to time there are openings in the trees where dense brush clogs the trail. After 3.1 miles, a spur path runs to Little Fish Shelter, which occupies a gloomy streamside clearing.

The main trail swings uphill, beginning its ascent of Skagit Peak. Upon reaching the mouth of the Elbow Creek valley, it begins to zigzag upward through a sparse woodland of Douglas-fir. There are plenty of openings on the way up, with southward views up Grizzly Creek. The trail climbs doggedly up the ridgeline, finally breaking out of the forest high above Elbow

Skagit Peak from the Three Fools Trail.

Creek. At the top of the switchbacks are views of Spratt Mountain and the other rugged peaks that line the Three Fools watershed. The path now turns north, climbing steadily above the edge of an old burn to reach the low saddle behind Skagit Peak. The saddle reveals vistas of Skagit Peak's rugged north face, and the stark crag to the north is Hozomeen Mountain.

The path swings onto south-facing slopes to bypass the next high summit, then ascends into a narrow col above Freezeout Lake. The barren summit that rises to the northeast is Freezeout Mountain. A healthy climb leads to the ridgetop above the lake. This is the highest point on the trail, with views to match. To the south, Nohokomeen Glacier is now visible on the north face of Jack Mountain; beyond it lie the heavily glaciated summits of the Colonial Peak massif. Looking westward, the sawtooth spires of the Picket Range rise beyond Mount Prophet, and farther north are the cloud-scraping summits of the Mox Peaks, Mount Redoubt, and Mount Spickard.

The trail soon drops onto southern slopes once more, making for a meadowy saddle where a small spring affords a rare opportunity to take on water. The path then crosses the vast alpine meadows above the Elbow Basin, traversing the slopes to reach a low pass at its head. Eastward views now encompass the summits of the Cascade crest. From south to north, the major summits are Shull Mountain, Powder Mountain, Three Fools Peak, Blizzard Peak, and Mount Winthrop. The first good look at timber that burned during the Elbow Basin Fire can be had at this point.

The path then drops into the steep and nameless drainage to the east for the long descent to Big Face Creek. After a short distance, a forgotten trail runs north to a lookout site above Welcome Basin. The main trail continues

Three Fools Trail

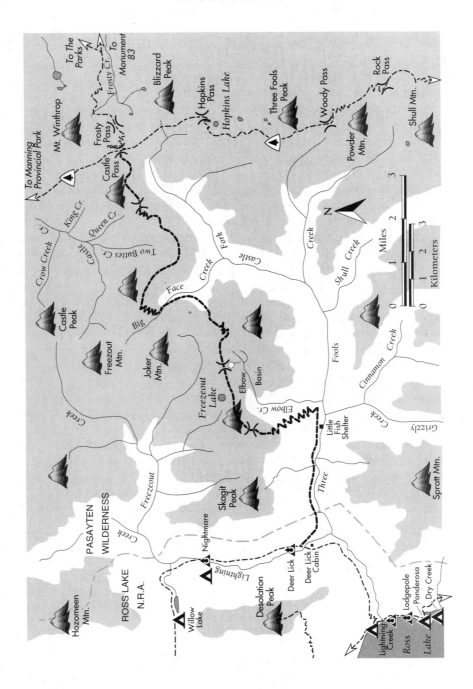

down, and the anemones of the upper slopes give way to clumps of brush farther down. The trail ultimately drops into heavy timber before entering the Big Face valley. Big Face Creek occupies a spectacular basin, bounded to the east by vast, grassy slopes and to the west by the sharply inclined sedimentary layers of Joker and Freezeout mountains. The trail traverses the western wall of the valley to reach a shallow ford of the creek in the midst of an open meadow. There is a good camping spot in grove of old spruce and fir at the meadow's north edge.

The trail passes this camp and follows the creek upward, becoming faint and overgrown with salmonberry in places. Upon drawing even with Joker Mountain, the path embarks on a hearty climb, zigzagging straight up the steep slopes to the east. The brush gives way to grassy swaths interfingered with stands of subalpine fir. At the top of the grade, the trail swings south for a long traverse across flowery grasslands. Ahead, the distant peaks of Ragged Ridge are mantled in glaciers, and can be seen between Crater Mountain and the northern horn of Jackita Ridge.

Upon gaining the ridgetop, the trail follows the crest of the divide, where once again there is evidence of the Elbow Basin Fire. After an initial descent the path surmounts two bald knolls that command spectacular views in all directions. Rugged peaks line the eastern horizon, the lone summits of Mount Ballard and Jack Mountain rise to the south, and the Picket Range crowds the far horizon to the west. As the trail makes its way down to the saddle at the head of Castle Creek, views of Freezeout Mountain, Castle Peak, and Frosty Mountain open up to the north.

The trail then swings across burned-over slopes that face southward, and the grassy glades between the snags yield the trail's finest views of the Cascade crest. After descending around a grassy bowl, the path drops into a low col above Queen Creek. Look back as the trail climbs away from this saddle, since a striking frieze of Freezeout Mountain and Castle Peak is presented here. The trail soon begins to descend, and before long it leaves the Elbow Basin burn for good. A loose subalpine forest yields farewell views of Jack Mountain and the peaks above the Castle Fork as the trail descends to meet the PCT at a poorly marked junction in Castle Pass.

54 Buckskin Ridge

Overview:	A long day hike or short backpack to Silver Lake, 12 miles round trip, or a longer backpack to the Middle Fork of the Pasayten River, 18.3 miles.
Best season:	Mid-July to mid-October.
Difficulty:	Moderate to Silver Lake; moderately strenuous beyond.
Elevation gain:	3,950 feet.
Elevation loss:	6,290 feet.
Maximum elevation:	7,300 feet.
Topo maps:	Slate Peak, Pasayten Peak (trail not shown); *Pasayten Peak, Washington Pass.*
Jurisdiction:	Pasayten Wilderness (Okanogan National Forest).

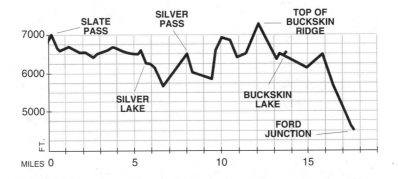

Finding the trailhead: From Washington Highway 20, follow the Harts Pass Road (see Hike 52) to Harts Pass. Turn right onto Forest Road 5400-600 and follow it 1.8 miles to the Slate Pass trailhead, at the second switchback.

Key points:
- 0.0 Slate Pass Trailhead.
- 0.1 Slate Pass.
- 0.6 Junction with Robinson Pass cutoff trail. Bear left.
- 0.8 Junction with Middle Fork Pasayten cutoff trail. Stay left.
- 5.9 Silver Lake junction. Turn right for Buckskin Ridge.
- 7.0 Trail makes two crossings of Silver Creek.
- 8.4 Silver Pass.
- 8.8 Floor of Threemile Creek valley.
- 9.9 Trail begins ascent of Buckskin Ridge.
- 12.7 Pass atop Buckskin Ridge. Trail descends into Point Creek basin.
- 13.2 Floor of Point Creek basin.
- 14.7 Buckskin Lake junction. Turn left for lake, or right to continue.
- 16.4 Trail begins final descent.
- 18.3 Junction above ford on the Middle Fork of the Pasayten. Turn right for the ford or left for Three Forks junction (1.2 miles, easy).

The hike: This trail follows a long series of ridges through subalpine parks and forests to penetrate deep into the Pasayten Wilderness. Hikers starting at Slate Pass commonly range as far north as Silver Lake, while a few horse parties venture up to Buckskin Lake from the north. The country between the two lakes receives few visitors, and some route-finding ability is needed to follow this portion of the trail. There are fine views all along the trail, but the best vistas are from the crest of Buckskin Ridge at mile 12.7. The fishing at Buckskin Lake is well worth the long trek.

From the Slate Peak road, follow the trail over Slate Pass and then down into a small alpine cirque. A faint track runs eastward from the foot of the basin toward Robinson Creek, while the main trail continues northward across flowery meadows and through copses of subalpine larch. Pleasant rills course down through the glacier lilies, and mountain views encompass the sawtooth ridge that rises above the Middle Fork of the Pasayten River. A connecting trail soon drops away toward the valley floor, while the Buckskin Ridge route continues its traverse across the slopes of Haystack Mountain.

Wooded ridges alternate with meadowy bowls, and mule deer and ground squirrels commonly are sighted as the trail makes its way northward. As the trail nears the end the ridge, grouse whortleberry becomes the dominant ground cover. This tiny relative of the huckleberry grows well in the wake of forest fires, and its tiny and delicious fruits are much prized by birds and small mammals. As the path makes a sharp ascent to surmount a finger ridge, look southward for views of distant Silver Star Mountain.

The path then drops steadily into a wooded basin, and a spur path soon runs south to the shores of Silver Lake. This pretty cirque lake is nestled at

Osceola Peak reflected in a shallow tarn.

the base of a small but rugged peak. The main trail follows the lake's outlet stream downward through pocket meadows bordered by stands of subalpine fir. After a zigzagging descent, the path makes tricky rock-hops across the two branches of Silver Creek, then turns uphill for the moderate ascent to Silver Pass. From the top of this wooded divide, the trail makes a short but steep drop to the head of Threemile Creek.

Here, avalanche paths reveal fine views of Pasayten Peak and the other rugged summits of Gold Ridge. The trail skirts the eastern edge of the basin, then climbs straight up the mountainside in the midst of an avalanche track. After a calf-burning climb, switchbacks finally intercede to give the trail a manageable gradient. The trail then turns north into the trees, now zigzagging up through a loose stand of gnarled whitebark pine. The limbs of whitebark pines are filled with resin, which gives them the flexibility to withstand the heavy winds that often occur near timberline.

At an unmarked junction, ignore the path that continues upward in favor of the fainter track that traverses northward across the slopes. Steep meadows yield views that encompass the distant summit of Mount Baker as well as the closer peaks of the Cascade crest. The track descends along an arid ridgeline to reach the foot of a blind basin, where the drainage is walled off by an old glacial moraine. On the far side of the basin, the path climbs the ridgeline through a loose growth of subalpine larch and fir to reach a high, windswept saddle atop Buckskin Ridge. In addition to sweeping westward views, the saddle reveals Osceola Peak directly across the valley to the east, with Monument Peak rising farther south above an intervening ridge.

The trail then zigzags down into the headwaters of Point Creek, with its loose stands of larches and its shallow snowmelt tarns. The trail descends to the lowermost tarn, then turns north onto a rocky slope. The boulders soon give way to grassy meadows, and the trail wanders across the slopes to enter the next declivity. This vale bears two drainages, and a spur path climbs into the far drainage to reach the shores of Buckskin Lake. This long, narrow body of water is guarded by sloping walls that rise to the heights of Buckskin Point above the head of the lake. Cutthroat trout are numerous and husky here, and provide lively angling at times.

Meanwhile, the main trail continues to sidehill across the mountainside, descending gradually below the foot of the lake as it crosses burned-over slopes. It soon enters a final drainage filled with aprons of loose rock and is guarded by a small but rocky promontory; watch for pikas and mountain goats here. After crossing the small stream that occupies the vale, the trail climbs a bit and then traverses across open, east-facing slopes. There are fine parting views of Monument and Osceola peaks until the trail disappears into the trees on its way to the descending ridgeline.

A long but moderate descent leads downward through the trees, following the crest of the ridge. The trail reaches its end at a junction beside the Middle Fork of the Pasayten River. The trail to the right drops down to a deep ford of the river then connects with the Robinson Pass Trail. To the left, a level trail runs northward for a short distance to reach the Three Forks area, with many trail junctions and bridges spanning the forks of the Pasayten.

Buckskin Ridge

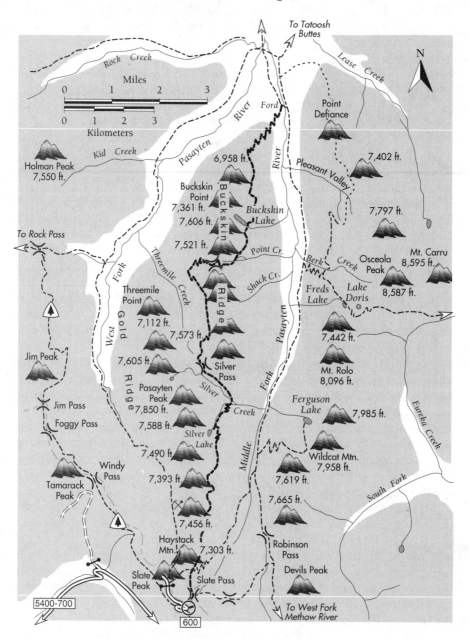

To Tatoosh Buttes

Rock Creek

Lease Creek

Miles

Pasayten River

Ford

Point Defiance

Kid Creek

6,958 ft.

River

7,402 ft.

Holman Peak
7,550 ft.

Buckskin Point
7,361 ft.

Buckskin Ridge

Buckskin Lake

Pleasant Valley

7,797 ft.

7,606 ft.

To Rock Pass

7,521 ft.

Point Cr.

Berk Creek

Osceola Peak

Mt. Carru
8,595 ft.

West Gold Ridge

Threemile Creek

Shack Cr.

Freds Lake

Lake Doris

8,587 ft.

Threemile Point
7,112 ft.

7,573 ft.

7,442 ft.

Jim Peak

7,605 ft.

Silver Pass

Pasayten Fork

Mt. Rolo
8,096 ft.

Jim Pass

Pasayten Peak
7,850 ft.

Silver Creek

Ferguson Lake

7,985 ft.

Eureka Creek

Foggy Pass

7,588 ft.

Silver Lake

Wildcat Mtn.
7,958 ft.

7,490 ft.

Windy Pass

7,393 ft.

Middle

7,619 ft.

South Fork

Tamarack Peak

7,665 ft.

7,456 ft.

Haystack Mtn.

7,303 ft.

Robinson Pass

Slate Peak

Slate Pass

Devils Peak

5400-700

To West Fork
Methow River

600

55 Ferguson Lake

Overview: A backpack to Ferguson Lake, 10.8 miles one way.

Best season: Mid-July to mid-October.

Difficulty: Moderately strenuous.

Elevation gain: 2,420 feet.

Elevation loss: 2,640 feet.

Maximum elevation: 6,990 feet at Slate Pass.

Topo maps: Slate Peak, Pasayten Peak, Mount Lago (trail not shown); *Pasayten Peak, Washington Pass.*

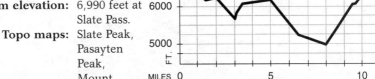

Jurisdiction: Pasayten Wilderness (Okanogan National Forest).

Finding the trailhead: The hike begins at the Slate Pass trailhead (see Hikes 52, 54).

Key points:
- 0.0 Slate Pass Trailhead.
- 0.1 Slate Pass.
- 0.6 Unmarked junction with faint trail to Robinson Creek. Turn right.
- 1.4 Nameless pass into Robinson Creek drainage.
- 3.0 Robinson Creek crossing.
- 3.2 Junction with Robinson Pass Trail. Turn left.
- 5.1 Robinson Pass. Trail descends toward the Middle Fork of the Pasayten River.
- 6.7 Junction with cutoff from Buckskin Ridge. Continue straight ahead.
- 8.0 Junction with Ferguson Lake Trail. Turn right.
- 9.7 Trail crosses nameless stream at junction with old Eureka Creek Trail.
- 10.8 Ferguson Lake.

The hike: This trek is beyond the range of day hikers, but makes a nice backpack into the Pasayten Wilderness for visitors who are interested in fishing and mountain scenery. The most direct path to the lake is via the trail that descends directly from Slate Pass to the Middle Fork of the Pasayten River, but the preferred route skirts eastward to take in Robinson Pass, vastly increasing the scenic value of the trip with less than a mile of additional hiking.

From the Slate Pass trailhead, follow the Buckskin Ridge Trail (Hike 54) for the brief climb over the ridgetop. The trail then descends into a meadowy bowl lined with talus slopes. Marmots are abundant here, and there are eastward views of Devils Peak and Robinson Mountain. At the bottom of the bowl, the trail skirts a copse of larches and a faint track runs eastward toward a nameless saddle. Turn right onto this trail, angling downhill across boulderfields, meadows, and timbered slopes to reach the broad, waterlogged lawns of the pass. Follow the cairns across the verdant swards of wildflowers to reach the far end of the gap,

Isolated valley near Ferguson Lake.

Ferguson Lake

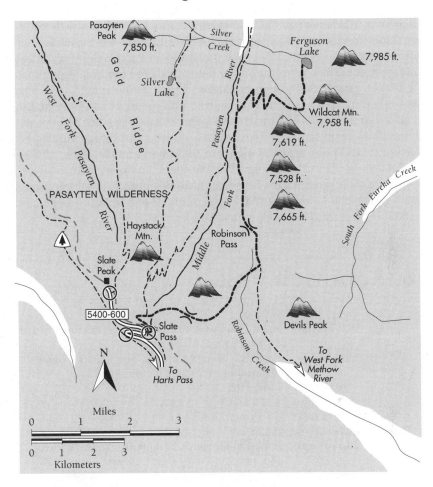

where the path angles northeast onto stony slopes.

The trail now descends across the sparsely timbered slopes of a nameless summit; some route-finding skills are helpful here since the trail is a bit faint in places. The loose woodland is interrupted frequently by shelves of bedrock, and there are fine views down the Robinson Creek valley, with Devils Peak presiding above its north side. After a rather gentle descent, hikers make a shallow ford of Robinson Creek, after which the trail climbs to join the Robinson Pass Trail.

Turn left as this well-beaten track climbs out of the old-growth subalpine firs and into a broad series of rolling alpine meadows. The path climbs moderately to reach the boggy flats of Robinson Pass, then descends on a northward tangent toward the Middle Fork of the Pasayten. During the descent, stands of fir alternate with lush avalanche slopes that offer westward views of Gold Ridge and Haystack Mountain. At the bottom of the grade, the cutoff trail from Slate Pass joins the main trail, which runs northward through a bottomland meadow and then treks 0.8 mile through the spruces to reach a junction with the spur trail to Ferguson Lake.

The old, mule-killer trail to the lake has been rebuilt recently, and now a series of long switchbacks carries the trail upward across a broad snowslide path. The open slopes provide unobstructed views of Pasayten Peak and the lesser summits that line the ridge to the south of it. The trail gains most of its altitude on this sunny, west-facing slope, then turns the corner onto a timbered northern exposure.

The path traverses through subalpine forest to the mouth of a narrow, open valley that is guarded by a soaring edifice of stone. The old Eureka Creek trail once departed from this spot, but it has long since disappeared. A shallow ford leads across the stream that issues from this picturesque vale, after which the path heads straight up the mountainside. After a brief but breath-stealing climb, the trail levels off to round an open ridge and drop into the floor of the cirque where Ferguson Lake lies beside grassy meadows. Its waters reflect the summit of Wildcat Mountain, and a strong population of rainbow trout offers fine angling possibilities.

56 Robinson Pass

Overview:	A long backpack from the Harts Pass Road to Three Forks, 25.6 miles one way.
Best season:	Early July to mid-October. The Beauty Creek waterfall is accessible by mid-May.
Difficulty:	Moderate.
Elevation gain:	4,130 feet.
Elevation loss:	2,450 feet.
Maximum elevation:	6,220 feet.
Topo maps:	Robinson Mountain, Slate Peak, Tatoosh Buttes, Mount Lago, Frosty Creek, Pasayten Peak; *Pasayten Peak, Washington Pass*.
Jurisdiction:	Pasayten Wilderness (Okanogan National Forest).

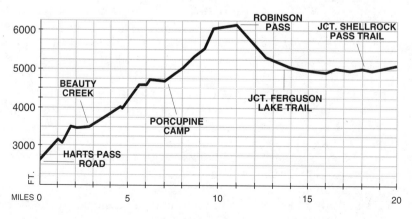

Devils Peak from Robinson Pass.

Finding the trailhead: Take Washington Highway 20 to the Mazama cutoff road, 11 miles west of Winthrop. After a mile, there is a T-intersection. Turn left, passing the Mazama general store. This is the Harts Pass Road (Forest Road 5400), which is paved as far as the Lost River, about 5 miles. The Robinson Pass trailhead is on a short spur road at mile 7.

Key points:

- 0.0   Robinson Creek Trailhead.
- 1.0   Trail enters Pasayten Wilderness.
- 1.2   Trail crosses Robinson Creek and follows north bank.
- 2.9   Trail crosses Beauty Creek below a large waterfall.
- 4.5   Trail crosses Robinson Creek and follows south bank.
- 5.1   Amey Creek.
- 6.1   Midnight Creek.
- 6.8   Trail fords Robinson Creek and follows north bank.
- 7.1   Porcupine Camp.
- 9.1   Junction with cutoff trail from Slate Pass. Continue straight ahead.
- 11.0   Robinson Pass.
- 12.6   Junction with cutoff trail from Buckskin Ridge. Continue straight.
- 13.7   Junction with Ferguson Lake Trail. Bear left.
- 18.0   Junction with Shellrock Pass Trail. Continue straight ahead.

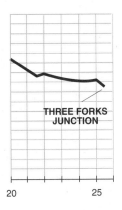

THREE FORKS JUNCTION

20   25

217

18.1 Trail crosses Berk Creek.
20.8 Trail crosses stream that drains Pleasant Valley.
22.4 Junction with ford trail that leads to Buckskin Ridge. Stay right.
23.5 Junction with abandoned Point Defiance Trail. Bear left.
25.1 Junction with Tatoosh Buttes Trail. Bear left.
25.6 Bridge at Three Forks junction.

The hike: This long trail links the West Fork of the Methow River with the forks of the Pasayten River. Most of the route is a long valley-bottom slog through the timber, but alpine meadows atop Robinson Pass and periodic avalanche slopes along the Middle Fork of the Pasayten yield fine mountain views. The roaring waterfall on Beauty Creek makes an excellent day-hike destination, and is open in early summer when the high country is still locked in snow. The entire length of Robinson Creek can be hiked in a long day by starting at Slate Pass and following the initial stretch of the Ferguson Lake route to connect with the Robinson Pass Trail, then hiking down the valley to the Robinson Creek Trailhead. (A car shuttle is required.)

The trek begins at the mouth of Robinson Creek as the trail runs north through a bottomland forest of Douglas-fir and ponderosa pine that is typical of the dry side of the Cascades. After a short distance, the path climbs heartily up the mountainside to attain a altitude that is several hundred feet above the valley floor. A split waterfall is visible from the brushy slopes, and across the valley are the cliff bands of Scramble Point. The trail ultimately levels off, and the valley floor rises to meet it. The path crosses the Pasayten Wilderness boundary in a floodplain stand of cottonwood, Douglas-fir, and cedar.

A bridge soon spans the rushing waters of Robinson Creek, offering the first views of Last Chance Point with its broad apron of talus and castellated crown of surreal spires and cockscombs. The trail crosses brushfields dominated by aromatic ceanothus bush, then reaches a stout bridge over Beauty Creek. A spectacular waterfall tumbles down the cliffs here, and a short distance beyond it an unmarked spur runs to the edge of a picturesque gorge chiseled into the stone by Robinson Creek.

The trail now continues upward through brushfields to reach a second bridge over Robinson Creek. On its way to Amey Creek, the path crosses avalanche scars that reveal the first views of Robinson Mountain. Watch for signs of massive rockfalls that have tumbled down from the sheer cliffs above the trail. Beyond Midnight Creek, the Douglas-firs give way to Engelmann spruce, which attain old-growth proportions in the fertile soils of the bottomlands. An ankle-deep ford leads across Robinson Creek, and beyond it are campsites beside grassy avalanche scars. As the trail continues up the creek, outbreaks of spruce budworm have opened up the forest, allowing views of the small peaks that rise across the valley.

A stand of old-growth subalpine fir surrounds the junction with a cutoff trail to Slate Pass. The main trail climbs gently onto vast and rolling slopes robed in verdant subalpine meadows. The stark cliffs of Devils Peak preside over endless swards of wildflowers as the trail makes its way to Robinson Pass. The pass itself is quite boggy, and scattered conifers are interspersed with wet

Robinson Pass

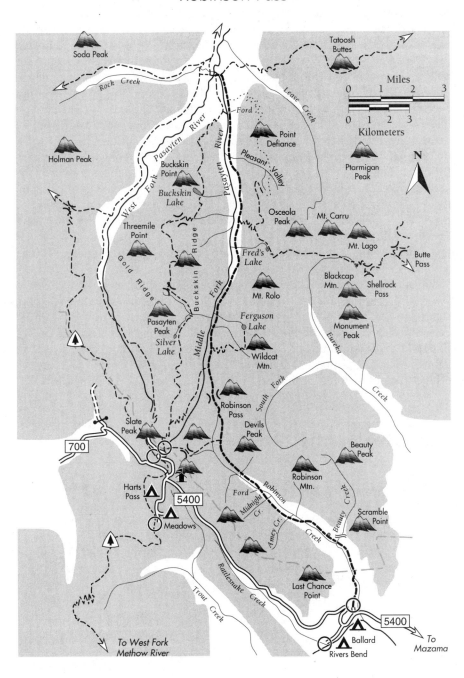

meadows. Views from the pass encompass the valley of the Pasayten's Middle Fork, with Slate Peak and Haystack Mountain rising above its headwaters.

A steady descent leads northward across the wall of the valley, and the trail bottoms out in a grassy meadow on the valley floor. Here, a cutoff trail runs southwest toward Slate Pass, and at the far edge of the clearing a well-beaten path leads to a riverside campsite. The trail then enters a scruffy forest of spruce, emerging 0.8 mile later at a junction with the Ferguson Lake Trail. Across the valley, timbered slopes rise to the rocky cockade of Pasayten Peak. Beyond this point, the forest becomes quite boggy, and gaps in the canopy admit shafts of sunlight into the understory. The path ultimately seeks the banks of the Middle Fork, and a number of campsites are sheltered beneath the streamside firs and spruces.

The path then swings away from the river, crossing a grassy slope beneath the rugged cliffs of Mount Rolo. The trees soon close in, masking views for several miles. Just before reaching Berk Creek, the spruces are replaced by lodgepole pines that grew in the wake of a massive wildfire that burned here. The Shellrock Pass Trail climbs away along the south side of Berk Creek, while the main trail continues its gradual descent along the edge of the valley. Along the way, avalanche paths reveal views of Buckskin Ridge, and groves of aspen grow in these sunny openings.

Beyond the stream that issues from Pleasant Valley, the mountains dwindle away into rounded foothills, and dense doghair stands of lodgepole pine shade the trail. A connecting trail departs from mile 22.4 to ford the Middle Fork and link up with the north end of the Buckskin Ridge Trail (Hike 54). The main path continues its forest trek, passing junctions with the defunct Point Defiance Trail and the Tatoosh Buttes trail just before reaching the bridge that spans the Middle Fork to reach the Three Forks junction.

57 Shellrock Pass

Overview:	An extended trip from the Middle Fork of the Pasayten to Shellrock Pass, 7.3 miles overall.
Best season:	Mid-July to mid-October.
Difficulty:	Moderately strenuous.
Elevation gain:	3,905 feet (west to east).
Elevation loss:	1,375 feet (west to east).
Maximum elevation:	7,500 feet.
Topo maps:	Mount Lago; *Pasayten Peak.*
Jurisdiction:	Pasayten Wilderness (Okanogan National Forest).

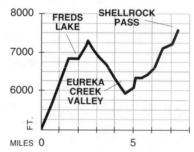

Finding the trail: From the west, follow the Ferguson Lake route (Hike 55) but instead of turning on the Ferguson Lake spur, continue north on the Robinson Pass Trail another 4.3 miles to the junction with the Shellrock Pass route. The east end is reached via a 19.1-mile trek on the Monument Trail.

Key points:
    0.0 Junction with Robinson Pass Trail. Shellrock Pass Trail starts climbing.
    1.0 Junction with old Point Defiance Trail. Bear right.
    1.8 Freds Lake.
    2.4 Pass above Freds Lake.
    4.5 Floor of Eureka Creek valley.
    5.0 Trail crosses Eureka Creek and follows south bank.
    5.4 Trail crosses headwaters of Eureka Creek and begins final grade.
    7.3 Shellrock Pass. Monument Trail leads eastward.

The hike: This remote trail journeys through some of the most rugged high country in the Pasayten Wilderness, linking the Middle Fork of the Pasayten River with the terra incognita of the Lost River watershed. The route is well traveled as far as Freds Lake, but beyond this point the trail has a low maintenance priority and is the exclusive domain of hard-core wilderness travelers.

From its junction with the Robinson Pass Trail, the trail to Shellrock Pass zigzags upward through a loose growth of lodgepole pine. There are fine views across the valley, featuring the low but rugged peaks of Buckskin Ridge. After a mile of climbing, the path reaches a junction with the Point Defiance Trail, which now exists only as far as Pleasant Valley. Our route bears right at the junction, climbing moderately across slopes that are shaded

Monument Peak above Eureka Creek valley.

221

Shellrock Pass

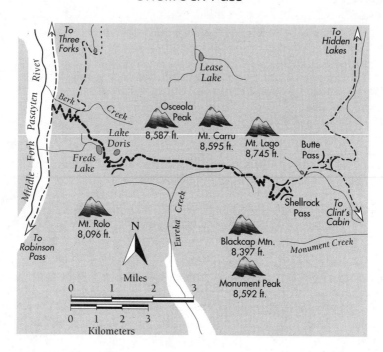

by an unburned forest of subalpine firs. The path soon strikes a gushing stream and follows it upward to Freds Lake. Rainbow trout cruise languidly in the emerald waters of the lake, and marmots frolic along its shores.

The trail skirts the north side of the lake, then zigzags up to the ridgetop through a scattering of subalpine larches. Gaining the top of the divide, the trail offers eastward views of Blackcap Mountain and Monument Peak across the deep Eureka Creek valley. Mount Rolo looms directly to the south, and the majestic peaks of Robinson Mountain rise beyond a saddle to the left of it. The views improve as the path climbs over a low knoll, where one can gaze up the headwaters of Eureka Creek and take in the barren, tawny summits that rise to the north.

After dropping swiftly to cross the brook that issues from Lake Doris, the trail descends gradually across the steep, meadowy slopes that wall off the Eureka Creek valley. The path bottoms out in a stand of subalpine fir on the valley floor, at a former junction with the long-abandoned Eureka Creek trail. The route now begins a gentle ascent up the floor of the valley, passing through a series of pleasant glades that offer fine camping possibilities. A little farther up the trail is a broad scar in the forest where an enormous avalanche mowed down the trees during the winter of 1995-1996.

In the midst of the tangled tree trunks, the trail makes a ford of Eureka Creek, then follows its south bank into a high alpine basin. Here, the path runs beside the shorelines of several shallow pools. Above the upper pool, follow the cairns as the

222

trail crosses the stream once more to reach the base of the grade to Shellrock Pass.

A steady climb carries travelers upward across broad aprons of broken rock and through stands of subalpine larch. After many well-engineered switchbacks, the trail traverses over to Shellrock Pass, where the barren landscape of naked rock stretches in all directions. Far to the east, a barren backbone of sedimentary rock rises beyond Monument Creek, while the stark summit of Blackcap Mountain soars skyward directly to the south. From here, the Monument Trail (Hike 58) descends into the valley to the east.

58 Monument Trail

Overview:	A day hike to the Lost River Gorge overlook (11.8 miles round trip) or a long backpack to Lake of the Woods (12 miles) or Shellrock Pass (19.1 miles).
Best season:	Late July to mid-October.
Difficulty:	Moderate to Eureka Creek; strenuous beyond.
Elevation gain:	8,130 feet.
Elevation loss:	3,130 feet.
Maximum elevation:	7,500 feet at Shellrock Pass.
Topo maps:	McLeod Mountain, Robinson Mountain, Lost Peak, Mount Lago; *Washington Pass, Mazama, Billy Goat Mountain, Pasayten Peak.*
Jurisdiction:	Okanogan National Forest, Pasayten Wilderness.

Lake Mountain from Pistol Pass.

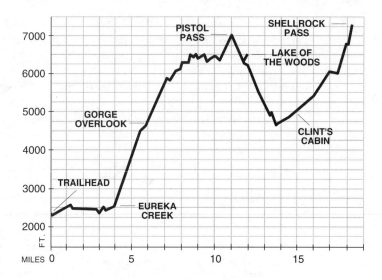

Finding the trailhead: Take Washington Highway 20 to the Mazama cut-off road, 11 miles west of Winthrop. After a mile, there is a T-intersection. Turn left, passing the Mazama general store. This is the Harts Pass Road (Forest Road 5400), which is paved as far as the Lost River, about 5 miles. The spur road to the Monument trailhead is 0.2 mile beyond the Lost River.

Key points:
     0.0   Monument Trailhead. Trail follows the Lost River.
     4.0   Trail crosses Eureka Creek to reach campsite on Lost River. Bear left.
     5.9   Overlook with view of Lost River Gorge.
   11.1   Pistol Pass.
   11.6   Junction with trail to Lake of the Woods (0.4 mile, moderate). Bear right for Monument Creek.
   12.6   Trail crosses stream that drains Lake of the Woods.
   13.7   Trail bottoms out in valley of Monument Creek.
   15.0   Clint's Cabin.
   15.2   Monument Creek ford.
   17.8   Junction with trail to Butte Pass. Bear left for Shellrock Pass.
   18.2   Basin below Shellrock Pass.
   19.1   Shellrock Pass.

The hike: This trail penetrates deep into the heart of the Pasayten Wilderness, first following the Lost River then running arid ridgetops northward to the head-waters of Monument Creek. The divide between Eureka Creek and the Lost River burned in 1986, and the trail has received scant maintenance after that point. The trailbed is in fine shape, however, and seasoned backcountry visitors will be able to find the way without much difficulty. A high overlook of the Lost River Gorge makes a good day hiking destination. Backpackers are advised to carry an overabundance of water if they approach the trail from the south; there

Monument Trail

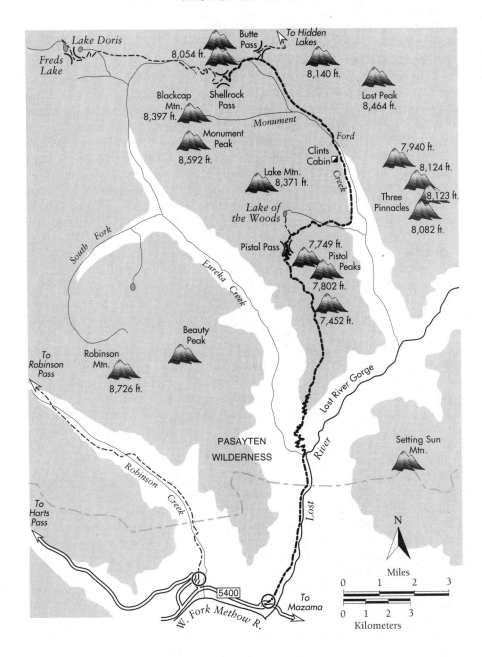

Lake Doris

Freds Lake

Butte Pass

To Hidden Lakes

8,054 ft.

8,140 ft.

Lost Peak
8,464 ft.

Blackcap Mtn.
8,397 ft.

Shellrock Pass

Monument

Ford

Monument Peak
8,592 ft.

Clints Cabin

7,940 ft.

8,124 ft.

Lake Mtn.
8,371 ft.

8,123 ft.

Three Pinnacles

Creek

8,082 ft.

Lake of the Woods

Pistol Pass

7,749 ft.

Pistol Peaks

South Fork

Eureka Creek

7,802 ft.

7,452 ft.

Beauty Peak

To Robinson Pass

Robinson Mtn.
8,726 ft.

Lost River Gorge

PASAYTEN

WILDERNESS

Lost River

Setting Sun Mtn.

To Harts Pass

Robinson Creek

Lost

N

Miles

0   1   2   3

5400

To Mazama

0   1   2   3

Kilometers

W. Fork Methow R.

is no surface water along the rigorous climb from Eureka Creek to Lake of the Woods, a distance of 8 miles.

The journey begins with a level trek along the timbered benches west of the Lost River. The forest here is a mixture of ponderosa pine and Douglas-fir. Both trees are well-adapted to the periodic droughts and fires that are so common on the east slope of the Cascades. About halfway to Eureka Creek, the benches give way to steep talus slopes that reveal the river and the foothills that surround it. Upon entering the Pasayten Wilderness, the trail drops to the river bottoms, where water-loving deciduous trees, such as cottonwood and western birch, are favored by frequent floods. The approach ends at the confluence of Eureka Creek and the Lost River, both of which emerge from impenetrable gorges. A stout bridge over Eureka Creek leads to the toe of the ridge that divides the valleys. There are good camping spots beyond the bridge on a spur path that leads down to the riverbank.

The main trail now begins its long and waterless grade to Pistol Pass. It initially zigzags upward across rocky and fire-prone slopes, climbing at a moderate but steady clip. There are fine views en route, featuring the mouth of Eureka Creek canyon as well as Mount Gardiner to the south. On the upper slopes of the ridge, bedrock and talus give way to grassy savannahs, and soon the glacier-clad summit of Silver Star Mountain peers out above intervening ridges to the south. Upon reaching the ridgetop, the trail arrives at a rocky overlook that commands good views of the Lost River Gorge. Day hikers should turn around at this point.

The next several miles present a mild route-finding challenge, since trail maintenance has been neglected in the wake of the most recent fire. The path follows the ridgeline to the base of the next summit, then zigzags up to the level ridgetop beyond. Ever-expanding views now encompass the bald summits of the Lost River divide, Monument Peak to the north, and unobstructed southward views of Silver Star Mountain. A tableau of spires and pinnacles crowds the southwestern horizon.

Blow-downs cease to be a problem as the path enters the older burn below the southernmost of the Pistol Peaks. The path drops onto the western slope of the ridge, where a sparse, post-fire growth of spruce, fir, whitebark pine, and larch allows superb views of Beauty Peak beyond the Eureka Creek valley. The trail undertakes small-scale climbs and descents as it works its way across the mountainside, then zigzags up a short but tiring pitch to reach Pistol Pass. From here, the striking summit of Lake Mountain rises above a small pool known as Lake of the Woods, and the barren summits of Lost Peak and the Three Pinnacles rise beyond the deep basin of Monument Creek.

The trail then zigzags down into the larch-filled basin below with views of the Pistol Peaks along the way. On the floor of the bowl, a signpost marks the faint spur path that runs westward to Lake of the Woods. A 10-minute side trip leads to the shore of this shallow pool, surrounded by a youthful forest of larch and fir. Meanwhile, the main trail glides gently to the floor of the basin, crossing a series of ponds and watercourses that dry up in late summer.

Upon leaving the basin, the path snakes down to the stream that drains Lake of the Woods, the first reliable water source since Eureka Creek. The trail drops steeply along its south bank, then crosses the stream and continues its rapid descent along the far bank. The firs and whitebark pines of the subalpine zone give way to a montane forest of lodgepole pine. The trail eventually swings north into the valley of Monument Creek, angling downward to the valley floor. It then runs upstream along wooded benches to reach the ruins of Clint's Cabin, which was built by trapper Clint Hanks. The cabin site is a good spot to camp, and a side trip down to the creek reveals interesting outcrops lining the watercourse.

Just above the cabin, a shallow ford leads across Monument Creek, and the trail continues its journey through grassy parks where aspens grow. The lodgepoles soon return, and through their boughs one can see the craggy cliffs that stretch between Lake and Blackcap mountains. As Monument Creek splits into two forks, the trail follows the more northerly branch toward Butte Pass. Views are hidden by an intervening ridge as the path works its way up through sills of bedrock that are robed in heather and studded with a sparse growth of subalpine fir.

After passing a marked junction with the Butte Pass trail, the main route swings westward. A rocky spur of Mount Lago rises ahead as the trail wanders through grassy glades. It soon strikes a sparkling brook, replete with waterfalls and lined with mosses and bog gentians. The path follows this stream up into a pure stand of subalpine larch, which soon opens up at a beautiful mere at the base of the peaks. The trail grows faint as it continues westward through lush meadows and stands of young larch; follow the cairns that lead gently upward into the rocky saddle to the south. There are superb eastward views of Lost Peak and Rampart Ridge as the trail tops the saddle. It then swings north across the talus to reach Shellrock Pass, where it becomes the Shellrock Pass trail (Hike 57).

ADDITIONAL TRAILS

A trail once ran over **Anacortes Crossing** to access the mine claims in Hells Basin. It has long since been abandoned to the brush.

The **Frosty Creek Trail** has been rebuilt over Frosty Pass. It is used mostly by horse riders and is quite muddy in the Frosty Creek bottoms.

A spur trail to **The Parks** climbs from Frosty Creek into vast meadows. It receives only sporadic maintenance, and its junction is unmarked.

The **Chuchuwanteen Creek Trail**, maintained sporadically, climbs vigorously from the mouth of Frosty Creek to Monument 83 on the Canadian border.

The **Rock Creek Trail** is maintained fairly regularly, but is prone to washouts in its upper reaches, as well as deadfalls and avalanche debris.

A long, muddy trail runs down the **West Fork of the Pasayten River**. It is the preferred route of horse parties bound for Holman Pass.

A cutoff trail descends from the Buckskin Ridge trail to the **Middle Fork of the Pasayten**. It is well maintained though less scenic than alternate routes.

The **Point Defiance Trail** receives occasional maintenance from the Shellrock Pass Trail junction to Pleasant Valley. Beyond this point, it has been abandoned and is littered with deadfalls.

The **Tatoosh Buttes** trail is an old sheep driveway. The grade to the top is steep, but the alpine country is quite scenic. It is maintained regularly.

The trail from the Canadian Border to **Hidden Lakes** is very popular with horse riders, and the remote lakes are paradoxically one of the few crowded destinations in the Pasayten Wilderness.

A path runs over **Butte Pass** from the Monument trail to Hidden Lakes, but it receives minimal maintenance and is littered with blow-downs.

The trail that once followed **Eureka Creek** has been abandoned for so long that it is difficult to find even a trace of it.

Rainy Pass and Surroundings

As Washington Highway 20 nears the crest of the Cascades, it enters a region of stark granite pinnacles and dense forests that thrive on frequent rains and fogs. The highway crosses two divides here: from the west, Rainy Pass, which leads into the valley of Bridge Creek, a tributary of the Stehekin River that ultimately pours its waters into Lake Chelan, then the even higher divide of Washington Pass, where the Early Winters Spires guard the rim of the Methow River watershed, which drains eastward into the Columbia River. The ranges seen from the road offer some of the most awe-inspiring scenery in the North Cascades. These are prime recreation lands; the timber is so spindly here that loggers have never bothered with it, and the rather marginal lodes of precious metals played out years ago. Nonetheless, the lands surrounding Rainy Pass inexplicably were declared to be unfit for national park status. Today, the area falls within an unprotected portion of the Okanogan National Forest, which has thus far done a fine job of preserving the wild character of the landscape.

The landscape here is defined by a geologic feature known as the Golden Horn Batholith. *Batholith* is Latin for "sea of stone"; the formation originated millions of years ago as a huge upwelling of molten rock through faults in the Earth's crust, which cooled below the surface. As the magma cooled and hardened into granitic rock, it contracted and vertical cracks or joints developed. These joints weakened the stone, and over the course of eons, frost shattering has exploited the vertical weaknesses in the rock. In this way, erosion has chiseled away at the great batholith to create towering walls and sharp stone needles.

As the Golden Horn granite cooled, some of the cracks in the newly forged bedrock were infused with mineral-rich, superheated water. This process resulted in the formation of veins of quartz in the bedrock, and some of these veins contained substantial quantities of gold and silver. Later, erosion would carry granules and small nuggets of gold away from the mother lode and down into the streams and rivers. As the goldfields of California played out, prospectors moved north along the mountains, and in the 1880s they found gold in the stream gravels of this remote corner of the North Cascades. News spread quickly, and a flurry of mining activity and stock speculation ensued. A few got rich, but most went broke. When gold was discovered in the Klondike, most of the Cascades miners abandoned their claims and journeyed north. Today, the ruins of old gold and silver mines can still be found to the north of WA 20, on the mountainsides of the Canyon Creek drainage.

Modern visitors will find that the real treasure of the Golden Horn is still here in abundance: a collection of fine day hikes that lead into an inspiring

Rainy Pass

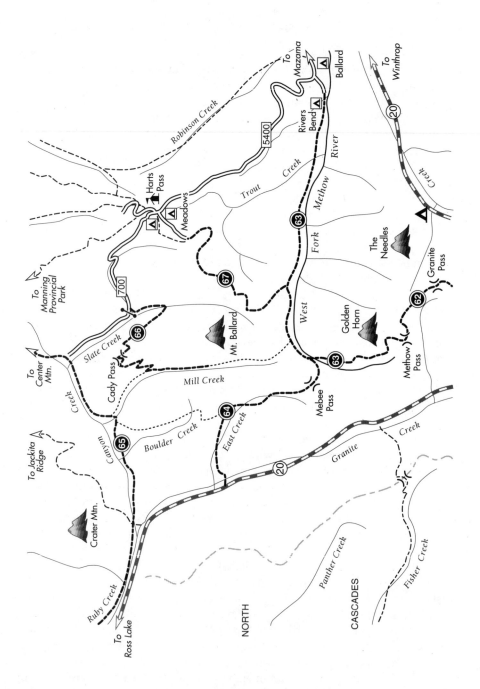

Overview

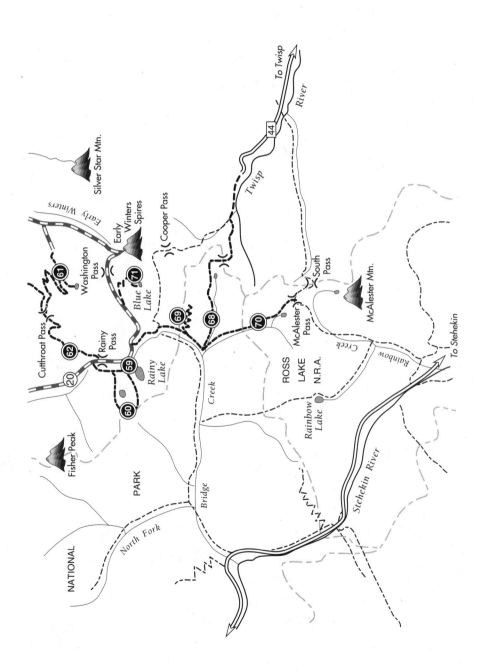

landscape of high peaks. Backpackers will discover that well-built trails also lead south down Bridge Creek into North Cascades National Park, where backcountry permits are required.

Services near Rainy Pass are nonexistent; the nearest place to get gas and supplies is Mazama, on the Methow River. It is 11 miles farther to Winthrop, the first real town. Traveling west from Rainy Pass, it is 38 miles to the company store at Newhalem and an additional 13 miles to Marblemount for gas and groceries. Roadside campgrounds also are hard to come by: the nearest Forest Service campground is 6 miles east of Washington Pass, and westbound travelers will have to drive 27 miles from Rainy Pass to reach Colonial Campground, which is run by the National Park Service. For more information, stop at the Forest Service visitor center in Winthrop.

59 Rainy Lake

Overview:	A short, wheelchair-accessible trek on a paved trail to Rainy Lake, 1.8 miles round trip.
Best season:	Late June to mid-October.
Difficulty:	Easy.
Elevation gain:	Minimal.
Elevation loss:	None.
Maximum elevation:	4,800 feet.
Topo maps:	Washington Pass; *Washington Pass*.
Jurisdiction:	Okanogan National Forest.

Finding the trailhead: The trail departs from the Rainy Pass picnic area at mile 157 on Washington Highway 20.

Key points:
    0.0 Rainy Pass picnic area.
    0.5 Maple Pass loop trail junction.
    0.9 Rainy Lake.

The hike: This short, paved trail starts at Rainy Pass and contours along the mountainsides to enter the glacier-carved cirque that bears Rainy Lake. It is a short, level trek that is well suited to wheelchairs.

The trail begins in a series of subalpine bogs and meadows where Engelmann spruce have taken root in the cool, damp soil. As the trail nears the halfway point, a pleasant series of waterfalls tumbles down through the forest, draining the outflow from Lake Ann in a hanging valley high above. The forest is now dominated by silver fir and mountain hemlock; watch for fairy bells, violets, and queen's cup lilies in the understory, as well as the delicate fronds of ferns.

At the end of the trail is a viewpoint at the foot of Rainy Lake. The lake's brilliant turquoise waters are fed by an impressive waterfall that descends

Rainy Lake.

Rainy Lake • Maple Pass Loop

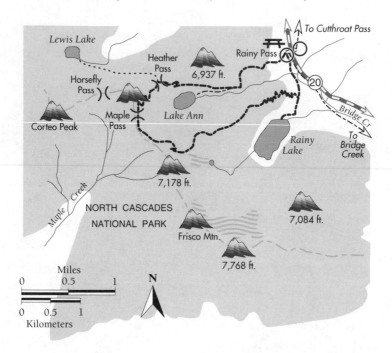

from Lyall Glacier. The towering crags of Frisco Mountain rise above the head of the basin. There is a fine population of good-sized cutthroat trout in the lake, but the brushy lakeshore makes fishing difficult without a boat.

60 Maple Pass Loop

Overview: A half-day hike to Lake Ann (3.8 miles round trip) or a longer day hike around the loop, 7.2 miles overall.

Best season: Late July to early October.

Difficulty: Moderate to Lake Ann; moderately strenuous beyond. The loop is strenuous if approached in a counterclockwise manner.

Elevation gain: 2,185 feet.

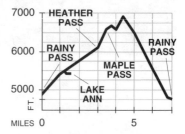

Looking south from Heather Pass.

Elevation loss:	2,185 feet.
Maximum elevation:	6,950 feet above Maple Pass.
Topo maps:	Washington Pass, Mount Arriva; *Washington Pass, Mount Logan.*
Jurisdiction:	Okanogan National Forest.

Finding the trailhead: The trail departs from the Rainy Pass picnic area at mile 157 on Washington Highway 20.

Key points:
- 0.0 Rainy Pass Day-use Area. Follow Maple Pass Trail.
- 1.4 Junction with trail to Lake Ann (0.5 mile, easy). Bear right for Maple Pass.
- 2.9 Heather Pass. Old trail runs east to Lewis Lake.
- 3.6 Maple Pass.
- 6.8 Junction with paved Rainy Pass Trail (0.4 mile to lake, easy). Turn left to complete the loop.
- 7.2 Trail returns to Rainy Pass Day-use Area.

The hike: This trail climbs from Rainy Pass to the much higher divide that runs west from Frisco Mountain. Both Rainy Lake and Lake Ann can be reached via short side trips from the loop, and adventurous hikers can try to trace the faint path from Heather Pass to Lewis Lake, which lies at the base of Corteo Peak. From the windswept alpine tundra of Maple Pass, there are fantastic views of jagged peaks in all directions. A new trail along the ridge that separates Lake Ann from Rainy Lake permits a loop trip that takes half a day for a strong hiker to complete.

From the parking lot at Rainy Pass, the trail zigzags upward through mature subalpine forest. The path soon turns south, traversing around the edge of a small cirque. Several avalanche paths face eastward toward the sharp spires of Stiletto Peak. Talus slopes soon drop away into the grassy floor of the basin, where marmots are often spotted among the boulders. As the path traverses onto the south wall of the bowl, sparsely timbered slopes offer excellent northward views. From right to left, the prominent summits are Whistler Mountain, Cutthroat Peak, and Tower Mountain.

The trail then strikes Lake Ann's outlet stream at a fine waterfall and follows it into a hanging valley carved by glaciers. The spur path to Lake Ann soon descends to the left. It runs through the timbered lower reaches of the basin, then breaks out into open country dotted with snowmelt ponds and wet meadows. Look backward as you approach the lake for views of the Early Winters Spires. The lake itself is bordered by low but rocky peaks that bear several small waterfalls down into the basin. Anglers will find fair fishing for undersized cutthroat trout.

Meanwhile, the trail to Maple Pass climbs gently but steadily through an ever-thinning forest. Emerging onto the slopes of a rocky spur, it reveals excellent aerial views of Lake Ann, with its footprint-shaped island. The gradient increases to a moderate ascent as the path reaches the lush meadows below Heather Pass. They are filled with wildflowers beyond counting; some of the more showy blossoms belong to aster, lupine, speedwell, phlox, columbine, and pink monkeyflower. An old trail climbs through the pass and continues west toward Lewis Lake, while the main route follows a newer track that surmounts a larch-studded outcrop overlooking the pass. From here, the tawny summits of the Pasayten country stretch away to the north, while to the west the turquoise waters of Wing Lake sparkle beneath the towering countenance of Black Peak.

The trail continues upward through the heather, charting a course high above Lake Ann. It crests the rounded divide at Maple Pass, with spectacular views all around. To the west, the towering summit of Corteo Peak rises above a cirque, flanked by Mount Benzarino to the left and Black Peak to the right. Far to the southwest are the glacier-mantled summits of Dome and Old Guard peaks, with the icebound cone of Glacier Peak rising in the distance. Watch for white-tailed ptarmigan as the trail turns southward and climbs along the ridgeline toward the rugged peaks of Frisco Mountain. It tops out on the high prominence above Lake Ann, then turns east to follow a spur ridge downward.

The barren, rocky country of the high alpine zone is soon replaced by lush meadows, and hikers get views of a deep-blue tarn in the hanging basin below. Jumbled spires rise to the east, and to the west are continuing views of Black and Corteo peaks. As the path continues down the ridge, it reveals a superb vista of Lyall Glacier, which unleashes its meltwaters to feed the magnificent waterfall that plunges to the turquoise waters of Rainy Lake.

The scattering of subalpine larches and whitebark pines soon gives way to a ragged woodland of mountain hemlock, gladed with swards of heather. The trail now plummets down the spine of the ridge, zigzagging downward as the mountain views dwindle into sporadic glimpses of peaks. Nearing the bottom of the grade, the path enters a lush forest. It joins the Rainy Lake trail at a marked junction; turn right for the 0.3-mile side trip to Rainy Lake, or left for 0.7 mile of paved trail that leads back to Rainy Pass.

61 Cutthroat Lake and Cutthroat Pass

Overview: A short day hike to Cutthroat Lake (2.8 miles round trip) or a longer day trip or short backpack to Cutthroat Pass (11 miles round trip).

Best season: Late June to mid-October for the lake; mid-July to early October for the pass.

Difficulty: Easy to Cutthroat Lake; moderate to Cutthroat Pass.

Elevation gain: 410 feet to the lake; 2,265 feet to the pass.

Maximum elevation: 6,815 feet at Cutthroat Pass.

Topo maps: Washington Pass (trail not shown); *Washington Pass.*

Jurisdiction: Okanogan National Forest.

Finding the trailhead: From Washington Pass, drive east on Washington Highway 20 for 4.5 miles to the Cutthroat Creek Road. Follow this paved road west for 1.5 miles to reach the trailhead and camping area at its end.

Key points:
- 0.0 Cutthroat Lake Trailhead.
- 0.1 Bridge over Cutthroat Creek.
- 0.9 Junction with spur trail to east shore of lake (0.5 mile, easy).
- 1.3 Spur trail to outlet of lake. Bear right for Cutthroat Pass.
- 4.4 Camping area in larch-filled basin.
- 5.5 Cutthroat Pass. Trail joins Granite Pass section of Pacific Crest Trail.

The hike: This wide and well-engineered trail makes an easy day hike to the lake. Because the sensitive heather parks that line the lakeshore are extremely susceptible to damage, camping is forbidden within 0.25 mile of the shoreline. Hikers who seek a more challenging trek can follow the steady but moderate grade that climbs to the crest of the divide at Cutthroat Pass. Here, the trail intersects the Pacific Crest Trail (PCT) just 4 miles north of

Cutthroat Lake • Cutthroat Pass
Granite Pass Highline

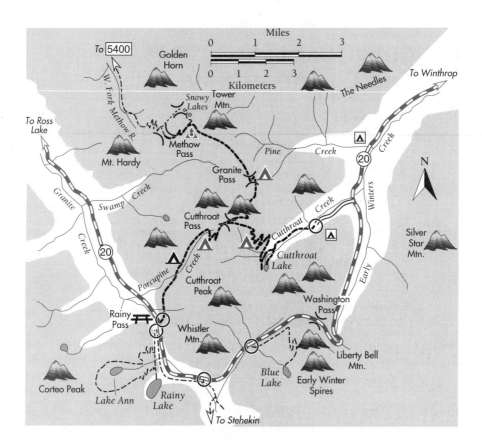

Rainy Pass (see Granite Pass Highline, Hike 62).

The trek begins by crossing a bridge over Cutthroat Creek and climbing gently through an open woodland of Douglas-fir and lodgepole pine. This entire valley burned long ago, and the resulting forest is comprised of fire-resistant or fire-dependent plant species. All along the way are fine views of the tawny crags of sedimentary rock that line the valley. As the trail continues upward, it passes through several isolated groves of spruce that were spared by the blaze. The groves reveal the pre-fire forest community that once covered the valley floor.

After 0.9 mile of traveling, the first spur path to Cutthroat Lake leads westward across hummocky parks to the eastern shore. A short distance farther, the main trail splits and the left fork leads to the north shore of the lake. Ringed by an open woodland of mountain hemlock and subalpine larch, the green waters of Cutthroat Lake are guarded on two sides by rugged mountains, the tallest of which is Cutthroat Peak. The lake is quite shallow, and as it fills with silt, meadows take over where fish once swam. Anglers will find fair fishing for pan-sized trout.

Cutthroat Pass Option. From a junction on the north shore of Cutthroat Lake, this trail makes two stream crossings as it begins a long series of gentle zigzags that carry it up the north wall of the valley. Through thinning forest, hikers get constant views of the surrounding peaks and sporadic glimpses of Cutthroat Lake. Near the top of the initial grade, the spires of Silver Star Mountain appear to the south above the intervening ridge.

At the top of the hill, the trail winds into a flat basin where subalpine larch are the dominant conifers. The strong winds at timberline rake the trees during winter, breaking off the topmost twigs so that the larches are prone to top-kill. When the dominant bud at the top of the tree breaks off, buds on the lateral branches are released from inhibiting hormones and start to grow vertically, competing to become the new dominant branch. There are excellent campsites in this basin, but surface water is unavailable from midsummer onward.

The path climbs onto the timbered slope to the east of the basin, passing among mountain hemlocks and subalpine firs. These slopes offer the finest views of Cutthroat Lake. The path soon navigates among rounded slabs of granite interspersed with swards of heather and dwarf blueberry. Watch for golden-mantled ground squirrels, which are abundant here. The trail rounds a shallow bowl to reach the crest of the divide, where it ends at a junction with the Glacier Pass segment of the PCT. The tops of the Early Winters Spires can now be seen to the south above an intervening ridge. To the west are views down Porcupine Creek toward the glacier-bound summits of Black and Corteo peaks.

62 Granite Pass Highline— Pacific Crest Trail

See Map on Page 238

Overview:	A day hike to Granite Pass, 15 miles round trip, or a backpack to Methow Pass, 10.5 miles one way.
Best season:	Early August to early October.
Difficulty:	Moderate.
Elevation gain:	2,970 feet.
Elevation loss:	1,240 feet.
Maximum elevation:	6,980 feet above Granite Pass.
Topo maps:	Washington Pass (trail not shown); *Washington Pass*.
Jurisdiction:	Okanogan National Forest.

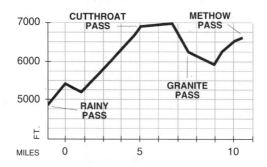

Finding the trailhead: The trail departs from the Pacific Crest Trail North trailhead, directly across the highway from the Rainy Pass picnic area at mile 157 on Washington Highway 20.

Key points:
0.0 PCT North Trailhead.
1.9 Trail crosses Porcupine Creek.
3.8 Upper Porcupine camp.
5.0 Cutthroat Pass. Junction with trail to Cutthroat Lake. Turn left.
5.8 Campsite on rocky spur.
6.9 Trail reaches heights overlooking Granite Pass.
7.5 Granite Pass.
9.5 Snowy Lakes horse camp.
10.5 Methow Pass. West Fork Methow Trail runs northward.

The hike: This segment of the Pacific Crest Trail (PCT) climbs high among the barren ridgetops and soaring granite spires north of Rainy Pass, staying above timberline for a high traverse to Methow Pass. The heights above Granite Pass are the highlight of the trip, offering staggering views of The Needles, a collection of fanglike spires of the Golden Horn granite. The

Snowy Lakes make a popular side trip for this trail, accessed by way trails from either side of Methow Pass. Travelers following the PCT will continue northward, following the West Fork of the Methow and Trout Creek Divide routings to reach Harts Pass.

From the PCT North trailhead at Rainy Pass, the trail runs northward across heavily timbered slopes. After passing a pretty woodland waterfall, the path crosses an open slope that offers the first views of the surrounding mountains. The path returns to the trees for the trek to Porcupine Creek, which is spanned by a footbridge. There is a small tent pad beside the bridge. The trail follows the stream upward into a sparsely wooded basin, with fine views of Cutthroat Peak along the way. Upon reaching the headwaters, the trail arcs upward above the treeline. It passes a well-developed camping area as it crosses the many rills that form Porcupine Creek.

Bidding farewell to a sparse growth of larches, the trail climbs into alpine country of heather and granite. The trail reaches the divide at Cutthroat Pass, where a spur trail drops away to the east toward Cutthroat Lake (see p.237). The main trail climbs gently on an easterly heading, passing through a landscape with huge boulders and twisted trees like those of an Oriental garden. Views are outstanding as the path reaches the tip of a steep spur ridge, with Cutthroat Lake lying in the basin below like a giant emerald and the pinnacles of Kangaroo Ridge and the Early Winters Spires rising above the ridgetops to the south. A hidden and waterless tent pad lies just above the trail at this point.

The path now runs north across barren slopes of broken rock, an alpine desert where only phlox and penstemon grow. Snowslips linger late into the summer here; carry an ice axe at all times. Silver Star Mountain can be seen to the southeast, buttressed by the craggy jawbones of Vasiliki and Snagtooth ridges. The trail soon passes above a high saddle that marks the edge of the Pine Creek watershed. As the trail descends toward the much lower gap of Granite Pass, there are inspiring views of The Needles rising beyond the headwaters of Pine Creek. Glacier Pass lies at the head of the glacier-carved trench now occupied by Swamp Creek. The sparsely wooded dells of the pass offer sheltered camping spots.

The trail now swings westward, descending briskly before beginning a high traverse of the Swamp Creek valley wall. The steep slopes are sparsely timbered with spindly firs and hemlocks. The majestic summits of Black and Fisher peaks are framed by the valley's mouth, and a tall but nameless peak rises above the far side of the abyss. Minor ups and downs lead to a pocket basin high above the valley floor. There is a horse camp here, and a way trail ascends northward to the spectacular Snowy Lakes, which occupy the alpine shelf between Tower Mountain and the Golden Horn.

After passing the basin, the main trail climbs a bit, then traverses across to the larch-bordered meadows of Methow Pass. The lack of water makes this pass a poor place to pitch a tent. The trail along the West Fork of the Methow River (Hike 63) rises into the pass from the north, a continuation of the PCT.

63 West Fork of the Methow River

Overview:	A backpack from Rattlesnake Creek to Methow Pass along the Pacific Crest Trail, 15 miles one way.
Best season:	Mid-July to mid-October.
Difficulty:	Easy to Horse Heaven; moderately strenuous beyond.
Elevation gain:	3,947 feet.
Elevation loss:	57 feet.
Maximum elevation:	6,590 feet at Methow Pass.
Topo maps:	Robinson Mountain, Slate Peak, Azurite Peak, Mount Arriva, Washington Pass; *Mount Logan, Washington Pass*.
Jurisdiction:	Okanogan National Forest.

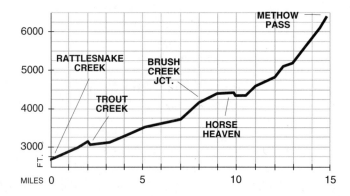

Finding the trailhead: Take Washington Highway 20 to the Mazama cutoff road, 11 miles west of Winthrop. After a mile, there is a T-intersection. Turn left, passing the Mazama general store. This is the Harts Pass Road (Forest Road 5400), which is paved as far as the Lost River, about 5 miles. After 8 miles, the road makes a hairpin turn, where a side road runs straight ahead toward River Bend Campground. Take the side road to its end, bearing right at the campground spur to reach the trailhead at Rattlesnake Creek.

Key points:
0.0 Trailhead. Trail crosses Rattlesnake Creek.
2.1 Trout Creek crossing.
8.0 Junction with trail to Harts Pass. Continue straight ahead.
9.7 Horse Heaven camp.
9.8 Junction with East Creek Trail. Bear left.
10.6 Trail crosses the West Fork of the Methow River.
11.0 Trail crosses Golden Creek and reaches Will's Camp.
12.8 Head of valley. Trail begins final grade.
14.8 Abandoned trail to Snowy Lakes. Continue straight ahead.
15.0 Methow Pass.

The hike: This trail is little known and rather neglected in its lower reaches. The stretches above Brush Creek are part of the Pacific Crest Trail (PCT), and are well-maintained and heavily traveled. There are improved camping spots all along the way. Expect forest hiking through spruce bottoms, followed by avalanche slopes in the middle reaches and subalpine forest for the climb to Methow Pass. (The river and pass are pronounced MET-toe).

The trail begins by crossing Rattlesnake Creek and ascending onto the burned-over terraces above the West Fork of the Methow River. The main valley constricts as the path follows the river upward, and the trail leads across steep slopes of talus that descend to the water. The open terrain offers fine views of the steep peaks flanking the valley. Upon reaching Trout Creek, the trail jogs northward to cross a tributary at the mouth of its narrow canyon. The trail soon returns to the river, but views of the water are now screened by cottonwoods and conifers. Talus slopes ultimately give way to wooded ridges, and a rich bottomland forest of western red-cedar and cottonwood shades several potential camping spots.

As the trail passes the mouth of the Leap Creek valley, it climbs onto higher slopes for views of the surrounding country. It then returns to the river in a grove of old spruce, where there is another good campsite on the riverbank. The route moves inland as it draws even with Cataract Creek, traveling through brushy country at the base of a ridge. It returns to the river just below its confluence with Brush Creek. Here, a series of switchbacks leads up the wall of the valley to a junction with the portion of

Mount Hardy guards the headwaters of the West Fork Methow River.

West Fork of the Methow River

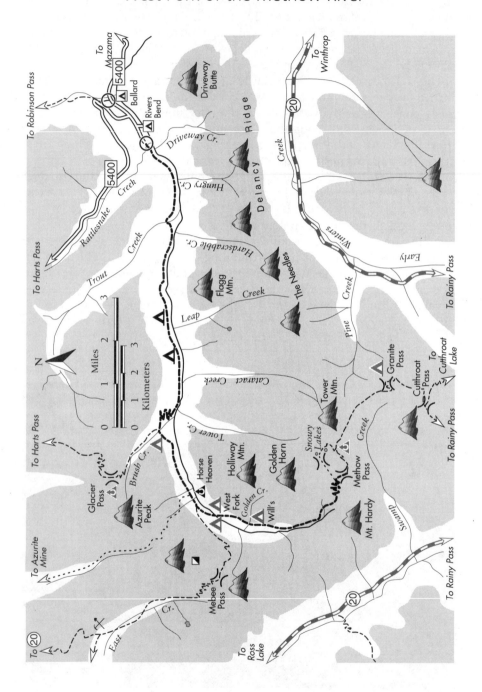

the PCT that runs north to Harts Pass (see Trout Creek Divide, p.255). The junction occupies a grove of old Douglas-fir just east of Brush Creek, and there is a tent spot tucked into a brushy pocket just beyond the stream.

The trail is now well trod as it embarks upon a long, level traverse above the floor of the valley. Stands of Douglas-fir cover the slopes, but numerous openings reveal views down the valley. The north face of Holliway Mountain slowly unveils itself across the river. The montane forest is soon replaced by a subalpine community of shapely spruces and firs. Broad avalanche tracks now interrupt the forest, extending down from the heights of Azurite Peak. There are fine views of Holliway Mountain as well as peaks farther up the valley. At the far edge of the second snowslide track, a spur path descends to Horse Heaven Camp in its riverside grove of tall spruces. This area is a favorite haunt of mule deer.

Just beyond the opening, the East Creek trail climbs away toward Mebee Pass, while the West Fork trail sticks to the lowlands on its way to a bridge over the river. Campsites sit on both sides of this bridge. The trail then climbs steadily through the forest before leveling off near Will's Camp, on the banks of Golden Creek. Another vigorous bout of climbing awaits, followed by a level stretch that lands the route back in the bottomlands. The forest is now dominated by silver fir, with a lesser contingent of older spruce overtopping them.

About 1.5 miles above the bridge, the ascent begins in earnest. Small avalanche paths descend from the slopes of the Golden Horn, breaching the forest canopy. Views are limited, however, until the trail reaches the head of the valley. Here, groves of mountain hemlock are interspersed with swards of heather and blueberry. The sheer cliffs of Mount Hardy loom threateningly above the south side of the valley, while the Golden Horn presides to the east. Nearing the headwall of the basin, the trail crosses a series of small streams where campsites can be found. It then zigzags steadily up the eastern wall of the basin, climbing out of the hemlocks to an altitude that favors subalpine larch.

At the edge of a boulderfield near the top of the grade, an abandoned spur path runs northeast through an alpine basin to reach Snowy Lakes Pass and its alpine tarns. The main trail swings up into Methow Pass, where golden-mantled ground squirrels frolic on fragile meadows bordered by larches. The segment of the PCT that extends southward from this point is discussed under the Granite Pass Highline (p.240).

64 East Creek

Overview: A day hike to the Gold Hill Mine, 8.8 miles round trip, or a backpack to the West Fork Methow Valley, 11 miles one way.

Best season: Mid-July to early October.

Difficulty: Moderately strenuous.

Elevation gain: 4,270 feet.

Elevation loss: 2,420 feet.

Maximum elevation: 6,700 feet at Mebee Pass.

Topo maps: Azurite Peak, Slate Peak; *Mount Logan.*

Jurisdiction: Okanogan National Forest.

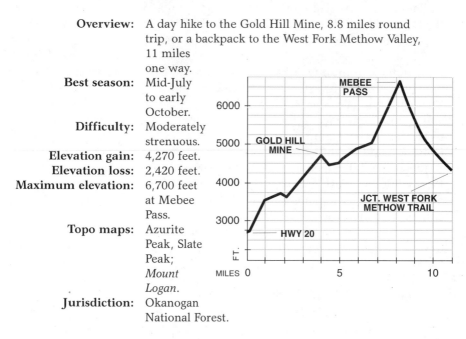

Finding the trailhead: The trail begins at the East Creek Trailhead, mile 144 on Washington Highway 20 (13 miles west of Rainy Pass).

Key points:
- 0.0 East Creek Trailhead.
- 2.2 Footbridge over East Creek. Trail follows north bank.
- 4.4 Junction with Boulder Creek Trail. Bear right to cross Gold Hill Mine site.
- 4.8 Trail fords East Creek and follows the south bank.
- 5.2 Trail returns to the north bank.
- 6.9 Bottom of grade to Mebee Pass.
- 8.3 Mebee Pass.
- 1.0 Trail joins the West Fork Methow Trail near Horse Heaven Camp.

The hike: This mostly forgotten trail offers a challenging trek from WA 20 to the headwaters of the West Fork of the Methow River. Along the way are several features of historical note, including the Gold Hill Mine and ruins of an old fire lookout above Mebee Pass. The early stretches of the trail have been rebuilt, and it is easy to follow as far as the Gold Hill Mine. Beyond this point, expect route-finding challenges; the trail over Mebee Pass receives low maintenance priority and is tough to follow in places.

From the parking area, the trail drops sharply to cross a stout bridge over Granite Creek. It then turns east, following the stream through shady bottomlands. After a brief ascent along the stream, the path climbs briskly

Peaks near the Mebee Pass lookout.

onto slopes that burned in a 1926 fire. The forest along the creek held more moisture and escaped the worst of blaze; old Douglas-firs were able to survive and reseed the area with their offspring. As the trail zigzags relentlessly upward, the forest becomes a pure stand of lodgepole pine so typical of burned-over sites in the drier parts of the Cascades. The trail climbs high onto the mountainside to avoid the stony gorge that guards the mouth of East Creek. During the ascent, bald knobs and a small talus field offer fine southward views of Beebe Mountain.

The trail then rounds the ridge onto the slopes above East Creek, climbing sporadically through a mossy forest of western hemlock. After a time, a steady descent leads down to the creek itself, and a footlog leads to the north bank. A streamside tent pad offers one of the few good camping spots along the route. The trail follows the stream eastward for a brief time, then climbs onto the slopes above. The southern exposure offers a drier microclimate, allowing Douglas-fir to dominate the forest. As the path nears the Gold Hill Mine, feeder streams descend through brushy openings with final views of the peaks to the west.

The trail tops out at a junction with the Boulder Creek trail. The ruins of the Gold Hill Mine are just beyond this intersection. A level pad of tailings bears the wreckage of collapsed structures and rusting mining equipment. The trail becomes faint beyond the mine site; cross the tailings and quarter downhill through the timber to reach a wide brushfield. The trail now runs straight downhill through the heart of the brush (follow flagging where possible). About halfway to East Creek, it crosses a tributary stream and continues downward along the eastern edge of the clearing. It levels off near the valley bottom, running eastward across two lesser avalanche slopes.

247

East Creek

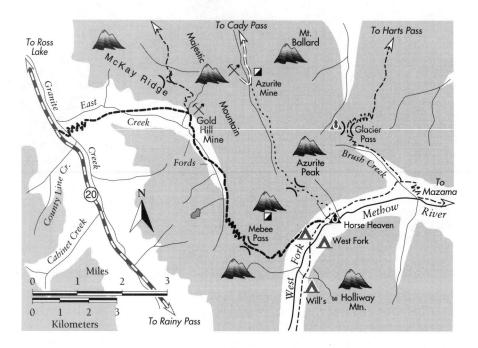

Upon reaching a grassy meadow, the path turns downhill again for a knee-deep ford of East Creek amid a riot of willows. It then climbs into the avalanche track on the south side and turns east for a short venture along the south bank. A loose forest of spruce and silver fir closes in around the trail, and soon a second ford leads back to the north bank. The trail now embarks on a long bottomland journey through forest. At the head of the valley, tidy avalanche paths interrupt the trees to reveal eroded ridges, stained yellow and orange by oxidizing metals in the bedrock.

The second snowslide slope is filled with wildflowers, and it marks the bottom of the grade to Mebee Pass. Short switchbacks lead steadily upward through a sparse subalpine woodland. Near the top of the grade, the trail enters the small alpine basin at the foot of the pass. Here, subalpine larch are scattered across slopes of heather and dwarf blueberry. The path zigzags up to Mebee Pass, overlooked to the north by a collection of daggerlike spires. Beyond the West Fork of the Methow River are the summits of Holliway Mountain and the Golden Horn. Adventurous travelers can scramble up the ridgeline to the north to reach the bleached ruins of a fire lookout that was built in 1934. From this lofty perch, hikers gain excellent views of the glaciers that adorn Ragged Ridge to the southwest.

From the pass, the main trail descends steeply into the basin beyond, then enters a heavy growth of mountain hemlock and levels off. Views open up again as the path strikes the western wall of the West Fork valley and angles down across its face. The imposing cliffs of Mount Hardy can now be seen above the head of the valley. The descent is rather steep at first, but soon becomes moderate as stony highlands give way to wooded slopes. As the trail continues northward, spindly subalpine trees give way to a robust montane forest. Two avalanche slopes near the bottom of the grade allow final views of Holliway Mountain and Mount Hardy. The trail ends at an intersection with the West Fork of the Methow River trail (p.242), just south of Horse Heaven Camp.

65 Chancellor Trail

Overview: A backpack along Canyon Creek from Washington Highway 20 to Chancellor Camp, 8.3 miles one way.
Best season: Late June to early November.
Difficulty: Moderate.
Elevation gain: 1,949 feet.
Elevation loss: 1,005 feet.
Maximum elevation: 2,855 feet.
Topo maps: Crater Mountain, Azurite Peak; *Mount Logan, Jack Mountain.*
Jurisdiction: Okanogan National Forest.

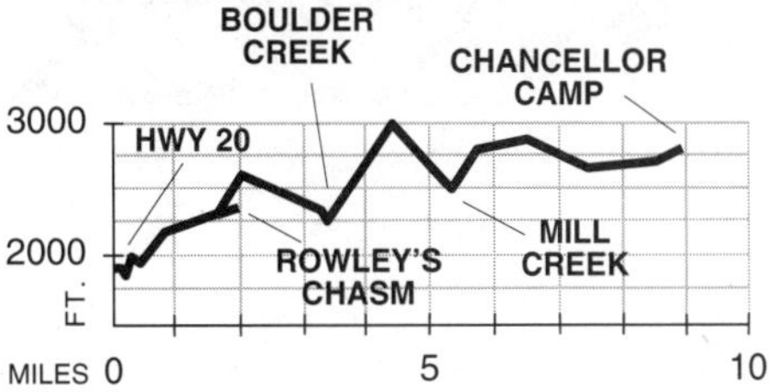

Finding the trailhead: The trail begins at the Canyon Creek Trailhead, at mile 141.2 on WA 20, 16 miles west of Rainy Pass.

Key points:
0.0 Canyon Creek Trailhead.
0.1 Trail crosses Granite Creek and turns southwest.
0.2 Chancellor Trail splits away to the right.
1.9 Junction with old Rowley's Chasm spur trail. Stay right.
2.2 Trail crosses Pete Miller Creek.
3.1 Junction with old Boulder Creek Trail. Continue straight ahead.
3.4 Trail crosses Boulder Creek.
5.4 Trail crosses Mill Creek.
5.7 Junction with abandoned Mill Creek Trail. Stay left.
6.8 Cedar Crossing. Bridge carries the trail to the west bank of Canyon Creek.
8.6 Converse Cabin.
8.2 Junction with Center Mountain Trail. Turn right to complete hike.
8.3 Trail crosses bridge over Canyon Creek to reach Chancellor Camp.

The hike: This route traces Canyon Creek through a historic gold-mining district to reach the old Chancellor Camp. The Slate Creek Road, which

Cabin at the confluence of Canyon and Granite creeks.

once offered access to Chancellor, has been closed 5 miles short of the campground due to washouts. Watch for the old cabins of prospectors along the way. Mountain views are scarce here, but the upper stretches of the trail offer lots of solitude.

The trail begins by crossing a bridge over Granite Creek, then makes its way downstream to a junction with the Chancellor Trail. A short side trip on the trail straight ahead leads to an old miner's cabin that guards the point where Granite and Canyon creeks join to form Ruby Creek. This cabin was dismantled and moved to this spot in the 1930s by the Forest Service, and it served for a time as a guard station.

Meanwhile, the Chancellor Trail itself splits away to the northwest, climbing steeply to enter the Canyon Creek valley. The ascent becomes moderate as the trail makes its way across the steep and heavily timbered slopes. Near the top of the grade, gaps in the forest canopy reveal a pretty waterfall that tumbles down the flanks of Crater Mountain. After 1.9 miles, the trail descends a bit to reach the Rowley's Chasm spur trail. A short distance down this side path is the spot where a bridge (since collapsed) once spanned a narrow cleft that dropped into a washed-out abyss. With slippery and uneven footing at the edge of the chasm, it is difficult to get a good view of the rift without endangering yourself.

The main trail now levels off, with easy traveling through the cedar-hemlock woodland. Several gaps in the forest along this stretch allow pleasant views up and down the valley. After crossing Holmes Creek, the trail descends almost to the floor of the main valley to make its crossing of

Chancellor Trail • Cady Pass

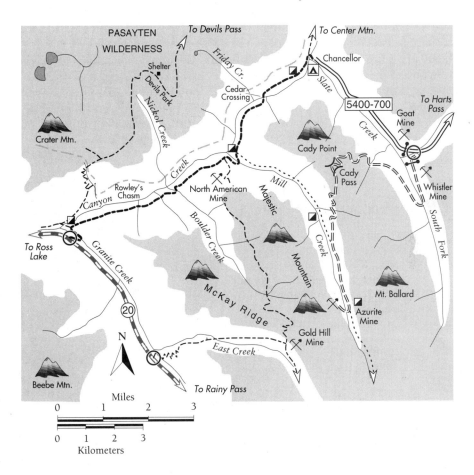

Boulder Creek. A steady ascent leads back onto the steep mountainsides for the moderate ascent to the mouth of the Mill Creek valley. Here, old trails run eastward, first the Boulder Creek trail and later the Mill Creek route on the far side of the stream. The ruins of an old sawmill lie below the trail at this point, and there are campsites along the stream. The trail adopts an old narrow-gauge roadbed, constructed in 1895 to link the Barron Mine with the sawmill, which provided the timbers needed to brace mine passageways. A gentle ascent leads to a cliff-hanging overlook high above Canyon Creek. Looking straight down the valley, hikers can see the north face of Snowfield Peak mantled in the billowy folds of Neve Glacier.

The old roadbed now enters a loose woodland of Douglas-fir, interrupted in several spots by steep talus slopes. Watch for waterfalls on the far side of the valley. The trail then descends gradually, and soon the Douglas-firs are replaced by a dense and shady stand of young cedar and hemlock. The descent steepens to a foot-pounding pace as the trail makes its way to the bottomlands at Cedar Crossing, where a rickety bridge leads to the far bank of Canyon Creek.

The path now ascends gradually through brushy openings beside the streamcourse. Willow and alder crowd the trail, and patches of thimbleberry are quite dense in places. Just before reaching Chancellor Camp, the trail passes the two-story Converse Cabin, which was associated with placer mining activities near Chancellor. The path then runs beneath a broad swath of talus, while Canyon Creek rushes through a picturesque series of rapids. A junction with the Center Mountain trail marks the spot where a bridge leads across Canyon Creek to the end of the trek at the camp.

66 Cady Pass

See Map on Page 251

Overview:	A day hike to Cady Pass (10.6 miles round trip) or a backpack to the old Azurite Mine, 10 miles one way.
Best season:	Mid-July to mid-October.
Difficulty:	Moderate.
Elevation gain:	2,590 feet.
Elevation loss:	1,940 feet.
Maximum elevation:	5,980 feet.
Topo maps:	Azurite Peak, Slate Peak; *Mount Logan, Washington Pass.*
Jurisdiction:	Okanogan National Forest.

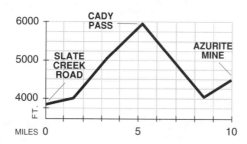

Finding the trailhead: Take Washington Highway 20 to the Mazama cutoff road, 11 miles west of Winthrop. After a mile, there is a T-intersection. Turn left, passing the Mazama general store. This is the Harts Pass Road (Forest Road 5400), which is paved as far as the Lost River, about 5 miles. It then becomes gravel, and is narrow and winding with many potholes as it makes the steep climb past Deadhorse Point to reach Harts Pass, 18.5 miles from Mazama. At the intersection atop the pass, go straight ahead on the primitive Slate Creek Road (FR 5400-700, high clearance recommended) for 5.5 miles to reached the well-marked trailhead.

Key points
- 0.0 Cady Pass Trailhead. Route follows closed road.
- 1.3 Bridge over the South Fork of Slate Creek.
- 5.3 Cady Pass. Old road starts to descend.
- 8.7 Unmarked junction with abandoned Mill Creek Trail. Follow the old road eastward.
- 10.0 Azurite Mine site.

The hike: This route follows the old mining access road that runs from Slate Creek over alpine Cady Pass to the Azurite Mine, in the Mill Creek valley. With recent interest in reopening the Azurite claims, travelers may meet an occasional four-wheeler along the way. The mine itself is a patented claim that is still active, and should be treated as private property. Stretches of the Mill Creek Trail leading down to Canyon Creek and over Azurite Pass have been abandoned and are no longer worth seeking out.

The trek begins at a road closure gate and follows the old roadbed upward above the South Fork of Slate Creek. After a series of minor ups and downs, the roadbed levels off, and gaps in the Douglas-fir offer fine views of Mount Ballard. Upon reaching the South Fork, a condemned bridge (easily passable to foot traffic) spans the water between two small cascades. The old road then climbs steadily through heavy timber, heading northwest toward Cady Pass. As the lowland forest gives way to subalpine firs and mountain hemlocks, views open up to reveal the northern buttress of Mount Ballard as well as the barren crest of Tatie Peak to the southeast. The sparse conifers are now underlain by thickets of huckleberry and white rhododendron.

As the track approaches the ridgetops, expansive views reach the bare ridges to the northwest, with the distant peaks of Joker Mountain and Castle Peak rising beyond them. Cady Pass burned over in the 1980s, and the few firs that survived the fire rise amid a mat of grouse whortleberry, dwarf blueberry, and lupine.

Upon cresting the pass, travelers gain spectacular views of the crags to the south and west. Looking eastward along the ridgeline, the summit of Mount Ballard peers out above an intervening spur. The glacier-carved trough that bears Mill Creek is stretched below, bounded by the craggy walls of Majestic Mountain. To the west are the twin mounds of Crater and Jack mountains, permanently mantled in snow and ice. Far to the west are a collection of distant spires. From right to left, they are Mount Terror, the rocky dome of Ruby Mountain, Paul Bunyan's Stump, and finally Colonial and Snowfield peaks cupping Neve Glacier.

The old road turns eastward as it descends into the valley of Mill Creek, and alpine meadows soon give way to arid brushfields that grew in the wake of the fire. Majestic Mountain provides a constant backdrop as the roadbed snakes downward through a series of hairpin turns. Looking up the valley, hikers can see the abandoned road grade on the lower slopes of Majestic Mountain leading to the upper portal of the Azurite Mine.

The road bottoms out as it nears Mill Creek, then begins its gentle climb

Mill Creek valley from Cady Pass.

up the valley. The old Mill Creek route joins the road at its low point, but is so overgrown with brush that it is nearly impossible to spot. As the main road follows the creek toward the Azurite Mine, isolated stands of tall silver fir and spruce are interrupted by broad swaths of alder, the legacy of frequent snowslides. The craggy countenance of Majestic Mountain looms above, a tangible presence throughout the latter part of the trek. Trail maintenance ends at the Azurite Mine site, with its dilapidated headquarters building of corrugated steel guarding vast piles of tailings on both sides of the stream. Mining began here in 1914, and more than $900,000 in gold was extracted before the mine finally shut down. There are good views of the valley's head just beyond the mine site.

67 Trout Creek Divide— Pacific Crest Trail

Overview: A day trip to the Azurite Peak viewpoint, 8.8 miles round trip, or a backpack to the West Fork of the Methow Trail, 10.6 miles one way.

Best season: Late July to early October.

Difficulty: Moderate south to north; moderately strenuous north to south.

Elevation gain: 1,005 feet.

Elevation loss: 3,125 feet.

Maximum elevation: 7,005 feet.

Topo maps: Slate Peak; *Washington Pass.*

Jurisdiction: Okanogan National Forest.

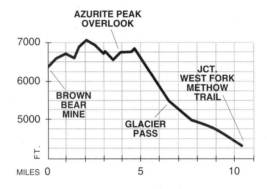

Finding the trailhead: From Washington Highway 20, follow the Harts Pass Road (see Hike 66) toward Harts Pass. Just before reaching the pass, turn left on Forest Road 5400-500, following signs for the Meadows Campground. Follow this improved gravel road for 2 miles to reach the trailhead at its end.

Key points:

0.0 Trailhead. Connecting trail leads upward.

0.1 Junction with PCT. Turn left to begin hike.

0.7 Trail crosses divide to enter Trout Creek watershed.

4.4 Trail reaches divide opposite Azurite Peak.

6.3 Glacier Pass and camps.

10.6 Trail reaches junction with West Fork of the Methow River Trail.

The hike: This segment of the Pacific Crest Trail (PCT) follows high ridgetops southward from Harts Pass, yielding excellent views before it drops toward Glacier Pass. It then follows Brush Creek to the West Fork of the Methow River. The low divide known informally as Grasshopper Pass lies just across

Trout Creek Divide

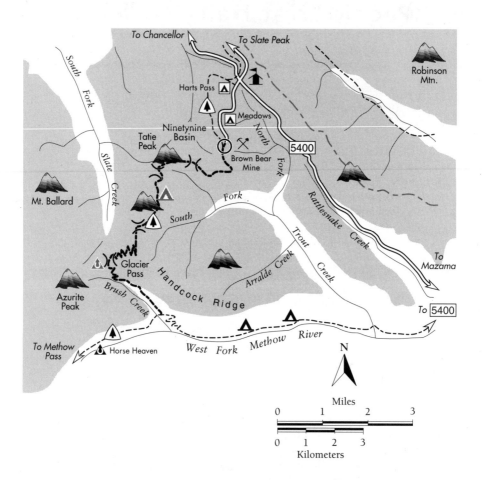

the valley from Azurite Peak, and its larch-studded meadows make an ideal destination for day hikers.

The trail begins above the old Brown Bear Mine, ascending moderately across a steep and rocky bowl. Marmots, pikas, and golden-mantled ground squirrels are abundant here, and a few subalpine larches rise from rocky moorings at the edge of the talus. The prominent massif to the east is Robinson Mountain. The upthrust strata of a rocky peak rise ahead, and the trail rises to surmount the ridgetop east of its summit.

Emerging high above the South Fork of Trout Creek, the trail offers a spectacular vista of the granite peaks of the Golden Horn batholith. Gardiner and Silver Star mountains rise along the eastern edge of the Cascades, with The Needles to the right of them. The craggy spires of Tower Mountain and the Golden Horn are next in line, followed by the distant and snowy summits of Ragged Ridge. A low gap at the head of the South Fork basin reveals the stark summit of Azurite Peak with its permanent collar of snow.

The trail now embarks upon a high circuit of the basin, crossing flower-studded meadows and arid slopes of shattered stone. A nameless summit guards the head of the basin, and an anticline, or downwarping of the rock strata, can be seen clearly in its east face. A shallow grade leads up to a saddle above the Ninetynine Basin, with its rainbow-banded peaks guarding a collection of shallow ponds in the meadows far below. Views from this point encompass the barren summits of the Pasayten Wilderness stretching northward to the horizon. A gentle descent leads to a pass above the Slate Creek watershed, and a short side trip to the top of the divide yields a stunning perspective of Mount Ballard as well as a distant view of Jack Mountain.

The path now skirts the base of the next summit, passing through sparse stands of larch and crossing broad talus slopes. There are several camps in sheltered spots along the way, with lingering snowfields nearby to supply drinking water. On the far side of the peak, the trail rises onto the long ridgetop known to some as "Grasshopper Pass," with its larch meadows and face-to-face views of Azurite Peak and Mount Ballard. The rusty tint on the ridge that links the two peaks is derived from the oxidation of iron-rich ores in the bedrock. Most day hikers turn around here.

The trail now winds southward, climbing a rugged ridgetop. Soon there are views of the Golden Horn and the nameless spires that guard distant Mebee Pass. Approaching its apogee, the path swings onto the west side of the ridge. It then begins a long descent to Glacier Pass, zigzagging down across steep and grassy slopes. These slopes play out into heather and fir parklands at the bottom of the grade, and small boulderfields provide habitat for pikas and marmots. After winding downward through subalpine forest, the trail finally reaches the level trough of Glacier Pass. There is a campsite in the trees beside the trail, but the horse camp occupies the prime location: a streamside meadow to the west beneath the gaze of Azurite Peak.

The trail soon drops into the Brushy Creek valley, where snowslides from towering cliffs have cleared the south side of the valley of all but the most supple shrubs. Enterprising beavers have been quick to exploit this mother lode of edible twigs; you can view their handiwork as the trail crosses talus slopes in the middle reaches of the valley. Pikas also live here, in the broken rock beside the trail. As the trail descends steadily across the north side of the valley, it enters tall brushfields of slide alder and mountain ash. The brush finally gives way to isolated stands of ancient spruce and Douglas-fir at the mouth of the valley. Hikers gain parting glimpses of The Needles and Tower Mountain as the trail completes its final descent to the West Fork Methow Trail.

68 Dagger Lake and Twisp Pass

See Map on Page 265

Overview: A long day hike or short backpack to Dagger Lake, 12.6 miles round trip.
Best season: Mid-July to mid-October.
Difficulty: Moderately strenuous.
Elevation gain: 4,628 feet.
Elevation loss: 3,124 feet to Twisp River Road.
Maximum elevation: 6,064 feet at Twisp Pass.
Topo maps: Washington Pass, McAlester Mountain, Gilbert; *Washington Pass, Stehekin.*
Jurisdiction: North Cascades National Park, Lake Chelan–Sawtooth Wilderness (Okanogan National Forest).

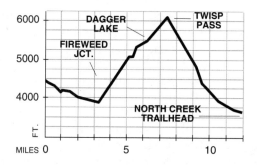

Finding the trailhead: The hike begins at the Pacific Crest Trail South Trailhead, at mile 159.2 on Washington Highway 20, 2 miles east of Rainy Pass.

Key points:

0.0 PCT South Trailhead. Cross highway to begin hike.
0.1 Junction with PCT inbound from Rainy Pass. Keep left.
0.8 Junction with Bridge Creek Trail. Turn left and cross State Creek.
0.9 Junction with old Bridge Creek Trail. Turn left.
1.0 Junction with Copper Pass Trail. Bear right.
2.0 Junction with Stiletto Peak Trail. Continue straight ahead.
3.3 Junction with trails to Fireweed Camp and McAlester Pass. Turn left.
6.3 Dagger Lake. Spur trail descends to hiker camp.
7.3 Twisp Pass. Trail leaves North Cascades National Park and enters Lake Chelan–Sawtooth Wilderness.
9.7 Trail crosses the North Fork of the Twisp River to join Copper Pass Trail. Turn right.
11.5 Road's End Campground.
12.1 North Creek Trailhead.

The hike: Dagger Lake is a shallow and weedy tarn at the edge of North Cascades National Park. Because it is easily reached in a short day's backpack from the highway, the lake is a popular destination: reservations for its two campsites fill up quickly on weekends and holidays. Dispersed camping is allowed without a permit east of Twisp Pass, within the Lake Chelan-Sawtooth Wilderness. This is steep country, though, and level camping spots with access to water are difficult to find.

From the Pacific Crest Trail (PCT) South trailhead, cross the highway and follow the main trail on a southeasterly heading. A moderate descent follows the highway through a forest of tall mountain hemlock. After a short distance, the PCT splits away to the right toward a bridge over Bridge Creek, while the trail to Dagger Lake veers left to continue along the east bank of the creek.

There is a fine Forest Service campsite as the trail crosses State Creek, and on the far side, a faint spur runs south to reach the ruins of an old drift mine on a bench above Bridge Creek. This type of mine comprises a vertical shaft sunk into loose alluvial gravels, shored up by timbers to prevent collapse. Once the shaft reached solid bedrock, where the heavy placer gold was concentrated, the richest deposit or "pay streak" was followed laterally by "drifting" horizontal shafts along the deposit of gold-bearing gravels until the paydirt petered out. An abandoned segment of the Bridge Creek Trail runs south from the mine site; the route to Dagger Lake follows the wider path that runs east from the junction above the mine.

The latter trail soon turns south at a junction with the Copper Pass Trail. A gradual descent through silver firs leads across the valley's edge, and occasional brushfields yield glimpses of Frisco Mountain. Just beyond the

Dagger Lake.

national park boundary, the Stiletto Peak Trail climbs away to the left, while the main trail descends quickly into the gloomy spruce swamps of the Bridge Creek bottoms. After a shady trek, a broad avalanche slope offers views of a thin waterfall on the flanks of Frisco Mountain. The broad bottomlands give way to wooded hummocks and swales as the trail progresses down the valley. It eventually reaches a well-marked junction with the connector trail linking McAlester Lake and Bridge Creek trails via Fireweed Camp.

Turn left here as the Dagger Lake Trail begins a steady climb up the mountainside. After a long slog through Douglas-fir woodland, the trail breaks out into a clearing filled with ceanothus bushes. To the south are views of the rocky peaks that line the head of the McAlester Creek valley. The path continues to climb, entering the valley of the East Fork of McAlester Creek. Initially it crosses snowslide tracks choked with alder, but later an unbroken forest of silver fir and spruce covers the mountainside.

The trail continues upward at a moderate pace and reaches the floor of an elevated basin. Here, runnels of clear water flow amid copses of mountain hemlock and heather-huckleberry parks. The manicured vegetation gives the effect of a Japanese garden, guarded by the soaring face of Hock Mountain. The woodland becomes more ragged as the trail glides upward to a spot above the north shore of Dagger Lake. The horse camp is above the trail here, while a spur path leads down to the hiker camp amid scattered spruces on the lakeshore. The marshy sedge flats around the water foster a burgeoning population of mosquitoes that are always biting, even when the smallish cutthroats that cruise the lake are not.

After passing the horse camp, the trail arcs upward, rounding the lake basin as it climbs steadily to the broad divide of Twisp Pass. Watch for marmots as the trail approaches the timberline. The trail leaves North Cascades National Park as it crosses the divide, and a faint way trail runs northward toward a high lake on the shoulder of Stiletto Peak. The main trail now descends into the Lake Chelan–Sawtooth Wilderness, crossing shelves of bedrock that alternate with brushy meadows. Lincoln Butte rises just to the north, and to the south is an ever-expanding panorama of the craggy peaks that guard the South Fork of the Twisp River.

The trail soon swings onto the eastern slopes of Lincoln Butte, descending more moderately across the open slopes covered alternately in brushfields and broken rock. The path enters a woodland of lodgepole pine as it nears the forks of the Twisp River. Upon reaching the confluence of the North and South Forks, the trail jogs westward as it descends to the North Fork, crossing the stream beside a junction with the Copper Pass Trail. Turn right as the route begins to descend more briskly across brushy slopes and through ragged stands of deciduous trees mixed with conifers. To end the trek, hikers can descend a steep pathway to reach Road's End Campground, or can continue east on the main trail for another 0.6 mile to reach the North Creek Trailhead.

69 Stiletto Peak

See Map on Page 265

Overview:	A day hike to the timberline meadows on Stiletto Peak, 9.2 miles round trip.
Best season:	Mid-July to mid-October.
Difficulty:	Moderately strenuous.
Elevation gain:	2,240 feet.
Elevation loss:	500 feet.
Maximum elevation:	7,400 feet at the old lookout site on the mountaintop.
Topo maps:	Washington Pass, McAlester Mountain; *Washington Pass, Stehekin.*
Jurisdiction:	Okanogan National Forest, North Cascades National Park.

Finding the trailhead: The hike begins at the Pacific Crest Trail South Trailhead, at mile 159.2 on Washington Highway 20, 2 miles east of Rainy Pass.

Key points:

- 0.0 PCT South Trailhead. Cross the highway to reach the trail.
- 0.1 Junction with the PCT inbound from Rainy Pass. Bear left.
- 0.8 Junction with trail that follows east bank of Bridge Creek. Turn left and cross State Creek.
- 0.9 Unmarked junction with old Bridge Creek Trail. Bear left.
- 1.0 Junction with Copper Pass Trail. Keep right.
- 2.0 Stiletto Peak Trail splits away from main trail. Turn left.
- 4.6 Trail peters out in subalpine meadows on shoulders of Stiletto Peak.

The hike: This seldom-hiked trail climbs from the Bridge Creek valley to subalpine meadows high on the flanks of Stiletto Peak. The trail disappears above timberline, but ambitious hikers can navigate upward by dead reckoning to reach the clifftop perch that once was the site of a fire lookout on one of the western summits. The entire trek can be completed in a long day of hiking.

From the Pacific Crest Trail (PCT) South Trailhead, follow the Dagger Lake route along the east bank of Bridge Creek. The Stiletto Peak Trail leaves from a signpost just beyond the national park boundary, and zigzags upward through a mature forest of silver fir. There are brushy openings as the path crosses small watercourses, with westward views of Frisco Mountain. The forest becomes patchy as the trail gains altitude, and the openings are carpeted with huckleberry bushes.

The path eventually reaches dry, south-facing meadows that offer views

Meadows atop Stiletto Peak.

of the many crags of Bowan Mountain. Continuing up into the subalpine zone, hikers can see the granite bones of the mountain begin to show through the veneer of vegetation. The lone summit of Whistler Mountain is now visible to the north, guarding Rainy Pass. As it nears the top of a level bench, the trail enters a series of lush meadows bedecked with wildflowers of all descriptions. The track is discernible for a short distance, then disappears in the midst of the meadows. The summit of Lincoln Butte is now visible to the east.

Adventurous hikers may follow the cairns upward, making a calf-burning climb to the mountaintop lookout site. Sheer cliffs drop away into the valley of Copper Creek, and all around are the jagged needles of the Golden Horn batholith.

70 McAlester Lake

See Map on Page 265

Overview:	A long day hike or backpack to McAlester Lake, 15.1 miles round trip, or a backpack to McAlester Pass, 8.5 miles one way.
Best season:	Mid-July to mid-October.
Difficulty:	Moderate.
Elevation gain:	2,230 feet.
Elevation loss:	790 feet.
Maximum elevation:	6,000 feet at McAlester Pass.
Topo maps:	Washington Pass, McAlester Mountain; *Washington Pass, Stehekin.*
Jurisdiction:	North Cascades National Park, Lake Chelan National Recreation Area.

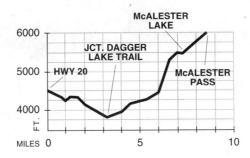

Finding the trailhead: The hike begins at the Pacific Crest Trail South Trailhead, at mile 159.2 on Washington Highway 20, 2 miles east of Rainy Pass.

Key points:
- 0.0 PCT South Trailhead. Cross highway to begin hike.
- 0.1 Junction with the PCT inbound from Rainy Pass. Keep left.
- 0.8 Junction with Bridge Creek Trail. Turn left and cross State Creek.
- 0.9 Junction with old Bridge Creek Trail. Turn left.
- 1.0 Junction with Copper Pass Trail. Bear right.
- 2.0 Junction with Stiletto Peak Trail. Continue straight ahead.
- 3.3 Junction with trails to Fireweed Camp and Dagger Lake. Turn right, then left to get onto McAlester Lake Trail.
- 4.1 Trail crosses East Fork of McAlester Creek.
- 7.4 Spur trail leads to McAlester Lake and camps. Bear left for McAlester Pass.
- 8.3 Junction with spur path to Hidden Meadows horse camp (0.7 mile, moderate). Continue straight ahead.
- 8.4 Spur trail runs west to High Camp.
- 8.5 McAlester Pass. Junction with South Pass and Rainbow Creek trails.

The hike: With fine fishing for small trout, McAlester Lake makes a good destination for a short backpacking trip. The trail continues up to McAlester

McAlester Lake.

Pass, linking with trails to Hidden Meadow, South Pass, and Rainbow Creek. The McAlester Lake trail is accessed most directly by the trail that follows the east bank of Bridge Creek (see Dagger Lake, Hike 68), but can also be reached via the more scenic Pacific Crest Trail (PCT) route.

To begin the hike, follow the Dagger Lake route along the east bank of Bridge Creek. The McAlester Lake Trail begins at a well-marked junction just east of Fireweed Camp, and climbs at a steady pace beside the rushing torrent of McAlester Creek. An open woodland dappled with the blossoms of lupine soon gives way to a closed-canopy forest of spruce and hemlock. The path soon rock-hops across several channels of the East Fork of McAlester Creek, then continues a moderate climb through a forest where queen's cup lilies grow. There is a pleasant waterfall on McAlester Creek before the trail crosses an open avalanche field. Look backward here for a view of Frisco Mountain.

After returning to the forest, the trail enters Lake Chelan National Recreation Area and soon begins to climb away from the valley floor. An old snowslide track, grown up with droopy Alaska cedars and spire-shaped subalpine firs, provides the next alpine scenery. From here, the craggy northern ribs of Bowan Mountain can be seen rising all around the head of the valley. The path now begins to climb in earnest, ascending steadily through a series of long switchbacks. A sparse forest of old mountain hemlocks allows glimpses of the neighboring peaks, but there is never an unobstructed view. The path finally levels off in the forested basin that bears McAlester Lake. The lake is hard to see from the trail; a side trip to the hiker camp is

Dagger Lake • McAlester Lake
Stiletto Peak • Twisp Pass • Copper Pass

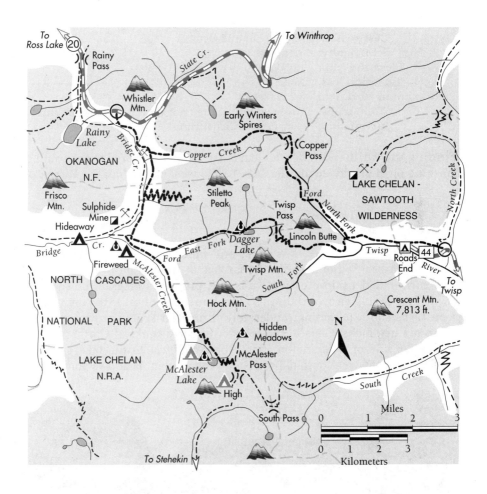

required for a good look. A rugged foothill rises west of the lake, and an abundance of small cutthroat trout cruise its greenish waters.

After passing the lake, the trail zigzags moderately up through the forest to reach the alpine tundra at McAlester Pass. High Camp is situated at the north end of the pass in a heavily impacted bog, while a spur trail runs northeast to the horse camp at Hidden Meadow. In the center of the pass, marmots guard the spot where the trail links up with the South Pass and Rainbow Creek trails.

71 Blue Lake

Overview:	A half-day hike to Blue Lake, 4.4 miles round trip.
Best season:	Mid-July to mid-October.
Difficulty:	Moderate.
Elevation gain:	1,050 feet.
Elevation loss:	None.
Maximum elevation:	6,250 feet.
Topo maps:	Washington Pass (trail not shown); *Washington Pass*.
Jurisdiction:	Okanogan National Forest.

Finding the trailhead: The trail leaves from a parking area to the south of Washington Highway 20 at mile 161, 1 mile west of Washington Pass.

Key points:
    0.0   Blue Lake Trailhead.
    2.2   Blue Lake.

The hike: This trail offers a short and modest trek in the vicinity of Washington Pass, climbing into the larches at timberline to reach a deep lake surrounded by impressive walls and pinnacles of granite. The trail begins by running eastward through subalpine forest beside the highway. It soon turns south, climbing moderately through a sparse growth of large mountain hemlocks. Gaps in the trees offer early peeks at Cutthroat Peak on the far side of Washington Pass. About halfway to the lake, the trail breaks out of the trees onto old rockslides mantled in meadows and fringed

Blue Lake.

Blue Lake

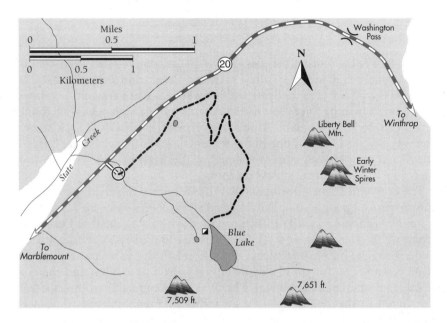

by subalpine larches. The surrounding peaks are now unveiled, stretching westward to include Mount Hardy and Black Peak.

The trail ascends gradually on a westward course, and the summit of Liberty Bell Mountain uncloaks itself to the east, flanked by the Early Winters Spires. Near trail's end, a rushing stream leads upward to the rocky shores of Blue Lake. This deep alpine tarn is guarded by imposing rock walls, and its translucent waters are home to abundant cutthroat trout. Camping is no longer allowed here due to the heavy impacts past visitors had on the fragile larch-heather community of the lakeshore.

ADDITIONAL TRAILS

The **Mill Creek Trail** is burned over and choked with fallen logs at its lower end and overgrown with alders near the Azurite Mine. Don't bother.

The trail from the Azurite Mine over **Azurite Pass** receives no maintenance and has been reclaimed by the wilderness.

The **Boulder Creek Trail** follows an old narrow-gauge route to the North American Mine site, then continues up the valley and over a pass to meet the East Creek Trail. Last cleared in 1980, it is hard to follow in the brushy avalanche tracks at the head of Boulder Creek.

The **Trout Creek Trail** is a hunter-access trail that descends from Harts Pass Road into the Trout Creek valley and visits several meadows.

The **Driveway Butte Trail** runs from WA 20 to an old fire lookout site above the West Fork of the Methow River. It opens fairly early in the summer, and is known for having lots of rattlesnakes.

The Stehekin Valley

Long before the North Cascades Highway was completed in 1972, centuries before miners flooded the valley of Ruby Creek and forged a path over Harts Pass to the north, Salish-speaking peoples were traveling well-worn trails along a rushing river that poured down from the high peaks and dumped its water into Lake Chelan. To the native peoples, the river was *Stehekin*, "the way through." It was one of the major trade routes across the Cascades. The Skagit people kept canoes stashed at the head of Lake Chelan to use after they crossed Cascade Pass on foot.

The Stehekin River (pronounced stuh-HEE-kihn) has held the interest of Euro-American people since the first British explorers came into this country in search of furs. Alexander Ross is credited with being the first European to penetrate the Cascades, and scholars surmise that in 1814 his Skagit Indian guides brought him over Cascade Pass to reach the valleys that drain into Puget Sound. The fur trade was never very profitable here, and the North Cascades remained a backwater. The next big boom came in the late 1880s, when gold in the region brought an influx of rough-cut prospectors who blasted mineshafts into the nearby mountains. This boom also faded quickly, giving way to a trickle of hardy settlers who carved homesteads out of the forested bottomlands of the Stehekin Valley. Human settlement has always been sparse, but the valley has been inhabited steadily over the last century by a self-reliant breed of subsistence farmers. Their current year-round population numbers about 100.

This spectacular valley at the head of Lake Chelan has consistently drawn sightseers from the far corners of the world. The original lodge here was the Field Hotel, established in 1892. It was dismantled in 1927 when a dam was built at the outlet of Lake Chelan, raising the water level by 21 feet and inundating the hotel site. Lumber from the Field Hotel was later used to build the Golden West Lodge nearby. In 1968, the Stehekin Valley was incorporated into the North Cascades National Park complex as the Lake Chelan National Recreation Area. The Golden West Lodge has become a National Park Service visitor center. Nearby is the North Cascades Stehekin Lodge and an array of small mercantile businesses. There is a bakery up the road a few miles that is not to be missed, and even farther north is the Courtney guest ranch, where lodging and meals can be had (reservations required). The Courtney family also runs short horse trips into the park. The Buckner Orchard, across from Rainbow Falls, is a historic fruit orchard established in 1912 and now maintained by the National Park Service as a historical attraction. The apples ripen in late September, and are free to anyone who can coexist with the black bears that also feed there.

The Stehekin's quaint charm depends upon its remoteness: the only cars in the area were brought in by barge over Lake Chelan. In the summer, a

Stehekin Valley Overview

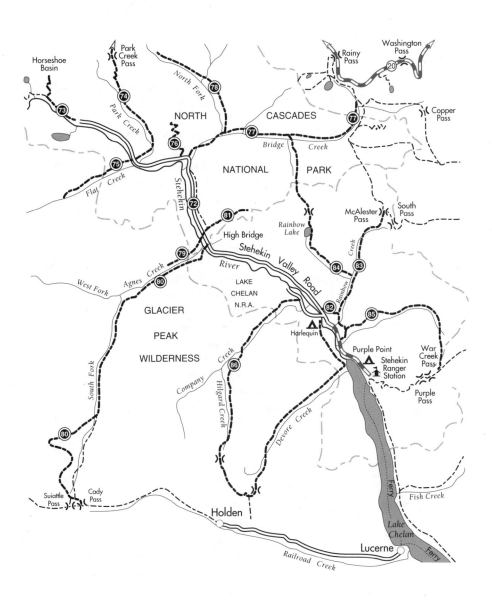

passenger ferry provides daily service to Stehekin (see p. 322 for details). Once there, a tour bus runs upvalley for a brief stop at Rainbow Falls. A longer hiker shuttle once ran the 22-mile length of the Stehekin Valley Road for a fee, providing access to trailheads (see the park newspaper for details). Floods in the winter of 1995–1996 washed out part of this road, and as of this writing the shuttlebuses were turning around at Flat Creek. As an alternative to the ferry, the hikes over Cascade Pass or down Bridge Creek are almost as fast (and cost less), and provide easiest access to the upper reaches of the Stehekin River. Other good routes into the Stehekin Valley include the South Pass Trail and the War Creek Trail, both of which originate beside the Twisp River.

Camping along the Stehekin Valley Road requires a free backcountry permit, which can be obtained at the Golden West Visitor Center. The backcountry of the Lake Chelan National Recreation Area has wilderness status, so motorized vehicles are prohibited outside the road corridor. Hunting is allowed within the Recreation Area, but all firearms are strictly prohibited on national park lands, which stretch northward from High Bridge. Park permits are required for all backcountry stays within both the national park and the recreation area, but permits are not required to camp within the neighboring Glacier Peak and Lake Chelan–Sawtooth wilderness areas. These areas fall within the domain of the Wenatchee National Forest.

Weather in the Stehekin Valley is typically warmer and drier than that found west of the range, with summer temperatures in the 90s common. Mountain weather is still unpredictable, though, and travelers should be prepared for chilly or wet weather, which may strike without warning. Ticks are rather troublesome pests in the Stehekin Valley, particularly abundant in spring and early summer. Rattlesnakes also live here, but they are reclusive and rarely present a real danger. Watch where you walk, and if you encounter a rattlesnake, remain still so it can retreat safely.

72 Stehekin Valley Road

Overview:	A gravel access route for hikers, bicyclists, and motorcyclists, 11.1 miles from High Bridge to Cottonwood.
Best season:	Mid-May to late October.
Difficulty:	Easy.
Elevation gain:	1,380 feet.
Elevation loss:	190 feet.
Maximum elevation:	2,750 feet.
Topo maps:	McGregor Mountain, Goode Mountain; *McGregor Mountain.*
Jurisdiction:	North Cascades National Park.

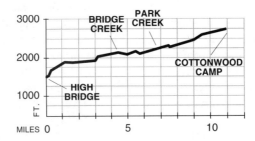

Finding the route: High Bridge marks the start of the route; take the shuttlebus or hike up the road 10.5 miles from Stehekin.

Key points:

0.0	High Bridge.
0.1	Agnes Creek Trailhead.
0.15	Agnes Gorge Trailhead.
0.2	High Bridge Camp.
0.7	Tumwater Camp.
0.9	Tumwater Bridge. Road now follows east bank of river.
1.7	Dolly Varden Camp.
3.1	Shady Camp.
4.2	Road crosses Clear Creek to reach Bridge Creek Camp.
4.4	Bridge Creek Trailhead.
4.5	Road crosses Bridge Creek to reach Goode Ridge Trailhead.
6.7	Road crosses Park Creek to reach Park Creek camp and trailhead.
7.0	Flat Creek Trailhead.
9.8	First of road washouts. Improvised trail follows river channel with several crossings.
11.1	Road ends at Cottonwood Camp.

The hike: This gravel trunk road runs from the boat landing at the head of Lake Chelan to Cottonwood Camp, following the Stehekin River all the way. Shuttlebus service once carried hikers along the entire length of the road, but floods during the winter of 1995 caused the road's closure at High Bridge. The buses currently run as far as Flat Creek, but resumption of shuttlebus service beyond this point remains in doubt. In the interim period, the road is open to hikers and horses, and mountain bikers and motorcyclists can reach a point about 2 miles short of Cottonwood Camp. All camping areas along the road are considered backcountry sites for permit purposes. Permits can be obtained free of charge from the Golden West Visitor Center or from other ranger stations around the North Cascades. Hikers on the Pacific Crest Trail (PCT) should note that the Old Wagon Road parallels the Stehekin Valley route from Bridge Creek to High Bridge, linking the two points by trail.

The trekking begins at High Bridge, and on the far bank of the river are two distinct trail junctions: first the PCT along Agnes Creek (Hike 80), then the short, dead-end Agnes Gorge Trail (Hike 79). High Bridge camp is on the opposite side of the road, with a long downward trek required to reach the river. McGregor Mountain is the stony massif to the east. The road climbs briefly, then levels off. It soon passes Tumwater Camp, sited above a roaring section of whitewater, then drops to cross the Tumwater Bridge. There are good views of the rapids from here. The road then climbs onto the bluffs east of the river, and here a cutoff trail links up with the Old Wagon Road, a connecting trail that parallels the roadway, slightly to the east.

The main road now descends to the riverbank, passing beneath overhanging outcrops and small waterfalls as the river courses through turbulent riffles and turquoise pools. Dolly Varden Camp occupies a picturesque riverside spot, while Shady Camp lies a mile upstream in a grove of old

Stehekin River at Tumwater Bridge.

272

Stehekin Valley Road

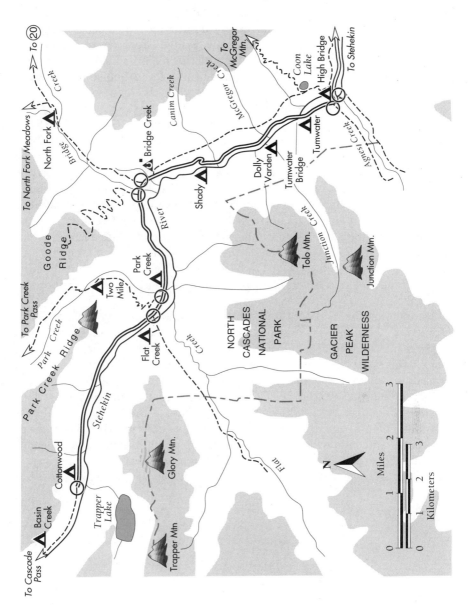

spruce and cedar. Beyond it, the road snakes high onto a wooded terrace, then continues north to find Bridge Creek Camp beside the limpid waters of a woodland brook, which is Clear Creek. Old cabins and a horse corral lie beyond the camp, and after passing these structures the road reaches a junction with the segment of the PCT that follows Bridge Creek (Hike 77). Bridge Creek itself is crossed a short time later, and this major tributary stream has carved for itself a deep channel in the bedrock. Its turquoise waters slide downward through a series of falls and deep pools, then swirl around a stony island just below the bridge.

On the far bank of Bridge Creek is a junction with the Goode Ridge Trail (Hike 76). The road now follows a great westward bend in the valley, climbing gently into a Douglas-fir woodland. Hikers get several views of the river along the way, and downriver views reveal the arid western face of McGregor Mountain. The trees begin to thin near Park Creek, revealing mountains ahead. Glory Mountain hulks to the south of the valley, while the summit of Booker Mountain guards its north side. The trail to Park Creek Pass (Hike 74) departs beside a creekside camp, and after climbing onto a rise, the Flat Creek route (Hike 75) splits away to the left. A short side trip long this trail is a must; within 100 yards there is a bridge spanning a small but breathtaking gorge on the Stehekin River. Flat Creek Camp is on a short spur trail on the far bank.

Meanwhile, the road continues upriver beneath the stony cliffs of Glory Mountain. About halfway between Flat Creek and Cottonwood, the river has adopted the roadbed as a flood channel. There are several tricky crossings beyond this point, and wheeled vehicles must stop here. The forest dwindles away into brushy bottomlands, and the blunt summit of Pelton Peak rises ahead. As the road approaches Cottonwood Camp, the summits of Trapper Mountain and Hurry-Up Peak can be seen above the low headwall that serves as a natural dam for Trapper Lake. The road ends in a riverside grove of Douglas-fir and cottonwood. Cottonwood Camp provides spots to pitch a tent, and from here the trail to Cascade Pass continues westward along the river.

73 Horseshoe Basin

Overview: A half-day side trip from the Cascade Pass Trail junction, 3 miles round trip, or a long day trip from Flat Creek, 15.5 miles round trip.

Best season: Late June to mid-October; Cascade Pass does not become snow-free until mid-July.

Difficulty: Moderate.

Elevation gain: 2,085 feet.

Elevation loss: None.

Maximum elevation: 4,840 feet at Black Warrior Mine.

Topo maps: Cascade Pass, Goode Mountain; *Cascade Pass, McGregor Mountain.*

Jurisdiction: North Cascades National Park.

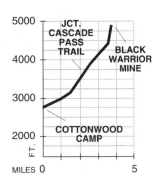

Finding the trailhead: The trail begins at Cottonwood Camp at the end of the Stehekin Valley Road.

Key points:

```
0.0  Cottonwood Camp Trailhead. Hike west on Cascade Pass Trail.
1.4  Basin Creek Camp.
1.5  Trail crosses Basin Creek.
2.2  Junction with Horseshoe Basin Trail. Turn right.
2.6  Horseshoe Basin.
3.7  Trail ends at portal of Black Warrior Mine.
```

The hike: This trek follows the abandoned mining road that once led to the Black Warrior Mine. The mine site is one of the finest examples of hard-rock gold mining activity in the North Cascades, and is listed on the National Register of Historic Places. It could hardly have been blasted into a prettier site: Horseshoe Basin is lined by steep cliffs, and impressive waterfalls tumble down them from the glaciers above. The Horseshoe Basin was originally reached via a moderate day trip from the end of the Stehekin Valley Road. Until this road is reopened, hikers will have to start their journey at the Flat Creek Trailhead and walk an extra 4.1 miles on the Stehekin Valley Road (each way). The Horseshoe Basin can also be reached by following the Cascade Pass Trail eastward from the Cascade River watershed, a round-trip journey that requires a minimum of two long days to complete.

From the well-marked junction, the Horseshoe Basin spur trail climbs vigorously across the north wall of the Stehekin Valley. After a short distance, the old roadbed swings into the valley of Basin Creek, which is filled with a

Horseshoe Basin

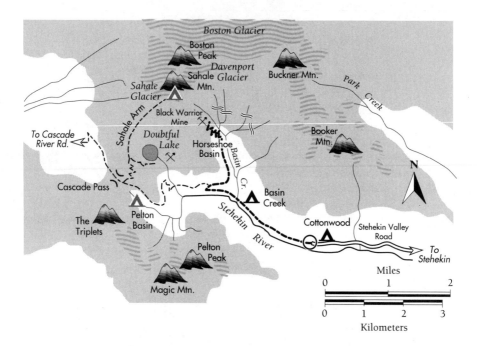

dense growth of slide alder. The climb eases as the trail makes its way up the valley, and soon offers spectacular views of the headwall that surrounds the Horseshoe Basin. More than a dozen breathtaking cascades grace the cliff walls, converging on the valley floor from Davenport Glacier on the flanks of Sahale Mountain as well as from permanent snowfields on Horseshoe Peak to the east of it.

Near the head of the basin, the alders give way to dense swards of fireweed that grow on the alluvial fan of Basin Creek. A southward glance reveals the majestic north face of Glory Mountain, with Trapper Mountain and Pelton Peak west of it. The old road now zigzags up the steep apron of boulders at the head of the basin, bound for the yawning mouth of the Black Warrior Mine. The entrance to the mine sits atop a mound of tailings, beside the base of one of the largest waterfalls. Long-lasting snow bridges make the final approach to the mine portal a hazardous one—beware of falling rocks from the cliffs above the portal.

Initially worked for gold in 1891, the Black Warrior Mine was abandoned after the initial gold rush subsided in 1914. The mine was reopened after World War II in response to surging silver and copper prices, but the operation fell prey to low-grade ore, avalanches, and rockslides. Living quarters and a generator shack were blasted into the rock at the mine's entrance and are still recognizable today. The cable tramway that once linked the road to a number of mines above the cliffs has long since fallen into ruin. The site is protected by federal law; it is illegal to deface or remove any of the artifacts.

74 Park Creek

Overview: A backpack from the Stehekin Valley to Park Creek Pass, 7.9 miles one way.

Best season: Late July to mid-October.

Difficulty: Moderately strenuous to Buckner Camp; strenuous beyond.

Elevation gain: 3,850 feet.

Elevation loss: 80 feet.

Maximum elevation: 6,100 feet at Park Creek Pass.

Topo maps: Goode Mountain; *McGregor Mountain.*

Jurisdiction: North Cascades National Park.

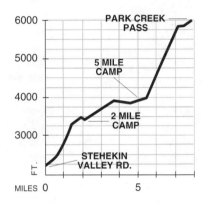

Finding the trailhead: The trail begins at Park Creek Camp, which can be reached via shuttlebus on the Stehekin Valley Road.

Key points:

0.0 Park Creek Camp.
1.4 Top of initial grade.
2.0 Two Mile Camp. Trail crosses Park Creek and follows east bank.
5.0 Five Mile Camp.
5.2 Buckner Camp. Trail begins ascent to Park Creek Pass.
7.9 Park Creek Pass. Thunder Creek Trail descends into valley beyond.

The hike: This trail forms one of the linkages between the Stehekin Valley and the outside world, with a challenging ascent over Park Creek Pass to the headwaters of Thunder Creek. Park Creek occupies a hanging valley that was gouged out of the rock by glaciers that flowed down from Buckner Mountain. As the planet warmed after the ice ages, these glaciers slowly receded, and now only small remnants of the once-massive river of ice remain at the head of the valley. The upper reaches of the trail yield superb alpine scenery, with sheer faces of rock rising on all sides of the upper basin. Buckner Camp makes a fine destination for day trippers bound upward from the Stehekin Valley; Park Creek Pass makes a better goal for backpackers.

The hike begins with a crossing of the Stehekin Valley lowlands, traveling through an open woodland of Douglas-fir to reach the base of Park Creek Ridge. As the trail zigzags up the slopes, the forest becomes denser, and

Buckner Mountain from the Park Creek Trail.

bigleaf and vine maples grow in the shady understory. Near the top of the grade, a brushy opening reveals the northernmost of the Seven Sisters beyond the Stehekin River. A final steep pitch leads to a rocky, bald top above the cliff-lined canyon of Park Creek. From here, views stretch southward to encompass the valley of Flat Creek, with LeConte Glacier at its head.

The trail then swings north onto the slopes above Park Creek, dipping and rising through arid savannahs of Douglas-fir. As it reaches cooler and moister exposures, the route enters a shady stand of spruce, hemlock, and silver fir. The trail now glides downward toward the tumultuous waters of Park Creek, and finds the lone tent site of Two Mile Camp nestled in a cluster of spruces. A footbridge leads across the stream, whereupon the trail embarks on a vigorous ascent of the slopes beyond. After a brief climb, the path levels off and continues up the valley, accompanied by the cliffs of Park Creek Ridge. With northward progress, broad openings reveal the first glimpse of Buckner Mountain at the head of the valley. Later, there are superb edge-on views of Booker Mountain.

After crossing a broad avalanche slope, the path enters a subalpine fir-spruce forest, and views disappear for a time. This woodland grades into a stand of old mountain hemlocks as the trail glides down to Five Mile Camp. Tent sites are located within the edge of the forest, beneath the towering cliffs of Booker Mountain. Just beyond the camp a series of avalanche meadows offers a stunning view of Buckner Mountain, with the several lobes of Buckner Glacier adorning its east face. Look north to see the castellated spires that mark the summit of Goode Mountain.

A short trek through the meadows leads to Buckner Camp, which has a

Park Creek

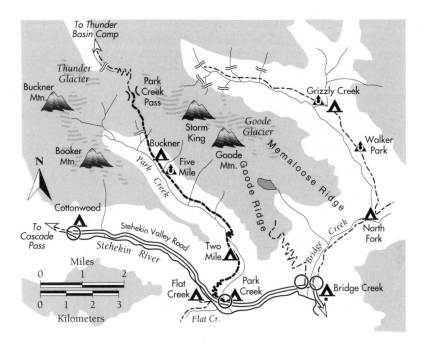

sweeping view of Buckner Mountain and its glaciers. Here, the trail turns away from Park Creek, climbing steeply toward a waterfall that issues from a notch in the north wall of the valley. The trail alternates between brushy avalanche tracks and narrow bands of timber as it climbs steeply up the mountainside. It levels off briefly as it enters a hanging vale, where the trees are replaced by lush swards of wildflowers and dense clumps of shrubbery.

The trail soon adopts a steep course up the mountainside, topping out in alpine fellfields below the cliffs of Goode Mountain. There are superb views of Booker Mountain from this point, and the glacier-clad summit of Buckner Mountain can again be seen above a low ridge. The filigree forms of subalpine larch rise from this ridge, brilliant green in summer and bright yellow as winter approaches. The path now ascends into a high basin of sedge meadows and heathery slopes, then climbs through the overgrown boulders to reach Park Creek Pass. Watch for marmots and pikas among the rocks, and look southward to a sea of jagged horns and arêtes that stretches westward from the shores of Lake Chelan. From the pass the Thunder Creek trail runs northward, bound for the Colonial Campground on the shores of Diablo Lake.

75 Flat Creek

Overview:	A day hike from the Stehekin River to the upper Flat Creek, 7 miles round trip.
Best season:	Late May to mid-October.
Difficulty:	Easy.
Elevation gain:	440 feet.
Elevation loss:	70 feet.
Maximum elevation:	2,520 feet.
Topo maps:	Goode Mountain (trail not shown); *McGregor Mountain*.
Jurisdiction:	North Cascades National Park, Glacier Peak Wilderness (Wenatchee National Forest).

END OF TRAIL

3000

2000

FT.

MILES 0   5

Finding the trailhead: The trail begins at a marked trailhead on the Stehekin Valley Road, which can be reached by shuttlebus.

Key points:
- 0.0 Flat Creek Trailhead.
- 0.1 Trail crosses gorge on Stehekin River and then meets spur trail to Flat Creek Camp. Stay left.
- 2.4 Trail enters Glacier Peak Wilderness.
- 3.1 Trail crosses west Fork of Flat Creek.
- 3.5 Trail ends on the bank of Flat Creek.

Flat Creek Valley.

Flat Creek

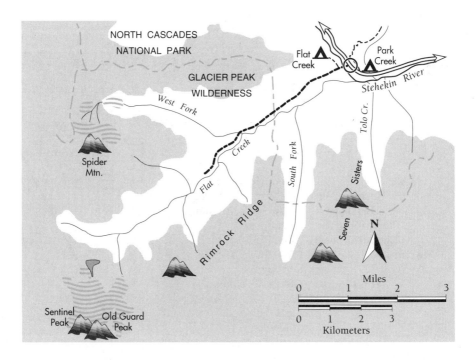

The hike: This short and level trail penetrates the valley of Flat Creek, a little-known tributary of the Stehekin River. It is a dead-end trail and receives little use. This is a good place for solitude seekers to fulfill their wilderness dreams. The upper reaches of the trail fall within the Glacier Peak Wilderness, where dispersed camping is allowed anywhere.

From the Stehekin Valley Road, the trail drops to a bridge over the river, which thunders through a shallow chasm at this point. A spur path runs north along the riverbank to reach Flat Creek Camp, while the main trail runs southward into the broad Flat Creek valley. It now embarks on a gentle but steady ascent across the slopes north of the creek. The coniferous forest soon falls away, replaced by broad swaths of alders punctuated by an occasional Douglas-fir of great age. Ahead, the craggy summit of LeConte Mountain guards the head of the Flat Creek drainage, while farther south are Sentinel and Old Guard peaks, mantled in the icy fastness of LeConte Glacier.

These are the last of the mountain views; the trail now descends into forested bottomlands on its way to the West Fork of Flat Creek. A footlog leads across the waters; steep banks make this a tricky crossing for horses. After a brief sojourn through the closed-canopy forest, the trail breaks out into brushy openings that are dominated by tall bracken fern. Ancient cedars and cottonwoods rise from the floodplain; some particularly large specimens grow near the end of the trail. Waterfalls on the far wall of the valley reveal themselves before the path dead-ends at a series of flood channels in the forest.

76 Goode Ridge

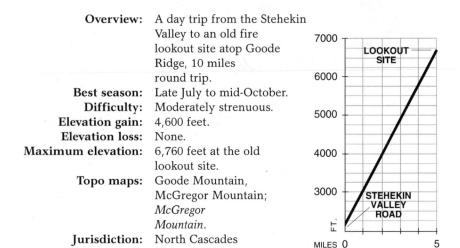

Overview:	A day trip from the Stehekin Valley to an old fire lookout site atop Goode Ridge, 10 miles round trip.
Best season:	Late July to mid-October.
Difficulty:	Moderately strenuous.
Elevation gain:	4,600 feet.
Elevation loss:	None.
Maximum elevation:	6,760 feet at the old lookout site.
Topo maps:	Goode Mountain, McGregor Mountain; *McGregor Mountain.*
Jurisdiction:	North Cascades National Park.

Finding the trailhead: The trail, accessible by shuttlebus, leaves the Stehekin Valley Road on the west bank of Bridge Creek,

Key points:
    0.0   Trailhead just west of Bridge Creek bridge.
    1.2   Trail crosses stream where water is sometimes available.
    5.0   Trail reaches former site of fire lookout atop Goode Ridge.

The hike: This trail provides a challenging and rewarding day trip from the Stehekin Valley Road to the alpine crest of Goode Ridge. The trail begins by zigzagging upward through a loose woodland of Douglas-fir, climbing at a measured pace. The forest understory is determined by soil moisture: dry areas are dominated by snowberry and low-growing kinnikinnick, while wetter spots support thickets of Douglas maple and, higher up, mountain ash. Douglas-firs are not as well-adapted to heavy snowfall as their higher-elevation cousins, and many of them have bent trunks known variously as "pistol butt" or "snow knees." This condition results when young saplings are bent to the ground by snow that is creeping downhill. Growth hormones stimulated by sunlight cause the slender trunks to grow straight up from their prostrate position, resulting in the odd curvature at the base of the tree.

Early views feature McGregor Mountain to the southwest and the sharp

Looking up the Stehekin Valley from Goode Ridge.

horn at the end of Heather Ridge to the south. These views are soon joined by the Seven Sisters, which rise farther up the Stehekin Valley. The trail then rises above the trees into an old burn, revealing panoramic views of Bridge Creek and the rugged summits that surround it. The summit of Mount Lyall can now be seen to the south. The trail zigzags steadily up the slope, then emerges unexpectedly onto a gentle shelf shaded by mountain hemlocks.

The respite is a brief one, since steep and open slopes beckon above. Ever-expanding views reveal Flat Creek and the glacier-clad summits of Sentinel Peak and LeConte Mountain at its head. With increasing elevation, the trail faces up the Stehekin Valley for views of Trapper and Johannesburg mountains and a crowd of lesser spires that rises between them. Nearing the summit, the trail reveals the blocky summit of Booker Mountain as well as Buckner Mountain with its sparkling glaciers.

The old lookout site occupies the summit of a long promontory that extends into the heart of the Stehekin Valley, with jagged peaks arrayed in all directions. Nearest of the peaks is Goode Mountain, with the long and rocky finger of Memaloose Ridge running southward from its base. The deep basin below bears Green View Lake, which can barely be seen, but the pretty waterfalls that descend from its outlet are in plain view. Grassy alpine swards fringed with larches beckon as picnic spots, but they are fragile; rest on the impact-resistant bedrock instead.

Goode Ridge

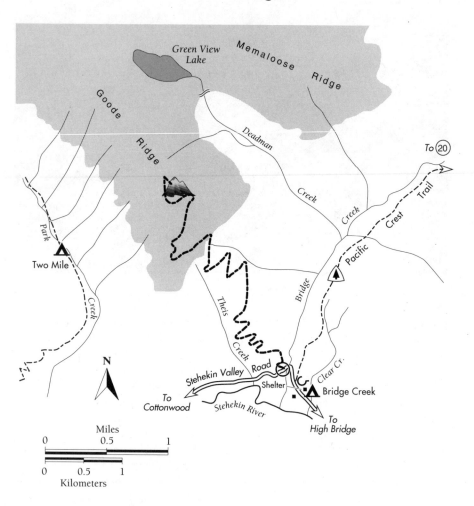

Green View Lake

Memaloose Ridge

Goode Ridge

Deadman Creek

To (20)

Pacific Crest Trail

Park Creek

Two Mile

Theis Creek

Bridge Creek

Clear Cr.

Stehekin Valley Road

Shelter

Bridge Creek

To Cottonwood

Stehekin River

To High Bridge

N

Miles
0   0.5   1

0   0.5   1
Kilometers

77 Bridge Creek

Overview:	A backpack along Bridge Creek from Washington Highway 20 to the Stehekin Valley Road, 11.1 miles total.
Best season:	Early July to mid-October.
Difficulty:	Moderate.
Elevation gain:	800 feet (north to south).
Elevation loss:	3,030 feet (north to south).
Maximum elevation:	4,400 feet at the PCT South Trailhead.
Topo maps:	Washington Pass, McAlester Mountain, McGregor Mountain; *Washington Pass, Stehekin, McGregor Mountain.*
Jurisdiction:	North Cascades National Park.

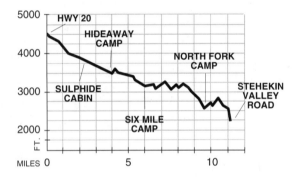

Finding the trailhead: The hike begins at the Pacific Crest Trail (PCT) South trailhead, at mile 159.2 on WA 20, 2 miles east of Rainy Pass. The trail emerges on the Stehekin Valley Road, 4.3 miles above High Bridge.

Key points:
- 0.0 PCT South Trailhead.
- 0.1 Junction with PCT inbound from Rainy Pass. Bear left.
- 0.8 Junction with trail that follows east bank of Bridge Creek. Turn right, following signs for the PCT.
- 0.9 Trail crosses Bridge Creek and follows west bank.
- 1.4 Trail enters North Cascades National Park.
- 2.5 Ruins of sulphide mining claim.
- 3.1 Junction with trail to Fireweed Camp, Dagger Lake, and McAlester Pass. Bear right.
- 4.0 Spur path descends to Hideaway Camp.
- 5.1 Trail crosses Frisco Creek.
- 5.5 Junction with trail to South Fork camps and Rainbow Lake. Continue straight ahead.
- 6.2 Spur path descends to Six Mile Camp.

Bridge Creek

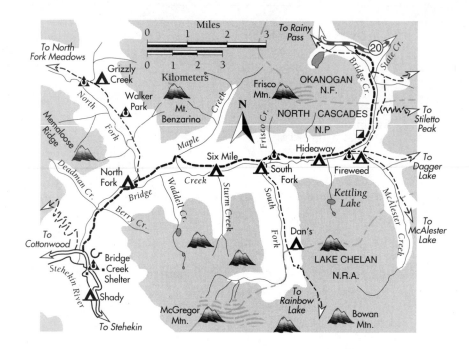

6.7 Upper end of Bridge Creek gorge.
7.6 Maple Creek crossing.
9.2 Junction with North Fork Meadows Trail. Continue straight ahead.
9.5 North Fork Camp. Trail crosses Bridge Creek and follows south bank.
10.5 Berry Creek crossing.
11.1 Stehekin Valley Road.

The hike: This major thoroughfare links WA 20 with the Stehekin Valley via a moderate descent along Bridge Creek. This is one of the fastest and easiest routes into the Stehekin and, unlike the ferries and floatplanes that serve this remote settlement, the Bridge Creek trail costs nothing. Possible side trips that depart from this trail include Dagger Lake, McAlester Lake, Rainbow Lake, and North Fork Meadows. The trail terminates near the Bridge Creek camp; from here, hikers can catch the shuttlebus to Stehekin for a small fee.

From the trailhead, cross the highway on the east bank of Bridge Creek to reach an unmarked trail junction. The path that crosses the creek from the west is the Pacific Crest Trail (PCT); turn left to follow it down Bridge Creek. The trail makes its way through a subalpine forest, following the highway for a time and then veering southward. The trail soon splits in two, and the resulting trails follow both banks of Bridge Creek. There is a camp spot to the left, and this trail continues southward to link up with the Stiletto

Peak and Dagger Lake (Hike 68) trails. Turn right for the Bridge Creek Trail, which descends to cross Bridge Creek before turning southward.

Old-growth grand and subalpine fir grow along the banks of the stream as the trail makes its way southward, and water ouzels flit along the rushing waters. The path traverses the lower slopes of Frisco Mountain, crossing avalanche scars that reveal views of Stiletto Peak to the east. Later, there are views down the valley toward the outlying buttresses of Bowan Mountain. Stands of tall timber alternate with the brushfields, and in the sunny forest openings the blooms of columbine, tiger lily, and lupine light the understory. As the valley bends around onto a westward heading, the trail passes a ruined cabin that was once part of the Sulphide Mine, which produced small quantities of silver and lead during the 1920s.

The path then makes its way across a broad brushfield that occupies an old landslide scar. Debris from the slide is piled up along the banks of Bridge Creek near its confluence with McAlester Creek. After returning to the timber, a connecting trail runs east past the Fireweed camps to join the McAlester Lake and Dagger Lake trails. The Bridge Creek Trail continues down the valley, descending gently across avalanche-scarred slopes north of the creek. As the path approaches Hideaway Camp, the crags of Memaloose Ridge become visible above the distant trees. The camp itself is down on the streambank in a secluded grove of conifers.

The trail now levels off, crossing open brushfields punctuated by narrow stringers of conifers and groves of black cottonwood. The granite heights of Frisco Mountain now rise above the trail, and tantalizing glimpses can be had of the more jagged crags down the valley. After crossing Frisco Creek, the brushfields offer views up the South Fork of Bridge Creek, with Bowan Mountain and the eastern outliers of McGregor Mountain above its headwaters. The path soon descends to a junction with the Rainbow Lake Trail; follow this side trail to the banks of Bridge Creek to reach the South Fork camps.

Beyond the junction, the path runs below timbered slopes. Although open slopes surround the trail, there will be no distant views for the next 3 miles. A spur trail soon descends through the nettles to reach Sixmile Camp in a picturesque creekside grove of spruce. The main trail now ascends gently across the mountainside, rising ever higher above Bridge Creek. The reason for the ascent becomes apparent as the path descends toward Maple Creek: the waters of Bridge Creek have cut an impenetrable gorge through the mountains, and jagged ribs of bedrock rise hundreds of feet above the water, barring all passage.

Maple Creek itself presents quite a spectacle, foaming down a torrential series of cascades beneath a forbidding landscape of cliffs and talus. A hiker bridge is suspended above the stream during the summer months, just above the horse ford. The trail then climbs again to reach a level pad that overlooks the main gorge. There are good views of the defile as the path continues its traverse across the high slopes, with occasional stands of Douglas-fir to provide patches of shade. Nearing the North Fork of Bridge Creek, the trail wanders out onto rounded slopes covered in ceanothus, allowing good views of the ragged summits to the west. It then descends steadily along the crest of a low ridge that separates the merging valleys. Lodgepole pine now dominates the landscape. The junction with the trail to North Fork Meadows is on an elevated bench between the streams; North Fork Camp is down at the confluence beside a striking waterfall on the North Fork.

A bridge now spans the main channel of Bridge Creek, and the trail will complete its journey on the south bank of the stream. Climbing across a rock face, the path reveals fine views of Mount Benzarino across the valley. After a brief ascent, the trail finds itself above a rocky gorge again. Just beyond Berry Creek, intervening hillocks screen off the main valley and the path runs through a narrow depression. The trees open up at the lip of a small, dry gorge that is overlooked by the stony countenance of McGregor Mountain. A backward glance reveals farewell views of Mount Benzarino and the rocky toe of Memaloose Ridge.

The trail passes a stagnant pond, then runs level through the forest to an overlook with views up the Stehekin Valley, featuring Booker, Sahale, and Johannesburg mountains, in order of increasing distance. The trail then loops downward through the Douglas-firs to reach its terminus on the Stehekin Valley Road, between Bridge Creek and the camp of the same name.

78 North Fork Meadows

Overview:	A day trip from Bridge Creek to the headwaters of the North Fork, 13.4 miles round trip.
Best season:	Mid-July to mid-October.
Difficulty:	Moderate.
Elevation gain:	1,600 feet.
Elevation loss:	120 feet.
Maximum elevation:	4,300 feet.
Topo maps:	McGregor Mountain, Mount Logan; *McGregor Mountain, Mount Logan.*
Jurisdiction:	North Cascades National Park.

Finding the trail: The trail departs the Bridge Creek Trail 0.3 mile east of the North Fork Camp, 1.9 miles above the Stehekin Valley Road and 9.2 miles downstream from Washington Highway 20.

Key points:
    0.0 Junction on Bridge Creek Trail just east of North Fork Camp.
    2.6 Walker Park Camp.
    3.2 Grizzly Creek hiker camp.
    3.3 Trail fords Grizzly Creek.
    3.4 Grizzly Creek horse camp.

Goode Mountain from the North Fork Meadows.

North Fork Meadows

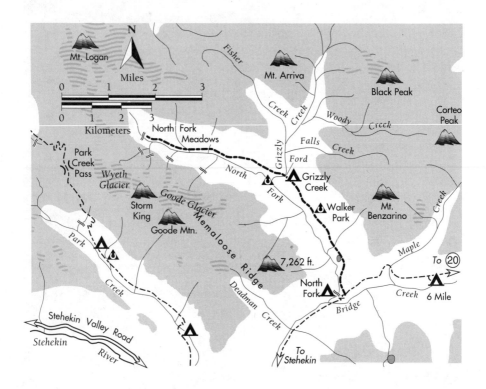

4.7 Trail enters North Fork Meadows.
6.7 Trail ends near large waterfall on the North Fork.

The hike: Of all the trails in the North Cascades, this route offers perhaps the most spectacular mountain scenery for the least amount of effort. It makes a gentle ascent along the North Fork of Bridge Creek to visit the stark crags of Memaloose Ridge and Goode Mountain. There are several camp-sites along the way, though the trail is most often hiked as a one-day side trip from North Fork camp on the Bridge Creek trail.

From its beginning on a wooded bench high above Bridge Creek, the trail climbs gently above the small gorge carved by the North Fork as it enters the Bridge Creek valley. A series of waterfalls roars far below, but the trees screen off the view. The loose woodland of spruce and Douglas-fir is underlain by a dense carpet of twinflower. The sparse forest canopy reveals views of Mount Benzarino as well as the more distant and rugged summits of Mount Arriva. The trail soon flattens out, passing above a boggy pond before it enters a mature forest of silver fir and hemlock. Through the widely spaced boles of the trees there are tantalizing glimpses of the spires of Memaloose Ridge.

The mountain scenery opens up dramatically as the trail reaches the brushy clearing of Walker Park. Stark pinnacles soar to the west, draped with snowmelt waterfalls, and Mount Logan can now be seen at the head of the valley. The Walker Park camp is in the trees just beyond the clearing. The path soon enters an old burn, where a sparse stand of lodgepole pine has taken root on the dry and sandy soil. Hikers gain continuing views of Memaloose Ridge, and can now see the southern bulwark of Mount Arriva up the Grizzly Creek valley. Just beyond Grizzly Creek Camp is a thigh-deep ford of this swift and brawling tributary stream. The forest on the far bank was left untouched by fire, and the graceful spires of spruce and fir provide ample shade.

This woodland soon gives way to vast brushfields, dominated by willow and alder but also featuring a healthy contingent of stinging nettle. The largest of the brushfields is spread below Goode Glacier, with impressive views of the summit of Goode Mountain, Storm King to the north of it, and the southern spurs of Mount Logan at the valley's head. At the far side of the brush is the first of the North Fork Meadows, a pleasant pocket of sedges at the base of an extensive talus slope. This is an excellent spot to stop for lunch, with views of the glacier and the waterfalls that course down from its toe. With the aid of binoculars, one might spot marmots in the rocks above the meadow.

The trail now climbs more briskly as it makes its way around a series of hidden waterfalls on the North Fork. Beyond the falls, the brush becomes less prevalent as grasses, bracken ferns, and sedge meadows come to dominate the valley floor. These meadows of the upper basin are excellent bear habitat. The already-splendid views continue to improve as the trail climbs steadily. The crags of Mount Benzarino and Corteo Peak can now be seen down the valley. Long waterfalls cascade down the western wall of the valley from Wyeth Glacier, which remains hidden from view. Lesser cataracts course through interesting outcrops on the eastern slope of the drainage.

As the valley makes a great bend to the east, sedge swards of brilliant green offer views of the summit of Mount Logan, with a multitude of cascades tumbling down from its brilliant snowfields. The trail ends here, at the foot of converging waterfalls on the facing cliffs and just below a rumbling cataract on the North Fork itself. Above the meadows are the jumbled spires and cliffs of Goode Mountain and Storm King, which soar above the valley in jagged pinnacles.

79 Agnes Gorge

Overview:	A half-day hike from High Bridge to Agnes Gorge, 5 miles round trip.
Best season:	Late May to mid-October.
Difficulty:	Easy.
Elevation gain:	430 feet.
Elevation loss:	190 feet.
Maximum elevation:	2,060 feet.
Topo maps:	McGregor Mountain, Mount Lyall (trail not shown); *McGregor Mountain.*
Jurisdiction:	North Cascades National Park, Glacier Peak Wilderness (Wenatchee National Forest).

Finding the trailhead: The trail leaves the Stehekin Valley Road between High Bridge and High Bridge Camp. Do not take the Agnes Creek trail (marked PCT), which is a different trail.

Key points:
   0.0   Agnes Gorge Trailhead near High Bridge Camp.
   1.2   Trail enters the Glacier Peak Wilderness.
   2.4   Overlook of Agnes Gorge and waterfalls.
   2.5   Trail ends beside Agnes Creek.

The hike: This trail makes an excellent short day hike from High Bridge, visiting waterfalls and a narrow gorge on Agnes Creek. The trail begins in the woodlands, providing superb examples of the influence of microclimates on forest communities. The dry, sunny hillsides at the mouth of the Agnes Creek valley are home to drought- and fire-tolerant species, such as Douglas-fir, ponderosa pine, manzanita, and kinnikinnick. As the trail progresses into moist, shady pockets, western red-cedar, grand fir, and mountain ash become the dominant trees. As the trail approaches the boundary of the Glacier Peak Wilderness, bigleaf maple becomes prevalent. Along with the aspens just beyond the boundary, they provide superb fall foliage in early October.

The forest soon opens up into a sparse growth of Douglas-fir and shrubs, and the jagged spires of Agnes Mountain rise in regal grandeur to the west. The trail now flirts with the edge of the Agnes Gorge for the first time, with its sheer walls of Skagit gneiss facing the wooded slopes of the near bank. After crossing a pretty woodland stream, the path begins to descend through an old-growth stand of grand fir, Douglas-fir, and western red-cedar. Steep cliffs now line both sides of the gorge, and a spur path leads to an old bridge footing for a humbling clifftop perspective of the chasm. There are no safety restraints here—stay away from the edge! The main trail continues straight

Waterfall in Agnes Gorge.

Agnes Gorge

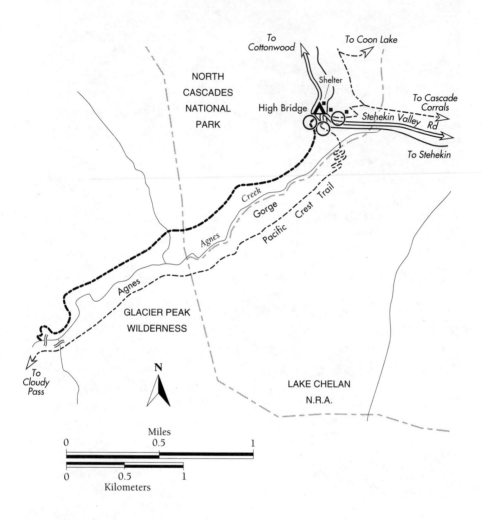

ahead, making a brief but rather steep descent to the water's edge at the upper end of the gorge. Here, a roaring cataract plunges into a turquoise pool, and hardy conifers grow from chinks in the rugged cliffs.

80 Agnes Creek — Pacific Crest Trail

Overview:	A backpack from the Stehekin Valley to Suiattle and Cloudy Passes, 21.7 miles one way.
Best season:	Early July to early October.
Difficulty:	Moderate to Hemlock Camp; moderately strenuous beyond.
Elevation gain:	6,440 feet.
Elevation loss:	1,640 feet.
Maximum elevation:	6,440 feet at Cloudy Pass.
Topo maps:	McGregor Mountain, Mount Lyall, Agnes Mountain, Holden; *McGregor Mountain, Holden*.
Jurisdiction:	Lake Chelan National Recreation Area, Glacier Peak Wilderness (Wenatchee National Forest).

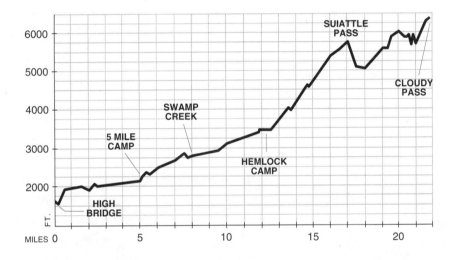

Finding the trailhead: The trail leaves the Stehekin Valley Road between High Bridge and High Bridge Camp.

Key points:
- 0.0 Trailhead on Stehekin Valley Rd.
- 0.2 Bridge over Agnes Creek. Trail now follows south bank.
- 2.0 Trail enters Glacier Peak Wilderness.
- 2.5 Campsite at junction with old spur to abandoned Agnes Gorge bridge.
- 4.8 Trail crosses Pass Creek.
- 4.9 Five Mile Camp. Junction with abandoned West Fork Trail. Bear left.
- 8.1 Trail crosses Swamp Creek to arrive at Swamp Creek Camp. Junction with abandoned Swamp Creek Trail. Follow main trail.
- 9.5 Cedar Camp.
- 12.4 Hemlock Camp. Junction with Upper Agnes Creek Trail (5.5 miles to upper junction). Turn right to follow preferred route.

12.7   Trail fords the South Fork of Agnes Creek.

14.7   Alpine basin below Sitting Bull Mountain.

16.3   Trail reaches camping area.

16.7   Upper junction with Upper Agnes Trail. Turn left to proceed directly to Cloudy Pass; turn right to follow preferred route via Suiattle Pass.

19.5   Suiattle Pass Camp.

20.0   Trail crosses Suiattle Pass.

20.3   Junction with cutoff trail to Cloudy Pass. Turn left.

20.6   Route re-crosses Suiattle Pass.

21.0   Junction with Upper Agnes Trail. Turn right for Cloudy Pass.

21.7   Cloudy Pass. Railroad Creek Trail runs eastward toward Holden.

The hike: This well-maintained segment of the Pacific Crest Trail (PCT) starts in the Stehekin Valley, then penetrates the heart of the Glacier Peak Wilderness. It follows the tumbling waters of Agnes Creek through bottomlands of old-growth conifers, with scant views of the mountains until the trail rises to the timberline at the head of the valley. Here, trails run over Suiattle Pass for views of Glacier Peak and over Cloudy Pass to link up with the trail that follows Railroad Creek to the retreat village of Holden. The trail receives few visitors until early September, when PCT through-hikers arrive on the scene.

The trail begins by descending to a bridge that spans Agnes Creek, which carries the volume of a small river. Hikers gain superb views of McGregor Mountain to the east and Goode Mountain to the north as the path leaves the Stehekin Valley, climbing moderately through open timber to avoid the cliffs of Agnes Gorge. A high perch overlooks the mouth of the gorge, and

Falls near Cedar Camp.

Agnes Creek

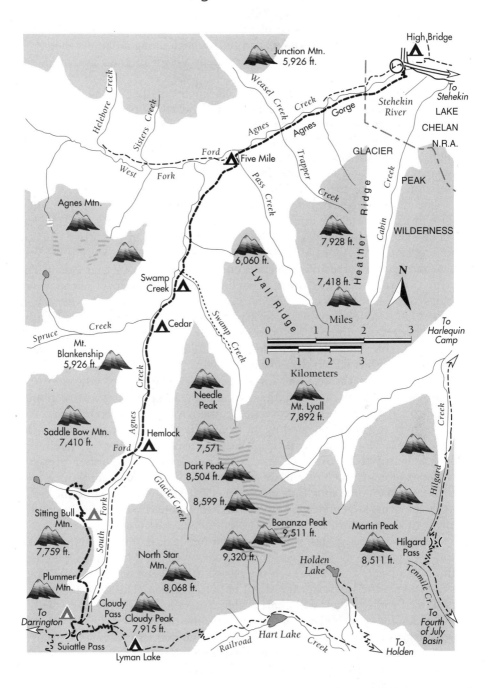

beyond it the trail completes its lazy climb and turns westward up the Agnes Creek valley. The route passes several impressive stands of old-growth cedar as it makes its way into the Glacier Peak Wilderness. There is a campsite at mile 2.5, where the roar of cataracts rises through the trees from the gorge below. Adventurous souls can bushwhack along an abandoned path to reach a cliffside aerie that offers clear views of the chasm and its thundering falls.

Meanwhile, the main trail continues up the valley, rising and falling through a sparse woodland of Douglas-fir and white pine. This latter tree rarely reaches maturity, falling prey to white pine blister rust as it reaches its full stature. There are tantalizing glimpses of Agnes Mountain, partly hidden by the treetops. The first major tributary is Pass Creek, bordered by ancient cedars and hemlocks. Just beyond it is Five Mile Camp, and the junction with the abandoned West Fork trail.

The Agnes Creek trail follows the great southward bend of the valley, climbing moderately as it moves inland. Sparse stands of pine and Douglas-fir indicate the locations of old burns. These breaks in the forest provide more glimpses of Agnes Mountain, but there is no clear view until the trail reaches the low gorge and waterfalls on the South Fork of Agnes Creek. The path soon returns to the forest, providing occasional glimpses of the water. Mossy groves of hemlock, pure stands of silver fir, and open woodlands of spruce and Douglas maple form a patchwork that is typical of a healthy forest ecosystem. Impressive groves of cedar appear as the trail approaches Swamp Creek. There is a camp here, but the trail that once ran east along this tributary has all but disappeared.

Easy trekking through the forest leads to Cedar Camp, where Spruce Creek pours in from the west. Agnes Creek now steepens its gradient, plunging through a series of small cascades formed by sills of resistant stone. The old-growth forest is breached by an avalanche slope as the trail passes the pale cliffs of Mount Blankenship. A larger brushfield farther on unveils the surreal spires of Needle and Dark peaks, while Saddle Mountain presents massive gables of rock on the west side of the valley. After climbing a rise, the forest takes on a subalpine character. The path then drops into the creek bottoms, where Hemlock Camp is sited in a superb stand of old-growth silver fir and western hemlock.

Just beyond camp, the trail forks. The left fork is the old Agnes Creek trail, which cuts off distance at the expense of scenery. It follows the creek through a boggy forest to reach the passes at the head of the valley. When snow covers the high country, it is the better option. The right fork is the preferred route, which will chart a high course across the western wall of the valley for superb views of the surrounding peaks.

It begins by following the South Fork through a strange and wonderful forest where stout trees grow atop massive boulders that have tumbled from the face of Saddle Bow Mountain. An ankle-deep ford leads across the creek, and soon the trail begins a long and steady upward grade. As it breaks out of the forest into open brushfields, the sawtooth crests of Needle and Dark peaks rise to the east, while the snow-dappled summit rising ahead is Sitting Bull Mountain. After leveling off briefly, the trail continues its ascent through the subalpine forest across from Sitting Bull. After a long detour into a nameless side valley, the trail reaches the open bowl at its head. There are breathtaking waterfalls here, and now the summit of Bonanza Peak can be seen beyond the toe of North Star Mountain. A low but rocky backbone links North Star with Cloudy Peak, which rises farther to the south.

Watch for marmots and pikas as the trail traverses southeast beneath the ramparts of Sitting Bull. The path soon resumes its climbing, ascending onto a high spur covered in heather. The journey is accompanied by fine views of Cloudy Peak and the indignant bleats of pikas, and there is a developed camp below the trail just before it enters a grove of ancient mountain hemlocks. After crossing a boulderfield overgrown with anemones and other wild-flowers, the trail begins a substantial descent into the basin at the foot of Plummer Mountain. Enormous boulders, some larger than a house, have crashed down from the towering cliffs to fill the floor of the basin. After threading its way through the fractured rock, the trail ascends into the forest for the final trek to the head of the valley. It reaches a signpost just 500 vertical feet below Suiattle Pass.

If it is raining or you are in a hurry to reach Cloudy Pass, turn left. Otherwise, bear right for a visit to Suiattle Pass followed by a steep and narrow traverse across the head of the Agnes Creek valley to Cloudy Pass. This route climbs steadily through heather-blueberry parklands and can be quite slippery when wet. After passing a camping area, the trail doglegs eastward to cross over the pass. After a short descent, there are jaw-dropping views of Glacier Peak as well as the jagged crest of Fortress Mountain to the east of it. After a few downward switchbacks, turn left onto the path that crosses through the lowest point on Suiattle Pass.

This trail soon descends across steep slopes, unveiling superb views down the South Fork of Agnes Creek as it bypasses a granite face. The track then climbs steeply, joining the main trail on its purposeful ascent to Cloudy Pass. The meadows below the pass offer views of Plummer and Sitting Bull mountains, while the tundra at the summit commands sweeping vistas of the upper basin of Railroad Creek, with its broad glaciers, majestic peaks, and sparkling lakes. From Cloudy Pass, the Railroad Creek trail (see p.324) descends to the tiny village of Holden.

81 McGregor Mountain

Overview: A brutal day hike or backpack from the Stehekin Valley to the summit of McGregor Mountain, 15.4 miles round trip.

Best season: Late July to mid-October.

Difficulty: Strenuous.

Elevation gain: 6,552 feet.

Elevation loss: None.

Maximum elevation: 8,122 feet at the summit of McGregor Mountain.

Topo maps: McGregor Mountain (trail not shown); *McGregor Mountain.*

Jurisdiction: North Cascades National Park.

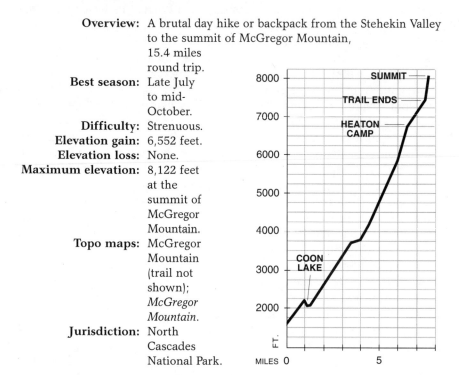

Finding the trailhead: The trail departs from the old High Bridge guard station, behind the buildings.

Key points:
- 0.0 Trailhead at old High Bridge guard station.
- 0.2 Junction with horse trail to Cascade Corrals. Bear left.
- 0.4 Junction with horse trail to south shore of Coon Lake. Bear left.
- 1.1 Coon Lake.
- 1.2 Junction with Old Wagon Road Trail. Turn right as trail begins ascent of McGregor Mountain.
- 2.1 Waterfall on Coon Creek.
- 6.6 Heaton Camp. Trail climbs above timberline.
- 7.3 End of maintained trail. Steep scramble route leads upward to summit.
- 7.7 Summit of McGregor Mountain.

The hike: This trek is for hikers who wish to push their limits and challenge themselves physically and mentally. A long climb leads from the floor of the Stehekin Valley to the base of the final pitch, which is an abandoned trail that is hard to locate and has dangerous dropoffs all the way to the summit. There is no easy way to approach this trek. Backpackers can camp at

Heaton Camp near the top of the grade, but hauling a full pack all the way up to this lofty aerie is a daunting prospect. Hikers who attempt the summit in a single day will be biting off more than 14 miles of steep trail, with scrambling and route-finding challenges thrown in at the top of the grade.

The trail begins by ascending the wooded benches to the east of High Bridge. Mountain views start early on this trail, with good views up Agnes Creek toward the sharp spires of Agnes Mountain. After a short distance, the Coon Lake horse trail departs to the right for even better views before reaching a bluff above the south shore of the lake. The main trail climbs northward through the ponderosa pines and Douglas-firs to reach the western shore of Coon Lake. This rare mountain wetland is an important staging area for waterfowl.

The trail rounds the north side of the lake and climbs to the base of McGregor Mountain. A long series of switchbacks carries the hiker ever upward through the scattered trees. There is a good overlook as the trail approaches Coon Creek, which tumbles down steep bedrock in a delightful waterfall. Views continue to improve as the trail climbs. Upon reaching an open shelf of rock at the 3,680-foot level, hikers gain views of the glacier-bound summit of Dome Peak to the west as well as Booker and Buckner mountains to the north. The rocky crags of McGregor Mountain tower high overhead, and the trail now snakes upward across ponderosa pine and Douglas-fir savannahs. This plant community is typical of valley bottoms on the arid eastern side of the Cascades, and its occurrence at such a high altitude is quite unusual. It attests to the warm and snow-free microclimate enjoyed by this south-facing slope.

Looking toward Sahale Mountain from McGregor Mountain.

McGregor Mountain

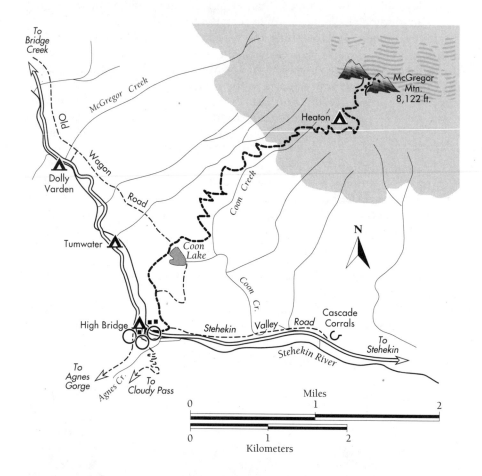

The trail soon passes a steep gorge on Coon Creek, then swings away from the stream. The next encounter with the stream comes in a narrow and brushy couloir that is swept free of timber by frequent avalanches. The trail now redoubles its climb, ascending pitilessly up the chute. Subalpine fir and larch announce the approach to the alpine zone, and lush swards of wildflowers soon carpet the streambanks. The trail ultimately rises into a barren bowl, filled with broken rock and guarded by the stark cliffs of McGregor Mountain. Watch for pikas amid the talus.

The trail then swings north onto a rocky arm, where it encounters Heaton Camp huddled in a ragged grove of larch and fir. Views from here encompass Sahale Mountain to the northwest, Mount Lyall to the southwest, and between them the distant and snowy crest of Glacier Peak beyond a sea of lesser crags. Above the camp, the trail continues upward, and finally peters out as a recognizable path atop the heather fellfields at the base of the cliffs.

The scramble route to the summit is really no more than a goat track, following cairns and arrows painted onto the rock up the loose scree and across narrow cliff ledges. Hikers with strong climbing and route-finding skills may find the route by looking due east, straight uphill from the cairn at the trail's end. A convex talus fan leads up to two couloirs that come slanting in from opposite directions. Climb southward across the talus, then traverse to the base of the left-hand (north) couloir to find the unmarked track slanting southward up a ledge of stone. The track snakes upward, rarely requiring handholds as it swings across open faces and ascends rocky spurs in preference to the looser rock of the couloirs.

The track reaches the mountaintop at a notch between major peaks; views extend eastward over barren crags and spires as far as the eye can see. The route now turns south across the top of Sandalee Glacier, then returns to the ridgeline at a low gap just below the summit. Follow the painted arrows up the spine of the ridge to reach the radio repeater that occupies an old fire lookout site on the summit. Views from here encompass most of the peaks within a 50-mile radius; highlights include Goode Mountain and Mount Logan to the north as well as the head of Lake Chelan to the south.

82 Rainbow Loop

Overview:	A half-day hike onto mountainsides above the Stehekin Valley, 4.6 miles one way.
Best season:	Mid-June to mid-October.
Difficulty:	Moderate.
Elevation gain:	1,050 feet (north to south).
Elevation loss:	1,090 feet (north to south).
Maximum elevation:	2,180 feet.
Topo maps:	Stehekin; *Stehekin.*
Jurisdiction:	Lake Chelan National Recreation Area (North Cascades National Park).

RAINBOW BRIDGE

SOUTH TRAILHEAD

2000

NORTH TRAILHEAD

1000

FT.

MILES 0   5

Finding the trailhead: Take the shuttle or hike the Stehekin Valley Road. The upper trailhead is 5 miles above the Stehekin landing, and the lower trailhead is 3 miles above the Stehekin landing.

Key points:
0.0 North Trailhead.
2.4 Junction with Rainbow Creek Trail. Stay right for loop.
2.6 Trail crosses Rainbow Creek.
2.8 Rainbow Bridge Camp.
3.2 Junction with Boulder Pass Trail. Stay right.
4.6 South Trailhead.

McGregor Mountain from the the Rainbow Loop.

The hike: The Rainbow Loop offers a rather short day trip that climbs onto the middle slopes of the mountains for views of the Stehekin Valley and the peaks that guard it. The journey is made chiefly by visitors who lack the time or inclination to attempt the more challenging day hikes in the area. It is easiest when approached from the north. An extra 1-mile climb up the Rainbow Creek trail leads to a high viewpoint that looks south across the head of Lake Chelan.

The trail begins by climbing modestly but steadily through a shady forest of Douglas-fir. Bigleaf maples occupy the wetter swales, and in early October they burst into a colorful display of fall foliage. On the way up, talus slopes provide glimpses of the surrounding country. Just after the trail completes its initial climb and begins traversing southward, a bedrock overlook below the trail provides panoramic views of the Stehekin Valley, where the river winds through its forested bottoms. The steep-walled peaks beyond the river are outriders of Sisi Ridge and Tupshin Peak.

After a long level stretch, the trail begins climbing once more. There is another viewpoint at the edge of a grassy hillside, after which the trail climbs to the top of a timbered platform. Now winding east into the Rainbow Creek drainage, the path crosses a grassy meadow dotted with ponderosa pines. The junction with the Rainbow Creek Trail is at the far edge of this meadow; follow it upward for 1 mile to reach a lofty overlook. Hikers who are pressed for time should skip the climb and follow the Rainbow Loop southward as it descends to cross a bridge over Rainbow Creek. There is a shady camping area on the far bank of the stream.

Rainbow Loop

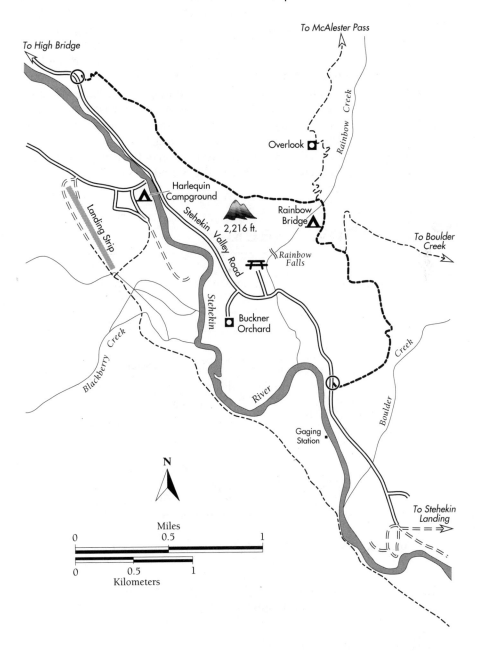

To McAlester Pass

To High Bridge

Rainbow Creek

Overlook

Harlequin Campground

Stehekin Valley Road

2,216 ft.

Rainbow Bridge

To Boulder Creek

Landing Strip

Rainbow Falls

Stehekin

Buckner Orchard

Boulder Creek

Blackberry Creek

River

Gaging Station

N

To Stehekin Landing

Miles
0
0.5
1

Kilometers
0
0.5
1

The slopes above the camp are studded with Douglas-firs that are dying from heavy infestations of parasitic mistletoe. The mistletoe, often called "witch's broom," causes twigs to grow in ball-shaped masses. Tupshin Peak rises dead ahead as the trail surmounts the next finger ridge, and atop the ridge is a rocky clearing overlooking the Buckner Orchard. McGregor Mountain rises prominently to the north. After passing a junction with the Boulder Creek Trail, the Rainbow Loop embarks on a steady grade that leads down the mountainside through stands of Douglas-fir and groves of bigleaf maple. It soon arrives at a clifftop perch that faces southward across the head of Lake Chelan. A long and steady descent leads to the mouth of the Boulder Creek valley. Here, the trail turns west to descend the gentle slopes that lead down toward the Stehekin River. The last portion of the trek runs through a sunny woodland to reach a trailhead on the Stehekin Valley Road.

83 Rainbow Creek

Overview: A backpack from the Stehekin Valley to McAlester Pass, 10.3 miles one way.

Best season: Early July to mid-October.

Difficulty: Moderately strenuous.

Elevation gain: 4,870 feet.

Elevation loss: 100 feet.

Maximum elevation: 6,000 feet at McAlester Pass.

Topo maps: Stehekin, McAlester Mountain; *Stehekin*.

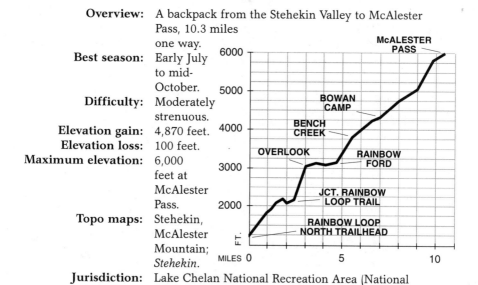

Jurisdiction: Lake Chelan National Recreation Area (National Park Service).

Finding the trailhead: Take the shuttlebus or walk to the Rainbow Loop upper trailhead, at mile 5 on the Stehekin Valley Road.

Key points:
- 0.0   Rainbow Loop North Trailhead.
- 2.4   Junction with Rainbow Creek Trail. Turn left for initial climb.
- 3.1   Overlook of Lake Chelan.
- 4.6   Rainbow Ford Camp. Footbridge leads to east bank of Rainbow Creek.
- 5.5   Junction with Rainbow Lake Trail. Stay right.

Lake Chelan from the Rainbow Creek Trail.

5.6   Bench Creek Camp. Trail crosses Bench Creek.

7.2   Bowan Camp.

8.2   Trail fords Rainbow Creek.

10.3 McAlester Pass. South Pass Trail climbs eastward and McAlester Lake trails drops away to the north.

The hike: This trail follows the Rainbow Creek valley through a rather arid forestland flanked by rugged foothills, reaching its terminus in the alpine meadows of McAlester Pass. The trek begins by following the initial leg of the Rainbow Loop (see p.303), which climbs briefly through timber then levels off to run southward across the base of Rainbow Mountain. After 2.4 miles, the path crosses a grassy slope to reach the junction where the Rainbow Creek Trail climbs away to the right.

A long but moderate climb leads up the grassy slopes of Rainbow Mountain. Views of the Stehekin Valley culminate at the 3.1-mile mark atop a viewpoint that offers sweeping views down Lake Chelan. Beyond this overlook, the trail turns north for good, entering the rocky lower reaches of the Rainbow Creek valley. The path climbs initially, then traverses across sparsely wooded slopes high above the creek. As the trail progresses northward, the valley floor rises to meet it, and there is a suspension bridge and a brushy camp at Rainbow Ford.

On the far bank, the path climbs vigorously through the brush, making it one of the hottest climbs in the North Cascades when the weather is sunny. There are fine views down the valley, featuring the peaks beyond the head of Lake Chelan: Castle Rock is farthest left, while Tupshin Peak can barely

Rainbow Creek

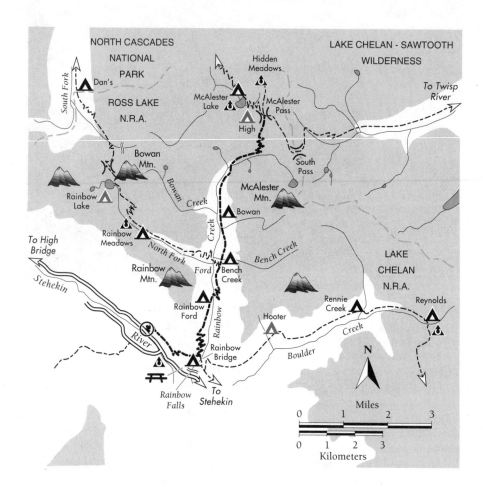

be seen at the far right. After a brief but grueling climb, the trail enters a pure stand of lodgepole pine and levels off. Here, the trail to Rainbow Lake drops away to the left, and Bench Creek camp occupies the hillside above the junction. Just beyond the camp, there is a shallow ford or a tricky rock-hop across Bench Creek.

A vigorous ascent then leads upward through the pines. An open avalanche path marks the top of this grade, with final views of the mountains to the south. Ascending moderately now, the path passes the mouth of the Bowan Creek valley, and the sharp southern spur of Bowan Mountain is framed by the gap. Lodgepole pines give way to a subalpine forest of fir and mountain hemlock, and the ridges that bound the valley are now girded with stout ribs and domes of granite. The trail reaches Bowan Camp some distance above its namesake stream, where there is a solitary tent site beside the trail in a grove of mature firs.

Continuing upstream, the trail passes several long and slender waterfalls on the west wall of the valley as it climbs along the edge of the forest. After a shallow ford of Rainbow Creek, the valley bends eastward and the trail crosses the lower edge of a vast talus slope. It then enters a stunted forest of mountain hemlock, where snow patches linger late into the summer and violets bloom in the deep shade.

After a while, the trail climbs onto south-facing slopes to begin the grade to McAlester Pass. Here, the warmer climate permits the hemlocks to grow to impressive proportions. The trail switchbacks steadily upward through the trees, which ultimately dwindle and are replaced by heather meadows and domes of bedrock. McAlester Mountain rears its regal summit directly across the valley, and far to the south are the jagged peaks along the crest of the Cascades. After passing through a notch guarded by subalpine larches, the trail wanders out into the broad wet meadows of McAlester Pass. Watch for marmots on the slopes to the east as the path makes its way to a signpost in the midst of the pass. The trail ends here, intersecting the South Pass and McAlester Lake trails just south of High Camp.

84 Rainbow Lake

Overview:	A backpack from Stehekin to Rainbow Lake via the Rainbow Creek trail (10.5 miles one way) or an extended trip from Rainbow Creek over a high pass to Bridge Creek (9.8 miles total).
Best season:	Late July to mid-October.
Difficulty:	Moderately strenuous.
Elevation gain:	2,770 feet (south to north).
Elevation loss:	3,270 feet (south to north).
Maximum elevation:	6,230 feet at the pass above Rainbow Lake.
Topo maps:	McGregor Mountain, McAlester Mountain; *Stehekin, McGregor Mountain.*
Jurisdiction:	Lake Chelan National Recreation Area, North Cascades National Park.

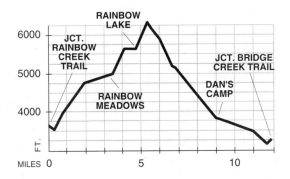

Rainbow Lake.

Finding the trail: The trail leaves the Rainbow Creek Trail at mile 5.5, just before Bench Creek Camp. It joins the Bridge Creek Trail at its halfway point near South Fork Camp.

Key points:
　　0.0　Junction with Rainbow Creek Trail at Bench Creek Camp.
　　0.4　Trail fords Rainbow Creek and climbs stiffly.
　　2.8　Rainbow Meadows hiker camp.
　　3.2　Rainbow Meadows horse camp.
　　3.5　Last campsites in the meadows. Trail starts climbing.
　　4.7　Top of grade.
　　5.0　Rainbow Lake.
　　5.7　Trail crosses pass into the valley of the South Fork of Bridge Creek.
　　7.0　Trail leaves Lake Chelan NRA and enters North Cascades National Park.
　　7.1　Dan's Camp.
　　9.6　Trail crosses Bridge Creek to reach South Fork hiker camp.
　　9.7　South Fork horse camp.
　　9.8　Trail ends at junction with Bridge Creek Trail.

The hike: This trail links Rainbow and Bridge Creeks via a high pass at the foot of Bowan Mountain, visiting the beautiful alpine tarn called Rainbow Lake along the way. It is most often traveled by backpackers during the course of extended forays into the backcountry to the east of the Stehekin Valley.

From the junction at Bench Creek camp, the Rainbow Lake Trail descends steeply to reach a ford of Rainbow Creek. In midsummer, the water is knee-deep and runs at a moderate pace. During spring runoff, the

310

Rainbow Lake

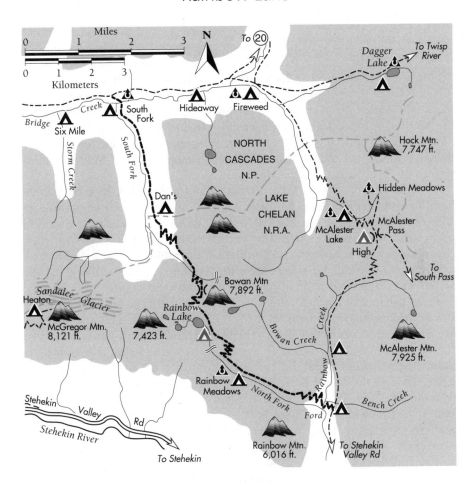

crossing is all but impassable.

On the far bank, the trail climbs onto open, south-facing slopes where ceanothus and kinnikinnick are the dominant plants. There are excellent views down-valley, featuring the sharp summit of Castle Rock. As the trail zigzags heartily upward, views across the Rainbow Creek valley reveal the rocky summits extending southward from McAlester Mountain. A few scattered clumps of Douglas-fir provide spots of shade, but for the most part the trail grinds upward under the heat of the sun. It ultimately seeks the banks of the North Fork of Rainbow Creek, and the ascent moderates as the trail follows the stream upward into a subalpine woodland of spruce and fir.

The first of several grassy meadows soon interrupts the forest, and the trail finds the Rainbow Meadows hiker camp in the trees a short distance beyond it. More expansive meadows lie ahead, filled with the blossoms of lupine, aster, and paintbrush. The horse camp occupies the lower edge of the second meadow, and there are more campsites beyond the third and largest meadow. Each of the meadows was created by avalanches from the rocky ridge above them, and periodic snowslides prevent the forest from encroaching into the openings.

The trail then begins to ascend the eastern wall of the valley, and old-growth hemlock and subalpine fir soon give way to open slopes. The trail zigzags upward at a purposeful pace, lit by the blossoms of penstemon. At the top of the grade, one can look southwest over a saddle in the intervening ridgetop for fine views of the glacier-mantled summit of Dome Peak. Agnes Mountain is the barren summit to the left of it, and the sawback ridges and the sentinel spire of Mount Lyall are visible above the ridgetop. The path now levels off and runs northwest across open slopes, with fine views of Rainbow Meadows and increasingly unobstructed vistas of Mount Lyall as well as of Tupshin Peak to the west of it.

Straight ahead, a waterfall courses across a rounded face of granite, heralding the approach to Rainbow Lake. This alpine gem is guarded by cliffs of white granite, the outliers of McGregor Mountain. The rugged summit of Bowan Mountain guards the eastern shore of the lake. Marmots cavort among the meadows and boulders at the foot of the lake, and there is a camping area on the far side of the outlet stream. Anglers will find that the waters are stocked with small rainbow and cutthroat trout.

From the foot of the lake, the trail zigzags up onto the talus apron below Bowan Mountain, then turns west for the final climb to a high pass. There are fine aerial views of the lake as the trail ascends, a fitting foreground for the broad panorama of peaks to the south. After crossing the divide, the path drops through a larch-heather community on its way toward the headwaters of the South Fork of Bridge Creek. Looking northward, hikers gain distant views of Black Peak, flanked by the lesser summits of Mount Benzarino to the left and Corteo Peak to the right. As the slope steepens, the path drops onto the western slope of Bowan Mountain, descending across a broad face of talus.

The trail bottoms out in a boggy meadow, which is fed by a beautiful waterfall that hangs in silver tresses down the cliffs to the east. A subalpine forest awaits at the meadow's edge, and the trail drops through it, following the banks of the rushing stream. After a brief descent, the trail levels off to cross an avalanche path, revealing the multiple peaks of McGregor Mountain lining the head of the valley. Look backward here for fine views of Bowan Mountain's solitary miter. The path then disappears into the forest once more for the long and zigzagging descent to the South Fork of Bridge Creek. Near the bottom of the grade, avalanche slopes offer astounding views of McGregor Mountain, with the pocket icefields of Sandalee Glacier draped across its north face.

The trail levels off in a meadow at the bottom of an avalanche track, and soon it reaches the banks of the South Fork. Just after entering North Cascades National Park, the trail encounters Dan's Camp in a stand of old spruce and fir. This is one of the few shady spots on the valley bottom; most of the forest has been periodically thinned by avalanches and low-intensity fires. The trail descends gently but steadily down the valley, finally reaching the main branch of Bridge Creek in a stand of old-growth spruce and cedar. A footlog leads to the South Fork hiker camp on the far bank, and the horse camp lies just beyond it. The trail then climbs into a brushfield to reach its end at a junction with the Bridge Creek Trail.

85 Boulder Creek

Overview:	A backpack from the Stehekin Valley to Lake Juanita via War Creek Pass, 11.6 miles one way.
Best season:	Early July to mid-October.
Difficulty:	Strenuous.
Elevation gain:	6,140 feet.
Elevation loss:	650 feet.
Maximum elevation:	6,920 feet (above Butte Creek).
Topo maps:	Stehekin, Sun Mountain; *Stehekin*.
Jurisdiction:	Lake Chelan National Recreation Area (North Cascades National Park), Lake Chelan–Sawtooth Wilderness (Okanogan National Forest).

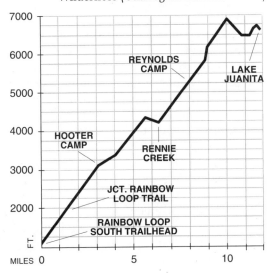

Finding the trailhead: Take the shuttlebus or walk to the Rainbow Loop lower trailhead, at mile 3.2 on the Stehekin Valley Road.

Key points:
0.0 Rainbow Loop south Trailhead.
1.6 Boulder Creek Trail splits away from Rainbow Loop. Turn right.
2.8 Top of initial grade.
3.1 Hooter Camp.
6.1 Rennie Camp.
6.2 Trail crosses Rennie Creek.

The hike: This primitive trail ascends into the valley of Boulder Creek and follows it to the timberline, where a steep climb leads over the high passes and into the Lake Chelan–Sawtooth Wilderness. The Boulder Creek drainage was the site of an immense wildfire during the summer of 1994, and although its tread was unaffected by the blaze, the trail has not received intensive maintenance since; deadfalls may bar the way. This fact, coupled with the insanely steep grades at the end of the trail, make this back-door route to the Chelan Summit a lightly traveled one.

The trek begins on the lower leg of the Rainbow Loop (see p.303), which climbs the gentle and loosely wooded slopes to reach the base of the mountains, then zigzags upward. There are several fine overlook points on the way to the junction with the Boulder Creek Trail, first offering views of Lake Chelan and the Buckner Orchard, and later a northward vista of McGregor Mountain. The Boulder Creek trail departs on a northward heading atop a wooded shelf, climbing first through a shady stand of Douglas-fir and later across grassy slopes. High on the mountainside, there are excellent views of Castle Rock and Tupshin Peak, and glimpses of Lake Chelan.

After a stiff 1-mile climb, the trail enters the Boulder Creek valley and the ascent eases (but does not cease). The route now enters the edge of the 1994 Boulder Creek burn. Here, the fire burned with low intensity and a number of thick-barked Douglas-firs were able to survive. Openings in the trees allow views up the valley; the jagged summit at its head is Reynolds Peak. The trail soon crosses a small stream and arrives at Hooter Camp, where a single tent pad has been carved out of the mountainside.

The trail now levels off for a time, passing across rocky and open slopes that offer the trek's best views of Tupshin Peak. It soon enters the heart of the burn, climbing steadily to maintain an altitude about 100 feet above Boulder Creek. The middle reaches of the valley are tedious and toilsome. The former forest has been transformed by fire into broad grasslands that offer scant relief from the heat of the sun. The old Rennie Camp was heavily damaged by the fire. Its trailside tent pads, easy to miss, are below the trail as it approaches Rennie Creek. This large stream is bordered by picturesque walls of bedrock.

The trail soon passes the mouth of the Butte Creek valley, guarded to the east by Lone Mountain. The next major stream to be reached is nameless, but is of enormous ecological significance in that it served as a natural fire-break during the Boulder Creek fire. Beyond it lies an unburned subalpine woodland of spruce and fir. The trail now exacts a heavy toll, climbing ever steeper as the valley makes its bend to the southeast. Grassy meadows ultimately yield views of Reynolds Peak, and the trail makes for its base to

Boulder Creek • Purple Pass

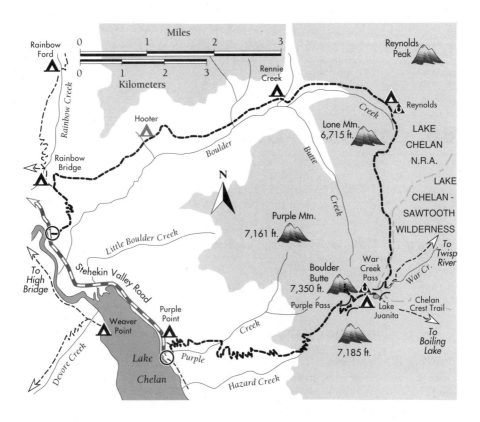

seek out Reynolds Camp. The camp is sited beside a picturesque meadow that offers northward views of Rennie Peak, with the bald spur of McAlester Mountain in the distance.

Views improve as the path continues its steep ascent. Soon it reaches the grassy basin at the head of Boulder Creek; take on water here because the remainder of the trek offers none. The path now swings westward to make an insanely steep climb of the ridge behind Lone Mountain. Larch meadows near the top of the grade reveal parting views of Reynolds Peak and the Camels Hump to the south of it. Upon gaining the ridgetop, the trail swings onto the western face for a high traverse of burned-over slopes high above Butte Creek. The rugged peak across the valley is Boulder Butte, while the lofty summits of McGregor, Buckner, and Goode mountains rise along the northern horizon.

A series of daunting upward pitches leads to the top of the War Creek divide, where hikers get southward views of Oval Peak as well as the lesser summit of Splawn Mountain at the head of the War Creek valley. The path now descends southward along the crest of the divide, then jogs west to

315

avoid a rocky knoll. Here, an unburned stand of spruce and larch occupies a rocky corner of the Butte Creek watershed. Soon the trail climbs across the head of the War Creek drainage, leaving national park land for a brief excursion through a corner of the Lake Chelan–Sawtooth Wilderness, which is administered by the Forest Service. Just below War Creek Pass, the Boulder Creek route feeds into the War Creek Trail; turn right for the short jaunt over the pass to Lake Juanita.

86 Company–Devore Creek Loop

Overview:	A long backpack over two passes in the Glacier Peak Wilderness, visiting Fourth of July Basin, 28.2 miles overall.
Best season:	Early August to late September.
Difficulty:	Moderately strenuous.
Elevation gain:	7,281 feet.
Elevation loss:	7,346 feet.
Maximum elevation:	6,638 feet at Hilgard Pass.
Topo maps:	Holden, Pinnacle Mountain, Stehekin, Mount Lyall; *Stehekin, McGregor Mountain, Holden, Lucerne.*
Jurisdiction:	Glacier Peak Wilderness (Wenatchee National Forest).

Finding the trailhead: The hike begins at the Company Creek Trailhead. Hike or take the shuttle to the bridge at Harlequin Camp, then walk across the bridge and up the main gravel road for 1 mile to reach the trailhead. The trek ends up at Harlequin Camp.

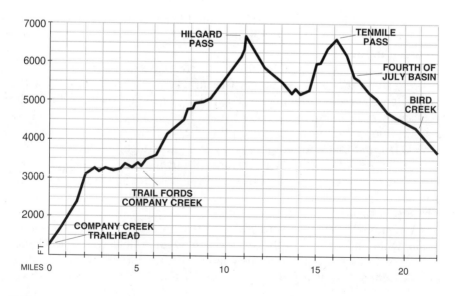

Key points:

 0.0 Company Creek Trailhead.
 1.4 Trail enters Glacier Peak Wilderness.
 5.1 Trail fords Company Creek.
 6.6 Trail enters valley of Hilgard Creek.
 8.5 Trail fords Hilgard Creek and briefly follows the west bank.
 8.8 Trail returns to the east bank of Hilgard Creek.
10.0 Trail crosses the headwaters of Hilgard Creek.
10.5 Bottom of the grade to Hilgard Pass.
11.0 Hilgard Pass.
12.0 Tenmile Creek valley floor.
14.4 Junction with abandoned Tenmile Creek Trail. Turn left.
15.2 Campsite in a high basin.
16.0 Tenmile Pass.
17.1 Trail crosses headwaters of Devore Creek, then follows the west bank.
19.1 Trail crosses West Fork of Devore Creek.
20.6 Trail crosses Bird Creek to reach Bird Creek Camp.
24.3 Top of grade that leads down to Stehekin Valley.
25.0 Junction with Stehekin River Trail. Turn left to complete the loop.
27.5 Trail crosses Blackberry Creek.
27.7 Junction beside Stehekin airstrip. Turn right for Harlequin Camp.
28.2 Hike ends at Harlequin Camp.

The hike: This loop trek combines trails along Company Creek, Devore Creek, and the Stehekin River for a multi-day journey into a remote corner of the Glacier Peak Wilderness west of Lake Chelan. The part of the route that falls within Forest Service lands has received minimal maintenance in recent years, a fact that discourages many visitors from going. Expect some brushy traveling in the middle reaches of Company Creek, a deep and difficult ford of Company Creek, and route-finding problems in the open grasslands at

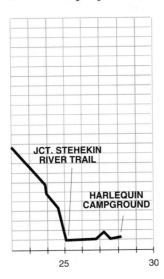

the head of Tenmile Creek. This is a journey of unparalleled wilderness quality, providing challenges and rewards in equal measure to the stalwart hikers who venture here.

The trek begins near the mouth of Company Creek, crossing the wooded floor of the Stehekin Valley then climbing steeply through an open woodland of Douglas-fir. There are fine views of McGregor Mountain here, and later the canyon of Company Creek appears as the trail rises onto gentler slopes north of it. Company Creek occupies a hanging valley, carved by a glacier that poured into the larger (and deeper) river of ice that coursed down the Stehekin Valley during the Pleistocene epoch. When the glaciers receded, the Company Creek basin stood 1,500 feet above the Stehekin River. During the intervening eons, Company Creek has carved this deep gorge through the bedrock to link the two valleys.

After entering the Glacier Peak Wilderness, the path levels off. It now traverses arid, south-facing slopes that provide superb views of the crags up the valley. Sable Ridge is the closer summit, and beyond it is Bonanza Peak with Mary Green Glacier on its left flank and the larger Company Glacier to the right of the summit. Douglas and bigleaf maples are prevalent in this area, providing splashes of fall color in late September. As the trail makes its final climb into the hanging valley, look eastward to see the rocky face of Rainbow Mountain.

The trail now levels off for easy trekking through a young forest of hemlock and silver fir. The respite is short lived, since the middle reaches of the valley are clogged with brush, and progress is impeded first by stinging nettles and later by boggy seeps. The forest returns for the final mile to the ford of Company Creek, where there is a campsite near the knee-deep crossing. Beware of swift currents and slippery rocks. On the far bank, the path climbs gently along the south edge of the valley. There is little brush aside from a few scattered patches of devil's club, and traveling is easy as the trail makes its way to the mouth of the Hilgard Creek valley.

As the trail rounds the corner and starts up Hilgard Creek, the rugged backside of Mount Lyall becomes visible to the north. Once in the Hilgard drainage, the trail crosses an old burn that has grown back in white pine and Douglas-fir. An avalanche slope reveals a summit of Sable Ridge, and as the forest grades into spruce and silver fir, there are tantalizing glimpses of Devore Peak up the valley. After several more brushfields, the path enters an old-growth stand of spruce, where stout boles rise at regular intervals from the tidy forest floor. After a considerable jaunt through the forest, an avalanche clearing marks the spot where the rather faint trail fords Hilgard Creek. Continuing upward along the far bank, a succession of snowslide meadows offers ever-improving views of Devore Peak, and the many regal summits of Sable Ridge present themselves one after the other on the opposite side of the valley.

The trail soon finds its way back to the east bank of the creek, where it completes its journey into the larch and heather basin at the valley's head. A sheer headwall guards the edge of the basin, and the faint path climbs to the base of it before turning east toward a narrow, vegetated slope. The ascent to Hilgard Pass begins with gentle switchbacks that cross slopes studded with anemones and other blossoms. The headwall is taller than it first appears, and soon the path zigzags steeply through narrow couloirs between the outcrops. Look west on the final pitch for a superb view of Martin Peak with its massive glacier. Atop the divide, heather meadows face north toward McGregor Mountain and south across the deep gulf of Railroad Creek to Tinpan and Buckskin mountains.

Below, the glacier-carved vale of Tenmile Creek stretches southward, and the trail zigzags steadily downward into the open grasslands of its headwaters. Route-finding talent comes in handy as the path is overgrown with grasses

Nameless peaks above Fourth of July Basin.

in many places. It charts a downvalley course to the east of the stream, and soon the open meadows give way to stands of ancient spruces. The trail approaches Tenmile Creek, then swings away from it as it climbs moderately across the avalanche scars to approach the mouth of a side valley that enters from the east. High on the timbered slopes is an unmarked trail junction; turn left as our route zigzags upward at a rapid pace. At the top of the grade, hikers get magnificent views of Copper Peak and Mount Fernow, which rise to the southwest in a crowd of jagged spires, rocky pinnacles, and sparkling glaciers.

The trail now turns eastward into a meadowy basin, then climbs the wooded slopes north of it. This is the realm of heather and subalpine fir, and the path makes its way through gently sloping glades to reach the broad gap of Tenmile Pass, which is wooded richly in fir and larch. The trail crosses the pass through a grassy window in the trees, with sweeping views down Devore Creek, which is flanked by bare and rocky summits. The trail now drops steadily through boulderfields and across vegetated slopes, robed in a dense mat of heather and dotted with copses of mountain hemlock and larch. There are superb views of the Fourth of July Basin during the descent, and of the stone pillars that rise above its western side.

The trail reaches the floor of the basin near its eastern edge, and gladed woodlands reveal the peaks to the east. The spruces and firs soon form a closed-canopy forest as the trail proceeds down the Devore Creek valley, and mountain scenery is limited to a few snowslide paths. The most scenic of these bears the West Fork of Devore Creek, with its waterfalls high above the trail, and higher still the bleached summit of Devore Peak. The trail has lost several hundred feet in elevation, and the forest is now dominated by

Company–Devore Creek Loop

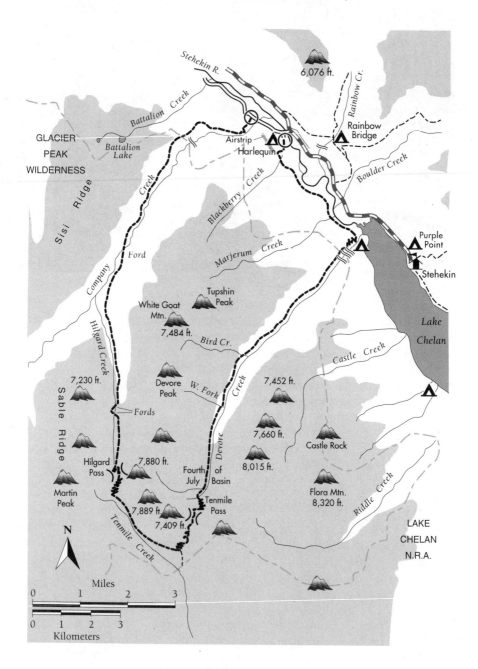

hemlock and silver fir. The path ultimately crosses Bird Creek, with a woodland camp spot on its far bank. Below this point, the valley supports a sparse forest of Douglas-fir that is underlain by low-growing shrubs. Groves of bigleaf maple become commonplace as Devore Creek plunges from its hanging valley toward the head of Lake Chelan. The trail now descends steep slopes high above the streamcourse.

After crossing the boundary into Lake Chelan National Recreation Area, the trail passes above the spectacular gorge at the valley's mouth. Several waterfalls are visible as the path zigzags down through Douglas-fir savannahs to reach the floor of the Stehekin Valley.

At a well-marked junction, a spur path runs south to Weaver Point Camp on Lake Chelan, while the loop route follows the Stehekin River trail northward for the remaining 3.2 miles to reach the road. A diverse bottomland forest contains such hardwoods as cottonwood, bigleaf maple, red alder, and aspen that provide fall colors in September. The river meanders close to the trail at several points along the way, first revealing Rainbow Falls across the valley and later unveiling the summit of McGregor Mountain. Upon reaching the end of the Stehekin airstrip, turn right twice as the trail runs east to the river, then follows it to reach the end of the trek at Harlequin Camp. From here, it is 1 mile by road to the Company Creek Trailhead.

ADDITIONAL TRAILS

The **Old Wagon Road** is a connecting trail that runs between Coon Lake and Bridge Creek, with access points at High Bridge and south of Dolly Varden Camp. PCT hikers use it as an alternate to hiking the modern road.

The **Cascade Corral Trail** is a horse trail that links Cascade Corral with High Bridge, following the road.

The **West Fork Agnes Creek Trail** has been abandoned and beyond its ford is completely overgrown with impenetrable brush.

The lightly traveled **Swamp Creek Trail** is difficult to follow, but it offers a scenic side trip from the Agnes Creek trail into the high country.

The **Stehekin River Trail** runs south from Harlequin Camp to the head of Lake Chelan, 3.5 miles.

Lake Chelan and the Sawtooth Country

The deep, blue waters of Lake Chelan extend for more than 50 miles from the semi-arid grasslands of the Columbia Basin into the heart of the North Cascades. About 17,000 years ago, the valley that now bears the lake was occupied by a river of glacial ice, which gouged the deep and narrow basin that now bears the lake. At the deepest point, the waters of Lake Chelan go down more than 1,500 feet.

A dam was constructed at the lake's outlet in 1921 to improve navigation for commercial vessels bound for the town of Chelan, Washington, and it raised the water level in the lake by 21 feet. During the early 1900s, barge traffic on the lake carried copper ore, timber products, and farm produce in from the hinterlands, and passenger vessels brought wealthy visitors to posh retreats along the lakeshore. Today, the waters around the town of Chelan teem with waterskiers and jet skis, while the upper reaches of the lake retain a more pristine aspect, flanked by precipitous slopes where only mountain goats venture.

The lake has seen a small armada of ferry boats, excursion craft, and barge traffic over the course of the last century. Today, the *Lady of the Lake II* plies the water, linking the town of Chelan with isolated outposts and Forest Service trailheads along the lakeshore. The express boat takes two hours one way to Stehekin and also stops at Lucerne. The regular ferry, which takes four hours one way, stops at Lucerne and also will make flag stops upon request. Driving 17 miles up the west shore of Lake Chelan to get on the boat at Fields Landing shaves an hour off the transit time. Long-term parking goes for exorbitant rates at either loading location. A note to campers: stove fuel is officially prohibited on the ferry—don't try to walk onto the boat with a jerry can of white gas. The store in Stehekin does sell white gas by the bottle.

At the head of Lake Chelan is the Stehekin landing, gateway to the Stehekin Valley and southernmost tip of the North Cascades national park complex. Most of the hikes in the Stehekin area are discussed in the previous section of this book, but the Purple Pass and Lakeshore trails discussed below lie within the jurisdiction of the National Park Service. Backcountry permits are required for all camping on national park lands in this area, and these permits can be obtained free of charge at the Golden West Visitor Center at the Stehekin landing. The ferry landing also offers a lodge with a restaurant, a camp store, and a small sporting goods concern.

To the west of the lake is the vast mountain fastness of the Glacier Peak Wilderness, administered by the Forest Service. Inquire at the Forest Service ranger station in Chelan for current conditions. This is a land of glacier-clad peaks, windswept passes, and valleys choked with brush and heavy timber.

Lake Chelan and the Sawtooth Country Overview

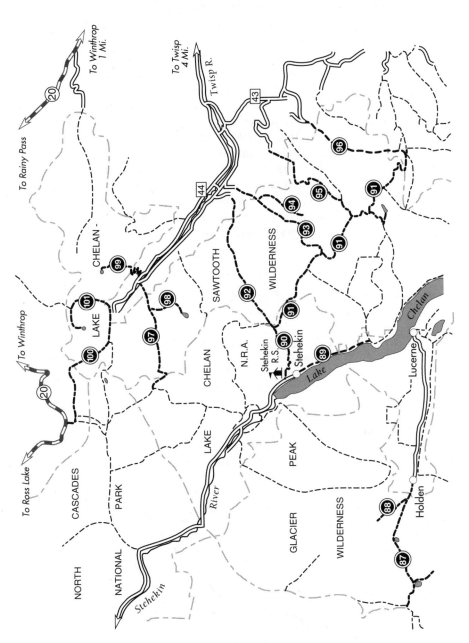

Logistical considerations make this area a good spot for extended backpacking expeditions. The primary western access point for the wilderness is the settlement of Holden, once a booming copper mine and now a retreat leased to the Lutheran Church. From the ferry landing that is Lucerne, a nominal fee gets you on the shuttlebus that runs to the historic company town of Holden. Tours and accommodations here are booked months in advance and are generally limited to guests at the retreat, but meals can be had at the dining hall, and there is also a sauna that is open to the public. A Forest Service camp is just west of the settlement.

East of the lake are the drier and more accessible peaks of Sawtooth Ridge, with vast timberline stretches of grassy meadows and copses of subalpine larch. Once the summer range of sheepherders, the range is now protected within the Lake Chelan–Sawtooth Wilderness. A number of manageable trails ascend from the Twisp River valley to the windswept ridgetops of Sawtooth Ridge, suitable for long day trips or short backpacks. Along the crest of the range is the Chelan Summit trail, which links any of the trails that rise from the east with less-traveled routes that descend to the shore of Lake Chelan. Here, there are flag stops where the passenger ferry will stop on request. Several Forest Service campgrounds wait along the Twisp River Road, and most kinds of supplies can be found in the village of Twisp. There is also a Forest Service ranger station in town.

87 Railroad Creek

Overview:	A day hike from Holden to Hart Lake, 9.2 miles round trip, or a backpack to Cloudy Pass, 9.7 miles one way.
Best season:	Early July to early October.
Difficulty:	Moderate to Hart Lake; moderately strenuous beyond.
Elevation gain:	3,575 feet.
Elevation loss:	361 feet.
Maximum elevation:	6,440 feet at Cloudy Pass.
Topo maps:	Holden, Suiattle Pass; *Holden*.
Jurisdiction:	Glacier Peak Wilderness (Wenatchee National Forest).

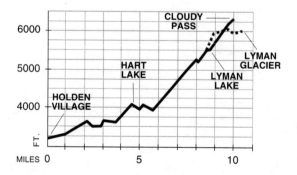

Lyman Glacier.

Finding the trailhead: Take the ferry to Lucerne and then the shuttlebus to Holden Village. The hike begins on the westbound Railroad Creek Road.

Key points:
- 0.0 Holden Village. Follow road westward.
- 0.3 Bridge to site of old Holden Mine. Continue straight ahead.
- 1.0 Road passes camping area and ends at wilderness boundary. Railroad Creek Trail runs westward from this point.
- 1.5 Junction with Holden Lake Trail. Bear left.
- 4.6 Trail reaches the foot of Hart Lake.
- 5.0 Campsite near the head of Hart Lake.
- 5.7 Rebel Camp.
- 6.2 Trail begins grade that leads to Lyman Lake.
- 8.6 Junction with Lyman Glacier Trail (2.2 miles, moderate). Continue straight ahead for Lyman Lake and Cloudy Pass; turn right for camping area.
- 8.7 Trail reaches foot of Lyman Lake.
- 8.9 Spur trail runs south along west shore of Lyman Lake. Turn right.
- 9.7 Cloudy Pass camping area.
- 10.1 Cloudy Pass. Connecting trails lead to Suiattle Pass and Agnes Creek.

This trail makes a long journey up Railroad Creek from the old mining camp of Holden to the alpine heights of Cloudy Pass. Railroad Creek got its name from the short inclined railway at the mouth of the valley, which transported copper ore down to waiting barges on Lake Chelan. The entire valley shows the influence of the miners: early prospectors burned most of the timber in a quest for gold; the copper mine at Holden came later and brought settlement to the valley; and the old company town has

325

become a Lutheran retreat that brings hundreds of visitors into the mountains annually. The Railroad Creek Trail offers an overnight getaway into the Glacier Peak Wilderness, replete with alpine lakes, waterfalls, glaciers, and superb mountain views throughout the trek.

The hike begins by following the gravel road that runs along the north bank of Railroad Creek, past the old ore-refining mill on the far bank and the stone curbs and stairways that are all that remain of the abandoned miner's village. The road gives way to trail at the wilderness boundary, and camping spots are scattered along the edge of a clearing. The sawtooth crest of Copper Peak reveals itself across the valley as the trail makes its way through a floodplain woodland of cottonwood and Douglas-fir. After passing a junction with the Holden Lake spur, the main trail rises out of the bottom-lands onto open slopes covered with willow and young aspen. Much of this valley was burned in the late 1800s by prospectors who sought to uncover veins of precious metals. Hikers get fine views of Copper Peak as the trail climbs steadily, then glides down to a footbridge over Holden Creek.

After passing through a stand of lodgepole pine, the trail breaks out onto the open slopes above a marshy flat. Beavers have constructed dams across Railroad Creek here, creating a number of ponds and canals. Shrubfields of mountain ash, Douglas maple, and willow now afford views of the craggy northern buttress of Dumbell Mountain. The trail soon undertakes a steady climb, passing quite close to a splendid cascade as Railroad Creek pours down the face of a gneiss outcrop. At the top of the grade, the trail reaches Hart Lake, and views open up to encompass Crown Point Falls at the head of the valley, with a rocky bulwark of Chiwawa Mountain rising beyond it. The trail crosses the rocky slopes above the lakeshore, passing a lone camping spot near the head of the lake. Here, a pretty peninsula rises across the water, clad in tall grasses and spruce copses. As the creek waters enter Hart Lake, they slow down and the coarse sediments settle out, extending the peninsula ever farther into the lake.

The trail now climbs high onto an alluvial fan, formed by spectacular cataracts that descend from Isabella Glacier, which remains hidden from view. Dropping back into the creek bottoms, the trail passes a second series of waterfalls to reach Rebel Camp in a streamside grove of ancient spruce trees. A clearing filled with spiraea awaits beyond the camp, with spectacular views of Dumbell Mountain and the slender waterfalls that descend from its heights. The path soon ascends into heavy brush, beginning a long grade that carries travelers past the headwall that bears Crown Point Falls. There are excellent views of the falls from several overlooks as the trail zigzags upward, and the mountain scenery continues unabated. At the top of the grade, look back for the trail's best views of Bonanza Peak.

The trail skirts subalpine firs beside a meadow-filled shelf, then switchbacks up beside a talus slope to surmount a second and smaller headwall. Upon reaching the upper basin, hikers pass a junction with the path to Lyman Glacier (discussed below) before reaching the foot of Lyman Lake. This vast and shallow lake is fed by the meltwaters of several glaciers,

Railroad Creek

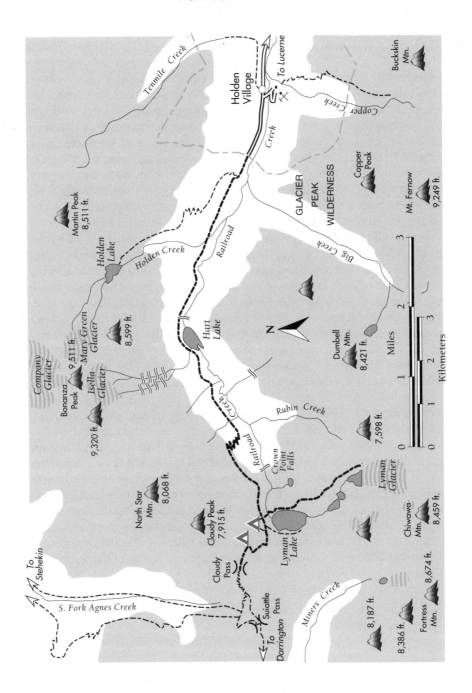

To Lucerne

Buckskin Mtn.

Holden Village

Tenmile Creek

Copper Creek

Copper Peak

GLACIER PEAK WILDERNESS

Mt. Fernow 9,249 ft.

Martin Peak 8,511 ft.

Holden Lake

Holden Creek

Railroad

Creek

Railroad

Big Creek

Mary Green Glacier

8,599 ft.

Hart Lake

N

Dumbell Mtn. 8,421 ft.

Miles

Company Glacier

Bonanza Peak 9,511 ft.

Isella Glacier

9,320 ft.

Railroad

Creek

Rubin Creek

7,598 ft.

Kilometers

North Star Mtn. 8,068 ft.

Railroad

Creek

Crown Point Falls

Lyman Glacier

To Stehekin

Cloudy Peak 7,915 ft.

Lyman Lake

Chiwawa Mtn. 8,459 ft.

S. Fork Agnes Creek

Cloudy Pass

Suiattle Pass

Miners Creek

8,187 ft.

8,386 ft.

Fortress Mtn. 8,674 ft.

To Darrington

327

which contribute a finely ground silt that gives the lake its turquoise hue. Hanging Glacier can be seen on a rocky spur of Chiwawa Mountain, while the much larger Lyman Glacier is hidden behind a low bluff at the head of the lake. There is a large camping area in the mountain hemlocks above the trail, while a spur route rounds the western shore of the lake for additional mountain views.

Meanwhile, the main trail turns north, climbing through copses of spire-shaped subalpine firs. As it breaks out onto the broad meadows below Cloudy Pass, there is a small campsite in the trees to the east. The Railroad Creek trail now swings westward for the final ascent to the pass. Views are spectacular along the way. The primeval upper basin of Railroad Creek is hemmed in by stark peaks, and Lyman Glacier and its lesser neighbors feed into shallow lakes. From the pass itself, hikers gain additional views of Plummer and Sitting Bull mountains across the Agnes Creek drainage. From here, the Agnes Creek trail descends into the valley beyond, and a cutoff path swings across the head of the valley toward Suiattle Pass.

Lyman Glacier Option. This narrow footpath is a must-see side trip for visitors who are camping at Lyman Lake. From the signpost, a footlog leads across Railroad Creek, whereupon the path climbs modestly onto a sparsely wooded bluff. There are fine views of Bonanza Peak to the northeast, and soon the trail offers panoramic vistas of Lyman Lake as it follows the eastern shore. As the trail climbs onto a tundra-clad rise, watch for even better views of Bonanza Peak's austere towers. To the north a spectacular landscape unfolds, with the turquoise waters of Lyman Lake stretched full-length below the white summits of Cloudy and North Star peaks. The twin peaks now visible through Cloudy Pass belong to Sitting Bull Mountain.

As the trail crests the rise, a primordial scene straight out of the Pleistocene epoch unfolds. Lyman Glacier lies at the head of the valley, descending from cliffs of iron-rich bedrock. Below it are a succession of terminal moraines, or ridges of waste rock bulldozed into place by the moving ice. They mark the successive surges and retreats of the glacier; some of the older moraines have become overgrown with heather and larch, while the more recent ones have dammed shallow meres of meltwater. The path runs eastward along the edge of the basin, then descends onto the outwash plain to reach an end at a cairn atop a sandy hillock. This perch offers superb views of the glacier's terminus, and of ice floes in the lake below its toe. The stark summit to the west is Mount Chiwawa; an upper lobe of Lyman Glacier graces its east face.

88 Holden Lake

Overview: A day hike or short backpack from Holden Village to Holden Lake, 11 miles round trip.

Best season: Mid-June to early October.

Difficulty: Moderately strenuous.

Elevation gain: 2,064 feet.

Maximum elevation: 5,290 feet.

Topo maps: Holden; *Holden*.

Jurisdiction: Glacier Peak Wilderness (Wenatchee National Forest).

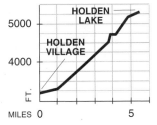

Finding the trailhead: The hike begins at Holden Village. See Hike 87 directions.

Key points:

- 0.0 Holden Village. Follow road westward.
- 0.3 Bridge to site of old Holden Mine. Continue straight ahead.
- 1.0 Road passes camping area and ends at wilderness boundary. Follow Railroad Creek Trail westward from this point.
- 1.5 Junction with Holden Lake Trail. Bear right.
- 2.4 Old road ends, giving way to trail.
- 5.5 Holden Lake.

The hike: This trail offers a long and challenging day hike to a high cirque lake beneath Bonanza Peak and Mary Green Glacier. Travelers who arrive in Holden in the afternoon will find that Holden Lake is an ideal destination for a short overnighter that allows you to make the next day's ferry.

To reach the lake, follow the Railroad Creek Trail (see p.324) to a marked junction in the bottomlands. From here, the Holden Lake trail follows an old roadbed up the north wall of the valley. The trees soon give way to brushfields, and initial views include Copper Peak to the south as well as Bonanza and Cloudy peaks farther up the valley. The old road ends at the first sizable stream, and from here a trail zigzags up the mountainside at a leisurely pace. The northern crags of Dumbell Mountain soon reveal themselves across the valley, and views down Railroad Creek encompass Buckskin and Tinpan mountains. After a long climb, the trail approaches a stand of conifers at the mouth of the Holden Creek valley. This stand turns out to be an open woodland of lodgepole pine, and the trail resumes its upward switchbacks upon entering it.

After a seemingly interminable climb, the trail turns north into the valley of Holden Creek. A dense stand of Douglas-fir and spruce provides shade as the trail makes its way to a small stream and crosses it. The path now leads

Holden Lake

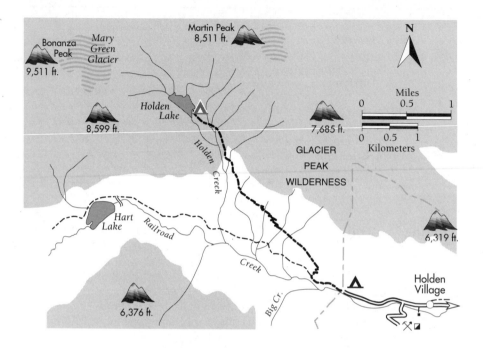

west through a beautiful stand of spruce and aspen. Striking Holden Creek, the trail turns north again and climbs across avalanche paths and through bands of subalpine forest. The openings reveal fine views of Mary Green Glacier, high on the craggy face of Bonanza Peak. After wandering through a stand of mature mountain hemlocks, the path finally breaks out into the subalpine parks that border Holden Lake. The lake itself is a scenic gem, nestled at the foot of the crags with slender waterfalls streaming down from the glacier above. To the east is the brooding summit of Holden Peak, visible from the lakeshore. Copses of spruce and fir shelter campsites inland from the lakeshore, and trout cruise the clear waters.

89 Chelan Lakeshore Trail

Overview:	A long day hike or short backpack from Stehekin to Moore Point, at the mouth of Fish Creek, 13.6 miles round trip.
Best season:	Mid-April to early November.
Difficulty:	Moderate.
Elevation gain:	1,050 feet.
Elevation loss:	1,060 feet.
Maximum elevation:	1,660 feet.
Topo maps:	Stehekin, Lucerne, Sun Mountain; *Stehekin, Lucerne.*
Jurisdiction:	Lake Chelan National Recreation Area (North Cascades National Park), Lake Chelan–Sawtooth Wilderness (Wenatchee National Forest).

Finding the trail: From Stehekin Landing, follow roads south past the Golden West Visitor Center and the fire cache to reach the marked beginning of the trail.

Key points:

0.0 Trail leaves Stehekin bearing southward along lakeshore.
0.5 Falls on Hazard Creek.
2.3 Trail crosses Fourmile Creek.
2.9 Trail crosses Flick Creek.
3.6 Flick Creek Camp.
3.7 Trail leaves Lake Chelan NRA and enters Lake Chelan–Sawtooth Wilderness.
4.4 Trail crosses Hunts Creek.
5.0 Trail reaches its highest point on Hunts Bluff.
6.1 Jeep track crosses trail. Continue straight ahead.
6.3 Junction with Fish Creek Trail. Bear right.
6.4 Trail crosses Fish Creek.
6.5 Junction with Moore Point spur trail. Turn right to complete the hike.
6.8 Moore Point camping area and boat landing.

The hike: This trail follows the eastern shore of Lake Chelan from the Stehekin visitor center all the way to the mouth of Prince Creek. This description covers only the first 6.5 miles of the trail, which offers the best scenery and is visited most often. The first 3.7 miles fall within National Park Service jurisdiction, beyond which the path travels through the Lake Chelan–Sawtooth Wilderness. There are privately owned parcels at various points along the lakeshore, and some have cabins on them. Treat them as private property. There are developed camping areas beyond Flick Creek (permit required) and at Moore Point, the end of the trek. Check yourself for ticks after the hike; they are particularly abundant in spring and early summer.

The trail begins as a level trek beside the water, with intermittent views of Castle Rock across the lake. There is a pretty waterfall at Hazard Creek, and just beyond it the trail runs out onto a rocky headland for superb views up and down the lake. Buckner Mountain is the snowy summit far up the Stehekin Valley, and its rocky neighbor is Booker Mountain. In the middle distance, McGregor Mountain presents an immense edifice of rock. The first major stream along the trail is Fourmile Creek, and the trail wanders inland here to cross an alluvial fan. Back on the lakeshore, the trail soon passes a private cabin and runs eastward into the woods to cross Flick Creek at the mouth of its rocky canyon. A moderate climb then leads to a grassy hilltop for more fine views of Lake Chelan. The Flick Creek shelter and camp occupies a sparsely wooded point farther to the south, offering a picnic spot with outstanding views.

After passing it, the trail leaves Lake Chelan National Recreation Area and enters the Wenatchee National Forest. The route now runs inland, climbing moderately through the trees. A side trip along Hunts Creek leads far to the east, after which the trail climbs onto a stony bluff for superb views of the head of the lake. The view continues to improve as the path charts a high and sometimes cliff-hanging course across the face of Hunts Bluff. To the southwest, magnificent crags rise in the Glacier Peak Wilderness beyond the settlement of Lucerne. The trail maintains its altitude to reach the great forested delta of Fish Creek. Pay attention to trail signs as the path crosses a

Castle Rock from the Chelan lakeshore.

Chelan Lakeshore Trail

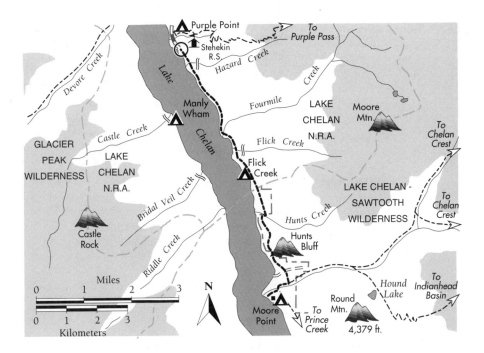

jeep road and later as the Fish Creek Trail splits away to the left. The lakeshore trail first follows Fish Creek toward the lake, then crosses a sturdy bridge and splits. To the left, the Lakeshore Trail continues southward toward Prince Creek, while our route follows a spur trail that runs down to meet Lake Chelan at Moore Point. This trail ends at a campground and boat landing that also boasts a log shelter.

90 Purple Pass

See Map on Page 315

Overview: A backpack from the Stehekin landing to Lake Juanita, 8 miles one way.

Best season: Mid-July to mid-October.

Difficulty: Strenuous.

Elevation gain: 5,810 feet.

Elevation loss: 305 feet.

Maximum elevation: 7,350 feet at Boulder Butte.

Topo maps: Stehekin, Sun Mountain; *Stehekin*.

Jurisdiction: Lake Chelan National Recreation Area.

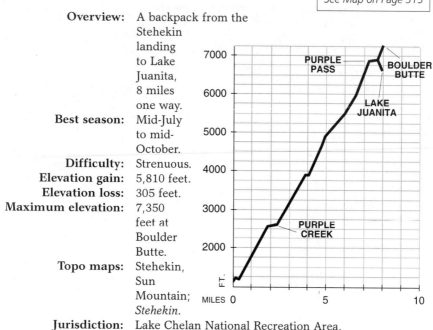

Finding the trail: The hike begins on the Imus Creek Nature Trail, which starts directly behind the Golden West Visitor Center.

Key points:
- 0.0 Golden West Visitor Center. Follow Imus Creek Nature Trail.
- 0.1 Trail crosses Purple Creek below waterfall.
- 0.2 Purple Pass trail splits away from Imus Creek Nature Trail. Turn right.
- 1.9 Second crossing of Purple Creek.
- 4.9 Abandoned spur trail descends to Cougar Spring.
- 6.0 Top of ridge.
- 7.4 Purple Pass.
- 7.6 Junction with Boulder Butte spur (0.5 mile, moderately strenuous). Stay right for Lake Juanita.
- 7.9 Lake Juanita camps.
- 8.0 Junction beside Lake Juanita. War Creek Trail runs northeast; Chelan Summit Trail runs southeast.

The hike: This trail is a seemingly interminable climb from the north shore of Lake Chelan to the subalpine parklands at the north end of the Chelan Summit Trail. Lake Juanita, a small and barren pond, lies at the end of the trek. The entire trail can be hiked in a single day, but it is a long and grueling journey. Backpackers commonly combine the Purple Pass trail with the

Looking through Purple Pass.

Boulder Creek route for a two- to three-day loop trip.

The trail is approached via the Imus Creek Nature Trail. Hikers may begin from the road just north of Purple Point Campground, or from the trail sign behind the Golden West Visitor Center. The latter option is more scenic, visiting the cool riparian woodland where Purple Creek plunges over a sill of resistant gneiss.

From the trail junction at the upper edge of Purple Creek's alluvial fan, the Purple Pass trail begins its long and steady climb on the grassy slopes beside the mouth of a rocky canyon carved by the creek. Initial views across the lake feature Castle Rock and Tupshin Peak. As the path climbs higher through a dense stand of Douglas-fir, forest openings reveal the summit of White Goat Mountain as well. After a considerable ascent, the trail swings east into the Purple Creek canyon. The riparian woodland along the water-course is comprised of water-loving hardwoods, dominated by bigleaf maple. Hikers can rely on this woodland for a colorful display of autumn foliage in early October.

After crossing Purple Creek, the trail runs south and soon climbs onto open savannahs populated by Douglas-fir and ponderosa pine. Scenic overlooks are commonplace as the trail makes a hot upward trek. To the north, a long vista up the Stehekin Valley is highlighted by the barren crags of McGregor Mountain and the more distant summits of Sahale and Booker mountains. Views of Lake Chelan stretch southward as far as the settlement of Lucerne, below the wooded dome of Domke Mountain.

· After almost 4 miles, the path runs eastward into the Hazard Creek drainage, still climbing. The ponderosa pines now fall behind, and views constrict to encompass only the peaks directly across the lake. Along the way, a signpost marks an abandoned trail that once accessed Cougar Spring; this path has been obliterated by a tangle of game trails and thickets of spiny hawthorn. Continuing upward, the trail ultimately rises to crest the ridgetop, which offers panoramic views. After a short climb, the path swings onto the high slopes above Purple Creek. The Douglas-firs are now replaced by a sparse woodland of subalpine fir, whitebark pine, and ultimately larch.

The final climb to Purple Pass is accompanied by expanded northward views, highlighted by the upthrust finger of Goode Mountain and the snowy massif of Mount Logan to the east of it. Grassy parklands stretch southward from the pass, interspersed with tidy copses of larch and spruce. As the path descends from the pass, there are fine views across the head of the Fourmile Creek basin, which is guarded to the east by Splawn Mountain and to the south by massive Moore Mountain. The poorly marked trail to Boulder Butte (outlined below) soon splits away to the left, while the main path continues its descent into the meadows beside Lake Juanita. There is a horse camp to the west of this small and shallow pond, while the hiker's camp occupies a rocky shelf along the south shore with splendid views of the surrounding peaks. A trail junction on the east shore of the lake offers access to Boulder and War creeks (to the left) and the Chelan Summit Trail (straight ahead).

Boulder Butte Option. This nearly forgotten but well-worn spur trail departs from the Purple Pass trail 0.2 mile east of the pass. It first runs northward across slopes of broken rock that are sparsely populated by subalpine larch. Watch for pikas as the trail crosses an east-facing bowl, then zigzags up to the summit of Boulder Butte. An old lookout site at 7,350 feet commands stunning views in all directions, encompassing McAlester Mountain to the northwest, Sun Mountain looking southward along Sawtooth Ridge, and the head of Lake Chelan with a crowd of crags rising beyond it.

91 Chelan Summit Trail

Overview:	An extended trek along the timberline meadows of Sawtooth Ridge from Lake Juanita in the north to Boiling Lake in the south, 19.5 miles.
Best season:	Early July to early October.
Difficulty:	Moderately strenuous.
Elevation gain:	6,250 feet (north to south).
Elevation loss:	6,030 feet (north to south).
Maximum elevation:	7,440 feet at the pass between Fish and Prince creeks.
Topo maps:	Sun Mountain, Oval Peak, Prince Creek, Martin Peak; *Stehekin, Buttermilk Butte, Prince Creek.*
Jurisdiction:	Lake Chelan National Recreation Area (North Cascades National Park), Lake Chelan–Sawtooth Wilderness (Wenatchee National Forest).

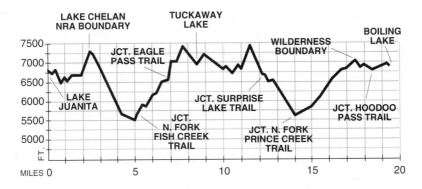

Finding the trailhead: The route is easiest to reach from the west via the Purple Pass (8 miles) and Boulder Creek (11.4 miles) trails. From the Twisp River side, it can be reached via War Creek (9.4 miles), Eagle Pass (8.4 miles), Scaffold Ridge (10.5 miles), the West Fork of Buttermilk Creek (9.0 miles), or Hoodoo Pass (7.8 miles).

Key points:

0.0	Trail junction at Lake Juanita.
2.4	Trail crests divide to enter Fish Creek watershed. It now leaves Lake Chelan NRA and enters the Lake Chelan–Sawtooth Wilderness.
3.3	Camp Comfort.
5.2	Junction with North Fork Fish Creek Trail. Continue straight ahead.
6.7	Ten Tree Camp and junction with Eagle Pass Trail. Bear right.
7.2	Trail crosses pass to enter East Fork Fish Creek drainage.
7.7	Second and higher pass.
8.9	Twin Springs Camp and junction with trail to Tuckaway Lake (1.2 miles, moderate) and Oval Pass (1.8 miles, strenuous). Bear right.
10.6	Junction with East Fork Fish Creek Trail. Continue straight ahead.

10.9   Junction with trail to Fish Creek Pass. Continue straight ahead.

11.5   Trail crosses pass to enter Prince Creek watershed.

12.4   Junction with Surprise Lake Trail (0.8 mile to overlook; 2.5 miles to lake; moderate). Bear left to stay on Chelan Summit Trail.

13.7   North Fork Prince Creek shelter.

14.1   Junction with North Fork Prince Creek Trail. Bear left.

17.4   Trail crosses pass into Middle Fork Prince Creek drainage and leaves Lake Chelan–Sawtooth Wilderness.

18.7   Junction with Hoodoo Pass Trail. Turn left for preferred route.

18.9   Junction with Boiling Lake cutoff trail. Bear right at hitchrack.

19.5   Boiling Lake.

The hike: This trail runs the length of the Lake Chelan–Sawtooth Wilderness, crossing the open larch parklands beneath the rugged peaks of Sawtooth Ridge. These high meadows were once the domain of Basque herders, who pushed their bands of sheep through the highlands of the Sawtooth country, then continued northeast into the Okanogan highlands. The trail can be accessed via a network of well-maintained trails that ascend from the Twisp River valley, or from steeper paths rising upward from Lake Chelan. Our description ends at Boiling Lake, just beyond the Wilderness boundary. The southern leg of the Summit trail to South Navarre is part of an ATV playground, a thoroughfare for dirt bikes and other mechanized traffic, and is thus a poor place for hikers to experience the wonder of the mountains.

From the larch-studded meadows at Juanita Lake, the trail runs southeast on a gradual descent across the head of the Fourmile Creek valley. It crosses grasslands where a few whitebark pines and subalpine firs grow. Views across the head of Lake Chelan extend from Castle Rock and Tupshin Peak in the north to the Chelan Mountains far to the south. Closer at hand, the rugged summit of Moore Mountain guards the south side of the Fourmile basin.

At the far edge of the drainage is a shallow basin, and from here the trail climbs aggressively through a stand of subalpine larch to gain the ridgetop and leave National Park Service-managed lands. The trail now turns south, growing faint as it follows the ridgetop through meadows and across bare ground. An old trailbed soon rises from the west to join the main trail; our route now drops onto the eastern side of the ridge. Clearings afford expansive views of Fish Creek's North Fork, with Deephole Spring rising in a meadowy pocket and sharp crags all around. Loftiest of these are Oval Peak to the east and the multiple summits of Sawtooth Ridge stretching away to the southeast.

The trail drops quickly into the basin below, bypassing Deephole Spring to bring travelers beneath the castellated spires of the nearest summit. After passing through Camp Comfort, the trail turns eastward. It soon reaches the lower mountain slopes that guard the head of the valley. A steady descent leads along the lower edge of a mountain grassland. Near the center of the valley, the trail enters a spruce-fir forest and the gradient lessens. An avalanche slope just before the North Fork junction offers views of the ranges to the west.

After intercepting the North Fork Fish Creek Trail, the Chelan Summit

Chelan Summit Trail

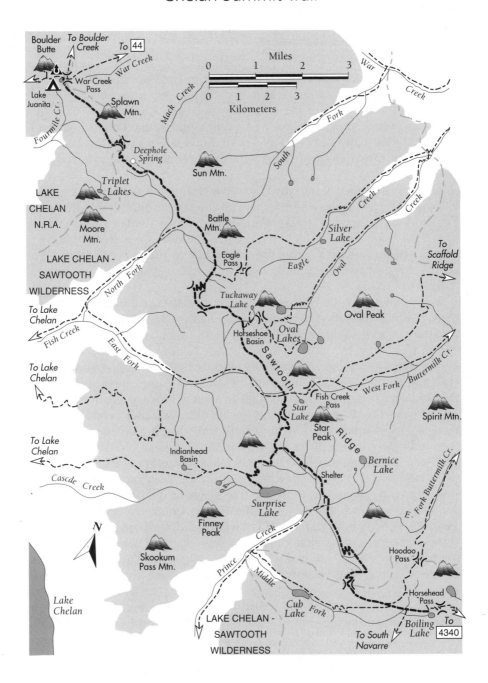

route climbs steadily through the forest. It crosses several open meadows near the head of the valley, but views are limited until the trail reaches the alpine meadows below Eagle Pass. Here, the rocky crags that surround the meadows tower above skirts of subalpine larch. There is a junction with the Eagle Pass Trail at Ten Tree Camp.

A vigorous climb soon leads over a high saddle to the west. The path then turns southwest and continues its ascent across the slopes beyond. A woodland of whitebark pine soon thins to become a grassy savannah, revealing a superb westward vista of the peaks beyond Lake Chelan. The path then crests an even higher ridgetop, and gains a panoramic view of Sawtooth Ridge with its many peaks rising above the East Fork of Fish Creek. The trail drops into a larch forest, then winds across open meadows to reach the Horseshoe Basin.

A spur path runs east into the Horseshoe Basin; it departs from a signpost in Twin Springs Camp, which is beyond the stream that drains the basin. The spur trail climbs a grassy slope beneath vast fields of broken rock. Watch for pikas and marmots among the boulders. In a shallow basin, a cairn-marked route runs across the north slope to Tuckaway Lake, while an abandoned trail climbs the south wall of the valley, bound over the ridgetop to the Oval Lakes.

Meanwhile, the main trail continues southwestward, climbing vigorously through the larches then zigzagging up along the edge of the talus. The trail tops out on larch-studded benches high on the shoulder of Gray Peak, then begins a long traverse across sparsely wooded slopes. The path loses several hundred feet as it crosses grassy meadows that offer stunning views of Star Peak and Baldy Mountain. The trail bottoms out within earshot of the East Fork of Fish Creek, then rises through an ancient grove of subalpine fir with a good campsite. It emerges in the spectacular meadows below Star Peak. Here, signposts mark the junctions with trails leading up over Fish Creek Pass and down the East Fork toward the shore of Lake Chelan.

After crossing the meadows, the trail makes a short but vigorous climb up to the larch-girt divide that stretches between Star Peak and Baldy Mountain. Atop the bald ridge crest, there are fine views of the rugged but nameless summits that crowd the edges of the Prince Creek watershed. The trail descends steadily onto terraces of larch parkland, then wends its way westward through a stand of subalpine fir. Upon reaching a beautiful meadow at the far side of the forest, hikers approach a signpost. The trail to Surprise Lake (see below) runs west, while the Chelan Summit Trail descends on an eastward bearing.

After dropping through the forest, the path turns southeast to descend gently across grassy meadows separated by strips of timber. Beyond a talus field, the Prince Creek shelter guards an open slope. The path continues downward to the junction with the Prince Creek Trail; follow the signs for Boiling Lake as the Chelan Summit Trail levels off in a montane stand of Douglas-fir and lodgepole pine.

After crossing a series of avalanche slopes, the trail strikes a mountain brook and follows it upward past picturesque pools and miniature waterfalls. Nearing the head of the valley, the path turns northeast to zigzag up through the pines toward what appears to be a low pass. Along the way, there are views of Finney Peak to the west. The "pass" turns out to be a blind amphitheater walled in by ragged cliffs, and the trail ascends into the meadows at its lower edge before turning westward toward the true pass. A level traverse leads across talus slopes and through sparse stands of larch to reach a hanging meadow at the far edge of the valley.

The path skirts the meadow's edge before climbing the final pitch to the windswept divide above the Middle Fork of Prince Creek, where the trail leaves the wilderness. Parting views of Star Peak are accompanied by a jumbled montage of fresh scenery: Martin Peak at the head of the valley, Old Man Mountain beyond the deep rift occupied by the Middle Fork, and Emerald and Cardinal peaks rising far to the southwest beyond the waters of Lake Chelan.

The trail now traverses arid and rocky slopes, offering views of Cub Lake in the valley below. It soon turns the corner onto grassier slopes, then descends to bypass a talus field. Just beyond the boulders is a junction with the trail to Hoodoo Pass, the first leg of a scenic high route to Boiling Lake that is recommended as the final leg of the trek. Follow this side trail eastward across meadows frequented by mule deer and black bear. Open meadows high in the basin have a camp with a hitchrail; the unmarked Hoodoo Pass trail continues east here, while a well-beaten trail runs south to Boiling Lake. This lake marks the end of the recommended route, and has a heavily developed camping area complete with picnic tables. The Chelan Summit trail, now frequented by motorized vehicles, turns south toward South Navarre Camp, while another wide dirtbike path leads southeast over Horsehead Pass.

Surprise Lake Option. The Surprise Lake trail begins by crossing attractive meadows interspersed with groves of spruce. After rising over a low knoll, the path makes its way around the head of a grassy bowl where marmots have taken up residence. A modest ascent leads upward, reaching the crest of a bare ridge that overlooks Surprise Lake after 0.8 mile. This large body of water lies within a hanging slot valley high above Prince Creek. The craggy summit of Finney Peak rises ahead as the trail traverses across grassy slopes toward the head of the valley. About halfway there, an intersection marks the spot where the Surprise Lake spur departs from the Indianhead Basin Trail and descends eastward to reach the grassy parklands at the head of the lake, for an overall distance of 3 miles.

92 War Creek

Overview: A backpack from the Twisp River to Lake Juanita, 9.4 miles one way.

Best season: Late June to mid-October.

Difficulty: Moderate.

Elevation gain: 3,670 feet.

Elevation loss: 90 feet.

Maximum elevation: 6,770 feet at War Creek Pass.

Topo maps: Oval Peak, Sun Mountain; *Stehekin, Buttermilk Butte.*

Jurisdiction: Lake Chelan–Sawtooth Wilderness (Okanogan National Forest), Lake Chelan National Recreation Area (North Cascades National Park).

Finding the trailhead: From Twisp, drive west on the Twisp River Road (Forest Road 44) for 14.8 miles. Turn left at the junction with FR 4430, veer

The approach to War Creek Pass.

War Creek

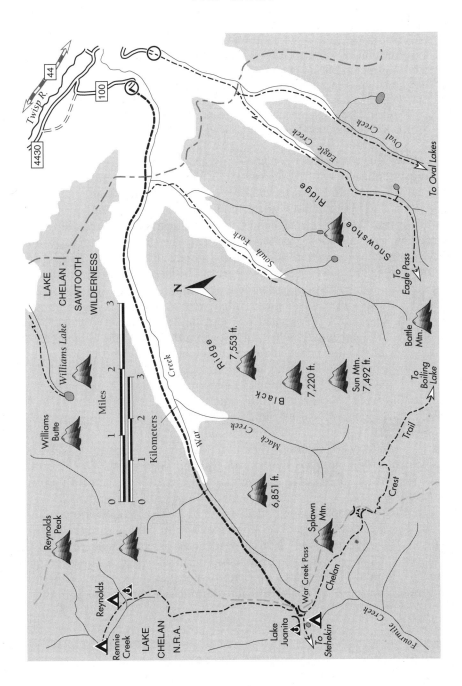

right after crossing the river, and turn left again at FR 4430-100. Follow this logging road for the remaining 1.5 miles to the trailhead.

Key points:
- 0.0 War Creek Trailhead.
- 1.8 Junction with South Fork War Creek Trail. Continue straight ahead.
- 5.4 Trail passes old cabin.
- 9.2 Junction with Boulder Creek Trail. Bear left for War Creek Pass.
- 9.3 War Creek Pass. Trail leaves Lake Chelan–Sawtooth Wilderness and enters Lake Chelan National Recreation Area.
- 9.4 Lake Juanita. Junction with Purple Pass and Chelan Summit trails.

The hike: This woodland trek passes through a diverse and beautiful selection of forest communities. It lacks mountain views, but represents the fastest and easiest route to the north end of the Chelan Summit Trail.

After a steep initial climb, hikers find that the timbered ridges lining the mouth of War Creek give way to the stark talus slopes of War Creek Ridge. The reddish boles of old ponderosa pines punctuate the slopes, and after 1.8 miles the trail reaches a junction with a spur running up the South Fork of War Creek. There are good campsites nearby. The main trail now follows the bottoms through a sun-dappled woodland of mature spruce and Douglas-fir. Farther up the valley, open parks filled with young aspen alternate with savannahs of old-growth Douglas-fir. Near the confluence of War and Mack creeks, the trail encounters a historic log cabin that was built to maintain the original telephone line between Stehekin and the outside world.

The trail now begins a long and monotonous grade to War Creek Pass. Heavy timber obscures the pinnacle that guards Mack Creek. Later openings in the trees reveal little more than timbered ridges. Halfway to the pass, the trail enters the 1994 Boulder Creek Burn. When the trees return, they will form a pleasant subalpine woodland. The trail climbs into a flat basin guarded by rocky crags, then ascends into the mixture of meadows, larches, and rock outcrops that guards the approach to War Creek Pass. A vigorous final pitch leads to the pass, and the Boulder Creek trail joins in along the way.

War Creek Pass marks the boundary of the Lake Chelan National Recreation Area, which is National Park Service domain. Permits are required for camping beyond this point. A brief descent across grasslands leads to the trail's end at a junction beside Lake Juanita. This tiny pool is surrounded by larch parklands. There is a campground on the western shore of the lake, and trails lead west to Purple Pass and south along the Chelan Summit.

93 Eagle Pass

Overview: A backpack over Eagle Pass to the Chelan Summit trail, 8.4 miles one way.

Best season: Early July to early October.

Difficulty: Moderately strenuous.

Elevation gain: 4,280 feet.

Elevation loss: 700 feet.

Maximum elevation: 7,260 feet.

Topo maps: Oval Peak; *Buttermilk Butte.*

Jurisdiction: Lake Chelan–Sawtooth Wilderness (Okanogan National Forest).

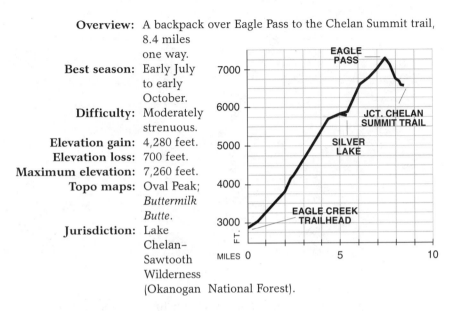

Finding the trailhead: From Twisp, drive west on the Twisp River Road (Forest Road 44) for 14.8 miles. Turn left at the junction with Forest Road 4430, veer left after crossing the river, and then turn right onto FR 4420-080. Follow this logging road for the remaining 1.5 miles to the Eagle Creek trailhead.

Key points:
0.0 Eagle Creek Trailhead.

2.0 Junction with Oval Lakes trail. Turn right for Eagle Pass. Wilderness boundary.

5.0 Junction with spur trail to Silver Lake (0.2 mile, easy). Continue straight ahead for Eagle Pass.

7.3 Eagle Pass.

8.4 Trail ends at junction with Chelan Summit Trail.

The hike: Arguably the most scenic trail to the Chelan Summit, this challenging route climbs through the valley of Eagle Creek, passing near Silver Lake on its way to the top of Sawtooth Ridge.

The trail begins by wandering up through the bottoms of Eagle Creek, which is loosely timbered in a diverse array of conifers and hardwoods. Upon reaching the confluence of Eagle and Oval creeks, the path zigzags up past the junction with the Oval Lakes trail and begins its long and viewless ascent to the high country. Thick timber surrounds the trail for the next 2.3 miles, finally relenting at the top of the grade as the trail passes a drift fence and enters a grassy meadow. There is a good campsite at the far edge of the

A nameless crag rises above Eagle Pass.

clearing. A brief climb through the trees leads to talus slopes that offer the first mountain views of the hike. Oval Peak rises prominently to the east, and a look down the valley reveals the distant domes of the Okanogan Mountains.

The trail soon levels off as it enters a hanging valley robed in a loose forest of subalpine fir, whitebark pine, and spruce. Along the willow-choked course of Eagle Creek, the trees open up into tidy meadows, which reveal themselves as the path drifts close to the water. A well-marked junction announces the departure of the Silver Lake spur trail, which crosses the parklands, makes a shallow ford (or a difficult leap) across Eagle Creek, and rises onto a heavily timbered shelf to reach the lake.

Meanwhile, the main trail continues its level journey up the valley, then climbs steadily to reach the whitebark pine savannahs high on the shoulders of a nameless peak that rises from Snowshoe Ridge. Superb views accompany the trail for the remainder of the trek, featuring Oval Peak and the nameless crags that guard the headwaters of Eagle Creek. The trail leads upward through flowery glades and stands of larch, finally climbing a steep pitch to gain the summit of Eagle Pass. A stark summit rises ahead, while a northward glance reveals the hulking massif of Gardiner Mountain and the pale summit of Silver Star Peak.

As the path descends into the grasslands to the southwest, westward views open up to reveal the sharp pinnacles beyond Lake Chelan. The path soon winds beneath a steep face of rock, then loops downward through larches and grassy glades to reach the floor of a meadowy basin. The trail ends here at a junction with the Chelan Summit route, and there is a good campsite beside a mountain brook just below the junction.

346

Eagle Pass • Oval Lakes
Scaffold Ridge

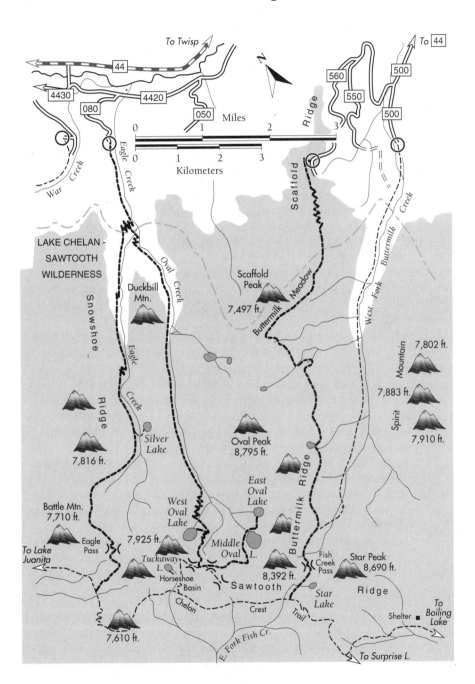

To Twisp

To 44

N

44

4430

4420

080

050 Miles

560

550

500

500

0   1   2   3

0   1   2   3

Kilometers

Eagle Creek

War Creek

Scaffold Ridge

LAKE CHELAN -
SAWTOOTH
WILDERNESS

Oval Creek

Duckbill
Mtn.

Scaffold
Peak
7,497 ft.

Buttermilk Meadow

West Fork Buttermilk Creek

Snowshoe

Eagle Creek

Ridge

Silver
Lake

Oval Peak
8,795 ft.

Mountain 7,802 ft.

7,883 ft.

Spirit

7,910 ft.

7,816 ft.

East
Oval
Lake

Battle Mtn.
7,710 ft.

West
Oval
Lake
7,925 ft.

Middle
Oval L.

Buttermilk Ridge

To Lake
Juanita

Eagle
Pass

Tuckaway
L.

Horseshoe
Basin

8,392 ft.

Fish
Creek
Pass

Star Peak
8,690 ft.

Sawtooth

Star
Lake

Ridge

Chelan

Crest

Trail

Shelter

To
Boiling
Lake

7,610 ft.

E. Fork Fish Cr.

To Surprise L.

94 Oval Lakes

See Map on Page 347

Overview: A backpack visiting all three Oval Lakes, 10.9 miles one way.

Best season: Early July to mid-October.

Difficulty: Moderately strenuous to West Oval; strenuous beyond.

Elevation gain: 4,850 feet to East Oval Lake.

Elevation loss: 1,170 feet to East Oval Lake.

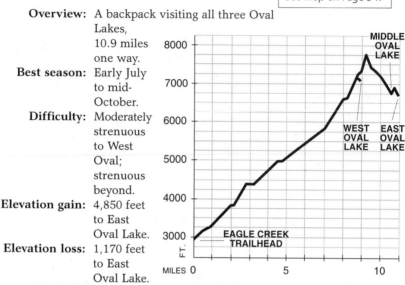

Maximum elevation: 7,700 feet above Middle Oval Lake.

Topo maps: Oval Peak; *Buttermilk Butte.*

Jurisdiction: Lake Chelan–Sawtooth Wilderness (Okanogan National Forest).

Finding the trailhead: The hike begins at the Eagle Creek trailhead; see the description on p.345.

Key points:

- 0.0   Eagle Creek Trailhead. Follow Eagle Pass Trail west.
- 2.0   Junction with Oval Lakes trail. Bear left. Wilderness boundary.
- 2.1   Trail fords Eagle Creek.
- 7.2   Bottom of grade to West Oval Lake.
- 7.9   Trail crosses outlet stream that drains West Oval Lake.
- 8.5   Junction with spur to West Oval (0.3 mile, moderate). Bear left for Middle and East Oval lakes.
- 9.1   Junction with abandoned trail to Horseshoe Basin. Bear left.
- 10.5   Middle Oval Lake. Trail crosses outlet stream.
- 10.9   East Oval Lake.

The hike: This trail climbs to a series of striking cirque lakes beneath the crest of Sawtooth Ridge. West Oval Lake can be reached in a long day hike, but the prettier lakes that lie beyond it require an overnight trip. The trail receives some use by horse parties, but for the most part the horses have had little impact on the landscape of this beautiful drainage.

The trek begins on the Eagle Pass Trail, a wide and dusty thoroughfare

Middle Oval Lake.

that follows Eagle Creek through a ragged woodland of Douglas-fir and ponderosa pine. As Oval Creek enters the valley from the southwest, the trail zigzags up to a marked junction at the wilderness boundary. Bear left onto the Oval Lakes trail, which soon crosses Eagle Creek via a ford of mid-calf depth or a scramble across slippery boulders. The path now tracks the steep gradient of Oval Creek, alternately switchbacking upward and traversing back to the stream. The dense growth of Douglas-fir offers scant scenery, and even when the trail crosses the shale slopes below Duckbill Mountain, there is little to see but forested ridges.

Beyond the scree slope, the stream gradient eases and the miles slide by effortlessly. The montane forest is soon replaced by a woodland of spire-shaped spruce and subalpine fir. The trail visits Oval Creek from time to time, revealing miniature waterfalls and crystalline pools. Near the head of the valley, the path passes beneath the towering edifice of Oval Peak. The path ultimately reaches a grassy meadow, and a spur path splits away toward a streamside camping spot.

The main trail now begins an arduous ascent across steep and timbered slopes. Atop a wooded shelf, the trail levels off and crosses the stream that issues from West Oval Lake. It then traverses to a second watercourse beneath a massive wall of stone, where it zigzags upward into the larches. A marked junction soon presents itself; the main trail is to the left, while to the right a spur trail climbs over a hillock and descends to West Oval Lake. Barren summits surround this high lake, and the sparse growth of whitebark pine and larch along the shoreline offers scant protection from the elements.

Meanwhile, the main trail adopts a steep grade as it climbs into a grassy vale, then redoubles its pace as it snakes upward along a barren spur ridge. There are outstanding views of Oval Peak from this point on. Plant life falls behind as the path climbs onto the barren scree at the base of Gray Peak. As the finger ridge joins the base of the mountain, an abandoned (but still passable) trail grade runs westward over a saddle and descends into the Horseshoe Basin, offering a linkage with the Chelan Summit trail. The main trail runs south, traversing across the scree to surmount a rocky col. Bear left as the path makes the steep drop into an open basin where rolling meadows are studded with groves of larch.

The trail runs roughly southward now, and steep descents alternate with level meanders across the meadows. A final descent through a spruce wood-land leads to the larch-studded flats at the foot of Middle Oval Lake. Guarded by towering peaks, this largest of the Oval Lakes is a superb place to camp. East Oval lake is nearby; to reach it, cross the outlet stream at Middle Oval and follow a path that first runs toward the lakeshore and then veers east to surmount a low and wooded hillock. A considerable descent leads to the shore of East Oval lake, which lies at the foot of Buttermilk Ridge and offers fine views of Oval Peak from its shoreline.

95 Scaffold Ridge

See Map on Page 347

Overview:	A challenging backpack along Scaffold Ridge to Fish Creek Pass and the Chelan Summit trail, 10.5 miles one way.
Best season:	Late June to mid-October.
Difficulty:	Moderately strenuous.
Elevation gain:	4,320 feet to Chelan Summit trail.
Elevation loss:	2,500 feet to Chelan Summit trail.
Maximum elevation:	7,500 feet at Fish Creek Pass.
Topo maps:	Hoodoo Peak, Oval Peak (trail not shown); *Buttermilk Butte.*
Jurisdiction:	Lake Chelan–Sawtooth Wilderness (Okanogan National Forest).

Finding the trailhead: From Twisp, drive west on the Twisp River Road (Forest Road 44) for 11 miles. Turn left onto the West Fork Buttermilk Road (County Road 1081), veer left at the split, and after 0.8 mile turn right onto Forest Road 43, following signs for Black Pine Lake. After 3.5 miles, turn

350

right onto FR 43-500, and turn right again at the next junction (unmarked) onto FR 43-550. This narrow road climbs onto Scaffold Ridge and splits. Take the right fork (560) and follow it to the wide spot near its end.

Key points:
    0.0   Scaffold Ridge Trailhead. Trail runs straight uphill.
    2.3   Trail enters Lake Chelan–Sawtooth Wilderness.
    2.6   Trail enters Buttermilk Meadow.
    3.9   Trail leaves Buttermilk Meadow.
    4.8   Trail crosses Spring Creek and begins steep ascent.
    6.5   Trail reaches nameless lake.
    9.0   Junction with West Fork Buttermilk Trail. Turn right.
    9.7   Fish Creek Pass.
   10.5   Trail ends at junction with Chelan Summit Trail.

The hike: This remote route follows the high country above the West Fork of Buttermilk Creek and then crosses Fish Creek Pass and descends to meet the Chelan Summit Trail. The Scaffold Ridge Trail receives light use from hunters and horsemen, and up to this time it has been largely ignored by hikers. It visits several beautiful but barren lakes along the way, and there are fine views all along the route. Route-finding skills are a must, since the trail receives light maintenance and is hard to follow in places.

After a killer ascent through the Douglas-fir and aspen savannahs, the trail runs southwest to reach a saddle atop Scaffold Ridge. The heavily timbered slopes of Scaffold Peak rises ahead, soaring upward out of sight. The path zigzags steadily up the ridgeline, and occasionally the spruces and lodgepole pines give way to grassy meadows that reveal distant views across the wooded foothills and tawny lowlands to the rounded peaks of the Okanogan Mountains. Near the top of Scaffold Peak, the trail levels off and makes its way onto south-facing slopes where sagebrush meadows afford superb mountain views. Star Peak, tallest summit on the granite backbone of Sawtooth Ridge, rises above the West Fork of Buttermilk Creek, and across the valley is the rugged crest of Spirit Mountain.

Entering the Lake Chelan–Sawtooth Wilderness, the trail glides down across the long band of grassland known as Buttermilk Meadows. Along the way hikers get superb views of the sheer north face of Oval Peak, and below it is a mantle of subalpine larch that turns brilliant gold in October. Upon reaching the bottom of the meadows, the trail climbs westward along its lower edge, shaded by the spreading canopies of mature spruce. There is a dependable spring just beyond the western end of the opening, and beyond it is an unmarked trail junction. Follow the heavily blazed lower path as the route-finding starts to get tricky.

The path wanders down through the formless folds of a gently sloping basin, then runs southward. The trail crosses a stream to reach the boulderfields at the base of a rocky and larch-studded spur of Oval Peak. Working its way along the lower edge of the talus, the trail skirts boggy meadows and then surmounts a low knoll to reach a camping spot beside a spring-fed creek. A steep climb ensues as the trail heads straight up the neighboring ridge, the same rocky spur that was visible earlier from below. As the path crests the ridgetop, take a short jog to the north, where granite outcrops offer fine views of Oval Peak.

A gentle descent now leads across whitebark pine savannahs; sporadic views encompass Spirit Mountain as well as the peaks of Sawtooth Ridge as far east as Mount Bigelow. After a number of minor ups and downs, the path climbs steeply to reach a shallow lake set among the larches below the northernmost horn of Buttermilk Ridge. Leaving the lake, the trail climbs briefly, then descends steeply through the subalpine woodland to reach the base of an impressive talus slope. The path follows the lower edge of this boulderfield and others like it, gaining elevation in steep spurts. Follow the cairns, blazes, and arrows sawed into the trees when the trail becomes difficult to follow.

After a long and vigorous ascent, the trail drops down to meet the West Fork Buttermilk trail at an unmarked junction. Turn right on the West Fork trail to continue the hike. The final and spectacular ascent to Fish Creek Pass is guarded by the regal summit of Star Peak. The barren col of the Fish Creek Pass is unmatched for scenic grandeur, with the granite faces of Star Peak soaring overhead, the turquoise mere of Star Lake nestled in the larch parklands below, and views of the angular crags of the Glacier Peak Wilderness far to the west. The trail now drops quickly across loess soil to reach the meadows below, then skirts far to the north of Star Lake as it descends gently to reach its end at a signpost on the Chelan Summit Trail.

Star Peak from the slopes of Scaffold Ridge.

96 Hoodoo Pass

Overview: A day hike to Hoodoo Pass, 13 miles round trip, or a backpack to the Chelan Summit trail, 7.8 miles total.
Best season: Early July to mid-October.
Difficulty: Moderate.
Elevation gain: 2,710 feet.
Elevation loss: 800 feet.
Maximum elevation: 7,450 feet.
Topo maps: Hoodoo Peak, Prince Creek; *Buttermilk Butte, Prince Creek.*

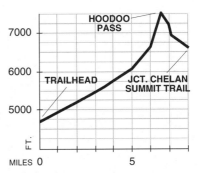

Jurisdiction: Lake Chelan– Sawtooth Wilderness (Okanogan National Forest).

Finding the trailhead: From Twisp, drive west on the Twisp River Road (Forest Road 44) for 11 miles. Turn left onto the West Fork Buttermilk Road (County Road 1081), veer left at the split, and after 0.8 mile turn right onto FR 43, following signs for Black Pine Lake. After 6 miles, turn right onto FR 43-400, following signs for Buttermilk Butte, and follow it for the remaining 2.5 miles to the trailhead.

Key points:
0.0   East Fork Buttermilk Creek Trailhead. Trail follows closed road.
2.2   Old road ends and trail fords East Fork of Buttermilk Creek.
4.5   Second crossing of the East Fork.
5.8   Final crossing of East Fork and bottom of grade to Hoodoo Pass.
6.5   Hoodoo Pass. Trail leaves Lake Chelan–Sawtooth Wilderness.
7.1   Horse camp. Junction with connector to Boiling Lake. Bear right for Chelan Summit Trail.
7.8   Trail ends at junction with Chelan Summit Trail.

The hike: This trail offers the shortest route to the south end of the Chelan Summit trail. Most of the trail has the tranquility conferred by wilderness status, but views along the way are masked by trees as far as Hoodoo Pass. Beyond this point, the trail enters alpine meadows that have been opened up to motorized vehicles.

For the first 2 miles of the trek, the trail follows an old road grade along the East Fork of Buttermilk Creek. Slide alder, ever the opportunist, has colonized the old roadway wherever there is sufficient groundwater. Talus slopes just beyond the wilderness boundary yield views of Hoodoo Peak and glimpses of Sawtooth Ridge, but for the most part the roadway runs

353

Hoodoo Pass

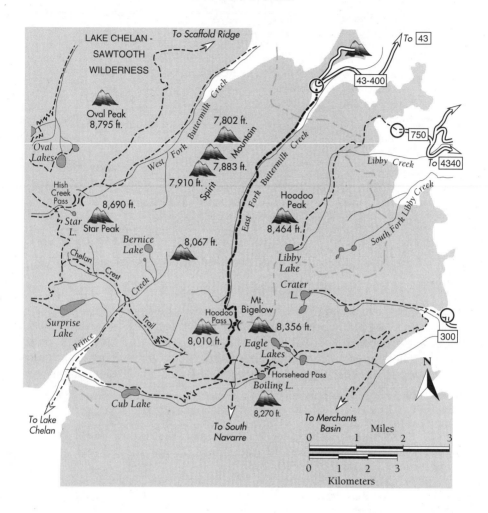

through a viewless forest. As the old road peters out, the trail fords the stream; hikers can clamber across the rocks just upstream. The trail now follows the watercourse closely, and its murmuring will be a constant companion as the path ascends gently through stands of spruce and lodgepole pine. The lodgepoles are the legacy of an intense forest fire that burned here in the early 1900s.

Above the burn, a more open forest of mature spruce provides a scenic counterpoint to the creek. After making a second crossing, the trail climbs moderately through open glades that provide glimpses of the surrounding mountains. The ground is saturated by seeps and springs, and horse traffic often churns the trail into a long succession of mud pits. There is a small camp beside the final stream crossing; this marks the bottom of the grade to

Hoodoo Pass.

The path now snakes upward through heavy timber, climbing steeply to reach the subalpine zone. Here, a fringe of larches gives way to a couloir of broken rock that has tumbled down from the blocky cliffs of Mount Bigelow. From the rocky heights of the pass, the eerie pillars of rock known as "hoodoos" can be seen on the mountainside to the south. The trail leaves the wilderness as it makes a surprisingly brief descent into the flat and grassy parklands to the south. It now wends its way down through the larch meadows to reach an unmarked junction beside a horse camp. To the left, a new trail traverses eastward to Boiling Lake. The old Hoodoo Pass trail runs southwest, providing fine views of the regal summit that rises to the north of Martin Peak as it crosses meadows guarded by ancient spruce trees. The trail ends as it joins the Chelan Summit trail in the upper reaches of Prince Creek's Middle Fork.

97 South Pass

Overview: A day hike to South Pass, 15 miles round trip, or a backpack to McAlester Pass, 9.9 miles one way.
Best season: Early July to mid-October.
Difficulty: Moderate.
Elevation gain: 3,120 feet.
Elevation loss: 370 feet.
Maximum elevation: 6,320 feet.
Topo maps: Gilbert; Stehekin.
Jurisdiction: Lake Chelan–Sawtooth Wilderness (Okanogan National Forest), Lake Chelan National Recreation Area.

Finding the trailhead: From Twisp, follow the Twisp River Road (Forest Road 44) west for 23 miles to the South Pass Trailhead.

Key points:
  0.0   South Creek Trailhead.
  0.1   Trail crosses Twisp River.
  0.2   Junction with spur trail from Horse Camp. Continue straight ahead.
  2.5   Junction with Louis Lake Trail. Continue straight ahead.
  7.5   South Pass. Trail leaves Lake Chelan–Sawtooth Wilderness and enters Ross Lake National Recreation Area.
  9.9   McAlester Pass. Junction with Rainbow Creek and McAlester Lake trails.

The hike: This trail offers one of the easiest hikes to a high pass in the North Cascades. It follows South Creek through the Lake Chelan–Sawtooth Wilderness, and beyond the divide enters Lake Chelan National Recreation Area, where National Park Service regulations apply. Louis Lake makes a fine side trip from this route (see p.358), and from trail's end at McAlester Pass it is an easy descent to McAlester Lake. Beyond South Pass are spectacular alpine meadows with views of McAlester Mountain and the distant peaks to the southwest.

After crossing a bridge over the Twisp River, the trail climbs onto a terrace where it is joined by a spur path from Horse Camp. The trail then enters the South Creek valley, climbing briskly to avoid a rocky gorge at the mouth of the valley. After a short distance, the climbing eases and the path makes its way through open timber that reveals the craggy peaks farther up the valley. A large brushfield offers views of a small but engaging waterfall. Just after the trees return, there is a well-marked junction with the Louis Lake trail.

Stands of mature spruce now alternate with open slopes populated by aspens, willows, and a variety of shrubs. The sharp peaks that run north from McAlester Mountain now present themselves to the west. After a long and gentle stroll up the valley, the trail climbs moderately across the headwaters of South Creek, on slopes cleared by an intense wildfire in 1970. Now wildflowers and low-growing shrubs populate the mountainsides, and superb views abound. The trail makes a few upward switchbacks, then swings south to cross a large talus slope where chipmunks scurry among the rocks. A zigzagging final pitch leads up through a brushy woodland of larch, fir, and mountain hemlock to reach South Pass, where the trail enters National

McAlester Mountain from the South Pass Trail.

356

South Pass • Louis Lake

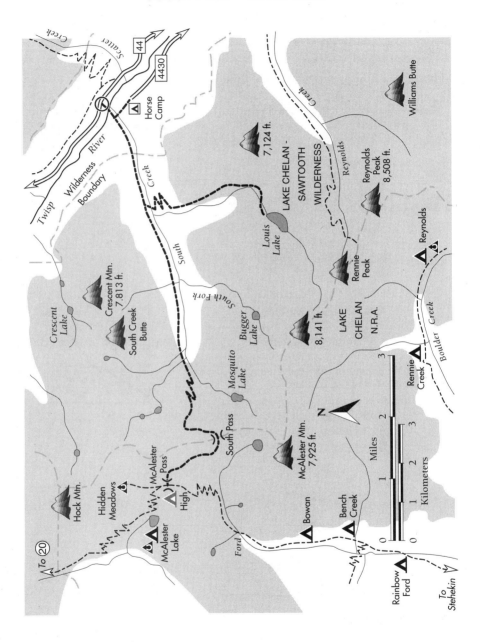

Park Service lands.

After passing through the notch, hikers emerge onto meadowy slopes across from McAlester Mountain. The path turns northward, traversing steep slopes robed in speedwell, phlox, lupine, and paintbrush. Views are superb during the level trek to the top of a flat promontory. Looking down Rainbow Creek, visitors can see Dome Peak and later Mount Lyall rising prominently among the distant peaks. Due west and closer at hand is the rocky tooth of Bowan Mountain. At the promontory, the trail begins to descend across flower-strewn swales that lead down to McAlester Pass. Watch for marmots as the path makes its final drop into the broad, grassy basin. A signpost marks the junction with trails to Rainbow Creek and McAlester Lake.

98 Louis Lake

See Map on Page 357

Overview: A day hike or short backpack to Louis Lake, 11.4 miles round trip.
Best season: Mid-June to mid-October.
Difficulty: Moderately strenuous.
Elevation gain: 2,210 feet.
Elevation loss: 40 feet.
Maximum elevation: 5,360 feet.
Topo maps: Gilbert; *Stehekin*.
Jurisdiction: Lake Chelan–Sawtooth Wilderness (Okanogan National Forest).

Finding the trailhead: From Twisp, follow the Twisp River Road (Forest Road 44) west for 23 miles to the South Pass trailhead.

Key points:
0.0 South Creek Trailhead. Hike west on South Pass Trail.
0.1 Trail crosses Twisp River.
0.2 Junction with spur trail from Horse Camp. Continue straight ahead.
2.5 Junction with Louis Lake Trail. Turn left.
5.7 Louis Lake.

The hike: This trail offers a manageable day hike in the South Creek basin, ending at a beautiful lake surrounded by cloud-scraping crags. Follow the South Creek route across the Twisp River and up the South Creek valley for 2.3 miles to a marked junction. The Louis Lake Trail descends to cross a

Louis Lake.

bridge over South Creek, where trailside tent sites are nestled in the timber. The next mile is a steady climb up the far wall of the main valley, through heavy timber of spruce and Douglas-fir. After passing a high overlook above the South Creek valley, the trail finally turns south into the Louis Creek watershed. The nasal cries of pikas drift down from the talus above the trail, and straight ahead sheer cliffs seem to wall off the valley.

The trail now passes through a dense growth of young conifers, climbing moderately along the east side of the basin. As the valley bends sharply to the southwest, the grade steepens and the route crosses snowslide meadows with fine views of the surrounding cliffs. Bending around onto its new heading, the trail crosses debris from an impressive rockfall and then levels off as it enters a full-grown subalpine forest. A footlog spans Louis Creek just below the lake, and the trail passes a number of fine campsites on its way to the shoreline. Louis Lake is a vast and impressive body of water, flanked by magnificent walls and peaks. Bring plenty of insect repellant, because the mosquitoes are murderous here.

99 Scatter Lake

Overview: A day hike or backpack to Scatter Lake, 8.8 miles round trip.

Best season: Early July to early October.

Difficulty: Strenuous.

Elevation gain: 3,750 feet.

Elevation loss: None.

Maximum elevation: 7,050 feet.

Topo maps: Gilbert; *Stehekin*.

Jurisdiction: Lake Chelan–Sawtooth Wilderness (Okanogan National Forest).

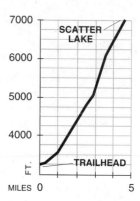

Finding the trailhead: From Twisp, follow the Twisp River Road (Forest Road 44) west for 22.2 miles to the Scatter Creek Trailhead.

Key points:
- 0.0 Scatter Creek Trailhead. Follow Twisp River Trail west.
- 0.2 Junction with Scatter Lake Trail. Turn right.
- 0.9 Trail climbs into Lake Chelan–Sawtooth Wilderness.
- 3.5 Forks of Scatter Creek.

The final approach to Scatter Lake.

3.9 Spur trail runs north to horse camp.
4.4 Scatter Lake.

The hike: A hike best saved for cool weather, the Scatter Lake Trail climbs 4,000 feet in 4.5 miles to reach the highest lake in the Lake Chelan–Sawtooth Wilderness. From the trailhead, follow the Twisp River Trail westward for a short distance to reach a sign marked "Scatter Creek trail." Follow this route, which climbs steadily atop an old logging road. It crosses south-facing slopes that bear selective cuts from the 1960s. This method of logging leaves a few mature trees untouched to reseed the cutover area. It is both more aesthetically pleasing and more ecologically sound than clearcutting. The trail leaves the old roadbed as it approaches Scatter Creek and begins a long and zigzagging ascent up the mountainside. A sparse woodland of Douglas-fir and ponderosa pine offers numerous views of the surrounding country. The Twisp River valley stretches below, guarded by barren peaks. As the trail gains altitude, hikers also get views up the South Creek valley.

After what seems like an interminable climb, the path dips into the Scatter Creek valley, but is still zigzagging upward as it crosses the wilderness boundary. The trail turns north for good beyond the boundary, entering a shady stand of Douglas-fir. The trail now embarks on a steep death march, mirroring the precipitous gradient of Scatter Creek. The onslaught continues as subalpine firs replace the montane forest of the lowlands, and grassy meadows soon offer southward views of the twin spires of Reynolds Peak. An old burn dating from 1929 can now be seen on the towering slopes of Abernathy Ridge across the creek.

After a final, steep scramble up a washed-out slope, the trail reaches the grassy benches where the stream forks. A stark prow of stone cleaves the valley in two, and the trail crosses the western fork and follows it upward through a gladed woodland of fir. After a steady climb, the path reaches grassy basin populated by larches, and a spur trail runs to a horse camp at the base of a waterfall. Scatter Lake lies not in this basin but on the shelf above the headwall, and the main trail soon begins its assault upon this final obstacle. Atop the final grade, larch-filled meadows and stagnant pools lead toward the shore of Scatter Lake. This deep pool lies at the foot of Abernathy Peak and is flanked on all sides by barren slopes of broken rock. Trout cruise the icy waters, and a fringe of larches lines the shoreline and the solitary island to provide a colorful counterpoint to the stark nakedness of the rock.

Scatter Lake • North Lake

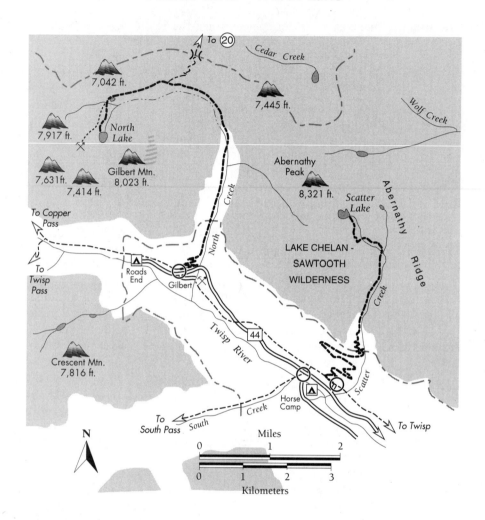

100 Copper Pass

See Map on Page 265

Overview: A day hike from North Creek Trailhead to Copper Pass, 12.8 miles round trip, or a trek to Washington Highway 20, 11.4 miles overall.

Best season: Late June to early October.

Difficulty: Strenuous.

Elevation gain: 3,030 feet (east to west).

Elevation loss: 2,440 feet (east to west).

Maximum elevation: 6,710 feet.

Topo maps: Gilbert, McAlester Mountain; *Stehekin*.

Jurisdiction: Lake Chelan–Sawtooth Wilderness, Okanogan National Forest.

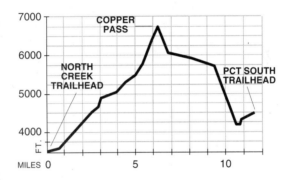

Finding the trailhead: From Twisp, follow the Twisp River Road (Forest Road 44) west for 25.3 miles to reach the North Creek trailhead. You can save 0.6 mile by parking at Road's End Camp and scrambling uphill behind the outhouse to acquire the trail.

Key points:

- 0.0 North Creek Trailhead.
- 0.6 Trail runs above Road's End Campground.
- 2.4 Junction with trail to Twisp Pass. Continue straight ahead.
- 3.9 Trail fords North Fork of Twisp River.
- 6.4 Copper Pass. Trail leaves Lake Chelan–Sawtooth Wilderness.
- 6.9 Headwaters of Copper Creek.
- 10.4 Junction with east Bridge Creek Trail. Make all right turns for remaining 1 mile (easy) to PCT South Trailhead on WA 20.
- 11.4 PCT South Trailhead.

The hike: This primitive trail is no longer maintained between Copper Pass and Bridge Creek, even on the eastern side where the tread is discernible, the uphill grades are brutally steep. Expect route-finding difficulties in the vast meadows of the Copper Creek valley; the route is most easily followed from east to west. At the mouth of the valley, alternate routes run north to intersect WA 20 at the State Creek culvert or down to Copper Creek and west to the trail along the east bank of Bridge Creek. Adventurous souls can combine this trek with Dagger Lake and Twisp Pass for a challenging two- to three-day loop.

The trek begins officially at the North Creek Trailhead, following a wide and dusty track above the road through the Twisp River valley. To save distance, hikers can climb the steep path that intersects the trail as it passes above Road's End Campground. The trail climbs vigorously for a while, leveling off as it enters the Lake Chelan–Sawtooth Wilderness. The forest is a ragged growth of Douglas-fir, with frequent gaps that reveal a rugged spur of Crescent Mountain to the south and the ragged tooth of Lincoln Butte above the head of the valley. As the trail passes the forks of the Twisp River, the gradual ascent steepens markedly and silver fir and spruce become the dominant conifers.

The trail soon reaches a junction beside a pretty waterfall on the North Fork of the Twisp. The footbridge leads to the Twisp Pass Trail, while the trail to Copper Pass lies straight ahead. A steady climb leads up through brushy openings, with the stern countenance of Lincoln Butte rising above the western side of the valley. A silent forest of Engelmann spruce soon closes in around the trail, shading the bottomland trek to a shallow ford of the North Fork.

The trail soon strikes a rushing tributary that tumbles through a series of cascades. A steep climb beside this stream leads past the ruins of a sod-roofed prospector's cabin and onto a wooded shelf. The trail wanders past the base of an impressive horn of stone, then begins to climb steeply through the edge of the forest. As the path enters a hanging valley, look southward for views of the spires Kangaroo Ridge. The path is deeply rutted as it climbs into subalpine brushfields of white rhododendron. Watch for marmots in the lowermost boulderfields, and for reclusive pika as the trail climbs into more alpine habitats.

As the trail climbs steadily above the timberline, look eastward to see the rank of rugged peaks that line the Twisp River valley: Lincoln Butte, South Creek Butte, and Crescent Mountain in order of increasing distance. A steep grade leads up to the barren col of Copper Pass, which commands westward views down the Copper Creek valley, with the rock walls of Stiletto Peak rising sheer to the south of it. Snaggletooth peaks rise to the north and east; these are the rear echelons of the Early Winters Spires.

A steep descent leads from the pass to the floor of an alpine basin. After fording the headwaters of Copper Creek, the trail grows faint as it traverses a level course across small alpine meadows bounded by copses of fir. There are a handful of potential campsites along the way. This is delicate country, so take pains to minimize your impact. The alpine meadows give way to a vast grassland that covers the steep north wall of the valley, with the stark cliffs of Stiletto Peak glowering down from across the creek. The faint track stays high on the slope as it skirts around clumps of alder that huddle in the

Stiletto Peak from Copper Pass Trail.

draws or wind-blasted copses of fir.

After a long stretch across open country, the trail reaches the first strips of conifers. A series of precipitous descents leads downward beside the mouth of the valley, with views of Frisco Mountain to the southwest. The beaten track soon bends northward toward the State Creek culvert on the highway; travelers bound for Bridge Creek should continue downward by dead reckoning to reach Copper Creek, then follow the faint prospector's trail to an intersection with the well-beaten trail along the east bank of Bridge Creek. Turn right to reach the PCT South Trailhead on WA 20.

101 North Lake

See Map on Page 362

Overview:	A day hike to North Lake, 9.6 miles round trip.
Best season:	Mid-June to early October.
Difficulty:	Moderate.
Elevation gain:	2,180 feet.
Elevation loss:	None.
Maximum elevation:	5,820 feet.
Topo maps:	Gilbert; *Stehekin*.
Jurisdiction:	Lake Chelan–Sawtooth Wilderness (Okanogan National Forest).

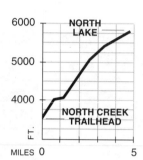

Finding the trailhead: From Twisp, follow the Twisp River Road (Forest Road 44) west for 25.3 miles to the North Creek Trailhead.

Key points:
- 0.0 North Creek Trailhead.
- 1.1 Trail enters the Lake Chelan–Sawtooth Wilderness.
- 2.5 Trail crosses North Creek.
- 3.4 Junction with Cedar Creek Trail. Keep going straight ahead.
- 4.3 Junction with abandoned trail to mine site. Bear left for the lake.
- 4.8 North Lake.

Meadows near North Lake.

The hike: This wide and well-tended trail offers a moderate day trip to a picturesque lake within the Lake Chelan–Sawtooth Wilderness. It is popular with horse parties; expect to share the trail with them.

The trail begins by zigzagging moderately up the slopes of the Twisp River valley, where selective logging has opened up the forest for fine views of Crescent Mountain crags beyond the river. After gaining 400 vertical feet, the path swings into the North Creek valley. Here, it crosses rugged slopes of broken rock with arid summits all around. As the trail gains altitude, backward glances reveal the graceful summits of Reynolds Peak. The talus slopes give way to meadows of rank grasses, and a scattering of aspens provides splashes of gold in early autumn. The summit of Abernathy Peak is now visible across the valley of North Creek.

As the valley makes a sweeping bend to the west, the trail crosses North Creek and there are camping spots on the far bank. An old burn has grown back in an open stand of lodgepole pine and subalpine fir, and hikers gain fine views of the granite crags ringing the valley. The trail offers level traveling to its junction with the Cedar Creek Trail, a primitive footpath that surmounts the rocky slopes to the north then makes a long forest trek along Cedar Creek to reach Washington Highway 20. The main trail continues westward, and the forest thickens to provide only fleeting glimpses as it passes the towering walls of Gilbert Mountain. Nearing the head of the valley, the path passes an enormous boulder in the midst of the forest. This is a glacial erratic, borne down from the mountain heights by the glacier that carved this valley during the Pleistocene. The ice deposited the boulder here as it melted away.

Beyond this geological oddity, the trail descends to skirt the edge of a beautiful subalpine meadow. Take a side trip to the campsite at its edge for spectacular views of the surrounding peaks, trimmed with larches that glow green in summer and turn a brilliant yellow in autumn. The trail passes a shallow pond at the upper edge of the meadow, then breaks into the open at the base of a cliff-lined cirque. Entering a shady stand of spruce, the trail passes a junction with the abandoned trail that once climbed to a mine site high above North Lake. The main trail ascends moderately to reach the lake, an emerald pool below the west face of Gilbert Mountain. There are fine campsites in the meadows along its eastern shore, and pikas sometimes call from the talus south of the lake.

ADDITIONAL TRAILS

The **Lower Railroad Creek Trail** parallels the road between Lucerne and Holden. It is brushy in places.

A long, seldom-traveled forest trek leads up **Cedar Creek** before crossing a wooded pass to reach the North Lake trail. There is a pretty waterfall at the 2-mile point.

A steep, occasionally maintained trail climbs from the Twisp River Road to **Slate Lake**.

The **Wolf Creek Trail** is a long forest trek to pretty meadows where cattle graze each summer. A stock and hunter access trail runs up the North Fork.

An unmaintained hunter access trail runs up the **South Fork of War Creek**.

The **Reynolds Creek Trail** is maintained infrequently. A long forest hike leads to a steep grade to a pass and fine westward views.

The **Williams Creek Trail** makes a steep climb to a subalpine lake.

A popular horse route runs from the boat landing at Moore Point along **Fish Creek** and its East Fork to link with the Chelan Summit Trail.

The **North Fork Fish Creek Trail** is a shorter route to the high country, with several fords that can be difficult in early summer.

A faint track climbs from the North Fork Fish Creek junction to a high cirque bearing **Bernice Lake**.

The **Horseshoe Creek Trail** is a short connector that links Twin Springs Camp with the East Fork of Fish Creek. It is prone to deadfalls.

The **Horton Butte Trail** climbs from Fish Creek to Round Lake in the wooded lowlands, then becomes faint as it climbs to an old lookout site with excellent views of Lake Chelan. It ends at the Indianhead Basin Trail.

The narrow and rocky **Indianhead Basin Trail** links Surprise Lake with the East Fork of Fish Creek via a high pass with excellent views.

A short connector follows the **North Fork of Prince Creek**, cutting off 2.5 miles to the Chelan Summit. Fords may be difficult during high water.

The **Prince Creek Trail** climbs 13.5 miles from a boat landing on Lake Chelan to the Chelan Summit Trail. It receives heavy horse use, and Cub Lake offers fishing along the way.

A steep footpath leads up the **Libby Lake**, at the southern edge of the

Extended Journeys

Many of the trails in the North Cascades are interconnected, allowing visitors to link them together for longer expeditions of varying length and difficulty. The expeditions described below represent only a small fraction of the possible treks. If you are of a more independent mindset, the information in this guide allows you to use your own imagination to put together an extended journey that is custom-tailored to your desires and abilities. It is a good idea to discuss your itinerary with local rangers and find out about prevailing trail conditions before you begin your hike. Be sure that you have all the necessary permits before you go.

BEAVER LOOP, 3–5 DAYS

This 35-mile route follows gentle valley bottoms with a few minor climbs, making it an ideal trip for beginning backpackers. This trek is not a true loop inasmuch as it requires a boat shuttle across Ross Lake from the mouth of Little Beaver Creek to return to the starting point. For parties who lack their own watercraft, the Ross Lake Resort provides a motorboat shuttle for a reasonable fee. Begin on the West Bank Trail, following it along the edge of Ross Lake to reach the mouth of Big Beaver Creek. The route now follows the Big Beaver trail into the hinterlands of North Cascades National Park's northwest corner. This trek is not known for mountain scenery, but the old-growth timber is unparalleled. A side trip to Whatcom Pass yields views of waterfalls and impressive glaciers and is highly recommended. To complete the trek, hike down Little Beaver Creek through even more ancient trees to reach the boat landing on Ross Lake.

COPPER RIDGE LOOP, 3–6 DAYS

This 29.9-mile route combines Hannegan Pass with a long, alpine trek along Copper Ridge, offering spectacular views. The return trip along the Chilliwack River features primeval stands of old-growth forest. Side trips include Hannegan Peak and Whatcom Pass for mountain scenery. Get permits early, because the campsites on Copper Ridge fill up quickly, especially on weekends.

WHATCOM PASS EXPEDITION, 6–9 DAYS

From its beginnings in the Nooksack River drainage, this route leads over three passes for a 47.6-mile-long, point-to-point trek through the northern section of North Cascades National Park to reach Ross Dam. Follow the Hannegan Pass route to Boundary Camp, then descend into the headwaters of the Chilliwack River as mountain views are replaced by deep forests. The challenging climb begins about halfway up Brush Creek on the trail to

Whatcom Pass. There are breathtaking waterfalls and glacier views on both sides of Whatcom Pass, including the magnificent Challenger Glacier. The trail then leads down the brushy valley of Little Beaver Creek. Heavy timber takes over as the trail approaches Stillwell Camp. From here, hikers can continue down Little Beaver Creek through ancient forests, cutting 12.2 miles from the journey but necessitating a boat shuttle down Ross Lake from the mouth of Little Beaver Creek. The preferred route runs over the low divide of Beaver Pass, then follows Big Beaver Creek through montane forests and cedar swamps to reach Ross Lake. Follow the West Bank Trail southward to end up at Ross Dam and a spur trail that rises to Washington Highway 20.

CASCADES CROSSING, 5–8 DAYS

This route makes an excellent week-long expedition of 44.2 miles, visiting some of the spectacular passes in the heart of the North Cascades. Worthy side trips include the Horseshoe Basin and Sahale Arm. The trek begins with a climb over Easy Pass, where larches guard lush meadows that look out over the jagged peaks. The trail then leads down into Fisher Creek, following it down into the forest for a long trek to the Thunder Creek valley. Follow Thunder Creek upward, with challenging grades as the trail climbs high over Park Creek Pass. A steep descent leads into the Park Creek valley for impressive views of Buckner Mountain and its glaciers. The route then leads down into the Stehekin Valley. It is necessary to follow the Stehekin Valley road westward for 4.4 miles to reach the beginning of the Cascade Pass trail. Travelers now follow in the footsteps of the Skagit and Chelan peoples as the trail crosses over the spectacular divide of Cascade Pass to reach the end of the Cascade River Road. History buffs can seek out the ruins of old gold mining structures near Skagit Queen Camp, in Horseshoe Basin, and at Doubtful Lake.

DEVILS DOME LOOP, 5–9 DAYS

This 40.4-mile route has received lots of publicity in recent years, and as a result it has become rather crowded by wilderness standards. The route follows the East Bank trail along Ross Lake, then turns inland and climbs vigorously to the alpine ridgetops of the Pasayten Wilderness. There are splendid views of Jack Mountain as the path climbs to the top of Devils Dome, and the alpine meadows and mountain scenery continue all the way to Devils Pass and beyond as the trail negotiates the steep climbs and descents of the Jackita Ridge Trail. Campers in the high country will find that water is scarce; the best sources and campsites are at the shelters at Bear Skull, below Devils Pass, and at Devils Park. After leaving the rolling meadows of Devils Park, the trail makes its way across the swampy shelf of McMillan Park and then passes the spur to "Crater Lake," a highly recommended side trip. A steep descent leads down to the mouth of Canyon Creek. Turn east here to reach the bridge to Washington Highway 20 and cut off 3 miles of hiking, or turn west along Ruby Creek to complete the loop on foot. A boat shuttle to Devils Creek camp on Ross Lake trims two days of hiking from the journey.

THE NORTH LOOP, 8-13 DAYS

This route of 76.5 miles offers a challenging wilderness journey on trails that require strong route-finding skills, and for this reason it is rarely attempted. Nonetheless, it covers some of the most striking and remote country in the Pasayten Wilderness, and is unmatched for untainted wilderness grandeur. From Hozomeen, follow the Lightning Creek Trail down to the mouth of Three Fools Creek. The route now follows the lightly maintained Three Fools trail through brushy bottoms and then up a long climb to the ridgetop behind Skagit Peak. Once in the alpine zone, expect the trail to be faint in places as the route runs eastward across the meadowy ridgetops to reach Castle Pass. Turn south here, following the Pacific Crest Trail (see Hike 52) along the timberline as it passes through Hopkins, Woody, and Rock passes. In the wooded defile of Holman Pass, turn west onto the little-used Deception Pass trail and follow it across the Canyon Creek basin then up to Sky Pilot Pass. After a low dip through Deception Pass, this trail winds upward to Devils Pass and a meeting with the Devils Dome Trail. Turn west and hike into the open meadows surrounding Devils Dome. After a long sojourn through the alpine tundra, the trail makes a long descent to Ross Lake. Arrange a boat shuttle to avoid 17.7 miles of hiking, or follow the East Bank trail northward to Lightning Creek and follow the Lightning Creek Trail back to Hozomeen.

FROSTY PASS LOOP, 3-5 DAYS

This 34-mile route begins and ends in Canada's Manning Provincial Park and crosses into the Pasayten Wilderness, requiring special clearance from U.S./Canadian Customs in advance. Begin at the Monument 83 Trailhead and follow trail markers for Monument 78. A notoriously muddy jeep road (closed to public vehicles) leads 7.4 miles to Monument 78 on the Canadian border. From here, follow the Pacific Crest Trail (see Hike 52) up a moderate grade to Castle Pass. Continue through the pass a short distance, then turn left on the Frosty Pass Trail, which climbs steadily for 2 miles to a high and windswept divide. The trail descends into the Frosty Creek valley, passing an alpine cirque on its way to the valley floor. A long trudge through boggy spruce forest leads down Frosty Creek.

Travelers who wish to visit The Parks will need to watch for a faint path the splits away to the north (it is the only such path). The main trail continues down the valley to a junction along Chuchuwanteen Creek. Turn north across the mouth of Frosty Creek as the journey leads down this small river, then crosses it and begins a vigorous climb. High on the ridgetops is Monument Spring, the last good campsite. The trail then crosses the border atop a bald foothill with superb views and several structures of historical note. The route then follows a closed fire access road (see Hike 41) down through endless trees to return to its starting point.

MONUMENT PEAK LOOP, 5–8 DAYS

This 44-mile trek covers some of the most remote territory in the Pasayten Wilderness, on trails that see little use and may pose route-finding challenges. Start on the Monument Trail (Hike 58) and plan to camp at the mouth of Eureka Creek, since the next 7 miles are a long and wearying grade with no surface water. After crossing the ridgetops, the trail drops to Monument Creek and follows it upward. High in the drainage, timberline meadows are guarded by subalpine larch. The route leads over the barren summit of Shellrock Pass, then drops into the Eureka Creek valley. Another steady climb leads over a second divide to Freds Lake. The trail then makes the long descent to the Middle Fork of the Pasayten River to meet the Robinson Pass trail. Follow it southward, up the modest grade to Robinson Pass, then down the timbered drainage of Robinson Creek. The route passes a spectacular waterfall on Beauty Creek before depositing hikers on the Harts Pass Road, just 2 miles west of the Monument Creek Trailhead. Start at Slate Pass and follow the Ferguson Lake routing for a point-to-point trek of 39 miles.

RAINBOW LAKE LOOP, 4–6 DAYS

This route can be approached with equal ease from Washington Highway 20 (28.5 miles overall) or the Stehekin Valley Road for a hike of 28 miles. It crosses two major passes, and visits Rainbow and McAlester lakes for high-country angling opportunities. Travelers approaching from the north will follow the Bridge Creek trail down to Fireweed Camp to intersect the loop. From Stehekin, follow the Rainbow Creek routing upward with fine views of the Stehekin Valley as the trail climbs the slopes of Rainbow Mountain. It then follows Rainbow Creek all the way to McAlester Pass. Worthy side trips from the pass include the even higher summit of South Pass as well as Hidden Meadows, a popular horse camp. The trail then passes McAlester Lake on its way northward on the trail of the same name. Turn west at the Dagger Lake trail junction; the route passes Fireweed Camp then joins the Bridge Creek trail for a downstream journey through broad avalanche slopes. Turn south again at South Fork Camp, following the Rainbow Lake trail up the South Fork Valley then heading over a high pass to reach Rainbow Lake. The trail leads down into Rainbow Meadows before returning to Rainbow Creek for the final leg of the trek.

SAWTOOTH RIDGE TREK, 3–5 DAYS

The routing selected here is only one of many loops that combine trails from the Twisp River valley with the Chelan Summit trail. It maximizes striking scenery and wilderness quality at the expense of ease and convenience. A two-car shuttle is required to span the distance between the trailheads. Though not strenuous by physical standards, this route of 23.1 miles demands good wilderness skills since it follows a faint and little-maintained trail along Scaffold Ridge. After visiting Buttermilk Meadows and a nameless lake, the trail joins the West Fork Buttermilk trail for the final ascent over spectacular Fish Creek Pass.

A descent through larch-studded meadows leads to the Chelan Summit trail. Turn north on this well-beaten route, hiking below the spine of Sawtooth Ridge through open meadows and stands of whitebark pine. At the mouth of the Horseshoe Basin, spur routes lead east to Tuckaway Lake and over the top of the divide to Oval Lakes. The main trail continues north, climbing over high passes with westward views of the peaks that guard Lake Chelan. After dropping into a pretty basin, the Eagle Pass Trail splits away to the east. Follow it over the divide and down into the pretty valley of Eagle Creek. After dropping into the timber, a short spur leads to Silver Lake, while the main trail carries the traveler down Eagle Creek to return to "civilization."

PACIFIC CREST NATIONAL SCENIC TRIAL, 10–16 DAYS

The seminal hiking trail of the North Cascades, this trail stretches for 2,627 miles between the Mexican and Canadian borders. Hikers who attempt the entire route usually start in April and reach the North Cascades in mid-September. Our coverage picks up the trail at Suiattle Pass; hikers who attempt the 107-mile northern stretch can access the pass via Railroad Creek. From here, the Pacific Crest Trail (PCT) follows the Agnes Creek routing, descending into forested bottoms and following Agnes Creek into North Cascades National Park. Through-hikers can catch a shuttle to Stehekin from this trailhead. To avoid hiking on the Stehekin Valley Road, cross High Bridge and follow the McAlester Mountain routing to Coon Lake. From its west shore, follow the Old Wagon Road northward. It emerges on the road just south of Bridge Creek. Next, follow the Bridge Creek routing through a brushy valley. Just before reaching Washington Highway 20, turn left for the shady hike to Rainy Pass and cross the highway there.

Hitchhike into Winthrop and arrange to meet the Customs agent at the ranger station for a permit to cross the border. From this point north, the PCT is now described under the Granite Pass Highline entry (Hike 62). It climbs up to the ridgetops and follows them north to Methow Pass. Here, it picks up the West Fork Methow Trail for a substantial descent into the bottomlands.

Turn left at Brush Creek; the PCT route is now covered under the Trout Creek Divide description (Hike 67). This trail climbs to Glacier Pass, then continues up to the alpine divide above Trout Creek. It remains at timberline all the way to Harts Pass; connecting trails stay west of the campgrounds and roads here. The trail then follows the Cascade Crest route along the top of the divide, running northward through alpine country. It begins to descend at the Canadian border and emerges at a trailhead in Manning Provincial Park.

APPENDIX A: DIRECTORY OF LAND MANAGEMENT AGENCIES

NORTH CASCADES NATIONAL PARK (ADMINISTERS ROSS LAKE AND LAKE CHELAN NATIONAL RECREATION AREAS)

Park Headquarters
2105 State Route 20
Sedro-Woolley, WA 98284
(360) 856-5700

Wilderness Center
Backcountry information/
permits for Ross Lake
National Recreation Area
Marblemount, WA
(360) 873-4500

North Cascades Visitor Center
Newhalem, WA
(206) 386-4495

Hozomeen Ranger Station
Ross Lake National Recreation Area
Hozomeen, WA
No telephone

Golden West Visitor Center
Lake Chelan National
Recreation Area
Stehekin, WA
(360) 856-5703

MOUNT BAKER—SNOQUALMIE NATIONAL FOREST

Supervisor's Office
(206) 775-9702
1-800-627-0062
TDD 1-800-272-1215

Mount Baker Ranger District
2105 Washington Highway 20
Sedro-Woolley, WA 98284
(360) 856-5700

Glacier Public Service Center
Glacier, WA
(360) 599-2714

**Heather Meadows
Visitor Center**
Heather Meadows
No telephone

OKANOGAN NATIONAL FOREST

Methow Valley Visitor Center
Winthrop, WA
(509) 996-4000
Wenatchee National Forest

Twisp Ranger Station
P.O. Box 188
Twisp, WA 98856
(509) 997-2131

Chelan Ranger District
428 West Woodin Ave.
Chelan, WA 98816
(509) 682-2576

BRITISH COLUMBIA PARKS

Manning Provincial Park
Box 3
Manning Park, BC V0X 1R0
Canada

Skagit Valley Provincial Park
Box 10
2950 Columbia Valley Highway
Cultus Lake, BC V0X 1H0
(250) 858-7161

Appendix B: Park Service Backcountry Camps

Ratings: 5 = Camp itself is a scenic attraction.
4 = Camp occupies a site of high scenic value.
3 = Camp occupies a site of modest scenic value.
2 = Camp has no scenic value or is an eyesore.

Notes: D = Boat dock.
S = Emergency shelter.
P = Picnic tables.

Camp	Rating	Sites/pads	Fires	Notes
Basin Creek	3	6/10	yes	
Bear Creek	2	1/2	yes	
Beaver Pass	2	2/5	yes	
Beaver Pass Horse	2	1/2	yes	
Bench Creek	3	3/7	yes	
Big Beaver	4	7/14	yes	D
Big Beaver Horse	2	1/3	yes	
Boundary	4	3/3	no	
Boundary Bay	3	3/3	yes	D
Bowan	3	2/6	yes	
Buckner	5	1/3	yes	
Buster Brown	3	3/5	yes	D
Cat Island	4	4/8	yes	D
Chilliwack	2	3/3	yes	
Copper Creek	3	3/3	yes	
Copper Creek Horse	3	2/4	yes	
Copper Lake	5	3/4	no	
Cosho	2	3/5	yes	
Cottonwood	2	4/4	yes	
Cougar Island	5	2/4	yes	D
Dagger Lake Hiker	4	1/3	yes	
Dagger Lake Horse	3	1/3	yes	
Dans	3	1/1	yes	
Deerlick Horse	3	1/3	yes	
Desolation	5	1/3	no	
Devils Creek Hiker	2	2/6	yes	
Devils Creek Horse	3	2/3	yes	
Devils Junction	3	1/2	yes	D
Dry Creek	3	4/6	yes	D
Egg Lake	4	3/5	no	

Camp	Rating	Sites/pads	Fires	Notes
Fireweed Hiker	3	2/4	yes	
Fireweed Horse	3	3/7	yes	
Fisher	5	3/5	no	
Five Mile Horse	4	3/5	yes	
Flat Creek	3	4/4	yes	
Flick Creek	5	1/1	yes	D,S
Fourth of July	4	3/7	yes	
Graybeal	4	2/4	yes	
Graybeal Horse	3	1/4	yes	
Green Point	3	7/9	yes	D
Grizzly Creek	3	2/2	yes	
Grizzly Creek Horse	3	1/1	yes	
Heaton	5	1/5	yes	
Hidden Cove	3	1/2	yes	D
Hidden Hand	3	3/6	yes	
Hidden Meadows Horse	4	1/4	yes	
Hideaway	3	2/8	yes	
High	3	1/2	no	
Hooter	2	1/2	no	
Hozomeen Lake	5	3/6	yes	
Indian Creek	3	2/3	yes	
Junction	4	3/10	yes	
Junction Horse	2	1/3	yes	
Lightning Creek	4	6/10	yes	D
Lightning Cr. Horse	4	3/6	yes	D
Little Beaver	4	5/9	yes	D
Lodgepole Horse	4	3/6	yes	D
Luna	3	2/3	yes	
Manly Wham	4	1/1	yes	D
May Creek Horse	3	1/3	yes	
McAlester Lake	5	2/6	yes	
McAlester Lake (Horse)	3	1/2	yes	
McAllister	3	5/12	yes	
McAllister Horse	2	1/2	yes	
McMillan	4	3/5	yes	D
Monogram Lake	5	2/5	no	
Neve	4	3/6	yes	
Nightmare	4	1/2	yes	
Nightmare Horse	4	1/3	yes	

Camp	Rating	Sites/pads	Fires	Notes
North Fork	4	2/17	yes	
Panther	4	1/6	yes	
Pelton Basin	4	3/5	no	
Perry Creek	4	2/4	yes	S
Pierce Mountain	4	1/1	no	
Ponderosa		2/5	yes	D
Pumpkin Mtn.	2	2/2	yes	
Rainbow Bridge	3	2/3	yes	
Rainbow Ford	2	1/2	yes	
Rainbow Lake	5	2/5	no	
Rainbow Meadows	2	1/3	yes	
Rainbow Meadows Horse	4	2/10	yes	
Rainbow Point	5	3/5	yes	D
Rennie	2	1/3	yes	
Reynolds	4	1/2	yes	
Reynolds Horse	3	1/2	yes	
Roland Creek	3	2/5	yes	
Roland Point	4	1/2	yes	D
Ruby Pasture Horse	2	1/2	yes	
Sahale Glacier	5	3/3	no	
Silesia	5	2/4	no	
Six Mile	4	2/8	yes	
Skagit Queen	3	3/5	yes	
Sourdough	3	1/1	no	
South Fork	4	3/11	yes	
South Fork Horse	3	1/1	yes	
Spencer	3	2/4	yes	D
Silver Creek	3	4/8	yes	D
Stillwell	3	4/9	yes	
Tenmile Island	5	2/4	yes	D
Thirtynine Mile	3	2/3	yes	
Thirtynine Mile Horse	3	1/4	yes	
Thornton Lake	4	3/5	no	
Thunder	4	2/4	yes	
Thunder Point	3	yes	D	
Thunder Basin	4	1/1	no	
Thunder Basin Horse	4	1/3	no	
Tricouni	3	2/4	yes	
Twin Rocks	3	4/6	yes	
Twin Rocks Horse	3	1/3	yes	
Two Mile	3	1/1	yes	

Camp	Rating	Sites/pads	Fires	Notes
US Cabin	3	4/6	yes	
US Cabin Horse	3	1/4	yes	
Walker Park Horse	5	2/4	yes	
Weaver Point	3		yes	D
Whatcom	4	3/3	no	
Willow Lake	3	1/2	yes	

FOREST SERVICE BACKCOUNTRY CAMPS

Camp	Rating	Notes	Camp	Rating	Notes
Anderson Lakes	4		Little Fish	2	S
Bear Skull	4	S	Lyman Lake	4	
Boiling Lake	4	P	Moore Point	4	B,S
Brush Creek	2		N. Fork Prince Cr.	3	S
Buckskin Lake	4		Upper Porcupine	3	
Camp Comfort	3		Rebel	3	
Camp Kaiser	5		Robinson Pass	3	
Cedar	3		Sauk Lake	4	
Devils Pass	3	S	Silesia Creek	3	S
Devils Park	4	S	Snowy Lakes Horse	4	
East Watson Lake	5		State Creek	3	
Ferguson Lake	5		Suiattle Pass	4	
Five Mile	2		Swamp Creek	4	
Fred's Lake	5		Ten Trees	5	
Glacier Pass	3		Tomyhoi Lake	3	
Glacier Pass Horse	4		Twin Springs	4	
Granite Pass	4		Upper Agnes	5	
Hemlock	4		Upper Porcupine	3	
Hopkins Lake	4		West Fork	3	
Hopkins Pass	3		West Watson Lake	3	
Horse Heaven	4		Will's	2	
Lake Ann	5				

About the Author

Erik Molvar first came to the North Cascades just after high school, as part of a volunteer trail crew. He then attended the University of Montana, gaining a bachelor's degree in wildlife biology with a minor in Native American studies. It was in Montana that Erik first began to write hiking guides, the first two of which were *Hiking Glacier and Waterton Lakes National Parks* and *The Trail Guide to Bob Marshall Country*. He obtained a master's degree in wildlife management from the University of Alaska at Fairbanks, where he published ground-breaking research concerning the ecology and behavior of moose in Denali National Park. More books followed his return to the lower forty-eight: *Hiking Arizona's Cactus Country, Hiking Zion and Bryce Canyon National Parks, Scenic Driving Alaska and the Yukon, Alaska on Foot: Wilderness Techniques for the Far North,* and *Hiking Olympic National Park.*

It was a sort of homecoming for Erik to return to the North Cascades. Working as a volunteer ranger as he completed the field research for this book, he hiked more than 1,380 miles of trails in the North Cascades, encompassing all of the trails covered here. It is his hope that his books will encourage responsible stewardship of our wildlands so that future generations can enjoy them.

Index

get
FALCON GUIDED

FALCON GUIDES ® are available for where-to-go hiking, mountain biking, rock climbing, walking, scenic driving, fishing, rockhounding, paddling, birding, wildlife viewing, and camping. We also have FalconGuides on essential outdoor skills and subjects and field identification. The following titles are currently available, but this list grows every year. For a free catalog with a complete list of titles, call FALCON toll-free at 1-800-582-2665.

HIKING GUIDES

Hiking Alaska
Hiking Alberta
Hiking Arizona
Hiking Arizona's Cactus Country
Hiking the Beartooths
Hiking Big Bend National Park
Hiking California
Hiking California's Desert Parks
Hiking Carlsbad Caverns &
   Guadalupe Mtns. National Parks
Hiking Colorado
Hiking the Columbia River Gorge
Hiking Florida
Hiking Georgia
Hiking Glacier & Waterton Lakes National Parks
Hiking Grand Canyon National Park
Hiking Great Basin National Park
Hiking Hot Springs
   in the Pacific Northwest
Hiking Idaho
Hiking Maine
Hiking Michigan
Hiking Minnesota
Hiking Montana
Hiking Nevada
Hiking New Hampshire
Hiking New Mexico
Hiking New York
Hiking North Carolina
Hiking North Cascades

Hiking Northern Arizona
Hiking Olympic National Park
Hiking Oregon
Hiking Oregon's Eagle Cap Wilderness
Hiking Oregon's Three Sisters Country
Hiking Pennsylvania
Hiking South Carolina
Hiking South Dakota's Black Hills Country
Hiking Southern New England
Hiking Tennessee
Hiking Texas
Hiking Utah
Hiking Utah's Summits
Hiking Vermont
Hiking Virginia
Hiking Washington
Hiking Wyoming
Hiking Wyoming's Wind River Range
Hiking Yellowstone National Park
Hiking Zion & Bryce Canyon National Parks
The Trail Guide to Bob Marshall Country

BEST EASY DAY HIKES

Beartooths
Canyonlands & Arches
Best Hikes on the Continental Divide
Glacier & Waterton Lakes
Glen Canyon
Grand Canyon
North Cascades
Yellowstone

n   *To order any of these books, check with your local bookseller or call FALCON* ® *at* **1-800-582-2665.**

FALCON®

Visit us on the world wide web at:
www.falconguide.com